# THE IDIOT AND THE ODYSSEY III

## TWENTY YEARS WALKING THE MEDITERRANEAN

**Joel Stratte-McClure**

Title and Cover Design: Author and photojournalist David Douglas Duncan (1916-2018).

Cover Photo: Walking the Mediterranean in Turkey.
(Credit: Liz Chapin)

3

The Idiot and the Odyssey III
Twenty Years Walking the Mediterranean

Published by
Freelance Ink Books

PO Box 994547
Redding, California 96099-4547

www.idiotandodyssey.com

ISBN: 978-1722683887

Designed by Aaron and Jenni Elise Patterson

Edited by Michael Knipe, London

# A NEW WAY TO SEE THE MEDTREK

Use your mobile phone to interact with *The Idiot and the Odyssey III: Twenty Years Walking the Mediterranean.*

Introducing scannable QR codes.

**iOS** devices, including iPhones and iPads.

For updated iOS devices, simply point your camera at the QR code and tap on the link.

**Android** users should use Google Assistant.

Having problems or curious? Go to bit.ly/2KSWPK2 for more info.

# Acclaim for *The Idiot and the Odyssey*

"This is one of those seductive books that, as you read, slowly insinuates itself into your consciousness and becomes more and more compelling...Stratte-McClure belongs to a generation that was entranced by the road journeys of Jack Kerouac and Robert Pirsig (*Zen and the Art of Motorcycle Maintenance*). These were journeys where the landscape and the exploration of the author's psyche were blended artfully...It is a high-wire literary act that is always in danger of collapsing into pretentiousness, but Stratte-McClure is so knowledgeable about the paths he walks and so sensitive to the history and landscapes around him that what he produces is not only an interesting travel book but a compelling story about a simple attempt to overcome a mid-life crisis and make some sense of the world."
– *Bruce Elder, Sydney Morning Herald*

"From the turquoise-tinted water and zillion-dollar yachts of Saint-Tropez to the intrigue of the Kasbah in Tangier, Joel Stratte-McClure takes the reader on a delightful spiritual journey around the Mediterranean that is filled with nudists and Buddhists, the obscenely chic and the exotic. *The Idiot and the Odyssey* is such a terrific antidote to the middle age melancholia that if Homer could do a sequel, Odysseus would probably jump ship to join Stratte-McClure's MedTrek." – *Craig Unger, Vanity Fair contributing editor, author of "House of Trump, House of Putin"*

"There must be simpler – and less strenuous – ways to get over a mid-life crisis following a divorce. Walking around the Mediterranean does seem to be a bit extreme. But American journalist and author Joel Stratte-McClure doesn't seem to be the type to take the easy way out." – *Diana Plater, Associated Press*

"Reading *The Idiot and the Odyssey* provides a hugely entertaining perspective of the world's oldest and greatest journey, conjured millennia ago by Homer. The books are a reminder that the Mediterranean, even today, is a wild and fascinating place." – *Tony Perrottet, author of "The Naked Olympics: The True Story of the Greek Games"*

"American Stratte-McClure is that rare bird among writers who can write a memoir that addresses the universal without sounding pompous or self-indulgent. Here is a man who tackles the most fundamental subjects with wit and profundity in equal measure." – *Toni Whitmont, Booktopia*

"Joel Stratte-McClure's *The Idiot and the Odyssey* is a wonderful book. By turns whimsical and profound – and more than occasionally laugh-out-loud funny – it defies all the conventions. It is at once an adventure story, a work of history, a philosophical treatise and an unflinchingly honest memoir." – *Harry Stein, author of "The Girl Watchers Club: Lessons from the Battlefields of Life"*

"Perhaps our perception of the world does not depend on the places we visit but the gait of our travelling. I never thought that, in an era obsessed with speed and technology, somebody could thrill me with his amusing observations, experiences and ruminations while tracing on foot the same route I travelled by car in 1968 to visit my aging grandfather at the other end of the Spanish coast. This is the best guide to the Mediterranean since Homer's *The Odyssey* and as informative as James Michener's *Iberia*." – *Princess Beatriz de Orleans Borbón, Spain*

"Having reveled in the sun, storms and special characters of the Mediterranean, I can attest to Stratte-McClure's insightful clarity. Without being tedious or sanctimonious, he introduces people and places as stereotypical, fantastic and ridiculous as could only be true in the Mediterranean. From one audacious and adventurous *minga* to another, I compliment him on his stable stride in an unstable but captivating region." – *Ethan Gelber, Lonely Planet author and president of BikeAbout the Mediterranean*

"The books *Idiot and Odyssey* titles suggests their tone: at once ambitious and self-effacing, literate and down-to-earth. Stratte-McClure is an erudite man whose lust for life is balanced by Buddhist wisdom, and he brings to each moment on his journey a genuine affection for all he encounters that is irresistible." – *Robert Speer, Chico (CA) News and Review*

"If you want to weave myth, magic, sharp-eyed travel writing and hilarious personal anecdote, you can't do better than *The Idiot and the Odyssey II* by Joel Stratte-McClure. This is a tale of walking around the Mediterranean, while sharing secrets with the locals, visiting the great monuments, quoting Plato, and watching the gods and goddesses of Homer's epic bubbling up from the ancient landscape and emerging from the blazing blue sea.
Stratte-McClure tromps with lovely, amazing aplomb along the coastlines of Italy, Greece and Turkey and makes you feel, hear, see and touch it all. Time presents no barriers, he skips from incident to incident as easily as a butterfly changing flowers, and the only thing that matters is his

enchanting story and sizzling detail...If you don't read this amazing book you are denying yourself fun, wisdom, and insight. Get it now." – *Lex Hames, author of "All Fall Down" and "Kill Club"*

"Contemplative and entertaining, *The Idiot* traverses a very contemporary Mediterranean shoreline – though Greek gods and goddesses pop up along the way. Much more than a guidebook, Stratte-McClure's tale is saturated with history and humor. This mid-life meditation will appeal to adventurers and armchair travelers alike." – *Linda Phillips Ashour, author of "Speaking in Tongues" and "Joy Baby"*

"The second volume of Joel Stratte-McClure's trilogy about hiking the Mediterranean is a delightful, offbeat guide to classical and coastal Greece, Italy, and Turkey. His MedTrek adventures were initially inspired by the break-up of his marriage and a spiritual crisis, but have now taken on a life of their own. The author is as wily, tenacious and gifted at finding the gold and surviving misadventure in his picaresque journeying as Odysseus himself. A wonderful storyteller, he is a genius at giving readers the sense that they are trekking with him on the paths of the gods with the blessings of the goddesses. Whether you're an armchair traveler or someone who loved the time you spent on the Mediterranean – you'll find this wise, entertaining, and must-have book a joy to own and read over many times!" – *Eve Siegel, author of "Success With Soul"*

"Like slow food, the Herculean hike around the Mediterranean by Joel Stratte-McClure – no idiot, for sure – seems an improbable ambition. Yet, inspired by Odysseus, Chinese philosophy and his own mid-life crises, the account of his adventures is a triumph of travel writing – entertaining, witty, perceptive and informative. An enchanting read." – *Marion Kaplan, photojournalist/author of "France: Reflections and Realities"*

"If, as the Greek physician Hippocrates said, 'Walking is man's best medicine,' then Joel Stratte-McClure's books prove it. Everyone who accompanies him will be healthier in mind and spirit. Slow down and read *The Idiot and the Odyssey*." – *Alex Belida, author of "Regrets Only: An Africa Journal"*

"This amazing account of human stamina and daring do, where mythological references merge with the author's experiences, creates a brilliant correspondence between past and present. Woven seamlessly in this tale are courage, curiosity and personal reflection, often against a historical or cultural context that shuns all pretence. The trek illuminates the human adventure, comprehension of the self and understanding of 'the other'." – *Constantine Christofides, Professor at the Institute for American Universities in Aix-en-Provence, France*

"Joel Stratte-McClure's didactic but sensitive voice simultaneously describes and contemplates the Mediterranean landscape he traverses and the individuals who inhabit it. He combines a knowledgeable guide's eye of historic and cultural detail with a tourist's awe of the fascinating scenery and people. Homer would love it!" – *Vince Tomasso, Classics Department, Trinity College*

"One man's travel narrative becomes one woman's guiding light." – *Judy Barnett, The Sunday Examiner, Tasmania*

Purchase all three books in *The Idiot and the Odyssey* series at amazon.com.

Watch hilarious video clips submitted by *The Idiot and the Odyssey* readers.

Listen to The Idiot hold forth during a one-hour radio interview with ABC.

Purchase PDFs of the books in *The Idiot and the Odyssey* trilogy.

*Dedication:*
*To the Mediterranean Sea and my many earthly and*
*godly companions on the path.*

*Disclaimer:*
*This book is a personal account of the author's experience,*
*insights and opinions during the third and final segment of his trek*
*around the Mediterranean Sea. The places, events and acid flashes*
*are generally factual, though the names and identifying details of*
*some participants have been changed to protect their privacy and*
*prevent lawsuits. The author alone is responsible for any errors.*

# VOLUME ONE

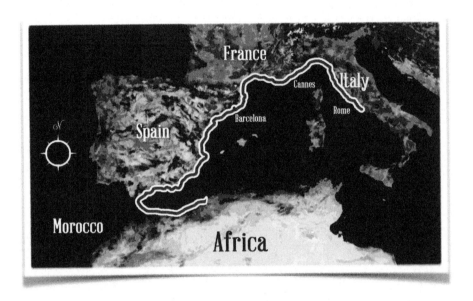

*The Idiot and the Odyssey: Walking the Mediterranean* takes readers on a 4,401 kilometer MedTrek through Morocco, Spain, France, Monaco and down the Italian coast to Rome.

# VOLUME TWO

*The Idiot and the Odyssey II: Myth, Madness and Magic on the Mediterranean* takes readers 4,401 kilometers from Rome to the boot of Italy, around the islands of Sicily and Crete, into the Peloponnese, up Mount Olympus, on to numerous Mediterranean islands and down the Turkish coast to İzmir.

# VOLUME THREE

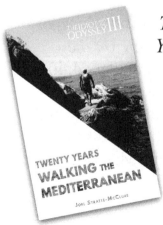

*The Idiot and the Odyssey III: Twenty Years Walking the Mediterranean* takes readers from Greece through Turkey, Cyprus, Lebanon, Israel and Egypt to Tunisia in the footsteps of Alexander the Great.

The Idiot and the Odyssey III

# CONTENTS

## Part Four
*Lebanon and Israel*

## Part Five
*Egypt and Tunisia*

**Bibliography**

**Acknowledgements**

**About the Author**

PREFACE

# Getting Arrested in Lebanon for Being an Israeli Spy

Two apparently undercover policemen, both with shaved heads and wearing jeans, look like any two young Lebanese men in their mid-20s and I think this is possibly a scam, maybe a robbery. But when I ask them for some ID, in response to their request that I show them my passport and answer some questions, they flash their plastic ID cards with **Internal Security Forces** emblazoned on them.

I calmly allow them to check my papers, which consist of photocopies of my passport and my California driver's license, and they joke with the people around the table that I'm a VIP American. The atmosphere and discussion are very casual and they tell me that I'll be able to continue my walk after they call their boss, whom they call "The Colonel," at the Saida office. Unfortunately, he tells them to bring me in.

It's obvious the second I enter the room that "The Colonel" doesn't like me and wants to prove to the young officers that he is vigilant and in control. He asks me not to cross my legs and instructs the ten plain-clothed cops in the room to go through the photos on my phone, investigate my GPS (Global Positioning System), check my phone calls and take my backpack apart.

"The Colonel," using French-and-English-speaking policemen to translate his questions from Arabic, is fixated on my high-tech GPS. This, he makes quite clear to his junior officers, indicates that I am a high-level spy capturing and recording state secrets involving people, places and things on Lebanon's coast. He tells them, citing his years of experience, that I am probably an Israeli spy and gloats, with a smug expression that indicates, "We've caught a big one here."

Within three hours, I have been transported from the beach, detained as a "suspicious foreigner," placed under arrest in Saida and transported to the top floor of the main ISF headquarters in Beirut, which I now consider a combination of the police, FBI and CIA in the US.

For the next six hours I'm interrogated by various officers using everything from a good cop/bad cop method, which lasts four hours, to forcing me to repeat my story, from start to finish, to various officials who each laboriously write everything down in Arabic while looking for inconsistencies. I begin to frequently point to a sign in the interrogation room that states I am entitled to a translator, a phone call and assistance. When I ask for a translator, the bad cop says, "I'm the translator," and I tell him that won't do. At this point, they are trying to pin everything bad going on in Lebanon on me. They've been through all of the photos on my phone, scoured and copied my Facebook account and my list of friends, and looked at my phones and analyzed my GPS, which they treated like a nuclear device.

The questioning becomes more intense as the night goes on and involves spying, gun running, mysterious phone calls to Belgium, drug use, my family, my profession, my books, my walking, the MedTrek, Buddhism, my life...

# PART ONE

## WALKING THE MEDITERRANEAN
## (IN THE FOOTSTEPS OF ALEXANDER THE GREAT)

*Meeting Alexander the Great*

*Running into Zeus and Alexander in Greece*

*Crossing the Hellespont with Alexander the Great*

*Rituals at Troy and Different Routes in Turkey*

# Meeting Alexander the Great

"All truly great thoughts are conceived by walking."
– Friedrich Nietzsche

"I think there was, at that time, no race of men, no city, nor even a single individual to whom Alexander's name and fame had not penetrated." – Arrian of Nicomedia

I first met Alexander the Great in the 1950s when I was nine years old and he was 23.

I was eating Rocky Road ice cream after a day of grammar school in Redding, California, and reading a book called *Myths and Legends of the Ages*. Alexander the Great was one of many characters featured in this, my favorite book. Even as a kid I realized that Alexander's quests, his exploits, victories and reign, dramatically altered the fate and future of the world.

Written in very large type with simple words – if you discount all of the Greek and Roman names of people and places – the story on page 54 of the book was entitled *The Gordian Knot: The Destiny of Alexander*. It recounted the tale of Alexander's 333 BC visit to Phrygia, a tiny kingdom that is now part of Turkey, located about 100 kilometers west of Ankara, the current capital.

According to Homer's *Iliad*, which was Alexander's favorite book (he became familiar with the long poem as a teen when he was tutored by Aristotle), Phrygia was famous for its wine and "brave and expert" horsemen. An important kingdom from 1200-700 BC, its capital Gordium had been the home of King Midas, the 8th-century BC king on whom the god Dionysus bestowed the golden touch.

Everything that Midas put his hands on, including everything he tried to eat, turned to gold and the story about Midas, called *The Golden Touch: The King Who Worshipped Gold*, is on page 49 of the influential book that taught me so much. Even as a child I understood that the story was about the dangers of excess and greed. One sentence, which often has me laughing at myself, has stuck with me since then: "The more gold the foolish man had, the more he wanted."

Gordius, Phyrgia's first king, had tied the Gordian Knot when he arrived in an oxcart at the kingdom's Temple to Zeus. The oracles at the temple, like oracles throughout the Mediterranean back in the day, could foretell the future and had prophesied about the famous knot: "Whoever undoes this wonderful work shall have the world for his kingdom."

Thousands of failed attempts to unravel the knot had been made for centuries but there was a huge buzz in the ancient world when it became known that Megas Alexandros, or Alexander the Great, would attempt to undo the knot once he had defeated the Phrygians and taken control of their kingdom.

There are two historical versions of Alexander's success, but my book claimed that he simply drew his sword, raised it above his head and cut the Gordian Knot in two with one "mighty stroke."

"It is thus that I unravel all Gordian Knots," Alexander cried before he left this town where archaeologists have uncovered civilizations from the Bronze Age through the Hittite, Phrygian, Persian, Greek and Roman epochs.

That might not be the truth.

Aristobulus of Cassandreia, a military engineer and Greek historian who accompanied Alexander the Great on his beat-the-Persians campaign, claimed that Alexander simply pulled out a wooden peg holding the cord together. And Plutarch, one of the most respected historians to chronicle Alexander's life, attests "How Alexander performed the feat in connection with this cord, I cannot affirm with confidence."

But who cares? What impressed me as a kid was the decisive and dramatic sword-cutting version. Strength, I thought in my youth, outdid cunning, though I gradually realized that both options have their merits depending on circumstances.

Throughout the night after Alexander "untied" the knot,

tremendous bursts of thunder and ongoing bolts of lightning were considered favorable omens. The following day, Alexander offered sacrifices to the gods, a staple of Greek custom and a habit he frequently exhibited during his travels. It appeared that the oracles' prophecy had merit when he and his army defeated the Persians and created one of the largest empires of the ancient world, though one without a capital or geographical center.

I had the book – it was still intact despite a few torn pages, some missing stories and ice cream stains from the 1950s – rebound over a decade ago. And although I've since read numerous more sophisticated versions of the myths it contains, it is this childhood book that initially sparked my interest in travel and quests, in Greek and Roman myths and in adventurers like Alexander, Jason and Odysseus. Their exploits not only captivated my childhood mind but also became a key part of my perspective on the world and influenced what I did and who I am.

Those adventures also played a part in the genesis of my idea to walk around the Mediterranean Sea (which is frequently called *Mare Nostrum*, Latin for "Our Sea"), and when I reread the book while writing *The Idiot and the Odyssey: Walking the Mediterranean*, the first of three books recounting my trek around the Mediterranean, I got the idea of following Alexander's footsteps. Hence, this third volume.

And how did Alexander learn about myths and legends in his day?

His teacher, the Greek philosopher Aristotle, gave him a personally annotated copy of the *Iliad*, which Plutarch called "the casket copy" because it would go with him to his grave. Alexander always carried that copy, written in Homer's original dialect, with him because he considered it a "perfect portable treasure of all military virtue and knowledge." He slept with it, and a dagger for self-defense, under his pillow.

"I am indebted to my father for living, but to my teacher for living well," Alexander told me in our first mythical conversation. "Born to the sword, I grew up respecting both sides on the Trojan War."

As I continue my ongoing 20-year walk around the Mediterranean Sea, I'm on my way to Alexander's birthplace in Greece to participate in the annual Alexander the Great Marathon, which was first run in 2006. Before the race, I plan to visit the site of Alexander's birthplace in Pella, to investigate the spot where his father was killed in Vergina, and to climb Mount Olympus to engage in another lively discussion with Zeus, the father of the gods. Then, if the signs are clear and the omens are favorable, I'll follow the King of Macedon's (Macedonia was known as Macedon in Alexander's day) footsteps across Greece into Turkey.

I also have one other goal on this last stage of the MedTrek, a personal goal dating back to that book I held in my eager hands at the age of nine. I want to find Alexander's tomb, a mystery that has been a baffling challenge for historians and archaeologists for centuries. No one knows where his remains remain.

I found Homer's home when I MedTrekked on the Greek island of Chios and I'm now looking forward to discovering the location of Alexander's last address. I'm an intrepid and tireless investigator, explorer and sleuth – I know I can find his final resting place. You may be aware that he died in Babylon and that Ptolemy, one of his generals, snatched the corpse and took it to Egypt to prove that he was Alexander's legitimate successor. The body went first to Memphis, then to Alexandria, then to Siwa and now he is buried in...well, keep reading.

I'd been living in France when I launched my MedTrek in 1998, but my base camp in 2013 was in California, where I had been training for a resumption of the Mediterranean walk with my partner Liz Chapin, one of the cheeriest women on earth despite (or perhaps because of) having worked for the United Nations World Health Organization in Geneva for over two decades. Liz has been invaluable to me in my travels, always providing good advice and sometimes accompanying me on the walks. We spent much of the California winter together preparing for the April marathon and our subsequent long-distance MedTrek.

However, when the time comes, we don't head directly back to Greece.

Instead we meander (the word is derived from the Maeander River, which I'll soon be crossing in Turkey) around Manhattan to get some background on Alexander the Great at the city's museums, and to enjoy some preliminary training for the next five months of MedTrekking. After that I go to London to explore a relevant exhibit at the British Museum to determine if Alexander might somehow have been buried under the lava in Pompeii when Mount Vesuvius erupted in AD 79, before I finally embarked for northern Greece.

This type of circuitous MedTrek training and preparation, which I call SideTrekking, keeps me from being overly obsessed and too linear about my project. At the same time, it creates a mounting sense of excitement about getting back on the actual path.

It turns out that Alexander the Great – although he never materialized in New York or London – is well known almost everywhere in the world and that quite a few people, from tourist guides and touts to academics and scholars, think they know where he's buried.

Still, why walk around the perimeter of Manhattan when I should be retracing the steps of King Alexander III of Macedon (his friends called him Alexandros, which is what he asked me to call him, or Al'skander or Sikander or Iskander), along the Mediterranean Sea from Greece to Egypt?

While the New York stopover is part of my training and research, I'm here because I was asked, almost a year ago, by a psychiatrist named

Harvey Berman if I wanted to lead a walk around Manhattan. Naturally I said yes and now consider it an appropriate launch to the next leg of my MedTrek. I timed the hike to coincide with an exhibit about Alexander at The Metropolitan Museum of Art and also hoped to meet with the New York author of a definitive-sounding book entitled *The Tomb of Alexander.*

You'll frequently encounter Alexander in this book – just as you met Odysseus, Homer and Athena (the goddess who counseled and mentored Odysseus during his endless wanderings and similarly aided me during my Mediterranean walkabouts) in my first two books – but don't worry: this is not another biography of Alexander the Great. It's the story of my walk in his footsteps over 2,300 years after his death.

But now I have a job to do in Manhattan. Our 31.87-mile (51.29 kilometer) circumnavigation of New York's best-known island, which I call a ManTrek, begins at the Bowling Green Subway stop in lower Manhattan just after the 6:20 a.m. sunrise on April 13. Typically, as an example of what I must admit is my shameless promotion, I show up wearing *The Idiot and the Odyssey II* T-shirt that I bought at my own online boutique. Liz, ever a good sport but a willing marketer too, appears in a rocking *Follow The Idiot* baseball cap. We're ready to face the rigors of Manhattan and the famous doubting scowls of New Yorkers.

The ManTrek's kick off reminds me of the initial start of the MedTrek early on New Year's Day in January 1998 at the Picasso Museum in Antibes, France. Then, as now, I expected scores of friends to join me, though then I wound up being accompanied only by Bogart, my yellow Labrador, and a spiritual goddess named Delphyne. Since that time, both solo and with a variety of interesting companions, I have walked 5,469 miles.

Many people vaguely promise to appear for our Manhattan escapade but at the beginning it is just me, Liz, Harvey the psychiatrist, my 100-year-old mentor Elliott Thompson and his wife Robin, a cyclist named Ashley, and Barbara Archer, who attended the Columbia School of Journalism with me in 1971.

Harvey sent me a countdown email a few days earlier and, like me, enjoys the anticipation, anxiety and energy of kicking off a new project. He's calculated distances and degrees of difficulty and confidently assures me that we'll complete the walk in eleven hours. Elliott symbolically walks the first hundred steps with us before, understandably, stepping aside while others gradually join the procession.

Most of the people accompanying me in New York have read, or say they've read, the first two books of the trilogy about my walk around the Mediterranean. We discuss how easy and safe it is to walk around an island or a sea compared to a more treacherous walkabout in unknown mountains or forests, where one can easily become disoriented.

"It's difficult to get lost on a MedTrek or a ManTrek because the sea or the river is always on your left or right," I say, as I explain how walking, and walking meditation, improve health and, according to some studies, enhance mental prowess and memory. "Just a few minutes walking is a great antidote to the risk of obesity, heart disease and stroke and usually burns more calories than you think. So a walk around Manhattan should extend your life by a few hours."

Someone mentions that there's a lot of conflicting advice about the type of shoes to wear, whether and how to stretch, and the pros and cons of step counters and activity trackers. I allude to the twelve simple instructions I sent Harvey and a few others before our ManTrek.

One of the people on the Manhattan walk asks, "Why, with all the options available, did you choose to call yourself The Idiot?"

Actually I credit *The Idiot and the Odyssey* title and The Idiot brand to one of my two former wives (I've never claimed that walking about the Mediterranean for 20 years is the key to a successful marriage – indeed it may be just the opposite) who had an epiphany at four in the morning.

She woke up, as though struck by a lightning bolt, shouted "The Idiot and the Odyssey!" and, almost immediately, went back to sleep. And, though the word "idiot," and its offsprings like "idiosyncratic," do not usually have positive connotations (think "babbling madman"), I shamelessly adopted and promoted the title and brand that played on the titles of Homer's two classic poems, the *Iliad* and the *Odyssey*.

Everyone starts the ManTrek energetically, pointing out landmarks and sharing their knowledge of Manhattan...about the High Line walkway; the damage from the Sandy Hook storm a few months earlier; the construction on the new World Trade Center; the history of buildings designed by Frank Gehry; the location of the Hustler Club; the fabulousness of the Chelsea Piers fitness center; the price of real estate; and lots more as we pass nifty chairs on the water's edge made of cement, wood or steel, picnic tables with chess games on them and lots of public toilets.

A friend meets us with coffee at West 70th Street, Sarah Chambers joins us near Grant's Tomb and Barbara Archer peels off around West 136th Street. By that time Harvey, who was celebrating his 60th birthday, had become our main concern. Thin, bearded and wearing tight jeans, Harvey looks like a younger Sigmund Freud on a serious march to higher meaning. I was hoping that he'd be able to maintain his quick pace because he had so enthusiastically suggested the walk at Elliott Thompson's 100th birthday party the previous May. However, by the time we had passed the George Washington Bridge, I was becoming more than a little worried about him. Harvey was carrying a giveaway bag with PROZAC written on

# TWELVE COMMONSENSE TIPS FOR MINDFUL MEDTREKKING

One of the reasons that I have such a delightful time walking around the Mediterranean Sea is because I keep it simple. Here are twelve commonsense tips that will enable you to have an equally pleasant and unencumbered stroll if you decide to walk around the sea, Manhattan or your neighborhood.

1. Adequately prepare, train and stretch to avoid, or lessen, aches, pains and injuries.

2. There is no hurry. Start slowly and walk at the speed of the slowest member of your party. For the record, I walk an average of 33 kilometers, or little over twenty miles, a day.

3. It is very difficult to get lost if you stay as close as possible to the sea or river. It will always be on your left or right.

4. Practice walking meditation, pick up litter, smile at strangers, do not argue (too much) with security officials and walk on behalf of all sentient beings.

5. Fresh water is the most important item in your backpack, which should be very light (I use a North Face Summit Series Verto 26 for day hikes). Don't worry; the load will get lighter after the first day out. You are what you carry.

6. Many things beyond your control – weather, logistics, illness, injury, topography, trail conditions and security officials – come with the territory. Accept that and be open to serendipitous events. It's imperative to be flexible, footloose and fancy-free, especially on the unpredictable and uncertain MedTrek.

7. There is more daylight during summer months but it is hot, tourists are everywhere and accommodation is more expensive and sometimes difficult to find. Try walking in April/May/early June and September/October.

8. It's fun to hike with friends but it's essential, and often much more interesting, to hike alone from time to time.

9. There's nothing more delightful than meeting strangers on the road.

10. Never reserve a room in advance and always be prepared to sleep on the beach, in a monastery, at a nudist colony or almost anywhere else. It's part of the game.

11. Forget the destination; take it a step at a time and don't worry about what's around the next curve. The goal is the path, the path is the goal.

12. Try to practice the relaxed attitude of the MedTrek in other parts of your life.

it, rather than a backpack, and he soon began to limp.

"I don't think I'm wearing the right shoes because I'm getting blisters and my back is killing me," Harvey confided to me.

"I know the feeling," I said sympathetically. "When this happens to me I don't hesitate to call it a day, go for a massage or a hot bath and take the next day off. Don't worry; Manhattan will be here the day after tomorrow."

We were all both disappointed and slightly relieved when Harvey did choose to drop out with his pal Ashley.

For most of the remainder of the walk it is Sarah, Liz and me.

When Liz had first told Sarah about the upcoming hike, she was enthusiastic from the get go. Sarah gets the award for the most bathroom stops in the most awkward places and positions of anyone who's ever hiked with me, around Manhattan or the Mediterranean. She provided an expanded definition to the phrase "pit stop" when she ducked behind parked cars, squatted near earth mounds, entered construction sites and disappeared under bridges. Fortunately she had time to take some classic photos of the ManTrekkers on the East River with the multiple bridges as a backdrop.

Oddly, as I walk along the Hudson, I sometimes get flashes of rivers I had forded or crossed on the Mediterranean – the Rhone in France, the Ebro in Spain, the Tiber in Italy. I feel that even as I circumnavigate Manhattan, I am still walking around the Mediterranean.

I was always confident that Liz could complete the long Manhattan hike and was delighted to see her marching with vigor until the last five miles. I'd told her about "the wall" that almost every walker hits after reaching the 40-kilometer, or 25-mile, mark. I'd even described how my son Luke once threw his backpack at me when he reached that frustrating distance in Italy. Karmically or coincidentally Luke phoned at just that moment and gave Liz a pep talk.

"No matter how painful it is, or how much you might want to stop, or how angry you get at Joel, you've just got to walk through it," Luke told her.

Ethan Gelber, who has biked around the Mediterranean, joined our threesome at East 78th Street and Barbara Archer rejoined us at East 63rd. Robin Thompson came on board at Houston Street and the last stragglers and remaining survivors celebrated with dinner at Smorga's on Stone Street when, a mere thirteen hours after our start, we arrived back at Bowling Green station.

High points of the Big Apple circumambulation?

The view of the Statue of Liberty caught in the light of the rising sun; the long approach to the symbolic George Washington Bridge; the walk through Inwood Hills Park at the tip of Manhattan; the stroll through a farmer's market on Isham Street; urban asides into a now-hip Harlem;

the photo of Liz and me backed by three bridges that stretch over the East River and the view of the Statue of Liberty at sunset. And, of course, the sight of well-known monuments like Grant's Tomb and the Cloisters.

Naturally Alexander the Great doesn't walk with us. That comes a bit later. But I sense his presence on the horizon because I am also in New York to find Seán Hemingway, Ernest's grandson. As the curator of the Greek and Roman collections at New York's Metropolitan Museum of Art, Seán has written several scholarly works about the mighty Alexander. And a few years ago, he generously took me through the museum and showed me a wealth of artifacts relating to the ancient Greeks.

"Alexander's conquests spread Greek civilization eastward throughout the lands of the former Persian Empire and changed the face of the ancient world forever, opening trade routes and encouraging cultural exchanges with far-reaching implications," he explained at the time.

Since then Seán had authored *The Tomb of Alexander* and curated an exhibit called "Pergamon and the Hellenistic Kingdoms of the Ancient World" that caused *The New York Times* to gush lyrically about Alexander's exploits.

"Alexander himself is everywhere in the opening gallery," enthused the *Times*, noting that a marble head sculpture made Alexander look "generically dishy with a designer haircut, Justin Bieber with gravitas."

That wasn't all. The usually sedate newspaper continued exuding superlatives about Alexander rather than spending much time detailing the exhibit's ten-feet high, 8,000-pound Hellenistic marble statue of Athena Parthenos. The *Times* claimed that Alexander moved beyond classical Greek culture "with the creative confidence of a superstar. Gorgeous and beauty-loving, culturally inquisitive and ravenous with ambition, Alexander embarked on what amounts to a world tour based on military conquest."

It added that "Two small bronzes suggest distinctive personas that Alexander, a born performer, wanted to market: in one he's a buff hunk inviting worshipful admiration, in the other an armored equestrian, eyes wide, hair flying, sword-arm raised."

Alexander was often thought to be, and often thought himself to be, god-like, if not a god. And he certainly had the looks for it. Curly blond locks (many gossipy scribes in ancient Greece called his hair "leonine"), melting liquid bluish grey eyes, a slightly ruddy complexion, his neck frequently tilted sideways to the left.

But *The New York Times* – comparing him with Justin Bieber and calling him a "superstar" and "buff hunk" – was more eloquent than most, though *The New Yorker* was equally enthusiastic.

"Alexander the Great conquered the Achaemenid Persian Empire and...unleashed perhaps the greatest economic stimulus package of all time," read a review of the exhibit in the magazine. "This tidal wave of wealth sloshed all around the eastern Mediterranean during the three centuries that followed, the era known today as the Hellenistic Age."

These weren't the first appreciative words about Alexander's good looks and historical importance.

"He was very handsome in person, and much devoted to exertion, very active in mind, very heroic in courage, very tenacious of honor, exceedingly fond of incurring danger, and strictly observant of his duty to the gods," wrote the historian Arrian of Nicomedia in his much-respected *Anabasis of Alexander* in the second century AD. In fact, Arrian wrote that narrative of Alexander's conquests to afford Alexander the same glory that Homer's *Iliad* did to Achilles.

Gosh, and I thought I was a fan.

But right now I'm more interested in Seán Hemingway's novel, *The Tomb of Alexander,* than in the exhibit. I want to see if he actually believes, as his novel concludes, that Alexander's body can be found in Rome.

The novel, which frequently cites the *Alexander Romance* – an illustrated collection of legends perhaps dating from the second century BC – places Alexander's crypt under the 13th-century Dominican Basilica di Santa Maria sopra Minerva, once the Roman Temple of Minerva (Minerva is the Roman version of Athena and *sopra* means above) near the Pantheon in central Rome. I'd already MedTrekked through Rome and visited both the church and the Pantheon, but had no clue at that time that Alexander might be there too.

Was he? I had to find out.

Disappointingly, when I ask for an interview, Seán tells me he isn't available to discuss whether, as he contends in his novel, I'll actually find Alexander's tomb in Rome. And he downplays the presence of Alexander at The Met.

"We don't have many artworks directly related to Alexander in The Met's Greek and Roman collection," he emails me. "But a search through The Met's collection online will no doubt yield all kinds of art works that may be of interest to you and your research."

The fact that he politely puts me off makes me think that (his fictional musings aside) he actually doesn't have a clue where Alexander is really buried. Or he is hiding a fabulous secret?

After the Manhattan walk, Liz returns to Geneva while I fly to London to visit a Pompeii exhibit at the British Museum before continuing to the birthplace of Alexander the Great in Greece.

The intriguing allure of the "Life and Death in Pompeii and Herculaneum" exhibit is its intimate characterization of daily life in the two Roman towns before their destruction by the eruption of Mount Vesuvius in AD 79. I thought the exhibit also might shed light on Alexander. If he might have been buried in Rome, as some academics contend, then Roman rulers seeking to keep him out of the public eye could also have hidden his corpse in Pompeii.

When I visit the exhibit during the week of Margaret Thatcher's funeral, I am both enchanted and horrified by full-sized representations of carbonized dogs and people (not actual human remains, but created by making molds during the excavation) that were obviously buried and killed almost instantly following the eruption in Pompeii.

"Is Alexander's buried body among them?" I wonder as I examine the carbonized bodies, food, swords, baby cribs, ornate lamp stands, jewelry, medical instruments, ceiling panels and household appliances. Together they all produce an eerie impression of humanity and a genuinely unsettling feeling.

I don't learn whether Alexander was there, but I always pick up something new and intriguing on these SideTreks. This time, besides all the vivid carbonizations pressed into my brain, my newly acquired knowledge turns out to be about love and sex during the days of Pompeii.

It seems, as a document at the exhibit contends, that the "Romans were generally comfortable with nakedness and with sexual scenes in art. Their homes were sometimes decorated with intentionally erotic images, such as phallic depictions and frescoes showing couples making love." And I leave amused by the odd fact that "Romans considered dormice a delicacy...when they were fat enough to eat, the mice would be stuffed, rolled in honey and poppy seeds and baked or fried."

"Who knew?" I wondered, as I begin to make a "The Weirdest Things The Idiot has Eaten on his Travels" list.

## FOOD SHOPPING

All this SideTrekking is a lot of fun, but New York and London are not where I am supposed to be. It's time to move on and I'm now ready to fulfill the promise I made to my readers at the end of *The Idiot and the Odyssey II.*

# MEDTREK MILESTONE #10

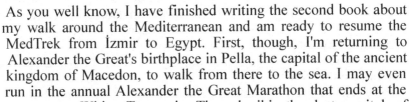

As you well know, I have finished writing the second book about my walk around the Mediterranean and am ready to resume the MedTrek from İzmir to Egypt. First, though, I'm returning to Alexander the Great's birthplace in Pella, the capital of the ancient kingdom of Macedon, to walk from there to the sea. I may even run in the annual Alexander the Great Marathon that ends at the White Tower in Thessaloniki, the last capital of ancient Macedon. Then away I go back to Turkey and down the shores of Syria, Lebanon and Israel into Egypt.

# See you in Alexandria!

# FOLLOW THE IDIOT

**American Author Follows Footsteps of Homer's Odysseus**

# CHAPTER PHOTOS

# CHAPTER MAP

# Running into Zeus and Alexander in Greece

"That he did not emerge a psychopath like Nero is one of
history's miracles."
– Mary Renault, *The Nature of Alexander*

"Macedon is too little for thee."
– King Philip II, Alexander's father

I savor a *bougatsa crema*, a delicious just-out-of-the-oven Greek pastry (it consists of mouth-watering semolina custard spread between thin but flaky layers of phyllo), on the Thessaloniki waterfront the moment that I return to Greece in the midst of the country's ongoing national economic meltdown.

I consider a *bougatsa crema* a justifiable culinary extravagance because of my ongoing and extensive MedTrekking exercise regime – and should probably admit that it's just one of many sweet delicacies that I regularly permit myself due to the uncountable number of calories I burn while walking around the Mediterranean Sea.

When I arrive, I immediately notice that my already inexpensive room at the Nea Metropolis Hotel costs 25 percent less than it did a few years ago when I first MedTrekked through this historic port towards Turkey. And that a ticket for the hour-long bus ride into town from the airport is now only 80 cents, though an employed Greek told me during the ride that "most Greeks now think 80 cents is too expensive."

There are bargains galore due to the country's economy-and-debt debacle. A cappuccino goes for only one euro, there are lots of ten-euro *prix fixe* menus in restaurants and "sale" signs shout from the dimly illuminated window displays in many stores. Though there are some closed shops, their front windows covered with graffiti-decorated cardboard or wood, what's most noticeable to me is that so much seems to still be working as usual amidst all the impending stories of doom and gloom.

Many open stores that I pass are packed with eager-looking shoppers and cafés are filled by large numbers of satisfied-looking customers sitting for hours over coffee in the mid-afternoon. The Greeks could nonchalantly take a day to drink a tiny cup of coffee even before the economic downturn. The buses are packed with joke-telling riders and there's construction underway to renovate and expand the wide seaside promenade.

The situation seems more like a yin-and-yang cyclical economic downturn than a blatant sign of a distressed economy in freefall collapse, or a country on the verge of a financial Armageddon, though the buzz on the cobblestone street from a woman my age is that "people are just scraping by; no one has money for a vacation and we're all trying to put on a brave face. These problems won't be solved during my lifetime."

I'm hardly a big spender when I'm on a MedTrek outing (all I ask for is a room with a view of the sea and Wi-Fi which, during the past fifteen years, has led to an average expenditure of just over $30 a night, often with breakfast included), but I don't enjoy saving a few euros at the expense of the economically struggling Greeks. Especially as I recall that the outlook was much brighter when I walked through Thessaloniki a few years ago to accomplish the twelve tasks given to me by the gods that I described in *The Idiot and the Odyssey II*.

Those arduous tasks, you might remember, were assigned to me by the sorceress Circe in Italy and included three pursuits in the northern part of Greece.

Here's the first one:

*"Meet with Zeus, the master of cloud, at the cave of his birth on Crete, visit him again at the top of Mount Olympus, and see him once more after you traipse through Troy at the top of Mount Ida in Turkey."*

I'd be a liar if I didn't confess that meeting Zeus, the father of the gods, on Crete, Mount Olympus and Mount Ida has been among the

38

highlights of my entire MedTrek project. And climbing Mount Olympus, 142-kilometers from here, to see Zeus and the other eleven Olympian gods in September 2009 was the most invigorating and rewarding of our three meetings. I described that climb up above the clouds to the peak of iconic and mysterious Mount Olympus as "one of the most enticing of the twelve labors prescribed by Circe...a delectable treat, right up there with a warm *bougatsa crema.*" Now that's a compliment.

I've scoured the history books and there's no indication that Alexander the Great (who frequently pointed out that he was a Macedonian, as well as a Greek) ever climbed the sacred Mount Olympus, though he was very active in Dion at the mountain's base, where he frequently held athletic contests and made sacrifices to the gods.

Dion gets its name from Dionysus, the influential god of the grape harvest, winemaking and wine who was/is in charge of "ritual madness and ecstasy" in Greek mythology. The village was best known for an athletic and theater festival called the Olympic Games of Dion that Archelaus first hosted here in the fifth century BC in honor of the nine Muses.

The Muses, incidentally, are Zeus' daughters and provided the inspiration for arts and sciences in Dion, then the shining symbol of ancient and powerful Macedon. And we all know that Alexander's mother Olympias was a fervent fan of bacchanalia (Bacchus is the Roman name for Dionysus), which made Dion a hot party town.

It was there that Alexander "often appointed prizes, for which not only tragedians and musicians, pipers and harpers, but rhapsodists also, strove to outvie one another; and delighted in all manner of hunting and cudgel-playing, but never gave any encouragement to contests either of boxing or of the pancratium," according to Arrian of Nicomedia, one of my go-to historians. Alexander was such an enthusiastic fan of the spot that he built the fortifications there and his Macedonian successors maintained the sanctuaries to Zeus, Demeter, Artemis, and other gods until things went downhill (as they always tend to in our impermanent world) when Rome conquered it in 167 BC.

I have a couple of days to spare before I get into marathon mode and, besides spending a mouth-watering afternoon in Dion, I plan to again climb majestic Mount Olympus and revisit the ancient capitals of Vergina, Macedon's first capital, and Pella, where Alexander was born, before undertaking the Alexander the Great Marathon.

Why do I return to again climb Mount Olympus when I had already met Zeus at the summit a few years before?

Because I want to consult the father of all gods to get his thoughts, ideas and, hopefully, his benediction before I launch my MedTrek in the footsteps of Alexander the Great. I want to refresh my conversation with the Master of the Heavens, and bask in his wisdom once more. It's always nice, I've learned, to let the gods have your back.

Retracing my steps in such a pleasurable place has other benefits. The day's auspicious meditation from Tao, which I read daily at dawn, puts it aptly: "After completion, come new beginnings. To gain strength, renew the root." So I return to the route to renew my root and, as my MedTrekking partner Liz Chapin, who will join me in Turkey, points out in an email, "you should walk with the Gods...seeking inspirational direction during your climb up Mount Olympus."

I need some inspiration because it won't always be easy to follow in the footsteps of Alexander, the son of Philip II, the shrewd and forceful king of Macedon, and his mother Olympias, a proud princess from Epirus. Some insights and snippets of wisdom from Zeus and his lightning bolts might help. I also want to learn from Zeus if, as Olympias constantly claimed and Alexander believed, it was he who actually fathered Alexander.

Was Alexander justified in believing he had heavenly origins, and could he justly claim to be divine? Or was Alexander, handsome, courageous and successful as he was, just another power-mad human conqueror that let his vanity overrun his reason? And if Zeus is the father of Alexander, will he admit it to me? Will he try to evade my question about Alexander's provenance or lie outright to me? And if he is lying and prevaricating, will I be able to tell? Someone who has been ruling the firmament for so long must become pretty good at hoodwinking and tricking everyone, both humans and gods. I have to nail Zeus with the question; I have to find out.

I want to find out too, if the all-seeing Zeus has any information about the location of Alexander's tomb. And I'm counting on him to give me general guidance for the last third of my MedTrek. That's why I am scaling Olympus once more.

During my four-hour walk from the mountainside village of Litóhoro (aka the City of Gods) through the Enipea Canyon to the Prionia trailhead, my breath is, as it always is on this climb, taken away by the natural beauty and the godly, mythical history of the majestic mountain. I frequently stop to relish nature, talk to spiders and other sentient beings, and marvel at my good fortune to be making this climb for the third time.

I'm again on the international E4 hiking path, one of the entrances into the National Park that goes along a river and passes the spectacular Enipea waterfalls. The mountain summit itself is still snow-capped in mid-April but I hope that Zeus, and perhaps one or more of the other gods living at the top (they include, in alphabetical order rather than prowess, Aphrodite, Apollo, Ares, Artemis, Athena, Hephaestus, Hera, Hermes, Hestia and Poseidon), might descend and meet me between the tree line and the snow-covered summit. I'm still mulling about what to ask and discuss with Zeus, and whomever else I might meet, during a possible lower-altitude consultation when I'm surprised to look up and see a group of three-dozen school kids in the path in front of me.

For just a moment, I wonder if these could be godlings or half-godlings themselves, perhaps the lost children of an ancient Olympian, ambling down the sacred mountain. I look closely for tell-tale superhuman signs. But no, the clothing is all wrong. There are no flowing white robes or laurels of leaves on their brows. These are just contemporary kids in jeans, T-shirts and bright polyester jackets.

"Why aren't you in school?" I ask, quite sensibly I think.

"This IS school for us today," a tweenage girl replies, mentioning that she just learned that, since 1938, Mount Olympus (the name in classical Greek means "the luminous one") has been part of a national park that includes 25 percent of all Greek flora, thirty-two species of mammals, and 108 species of birds. "Do you have anything to teach us? We've been told that everyone has something to teach!"

I'm wearing my *The Idiot and the Odyssey II* baseball cap and this, plus the fact that I tell them I'm from California, sparks some interest in my find-a-god climb, the ongoing MedTrek, my pursuit of their Greek hero Alexander and my books. I spend twenty minutes replying to their questions as we look down on the valleys below Mount Olympus.

Like most Greek kids, these students have, compared to most Americans their age, an intimate grasp of history, particularly Greek history and mythology. They are mesmerized by my tales of everything Homeric, though I don't tell them about the scene in my second book when I slept with Helen of Troy (that was another one of those challenging twelve labors).

They love the stories about how three drunken Gypsies in Italy robbed me and how my son Luke and I lost our passports in the sea in Morocco after walking through fields of marijuana growing taller than we are. They can't get enough about the Sirens and the Cyclops' cave in Italy, the cave in which Zeus was born on Crete or my meeting with the Oracle of Delphi, the Greek Orthodox monks on nearby Mount Athos (where none of them had been) and my swim across the Hellespont.

Before they go down the path, the high schoolers take a group photo which later that day, when it's posted on Facebook, gets scores of "likes" from all their classmates. A decent omen, I figure, in the era of social media.

After a few hours, I reach the refuge where I found shelter from a lightning storm during my first assault on the 2,917-meter (9,570-feet) Mount Olympus. I stop for a rest, munch on a quick snack, gulp down a hot cappuccino from the thermos in my pack, and push onward. As I climb, I'm full of anticipation, my heart is in my throat, my excitement steadily rising. An hour later I swing around a towering rock near the crest, and there he is, standing in the path, spanning the trail, spanning the entire world, as only Zeus can. I am thunderstruck but happy. He's as splendid as ever, as awe-inspiring as before.

Standing there with his feet pressed on the trembling ground, this is one staggering apparition. He has a long silvery beard that looks like it might suddenly burst into a karmic flame, setting the whole earth on fire. He's wearing a long white toga-ish robe draped over one shoulder that reveals a lot of heavenly muscle, sinew, and skin. His legs are like tree trunks, his pecs like iron bars, his biceps ripple like wild waves on the sea. And handsome? – oh, handsome does not even begin to describe this dashing and overpowering man, er, god. Finally there are the eyes, cold pieces of hard blue steel, looking as if they were cut out of the heart of a frozen stream. His gaze radiates out in fierce, piercing jabs that go right through me. I'm rattled, I admit it, but I manage to stay on my feet.

For lack of a better comparison, Zeus still resembles Charlton Heston in the 1956 version of *The Ten Commandments*. He has the same earthshaking presence and the same ear-splitting voice. Both a god and an actor to be reckoned with. But, of course, Zeus goes far, far beyond Heston who (sorry to shatter your illusions) was only human and made, like the rest of us, of mortal, mucky clay. This is something different; this is the god-stuff, standing before me. I feel a queasy, shaking, skittering sensation in my gut like nothing I have ever felt before – more, for some reason, than when I encountered him before. Everybody, gods and men and me, respects Zeus. Soldiers often pray to him (one of the 24 books of the *Iliad* is entitled by a modern translator as *The Battle Swayed by Zeus*) and his power is continually underscored by Homer and other gods.

"I would not dream of pitting all the rest of us gods against Lord Zeus," said Poseidon, the god of the sea, earthquakes and horses. "He overmasters all."

"Wellllllllll???!!!!" Zeus rumbles, his voice like a rolling thundercloud, like a hail of arrows slicing through my heart. But I stand still. I have my questions ready.

I last saw Zeus when we met, in an encounter described in the last chapter of *The Idiot and the Odyssey II,* at the top of Mount Ida in Turkey. He told me then, as we entered the baths attended by various nymphs at a meeting set up by my mentor goddess Athena, who was born from the aching head of Zeus, where I should go on the MedTrek in the years ahead.

Today I don't beat around the bush (actually there are no bushes at this altitude and Zeus has always been a direct and get-to-the-point kinda god) and ask the father of all gods whether he had anything to do with the birth of Alexander the Great.

"Did you happen to impregnate Olympias on her wedding night?" I ask, referring to the claim by Alexander's mother that she felt a thunderbolt on the night she conceived her son. "Olympias dreamt there was a crash of thunder, that you entered her womb in the form of a thunderbolt, that there was a blinding flash from which a great sheet of flame blazed up and that the result was Alexander. Any truth to that?"

Olympias – whom Plutarch describes as "a woman of a jealous and implacable temper" but whom Alexander believed was, as British philosopher Bertrand Russell wrote in the last century, "like some lady of Greek mythology beloved of a god" – frequently used an array of embarrassingly colorful adjectives and superlatives to describe how Zeus made love to her. She usually didn't give much, if any, credit to Alexander's natural father, although on King Philip's side of the family Alexander was descended from Herakles ("Hercules" in Latin).

"You know from our earlier meetings that I don't talk about my private affairs or how I've impacted specific individuals," Zeus tells me *sotto voce*. "But it's clear that what Megas Alexandros accomplished in less than thirty-three years was definitely superhuman, though he was not, of course, immortal."

Some people forgive Alexander the Great for thinking, as his mother insisted, that he might be immortal.

"Alexander's career was so miraculous that he may well have thought a miraculous origin the best explanation of his prodigious success," posited Bertrand Russell.

There were indications pointing in that direction from the outset. And, of course, it was great propaganda.

On the day Alexander was born, King Philip, his earthly and royal father, learned that his troops had won an important battle, that his racehorse placed first at the Olympic Games, that a fiery comet had been sighted in the sky above Mount Olympus and that the Temple of Artemis at Ephesus in Turkey was destroyed by fire, allegedly while its priestess was absent to assist at Alexander's birth. That's quite a list of noteworthy, possibly magical events. Could it all just be coincidence? Or was Zeus's mighty finger scrolling across the heavens, leaving cryptic – or not so cryptic – messages about the birth of his son?

These signs were interpreted by some as definite indications of a divine birth.

"You know, king of all gods," I inform Zeus just in case he doesn't know or has forgotten all the details about Alexander's time on earth, "Plutarch contended that Alexander didn't actually tell people that he was your son, but said, 'it is apparent that Alexander himself was not foolishly affected, or had the vanity to think himself really a god, but merely used his claims to divinity as a means of maintaining among other people the sense of his superiority.'

"Anyway, maybe you can resolve the long-time conundrum about where Alexander is entombed today," I ask Zeus. "How can I find him, or his remains?"

"What The Idiot should do now is follow in the tracks of that *Iliad* lover and Homerophile, Megas Alexandros, who first went from Macedon to Troy," said Zeus, who doesn't look a day older than when I last met him a few years ago. "Walk with him to the Hellespont. But instead of going to Persia, you should simply continue along the windy and difficult coast of Turkey and then through, if things have calmed down by the time you get there, Syria, Lebanon, and Israel to enter Egypt."

Zeus seemed a little smug on that last point, perhaps implying that he could predict the future but refusing to share his inner knowledge with me.

"Walk on the Egyptian coast toward Libya and go to Siwa, the oasis in the Egyptian desert, where the Oracle of Ammon will give you specific information about Alexander's divinity and where he is now buried," Zeus continues, not mentioning that Alexander had also gone to Siwa. "You'll have the details you need before your 20-year odyssey is completed. And don't worry about the obvious dangers in the Middle East; we gods will look after you if you complete the marathon."

In retrospect, it seems inevitable that Alexander (no one would dare call him Alex), who assumed the throne after his father was murdered, would become my mentor and guide for the final ramble through Macedonia, Turkey, Cyprus, Syria, Lebanon, Israel, Gaza, Egypt, Libya and Tunisia.

According to erudite author Anthony Burgess, the name Alexander means "the defender of men." Burgess called Alex, the main character in his book *A Clockwork Orange*, "a comic reduction of Alexander the Great slashing his way through the world and conquering it."

I can identify with that, especially the slashing and conquering approach.

Alexander's quest, which ended with his death at 32, was right up my adventurous pre-pubescent alley and prompted me to imagine myself as a participant and hero in some of the mythological anecdotes. I coined the phrase *me-thology* to describe my new, exciting, exalted state. That's nothing new because Alexander himself constantly imitated heroes like Achilles, Hercules and Dionysus.

"Why should I not compare myself to Hercules?" Alexander asked me once about the divine hero that embodied classical masculinity and whom he clearly envied.

"I know the feeling," I replied as we conversed on the stone steps before the Temple of Hera. "I often imagine myself as Odysseus with his many strengths and weaknesses. And sometimes I even think I'm you and try to emulate your many attributes."

"It's always nice to have role models," Alexander replied. "But no one stays on a pedestal forever."

I'm not sure Zeus would agree.

After getting a dose of godsend and godspeed on Mount Olympus, and eating a hearty chicken and eggplant dinner freshly whisked off an outdoor barbecue spit in Litóhoro, I make my way to the palace and necropolis in Vergina, ancient Macdeon's first capital that was also once called Aigai and was a city of scattered settlements. Although the palace is still being "renovated," the multimedia museum and tombs under the burial mounds are replete with deathly treasures and a big draw for contemporary visitors.

As I leisurely wander around the fourth-century BC palace, or what's left of it, it's easy to see why hilltop Vergina was the capital as early as the tenth century BC when it was an important stop on a trade route heading to the east. Caravans of horses, donkeys and camels paused here, loaded up with trade goods, before heading off into the fierce deserts and mountains to the east. I recall that the Vergina Sun, a popular solar symbol between the sixth and second centuries BC featuring sixteen triangular rays, was the historical royal emblem of the old Macedon – and became prominent again in the late 1900s.

Vergina can still boast of quick-running rivers, an elevated location and a rich verdant soil that has turned everything, except today's persistently barking dogs, a delightful dark green. A sign says that the palace, which was once the largest building in Greece, is closed for renovations until 2008 (the palace was still gated and padlocked during this visit in 2013, a situation everyone blamed on the shattered economy) but I scamper along the fence and circle the perimeter to get a look at the renovation work and ongoing archaeological digs.

Judging from the uncut overgrowth, I'm one of the few people to attempt this stroll recently and I draw the first blood of this MedTrek outing when my legs (I'm wearing shorts) are slashed by proliferating thistles and briars.

As I imagine how the stately palace would have looked with its high walls and a grandeur transmitted by sanctuaries, temples, altars, *stoae* and votives dedicated to the gods – I remind myself that in King Philip's and Alexander's day, Vergina was far from the influence of the democracy of Athens. Indeed, the Macedon king was considered the absolute father and master of his subjects, whether they were in Vergina or Pella.

The king at that time carried on the epic Macedonian tradition of being "a leader in war, guarantor of law and order, a carrier of divine blessing, sacred and sacrosanct." And during the mid-fourth century BC, Macedon was a formidable power whose royal court became a leading center of Greek culture.

Although King Archelaus abandoned Vergina and moved the royal digs to nearby Palaia Pella, or Old Pella, in the fourth century BC, the theater in Vergina was still used as a royal event venue. I reflectively stand at the exact spot where King Philip II – Alexander's father, who came power in 359 BC and was known to be one of the best military commanders of his era – was standing in 336 BC to celebrate his daughter's wedding. I'm in a reflective mood, wondering what the stout old fellow himself might have felt, standing here, so long ago.

Despite being heavily battle-scarred and blind in one eye, I imagine that Philip was feeling pretty good on that late afternoon.

Using a combination of diplomacy, military reorganization and innate skill, he had transformed Macedon, which was about the size of New Jersey, into a major power and significantly expanded his empire, defeating enemies and tribes in different city states and regions throughout Greece. He had introduced innovative forms of warfare – including improved catapults and siege machinery and an infantry that equipped each soldier with an enormous spike known as a *sarisa* – and provided his armies with the latest military technology. And he had just sent 10,000 of his troops into Asia to attack the Persians who had invaded Greece centuries before.

Although some said that Philip had too many wives and drank too much booze, these traits were not considered extreme in those days.

Polygamy had been a customary practice by Macedon kings since it was introduced by Persian invaders in 513 BC and Philip had seven wives for political, military, romantic and sexual reasons. Although when Philip, age 46, fell for a Macedonian woman named Cleopatra, who was aged only 16, Alexander felt it disgraced his mother and there was a family spat and physical separation.

That didn't bother the king.

"I'll marry the girl if I want," the king told his disgruntled son about his teen bride, "and I'll have as many sons as I want and there's nothing you or your harpy mother can do about it!"

Most Macedonians were prodigious consumers of alcohol and extremely proud of their brazen and excessive drinking habits during an era when wine for breakfast was the norm and all-night partying the usual program. Philip, like any decent king, led the way. He once fell down due to too much drink, causing Alexander to comment: "This is the man who is going to take you from Greece to Persia? He can't even make it from one couch to the next."

"At one point my father screamed at me 'Get out of my palace! You're exiled, you bastard! Banished from the land! You're not welcome here! You're no son of mine'," Alexander recounted.

A bit later, after I get to know you better, I'll let you in on a discussion I had with Alexander about whether he and his father were just two of the boys or full-blown alcoholics.

So what could go wrong at the wedding?

I linger at the exact spot where Alexander's father was killed by an assassin's dagger that day and recall that the alleged murderer was Pausanias, one of King Philip's bodyguards. Pausanias and a number of accomplices were rounded up, though there was (and still is) gossip and suspicion that Alexander and his mother played a part in the assassination, primarily because they were sick of Philip's drinking, philandering and multiple marriages.

Alexander was also a suspect because his relationship with his father had soured. He was not only upset with the way his mother had been treated, but also wasn't sure that he would accede to the throne and, as palace gossip had it, was even jealous that his battle-victorious father was on the threshold of everlasting fame. Although Alexander saved his father's life in one skirmish and was usually treated as Philip's rightful heir, this was a time when kings feared their sons and would often kill them to prevent a challenge to their throne.

At the same time, Alexander had been groomed as Philip's heir. At 16 he ran the government of Macedon when his father marched against the people of the city of Byzantium and at 18 he fought alongside his father in the battle of Chaeronea to defeat Athenians, Thebans and other Greek *poleis*, or city states. He had even become an honorary citizen of Athens during his only visit there and an oak tree on the Cephisus River had been named Alexander's Oak because it provided shade for his tent.

Alexander denied that he had anything to do with his father's death and later contended that the Persian king, Darius III, "paid assassins in gold coins to murder my father, our king, in a most despicable and cowardly manner."

Not that the assassination should have surprised anyone, because succession in Macedon was usually determined by assassination, murder, or death in battle. In fact, Alexander the Great, presuming he wasn't poisoned, is one of the few Macedon rulers who might have had a natural death.

He did not start a trend, sad to say. His own son and heir Alexander IV, as well as his wife Roxana, were both murdered by a future king of Macedon after Alexander's death. That terminated Alexander's line and, for good measure, the new king also had Olympias, Alexander's mother, executed.

Funerals were both expressions of honor and periods of mourning in those days and Alexander, now King Alexander III, deftly handled his father's rites and was responsible for his impressive (and now-visitable tomb) at Vergina, where he hosted an officially Homeric state funeral. Philip was entombed, after being cremated on a magnificent funeral pyre, along with his favorite armor, art, ornaments and table settings – all required for the eternal feast that follows death, say ancient traditions.

I scamper down to the tombs and necropolis and enter the Great

Tumulus, a museum/mausoleum under a prominent burial mound. I spend a meditative hour walking around the rich, impressive underground tomb marveling at the frescoes, vases, weapons, jewelry and other treasures embodying Philip's reign.

Vergina fell into decline after its defeat by the Romans in 168 BC and this royal tomb wasn't uncovered until excavations began in the 1970s. Today the descriptive wall paintings and elaborate decorative arts produced for the Macedon royals remind me that this was the apex of Greek culture when Alexander became king.

If I was dubious about visiting Vergina after my thwarted attempt to see the still-under-renovation palace, the site of King Philip's murder and visit to the illuminated darkened underworld turned me into a fan. Go there!

At 20, the stocky and short Alexander (he wasn't tall but was never characterized as the BC equivalent of Napoleon), already a charismatic and decisive leader, was proclaimed king. At 22, he confidently took supreme command of the Macedonian forces to lead the expedition against the Persians in Asian Minor.

He consulted the oracle of Apollo at Delphi and was told, "You are invincible, my son" before he began his own odyssey to successfully conquer much of the known world and create an empire that stretched from Greece and Asia Minor through Egypt and the Persian empire in the Near East to the border of India.

"He was driven by his overbearing mother and fearfully mastered by love of fame," wrote Arrian of Nicomedia.

I arrive in nearby Pella the day before the 8th International Alexander the Great Marathon, a 42.195-kilometer race that follows contemporary tarmac roads flanked by pastures, fields and villages to the iconic White Tower on the Thessaloniki seaside.

Typically, in Pella's Alexander the Great Square, a statue of Alexander riding his long-time equine companion Bucephalus regally hovers over the start of the marathon bearing his name. Beardless, mythically handsome with flying golden locks, Alexander the Statue makes our hero look like he was destined to crave glory, love fame, live hard and die young.

The story of Alexander's acquisition of his horse Bucephalus is right up there with the Gordian knot in terms of fable and lore. Legend says the way he acquired the horse was the first time that Alexander demonstrated his personal determination, taste and greatness in public. The horse was crucial to the development of the man. As someone who rode horses as a kid, I like that thought.

Here's the short version:

Philonicus the Thessalian brought a chestnut-colored stallion with four white stockings to sell in Pella but King Philip, and apparently all of the king's horsemen, deemed the steed unrideable and unmanageable.

"Who would want such a beast?" King Philip scowled when he looked at the horse. "I already have a wife!"

Alexander, then about ten years old, apparently saw something his father and everyone else did not. He felt that the horse was simply "afraid of its own shadow" and could be tamed.

"What an excellent horse do you lose, for want of address and boldness to manage him!" Alexander, accompanied by his best friend Hephaestion, told his father. "I could manage this horse better than others do."

"Do you reproach those who are older than yourself, as if you knew more and were better able to manage him than they?" his father asked him.

Alexander, goes the tale, promptly threw himself on the horse and galloped away bareback, holding on with nothing more than his knees, his hands gripping the horse's mane. The crowd broke into applause when he safely returned and King Philip, impressed by his son's bravery and capability, bought the untamed horse, called Bucephalus or Oxhead in deference to his breeder's brand, for his son.

It was at this propitious moment, when Alexander returned from his gallop across the plain that, according to Plutarch, King Philip made the much-cited comment "O my son, look thee out for a kingdom equal to and worthy of thyself, for Macedon is too little for thee."

Looking at the statue of Alexander on the day before the race I am reminded that he rode Bucephalus at the famous Battle of Gaugamela in Persia and kept him until the horse, then about 30, died in 326 BC. In the steed's memory, Alexander built a city on the bank of the Jhelum River in Pakistan and named it Bucephalia.

Alexander also built another city and gave it the name of his favorite dog, Peritas (after the Macedonian month of January), who had saved his life at Gaugamela by leaping in front of a Persian elephant and biting its trunk.

According to Plutarch, compassion for animals is a sign of a superior man and Alexander's regard for Bucephalus and Peritas, and the extreme way he was affected by their deaths and honored them, was rare during those times.

Maybe I'll find a dog to join me on this MedTrek outing, perhaps a reincarnation of Bogart, my yellow lab who was with me on the MedTrek when I set out from Antibes so many years ago.

The next morning at daybreak, the buzz of excitement before the start of the marathon is reminiscent of the horse fairs when dealers came from Thessaly, Thrace, Epiros and across the Hellespont to sell or swap steeds in Pella. I recall the source of the word marathon, which gets its name from a village on the plain of ancient Greece northeast of Athens. Marathon was the site of a major Athenian victory over the Persians in 490 BC and the name was adopted for a long run after a messenger named Pheidippides ran from there to Athens, a distance of about 40 kilometers, about the length of a contemporary marathon, with news of the victory. Poor Pheidippides, the marathon messenger, dropped dead of exhaustion after delivering his all-important news. Hopefully I will have a somewhat kinder conclusion at the end of my marathon.

My daily Tao reading suggests: "Once we find the true path of today we must walk it with the same determination as the ancients." So I plan to attack the Alexander the Great Marathon as though I am, compared to most of the other runners, ancient. That is, I plan to leisurely walk, not jog or run, the entire way.

The statue of Alexander seems to want to come to life this morning and just be another one of the boys in the crowded marathon. I imagine Alexander, his hair crowned with gold laurel and his purple cloak clasped with jewels, dismounting to hobnob with the rest of us before the start of the race.

Alexander's tutoring by Aristotle presumably prepared him for such social and philosophical eventualities as fitting in at a marathon at the last minute. I'm sure, if he actually were here today, he would probably be president of the Zeus Runners Club and the star of the show, firing the starting pistol himself at precisely 8 a.m. He would set off with the crowd, let his soldiers and commoners take the lead and then, near the end of the race, catch up with them all and pass the pack to easily come in first.

"That's the king!" some onlooker at the finish line would shout. "He's not even exerting himself, just getting some exercise. He can't bear to dawdle."

I'm not the only one surprised by Alexander's informal bearing and social ease. For a conqueror and a man with absolute powers, he was surprisingly egalitarian.

"Nobody had prepared me for the freedom of speech the king permitted," Bagoas, a eunuch in Alexander's employ after Alexander defeated the Persians, told author Mary Renault in her book *The Persian Boy*. "They called him Alexander, without title, like one of themselves; they laughed aloud in his presence, and far from rebuking them he joined in. The best you could say was that when he spoke, nobody interrupted him."

I am surprised, as I give a last glance over my shoulder as the race begins, to hear Alexander speak for the first time. The gorgeous blonde head seems to tilt back a notch and silver words escape the gracious lips. The statue is alive for a moment.

"May God keep you away from the venom of the cobra, the teeth of the tiger, and the revenge of the Afghans," Alexander says to me.

"Godspeed and good luck."

As the marathon kicks off, with one American competitor in a cowboy hat wearing a shirt promoting Marathon, California, and some Greeks wearing Alexander the Great-era helmets, I walk only a bit faster than my usual five-kilometer-per-hour pace.

I'm in no hurry and wonder how, when Alexander and his troops took this route, they forded wide rivers like the Axios and what the land looked like then with no roads or cars (which are pleasantly banned today), with no factories, bus stops or porta potties. I'm sure that some of the goats and sheep I pass are descendants of those that grazed these same pastures during Alexander's day.

Why aren't I running?

I used to run ten-kilometer and half-marathon races but quit when I began the MedTrek in 1998. My goal today is simply to relax, enjoy the walk to Thessaloniki and not make a commotion if Alexander passes me.

After an hour or so, when most of the runners have streamed, steamed or screamed by me, I'm going at my own pace and only occasionally pass people who've stopped or dropped out of the race. However, I'm cheered on, somewhat lamely I must admit, by anyone who sees me and there's another walker competing with me for last place. There are 12,000 runners participating in the marathon and shorter races that day, so bringing up the rear and finishing last would be quite a distinction.

The race goes due east and is gradually downhill, starting at around 45 meters above sea level and ending less than a meter above it. There are some very gentle undulations, but no significant climbs and I don't permit a headwind I encounter at the 27th kilometer to bother me too much.

The route, on a slightly cloudy day, is not particularly interesting. Most of it passes through scrub and farm land, with the odd industrial area. But there are numerous feed stations supplying water, isotonic fluid, bananas and, at a few, energy gels.

The terrain, once we pass the fields and enter the suburbs of Thessaloniki, is forgettable until we get to the sea, where I recall that Greece's second largest city and port was founded in 315 BC and got its name from Alexander the Great's half-sister.

The last 1.5 kilometers to the finish along the waterfront in Thessaloniki are lively and inspiring. It is during this part of the race that I reflect about Alexander's fascination with Homer and his fixation on Hercules, Achilles and other Homeric heroes. Not that this is odd – a list of historic Homerophiles also includes Julius Caesar, Napoleon, Lawrence of Arabia, Lord Byron, James Joyce, Nikos Kazantzakis and Princess Sisi of Austria.

That was when I realize it might not be as difficult for me to follow in the footsteps of Alexander, in Egypt or elsewhere, as I had thought. Perhaps I had been over-estimating the task and under-estimating myself. Although it would be vainglorious to compare myself to him, I figure we're starting out with some things in common.

Alexander, like me, arrived under the sign of Leo and was raised with an abundance of motherly love, though Olympias was much more possessive and dictatorial than my mother Helen.

Alexander was born in the Macedon forests far away from the glitz and glamour of Athens and the Acropolis. I was born in North Dakota where glitz and glamour still aren't part of the vocabulary.

Alexander had the *Iliad* and I have *Myths and Legends of the Ages*.

Alexander wasn't Greek, wasn't Christian and didn't speak with an Athenian accent. Ditto for me on all three counts.

Alexander, devout and schooled in the cosmology of the time, had an unwavering faith in oracles and began each day with sacrifices to the gods. I may not be as devout, but I follow a spiritual path. I begin each day with meditation, making a dedication on behalf of "all sentient beings," and I've never met an oracle that didn't interest me.

Alexander would be declared a god by the Oracle of Ammon in Egypt and often boasted that he was descended from Hercules, Achilles, Dionysus and Ammon. I have a habit, at some California cocktail parties, of claiming that too.

Alexander never went to bed early and never got up late. "One should learn to do without sleep; it's useful in war," he tells me. "We ought to be thankful to the gods for making us men." I have the same attitude, especially about getting up early.

We are both compulsive, disciplined and punctual. "Alexander could tolerate anything but a delay," said Curtius, one of his generals. I'm no different.

And, though we'll get into his sexuality later, we both like sex. "Sex and sleep alone make me conscious that I am mortal," Alexander frequently declared.

"In regard to the pleasures of the body, he had perfect self-control and regarding those of the mind, praise was the only one of which he was insatiable," wrote Arrian of Nicomedia.

Yeah, I know the feeling, though I'm still attempting to master perfect self-control.

Naturally Alexander had his detractors.

Demosthenes, an orator from Athens, called him a child and compared him to a fool. More recently, in 1882, A. W. Benn was even more caustic in his assessment in his book *The Greek Philosophers*: "It would be unfortunate if philosophy had no better testimonial to show for herself than the character of Alexander. Arrogant, drunken, cruel, vindictive and grossly superstitious, he united the vices of a Highland chieftain to the frenzy of an Oriental despot."

Emil Ludwig, in *The Mediterranean*, called Alexander "a leonine barbarian who inherited power, carried it to the ends of the earth, and left behind him an empire that was bound to fall apart forthwith."

Hey, you can't please everyone.

My pedometer reads 42.17 kilometers when I finish the Alexander the Great Marathon after a long walk on hard tarmac that reminds me of my 51.29-kilometer meander around Manhattan only eight days earlier.

Teklu Geto, the Ethiopian who wins the Alexander the Great Marathon in 2013, has a time of 2:19:29 but it takes me, walking the entire way, 7:29:46. I finish second to last but that doesn't seem to bother Alexander or me. After all, we both have a much longer way to go.

"With the right attitude, self-imposed limitations vanish," Alexander winks when I cross the finish line.

# FOLLOW THE IDIOT

## CHAPTER PHOTOS

## CHAPTER MAP

# Crossing the Hellespont with Alexander the Great

"The world is yours! Take it!"
– Olympias, Alexander's mother

"Let us conduct ourselves so that all men wish to be our friends and all fear to be our enemies."
– Alexander the Great

After the marathon, the next day's leisurely MedTrek outing is a pleasant return to my favorite pastime – walking the shore that surrounds the Mediterranean Sea – after 18 months spent writing, editing, producing, promoting and marketing *The Idiot and the Odyssey II* in the United States, France and England.

My walk on the seaside starts at Thessaloniki's ferry terminal in the main port, one of the largest seaports in Greece and a hub of shipping activity in the Aegean Sea. I check the schedule and learn that there is now only one ferry a week to Chios, the Greek island where Homer was born, and from there to İzmir in Turkey, where I ended my last MedTrek outing just over a year ago in 2012. A shipping agent informs me that, due to the economic malaise, there are about forty percent fewer voyages on that route, and on most routes, than a year ago.

This too, I figure, will be shrugged off by the ever adaptable Greeks.

I again stroll past the White Tower where I finished the marathon in next-to-last place, continue along the peacefully pleasant seaside past a colorful fishing port and slip into a contemporary concert hall to check out an art exhibit dedicated to music during the time of the Ancient Greeks.

Retracing the steps of my initial MedTrek through Macedonia a few years ago, I again drop into the Archaeological Museum of Thessaloniki that traces the Macedonian culture from the prehistoric ages to late antiquity. I also do a quick walk-through of the Folklife and Ethnological Museum of Macedonia-Thrace; skirt by the site of a Roman agora, which was the administrative sector of town in the second century AD; and drop into the Museum of Byzantine Culture.

I pass the office of the Holy Mount Athos Pilgrim's Bureau where I obtained the entry permit that allowed me to spend a week on the revered, sacred and womanless Mount Athos, the male-only, monk-abundant center of the Eastern Orthodox religion. And in Kalamaria, about seven kilometers down the coast, I admire an intriguing public herb garden with eight square plots each featuring a different herb – including mint, thyme and sage – in the shadow of a flamboyantly painted apartment building.

Although I MedTrekked along this part of the coast after I first climbed Mount Olympus and returned in 2010 when I MedTrekked throughout the Mount Athos peninsula, I'm now more consciously following the winding Mediterranean shoreline in the footsteps and company of Alexander the Great, rather than retracing the old pathways of Homer and Odysseus. It amuses me to compare Alexander to Odysseus as I look out to the windswept water.

Alexander and I left Thessaloniki a couple thousand years apart to walk to what is now Turkey, and though he had thousands of men with him and I am strolling solo, we both saw the same sea and similar terrain. Alexander always enjoyed being near the sea (he once insisted to me "the Great Sea encircles the whole earth") and talked about its importance during his boyhood when he liked "messing around" with boats.

And the man knew how to move an army. Much to my astonishment, it took him only twenty days marching with 43,000 soldiers and 3,000 horses and horsemen, to reach the Gallipoli peninsula in what was then Thrace. He had provisions for only thirty days, little money, lots of debt and a vast Persian Empire to confront.

When I asked what inspired and sustained him, he replied simply, "My hopes."

It is thrilling and emotional for me to realize that Alexander passed the same way I did when he left Pella in the spring of 334 BC. But the two places that impress me most on this portion of the MedTrek – Mount Athos and Gallipoli – had little religious or historic significance when Alexander walked by because Christianity wouldn't exist for another four hundred years and World War I hadn't been fought.

I wonder what Alexander would have thought if he, like me, had spent a week traipsing from monastery to monastery talking to monks and joining them in their prayers at Mount Athos. And whether he would have been impressed or disgusted by the callous battles, killing fields, expansive cemeteries and vivid memorial reminders at the slaughterhouse called Gallipoli.

He almost surely would have been amused that I joined a few hundred swimmers from throughout the world to swim across the Hellespont and in so doing move the MedTrek from Europe into Asia. I was inspired by Lord Byron who made the same swim in May 1810, to prove that Leander (swimming nightly to his beloved Hero on the opposite shore) could do it in ancient times – which then kicked off a swim-the-Hellespont craze in the 19th century. Incidentally, congratulations to Bo Derek, the actress who starred in the film "*10*" in 1979, for successfully completing that tricky current-challenging swim a few years after I did.

Today, during a somewhat leisurely and reflective 31-kilometer walk, I have a chance to get close and personal with Alexander. I particularly want to find out more about his private education under the tutelage of Aristotle, the renowned philosopher who began educating the future king when he was 13.

Why did Aristotle bother to teach a youngster?

Not because Alexander showed unusual academic accomplishment or philosophical promise but because King Philip told Aristotle that if he took the job he would rebuild Stagira, Aristotle's birthplace that had been destroyed by Philip's armies. You don't have to be the world's top thinker to accept that deal.

Alexander studied for three years under Aristotle, usually at the temple of the Nymphs at Mieza (called Lefkadia today), where I was shown Aristotle's stone seats, the paths where teacher and student took walks together and a modern stone sculpture of Aristotle in the garden. Alexander tells me that Aristotle taught him how to debate and equipped him with the skills to discuss virtually every topic under the sun, from politics, ethics and justice to friendship, enjoyment and love. The two frequently debated, from dawn until dusk, a variety of issues, ranging from concoctions of medicinal herbs to the physical appearance of heaven.

It was to the bearded Aristotle's home schooling, says Plutarch, that Alexander owed his inclination to practice medicine, which proved to be a bonus during an Asian military campaign with few medics in his army. When any of his men were sick or injured, Alexander would often personally prescribe a diet, a nostrum or other remedies to treat their affliction. He fastidiously kept a notebook of salves and draughts to treat fevers, wounds and broken limbs. That was a skill, I tell him, that really impressed me.

As we walk I confide to Alexander that I'd been doing a lot of research about him and had read accounts and well-known histories not only by Plutarch and Arrian of Nicomedia but also by Curtius, Diodoros and Justin as well as pertinent documents by Aelian, Athenaeus, Polyaenus, Strabo and other historians. I had scoured the *Metz Epitome*, an anonymous Latin work that describes Alexander's Asia campaigns in great detail, and read many contemporary works, including excellent fiction and non-fiction by Mary Renault.

I watched Colin Farrell play Alexander in Oliver Stone's 2004 film and even caught the "ultimate cut" of the movie on its tenth anniversary in 2014. Remember the film? I tell Alexander that one reviewer wrote, "Alexander the person was great. This play (I call it a play because he doesn't have a clue what a movie is) isn't." He laughs.

Plutarch and Arrian are my most reliable go-to guys concerning Alexander and are responsible for many of the facts and conjectures that I'm sharing with you. Their appreciations, comparatively early in the history of journalism and literature, are remarkably detailed and they agree on lots of facts (which, of course, does not mean that they're true).

Why do so many people, including me, have this fascination with Alexander?

"There is no other single individual among Greeks or barbarians who achieved exploits so great or important either in regard to number or magnitude as he did," said Arrian of Nicomedia, who wrote the *Anabasis of Alexander* during the reign of Hadrian in the second century AD.

Plutarch, who wrote *Parallel Lives* about numerous historical personalities at the beginning of the same century, took a more personal approach because "sometimes an expression or a jest, informs us better of their characters and inclinations, than the most famous sieges, the greatest armaments, or the bloodiest battles whatsoever."

Despite his reputed vanity, Alexander, who hosted an array of athletic games and made numerous sacrifices to Zeus before leaving Thessaloniki to traipse along the coast of Thrace, doesn't seem too impressed by my research or, at this stage, want to reveal too much about himself. Though that, I promise you, will come later.

During our walk beyond Thessaloniki, Alexander quotes Homer on war, heroism and honor while gradually regaling me with details of his instruction by Aristotle who, then in his 40s, was perhaps the most highly regarded philosopher of the day. Among other things, Alexander asserts as we pass the first sign for the much-publicized Macedonia Wine Route, Aristotle gave him another reason to invade Asia.

"Although an inferior race, the Persians control at least four-fifths of the known world," Aristotle told Alexander. "They rule and we sit around like frogs! If only these frogs could look outward from their favored position in the center, Greece could rule the world...and lift us from our frog pond."

Even before his father was assassinated, when Alexander was in his teens, he began meeting visiting foreign emissaries and gleaning information about Persia and the world beyond Macedon.

"Aristotle's education gave me many things, including the ability to entertain the ambassadors from the king of Persia, in the absence of my father and enter into conversation with them," Alexander tells me. "I inquired of them the nature of the roads into inner Asia, the character of their king, how he carried himself to his enemies and what forces he was able to bring into the field. Thinking I was merely an inquisitive child, they became my spies in their own country."

Alexander always wanted to know more about everything and one of my favorite stories concerning his unquenchable thirst for knowledge occurred many years later when he was in India, where he added elephants to his army.

Plutarch recounts that Alexander, eager to be intellectually challenged, had taken ten Indian philosophers, known as Gymnosophists, prisoner and asked them eternally unanswerable questions about life, death and the afterlife. He was so impressed with their answers, wit and conclusions that he gave them gifts and released them.

According to Arrian, the Gymnosophists also told Alexander not to be too proud because he was, like the rest of us, merely human "and very soon you too will die, and will possess no more of the earth than suffices for the burial of your body."

Callisthenes, a great-nephew of Aristotle and his royal archivist, joins us for a short portion of our walk and tells me that most scholars correctly credit Aristotle for giving Alexander a strong foundation for his fruitful career as king, military strategist and human being.

Callisthenes wasn't alone in crediting Aristotle.

"I doubt that Alexander, and the sense of adventure and excellence that he pursued, would have existed without his exposure to Aristotle and Homer," octogenarian Kathryn Hohlwein, who created Readers of Homer to introduce the *Iliad* and *Odyssey* in various languages to participatory audiences throughout the world, told me during one of our meals in Sacramento, California. "It's safe to say that Aristotle influenced Alexander's mission and vision and helped make him so brave, so beautiful and so everything else."

Georg Wilhelm Friedrich Hegel, the German philosopher, felt that Alexander's career was the embodiment of the Aristotelian philosophy, but not everyone was quite as impressed.

"Alexander was an ambitious and passionate boy, on bad terms with his father and presumably impatient of schooling," wrote Bertrand Russell in *A History of Western Philosophy*. "I cannot imagine Aristotle's pupil regarding him as anything but a prosy old pedant, set over him by his father to keep him out of mischief...I do not see anything else in Alexander that could possibly have come from this source...I suspect that Aristotle, to the end, thought of him as 'that idle and headstrong boy, who never could understand anything of philosophy'."

Whatever Aristotle's influence, this was the inspiring pitch that Alexander gave his troops when they left Thessaloniki:

"Youths of the Pellaians and of the Macedonians and of the Hellenic Amphictiony and of the Lacedaemonians and of the Corinthians...and of all the Hellenic peoples...Join your fellow soldiers and entrust yourselves to me, so that we can move against the barbarians and liberate ourselves from the Persian bondage, for as Greeks we should not be slaves to barbarians."

That sounds like a good reason for him to walk around the Mediterranean Sea. And during the next eleven years, Alexander defeated the Persian Empire in western Asia and Egypt and continued into Central Asia to the Indus River valley.

As we march through the Chalkidiki Peninsula I tell Alexander about the second "local" task given to me by Circe:

*"Get some contemporary spiritual guidance by consulting with the monks on Mount Athos. Ask them to pray for your worst enemies, kiss the icon of all icons and climb to the summit of the mountain."*

Alexander doesn't have a clue what I am talking about, of course, so I give him a quick course in Christianity and describe the evolution of *Ágio Óros*, as the Greeks refer to the Holy Mountain, considered the holiest place on earth by the Eastern Orthodox Church since AD 963.

During that conversation, which must have sounded totally surreal to someone versed in the pantheon of Greek gods and obviously unaware of the future existence of Christ and a text called the Bible, Alexander tells me that Aristotle taught him about Lao Tsu, the Chinese philosopher and founder of Taoism born in China in 604 BC, and he tosses out a couple of aphorisms to prove it.

"Lao Tsu said in the *Tao Te Ching* that 'a good walker leaves no tracks' but that's definitely not going to be true in my case," Alexander jokes.

I reply that another Buddhist practitioner, Deng Ming-Dao, said that 'wise people travel constantly and test themselves against the flux of circumstance'."

Then I get a little more profound and mention walking meditation, a concept that Alexander definitely isn't familiar with but which has been a guiding principle for me throughout the MedTrek.

"I know a Vietnamese Buddhist, Thich Nhat Hanh, who wrote a book called *The Long Road Turns to Joy: A Guide to Walking Meditation*," I said, "and he claims that 'walking meditation helps us regain our sovereignty, our liberty as a human being. We walk with grace and dignity, like an emperor, like a lion. Each step is life'."

"I like the bit about the emperor and the lion," says Alexander smiling, when we are less than a hundred kilometers from Thessaloniki on the easternmost of the three promontories on the Chalkidiki Peninsula that, besides Mount Athos, include Kassandra and Sithonia.

Alexander tells me that nearby Olynthos, conceived by Hippodamus of Miletus and built on a geometric design known as the Hippodamean system, is perhaps the most important ancient cultural center in Chalkidiki. With streets and avenues in a checkerboard square pattern, Olynthos was inhabited long before Athens or Sparta and ruled by the Bottiaeans from the seventh century BC until the Persians conquered it in 479 BC.

I respond that when I was here before I climbed to the citadel in the *paleá póli*, or old town, and looked down on what was once the eastern boundary of ancient Rome's European empire. Although Alexander once again doesn't know what I am talking about, I mention that it was in Olynthos in AD 49 that Saint Paul addressed his epistle to the Philippian Christians, and that the Muslim *imaret*, built in the town in 1817 by Mohamed Ali Pasha and run by Islamic *sheikhs* to house the poor, is now a luxurious hotel. Then I have to give to him an explanation about the founding and evolution of Islam and a description of hotels. Whew!

When we MedTrek past Mount Athos, I describe how I spent a week walking through the holy promontory visiting different monasteries for a night or two, talking (or trying to talk) to monks from Russia, Serbia, Romania and Bulgaria, and imported workers from almost everywhere who spoke some English. I try to describe how much I enjoyed the magic spirituality of an enclave that is separated from the mainland by an almost impenetrable forest and a long security fence.

I mention some advice I was given in Litóhoro on an earlier visit about my upcoming stay in Mount Athos.

"Go to Athos for the magic of the mountain, not for the monks," a woman of my age told me about the holy land that operates under a charter granted by the Byzantine emperor at Constantinople over 1,050 years ago.

"Incidentally, if you want to hit it off with any Greek, tell them you're going to Mount Athos and will pray for them. They'll love you forever."

Then I explain to Alexander that there are no females on Mount Athos and, despite occasional protestations, no one expects females to ever be allowed on the promontory. That's the way it's been for over a thousand years, I tell him.

"That doesn't sound right to me," says Alexander.

"The ban is officially due to the Orthodox Church's desire to honor the Virgin Mary and their contention that Christ gave the peninsula to his mother as her private garden," I explain. "All other women are excluded in order to more properly respect Mary, though there have been a few exceptions for short periods."

As I said, Alexander doesn't completely understand what I am talking about (that's one problem with being born BC instead of AD) and displays only vague interest in the quasi-autonomous religious state, including my climb to the top of the mountain, until I describe the food and scrumptious meals served at one of the Mount Athos monasteries. I go into detail about the ornate dining room and a lunch that included spaghetti, coleslaw, quiche, bread, cheese, wine, and fruit and vegetables from the well-tended terraced gardens. He hasn't heard of most of those dishes, but the new words, especially quiche and spaghetti, intrigue him.

Alexandros and I continue to the town of Amphipolis on the Strymon River, where three of his admirals had lived, and where he stopped for a day while he made final preparations for his entry into Asia. Alexandros reminds me that his father had sent an advance force across the Hellespont in 336 BC and says he expects to hook up with them immediately after he visits Troy.

Then he gives me a rundown on his soldiers, including his personal Companion unit of senior officers that consisted solely of trusted Macedonians. He says Cretans were exceptional archers, Thessalians were the most effective cavalry unit and Yuruks were good marchers.

"Did you have a clue that you would create an empire that stretched from Mount Athos to the Himalayas and launch a new era known as the Hellenistic Age that led to the nearly global proliferation of Greek culture and ideas and endure for centuries?" I ask.

He smiles.

As I mentioned, my average walking distance during almost twenty years is a little above thirty kilometers, or just over twenty miles, a day depending on the topography, weather, location and my mood. Alexander is in more of a hurry and moves at a much faster pace.

When we get beyond Mount Athos, after I again bid adieu to Dieu, I tell Alexander about the third task given to me by Circe in this part of Greece:

*"Traipse through Thrace before MedTrekking through the killing fields of
Gallipoli. Then swim from Europe to Asia across the Hellespont in the
wake of Leander and Lord Byron to arrive in Troy to meet Hector, the son
of King Priam who was slain by quick-to-anger Achilles."*

"I too am anxious to get to Troy," Alexander informs me as we
continue our journey. "I've read more about it than any place on earth."

We walk into bustling Kavála – a city in northeastern Greece
known at various times in the past as Philippi (honoring Alexander's
father), Neapolis, Christoupolis and Bucephalos (named after Alexander's
horse) – where the Alexander the Great Airport is obviously named after
Alexander.

I remember, when I walked through here a few years ago, how
enthused I was about crossing into Asia.

Even more thrilling, a bit further along and three kilometers
southeast of the Ismara ruins, is the exact spot that Odysseus ran into the
Ciconians after leaving Troy. When I MedTrekked through here before I
stumbled on a sign that said "Ulysses Stream" after descending from
climbing Mount Ismara. I recall that there's an interesting camel-shaped
formation not far from here called Perota Rock. I figure this will excite
Alexander too and we take a slight detour.

This strip of seaside in Thrace – "that fertile country, billowy
grassland, nourisher of flocks" as Alexander recalls from the *Iliad* – is
where Odysseus first landed on his way home following the Trojan War
and lost numerous members of his crew to the Ciconians.

It's certainly easy to understand why he landed here. Although the
winds are reputed to be thrashers (one description in the *Iliad* is "the north
wind and west wind wailing out of Thrace in squall on squall, and dark
waves crest, and shoreward masses of weed are cast up by the surf"), the
sea is calm today and the rolling hills, gleaming boulders, open spaces,
and groves of trees all appear very pastoral and welcoming.

Alexander and I sit for a while and visualize Odysseus' bloody
encounter with the pesky Ciconians, a tribe that fought on the Trojan side
in the war. Things started off on the right foot when Odysseus and his crew
"stormed the place and killed the men who fought" while taking the
women and children as slaves. But then they threw an over-exuberant and
premature victory celebration. "Sheep after sheep they butchered by the
surf" until "the main force of Ciconians…an army trained to fight on
horseback" arrived "with dawn over that terrain like the leaves and blades
of spring" and killed six men on each of Odysseus' ships.

It was the first of many embarrassing incidents for Odysseus on
his homeward journey.

"I love a good party to celebrate a victory," Alexander says. "But
since I first read about this battle many years ago, I've insisted on the

complete defeat, or total surrender, of the enemy. War isn't for monks or Christians."

Little did he know how many wars would be fought, and how many people would be killed, in the name of Christianity, Islam and other religions.

I do have one slightly embarrassing incident myself just after this. I am very excited about getting to Alexandroupoli because I presume it too was named, like so many other cities, for Alexander the Great. I recount this to Alexander as we walk together.

"I didn't name that village after myself," he says, looking at me like I am an idiot.

"Who did?" I ask him.

It turns out Alexandroupoli was founded as a small fishing village in the early 19th century (when what is now northeastern mainland Greece was still under the rule of the Ottoman Empire) by fishermen from two nearby villages. It was at first called Dedeağaç but in 1920, King Alexander I of Greece visited the city, and the local authorities decided to rename it Alexandroupoli ("City of Alexander") in his honor.

"Sorry," I apologize to Alexander, "but the confusion is understandable. I'm not an idiot."

"I'm not so sure," he says.

Alexandroupoli notwithstanding, it's still true that there was a virtual mania for naming localities after the big man, back in the day. There are over 70 towns named for Alexander, including Alexandria in Egypt, Iskenderun in Turkey, Iskandariya in Iraq and Alexandria on the Indus in Pakistan – and they all helped to introduce Greek speech and customs to Asia. Greek became the *lingua franca* of the civilized world and Alexander made efforts to ensure that each city had Greek temples, a garrison, a public square, a council chamber and a theater.

Then I tell Alexander about ongoing confusion over a former Yugoslav republic to the north that, when it was founded as an independent country with just two million people in 1991, was called the Republic of Macedonia. Taking that name seemed to personally offend everyone in Greece, creating an ongoing dispute already lasting almost three decades.

"They really upset a lot of people when they used the Vergina Sun on their flag but things calmed down when they revised the design in 1995," I tell Alexander, referring to the sun symbol on a larnax containing the bones of a member of the royal family of Macedon.

I inform him that in early 2018 the Republic of Macedonia agreed to change the name of its main airport (Macedonia) and highway (Macedonia) in an effort to resolve the issue.

"But the buzz from the capital Skopje," I tell him, "is that not far from the current Greek border, they found coins stamped with your visage, which they think gives them a right to use the name."

"They were part of my empire," Alexander agrees. "But so were many other countries and they don't call themselves Macedonia. Who's their king? Maybe I can work something out."

Although the Republic of Macedonia tentatively agreed in a deal with Greece in June 2018 to call itself the Republic of North Macedonia, I suggest that perhaps it should change its name to the Republic of Alexander.

"Why not?" says my companion, "That would end the dispute."

He needn't say more. He smiles the sly, contented smile that only someone who has kicked ass around the world can smile.

The Odyssean battle skirmish with the Ciconians seems tame in comparison to what we observe on our Gallipoli walkabout after we cross the current Greek-Turkish border and continue on the seaside towards the strait that connects the Aegean Sea to the Sea of Marmara – not only separating Europe from Asia but also dividing Turkey into Asian and European sections.

"European" Turkey today makes up only three percent of the country's total land area but it includes the Gallipoli Peninsula where more than 120,000 soldiers – primarily Turkish, ANZAC (Australian and New Zealand Army Corps), British, French and Indian – were killed during a barbaric and brief World War I campaign.

"They went like Kings in a pageant to their imminent death," wrote poet John Masefield about the Allied troops who were trying to take over the Turkish passage to Istanbul and the Black Sea.

A 127-square mile (33,000 hectares) Gallipoli Historical National Park is now "reserved forever as a resting place for soldiers who fell in the First World War."

"This is one of the most moving and most frightening places I've visited on the entire Mediterranean," I tell Alexander, mentioning that since I MedTrekked here I had visited an intriguing "Gallipoli: The Scale of Our War" exhibit at the Te Papa National Museum in Wellington, New Zealand.

"The Gallipoli campaign claimed the lives of 2,700 New Zealand soldiers – a whopping number for a small country," I tell him. Then I give him a vivid evocation of the days I spent wandering around the battlefields, beaches, hillsides, museums, cemeteries and memorials of Gallipoli while MedTrekking through the area.

"Since your day not much progress has been made when it comes to men killing men during World War I battles," I point out to Alexander, who obviously passed through Gallipoli without knowing what carnage would be wrought in these killing fields. "It was humanity at its worst."

"War is not a game," Alexander responds. "That's why I personally fought in every battle with my men and why I carry the scars to prove it."

I rarely pause long in one spot while MedTrekking, but Gallipoli seemed to demand that I stay. I had to learn the whole terrible, difficult, heart-breaking story.

Alexander and I are now walking through the killing fields with slow, somber, appropriate steps. Even he seems stilled and silenced in this awful place. One memorial commemorating the battle, essentially a vast graveyard with rows and rows of white stones on green grass hills that dip down towards the blue-green sea, is the sort of place that sinks into your bones, burns cruel etchings in your mind, seizes your soul, and only slowly retreats from your memory. A strange silence like a mammoth hand descending comes down on us as we solemnly enter the gate.

When we reach the Helles Memorial at the tip of the Gallipoli Peninsula on the Aegean Sea, I describe to Alexander how I swam across the Hellespont, or Dardanelles as it is also known today.

"It was Circe who instructed me to swim across the Hellespont four years – and more than 4,000 kilometers – ago," I tell him. "I had to succeed, or perhaps simply not drown, in order to MedTrek into Troy."

Troy, of course, was the site of the decade-long Trojan War that began in 1194 BC and Alexander thought it was pretty cool (no, he didn't actually use the word "cool" but I know that was what he felt in his heart) that Circe told me to go there to "meet Hector, the son of King Priam who was slain by quick-to-anger Achilles."

Completing the 4.5-kilometer crossing in the wake of Leander (who, according to the Greek legend and myth as recounted by the Greek writer Musaeus, swam across the Hellespont every night to consort with his lover Hero, a priestess of Aphrodite) could potentially have been the most difficult labor that Circe gave me depending on the conditions of the water.

Swimming from Eceabat on the European side to Çanakkale in Asia certainly required more physical and mental preparation than most of the eleven other footloose tasks.

The crossing was a rite of passage – and much easier than I expected because the weather and water conditions were excellent. That made me think of King Xerxes of Persia, whose armies crossed the Hellespont into Europe on a bridge of boats in 480 BC; and author Patrick Leigh Fermor, who made the swim on his 70th birthday.

In 2017 I attended the 50th reunion of Stanford University Men's 1967 NCAA Swimming Champions at the Sierra Camp on Fallen Leaf Lake near South Tahoe, California. The reunion honored Jim Gaughran, the Hall of Fame coach who took Stanford to its first-ever NCAA title.

Now 84, and in better shape than some of his younger paddling protégés, Gaughran was an Olympic water polo player in 1956, Stanford's swimming coach from 1960 to 1979 (I attended from 1966-70) and a mentor/friend to scores of former Stanford swimmers. His key to a long life: "Swimming and diet."

Before the reunion ended, The Idiot invited the coach and fellow Stanford swimmers to join him on the November MedTrek in Egypt, where they could take daily dips in the Mediterranean Sea.

# WHY DIDN'T THE IDIOT SWIM AROUND THE MEDITERRANEAN SEA INSTEAD OF WALKING AROUND IT?

Alexander didn't swim across the Hellespont but, after making a sacrifice to the gods to get their "backing" for his expedition and its success, he took the helm of a ship after his twenty-day, 300-mile march to Sestos on the western shore of the Hellespont. His army crossed using merchant ships and 160 triremes, the three-banked warships that originated in Phoenicia.

Along the way he sacrificed a bull to Poseidon, the god of the sea, at the middle of the channel and poured wine into the strait from a golden goblet to placate the Nereids and to "guarantee" a safe crossing.

When he reached the other side, Alexander cast his spear towards shore to dramatically claim the continent as "spear-won." He stepped out of the ship in full armor, with a flamboyant plume of white feathers attached to his helmet, and erected tall altars to Zeus, Athena, Poseidon and Hercules as thanksgiving "to the gods who had brought him so far as a conqueror, and as memorials of his own exertions."

"I imagined myself a contemporary Achilles on the way to visit Troy," he confides to me. "And I thought of all the action in Homer's works as I made the crossing."

Alexander then wrote a telling letter to the Persian king Darius: "Your ancestors invaded Macedonia and the rest of Greece and did us great harm, though we had done them no prior injury. I have been appointed *hegemon* of the Greeks, and invade Asia to take vengeance on Persia for your aggressions..."

Place names were different then, of course. There was no country called Turkey but rather the Persian Empire and kingdoms with names like Phrygia and Cilicia.

Further to the east, on the other side of the Sea of Marmara, is the Bosporus, which the ancient Greeks referred to as the Thracian Bosporus, and it's imperative that you know that its name is derived from the same word as Alexander's horse's name and means "ox ford" or "ox passage."

Why? Is that where oxen like to cross from Europe into Asia? Not quite. The name comes from a myth about Io's travels after Zeus turned her into a cow for her protection. Io, a priestess and one of Zeus's mortal lovers, endured the transformation to hide from Zeus's wife.

Once in Asia, once he crossed the Hellespont, Alexander neither looked back at, nor ever returned to, Europe, Macedon or his mother.

# FOLLOW THE IDIOT

**CHAPTER
PHOTOS**

**CHAPTER
MAP**

# Rituals at Troy and Different Routes in Turkey

"O fortunate youth, to have found Homer as
the herald of your glory!"
– *Alexander the Great at the tomb of Achilles in Troy*

"He was the hero, friend, father of the soldier and the
threatening, angry, terrorizing, melancholy king."
– Fritz Schachermeyr, *Alexander der Grosse:
Ingenium und Macht*

Alexander and I both think of Homer, the colorful and exciting panorama of characters and gods in the *Iliad* and the *Odyssey* and details of the Trojan War when we cross the Hellespont and approach Troy. You might recall that when I recounted my overland MedTrek from Thessaloniki to Troy in *The Idiot and the Odyssey II*, I mentioned that I imagined myself walking alongside Alexander and his troops.

That's what I do until I get to the other side of the Hellespont.

After my swim, I bid goodbye to Alexander and the gigantic replica of a Trojan horse – a prop used in the film *Troy* starring Brad Pitt in 2004 – on the beachfront promenade in Çanakkale. I MedTrek west along the shore of a mirror-smooth Hellespont through richly cultivated countryside and ford the legendary Scamander River to reach the edge of the Aegean Sea. Then I cut cross-country for seven kilometers to the famed city of Troy before seriously kicking off my walk along Turkey's meandering coastline.

When, after 25 kilometers, I climb a hill and enter the ruins of Truva, as the Turks call Troy, I immediately encounter another gigantic fake Trojan horse. These faux Trojan horses are something that Alexander missed but I told him all about them before we went our separate ways.

More important than encountering another Trojan horse in Troy is the fact that I again meet my mentor goddess, the ethereal Athena, and get the lowdown on a variety of little-known details relating to Alexander's visit.

The grey-eyed, spear-carrying Athena greets me with her distinguished left-eye wink and, as she did when we met in Rome a decade ago, appears in the guise of a tour guide. This time the earthly name of the goddess of wisdom, warfare, arts and crafts is Mustafa Askin, one of the best-known male guides in Troy. His family owns the nearby Hisarlik (it means "castled place") Hotel, where I stay in a room named after King Priam, who reigned over this "god-built bastion" on a steep and windy plateau.

The goddess guide, who actually once appeared as herself in Italy where I took the iconic photos of her posing next to Doric colonnades at pastoral Paestum, conveys all sorts of surprising information about Alexander's stay while we walk amid the ruins.

"I was here when Alexander the Great arrived in this part of Anatolia, which was known as the Troad, or "land of Troy," back in the day. He was wearing a gold crown and didn't take a slow, meditative walk through the battle site like you did but instead 'ran oiled and naked around the tomb of Achilles, donned some of the arms preserved in my temple and made grandiose plans for embellishing the city'," says the goddess, slightly misquoting a passage she had fed to the author of a book called *The Gold of Troy*.

"Alexander immediately made offerings of twelve gold chalices to me because I'm the patron goddess of Troy," Athena continues. "Then he laid a wreath on the tomb of Achilles and, with his best friend Hephaestion, paid tributes with garlands at the tomb of Achilles' companion Patroclus. In fact, Alexander frequently compared his friendship with Hephaestion to the relationship between Achilles and Patroclus."

That wasn't all. The goddess has much more to tell me about this redoubtable human. She seems to admire him, at least as much as any godlike being can admire a mere mortal. It is a bit hard to keep my mind on her words as I gaze at the astounding physique of this beautiful god-woman-man, and feel Athena's cold grey eyes sweeping over my all-too-human and aging skin. But I try.

"As he stood by me, Alexander said he was able to visualize the entire Trojan war occurring in front of his eyes on the plain below with the cast of thousands that Homer describes in the *Iliad*," recounts Athena as we chat under a fig tree. "He told me the *Iliad* was a much more important poem to him than the *Odyssey*, which is just an adventure story, because it is about war, tragedy, friendship, grief, honor, drama, and existence itself. For Alexander, the *Iliad* was history, not myth."

In case you've forgotten, let me remind you that the main players in the *Iliad* were the Achaeans/Argives/Danaans, as the various Greek tribes were called at the time. Their team included the fearless and proud warrior Achilles, the haughty commander Agamemnon, and Achilles' best pal Patroclus. On the Trojan side, Hector, the son of King Priam of Troy who was killed by Achilles in vicious face-to-face combat and whose funeral rites conclude the *Iliad*, was the lead character with key supporting roles by Helen, Paris (he's the prince who swept Helen off her feet), and the king.

"Alexander poetically recited a number of animalistic descriptive phrases from the *Iliad* to me as we walked around the city," Athena continues. "He said the Trojans were like 'cranes at dawn descending, beaked in cruel attack' while the advancing Greek army resembled a swarm of 'geese, cranes, and long-throated swans in the Asian meadow' as they 'came on in silence, raging under their breath' while 'yanking the horse's heads, lashing their flanks.' He seemed to know the text by heart."

"Alexander," says the goddess, "also described chariot skirmishes while 'dust rose underfoot as thudding hooves of horses shook the plain and men plied deadly bronze.'" She went into detail about Patroclus putting on Achilles' flashing bronze and outfitting himself with greaves, a cuirass, a solid shield, a plumed helmet, two shining spears, and a silver-studded blade as he rode off towards Hector and his undoing.

"Alexander was very emotional when he repeated Patroclus's last words to Hector before he died: 'No long life is ahead for you. This day your death stands near, and your immutable end, at Prince Achilles' hands'," says Athena. "And before he left he sent garments and other spoils to Athens with a messenger who was told to declare: 'Alexander won these from the barbarians who inhabit Asia'."

Athena tells me that fossils, fishhooks, and other artifacts found within Troy's first three layers prove it was once located on the seaside. Today's distance from the sea, she adds, is primarily due to siltation from two rivers that gradually turned the surrounding flats into a swamp and, finally with time, *terra firma*.

"Nine different levels, or layers, of Troy were constructed between 3000 BC and the early fourth century AD," Athena explains while pointing out remains from the different epochs and describing some of the discoveries found during the digs by archaeologists, including a chest-protecting, oxhide-aproned shield and helmet similar to the one worn by Odysseus. "The different walls, dated by the workmen during construction, are the easiest way to assess the evolution of Troy.

"The Trojan War probably occurred in the 6th or 7th layer of Troy," Athena goes on, adding that the period when Greeks ruled Troy created its 8th layer. "The battle Homer describes was certainly not the first war here, because arrowheads and *pithoi* were found from earlier periods when this was known as Wilusa, the Hittite name of Troy."

There's no question that Alexander had a better view of Troy than I do and apparently there's still a lot more to see.

"Ninety percent of Troy has still not been excavated, and you haven't seen anything yet," my mentor adds as she points to a slanted entry ramp from Troy II constructed in 2500 BC. "I think the most exciting discovery will be the graveyards of Homeric Troy to provide further proof that Troy was an important city – smaller than Babylon or Hattusa but bigger than Mycenae. Come back in another century."

Alexander's visit inspired Julius Caesar to make the pilgrimage to Troy (Alexander's megalomania was admired and emulated by leaders like Caesar and Napoleon) and when Caesar approached the Xanthus River he was told, "This is where they brought Hector's body! Be careful not to offend his ghost."

Caesar, who apparently feared ghosts, built an altar, burned incense on it and prayed to the gods guarding the sacred site, promising that he would rebuild the crumbling walls.

In fact, the list of historic Homerophiles who visited Troy before me goes back well before Caesar. Herodotus dropped by in the fifth century BC, Scylax of Caryanda was a fourth century BC tourist and Strabo, a well-known geographer and historian of the era, was here in AD 21. More contemporary visitors included Napoleon and James Joyce, who named each chapter in *Ulysses* after a person or event in Homer's *Odyssey*.

"Madmen and emperors came to Troy," concluded Robert Payne, author of *Gold of Troy,* noting that Virgil and Homer had created myths that "had the power to kindle the imaginations of men."

Each visitor saw a different Troy, of course, and that reminds me that we're all bound to miss something when we walk on the Mediterranean. The legends, the stories, the people, the cities and the monuments pile up. You can't catch them all.

Eric Newby, who wrote *On The Shores of the Mediterranean* in

1984, said that "all travelers on the shores of the Mediterranean eventually recognize how much we missed simply by being unobservant and how much more by being born 150 years or so too late."

I'd make that 1,500 years too late.

Before I leave Troy, Athena, the Hope of Soldiers, politely suggests that I again climb to the top of Mount Ida, where I had a conversation with Zeus on an earlier MedTrek. Athena believes that the tree-covered, multi-flowered, bee-hived national park on top of the mountain is the best source of oxygen in all of Turkey and strongly suggests that it might be the best place to restore my body and soul.

"It'll rejuvenate you for the rest of your walk in Turkey and beyond," Athena says.

The next morning, I sit reflectively on a crumbling Trojan wall overlooking fields of sunflowers and gaze towards the Xanthos and Scamander Rivers. Homer described the blue Xanthos as an "eddying and running, god-begotten wondrous river" and the Scamander starts on Mount Ida – where, it's written many times in the *Iliad*, things were controlled by "O Father Zeus! who rul'st Ida's height" – and flows into the Hellespont north of Troy.

Then I casually walk through tomato, corn and melon fields, and fig and olive orchards, down to the wine-dark sea. The pastoral flower-filled morning comes to an end when I confront a monstrous cement plant that, from the distance, resembles a gigantic ship. About 15-kilometers from Troy, it conceals any beauty that might once have been related to Besik Bay.

"Is this the lovely bay where Achilles and the Greeks kept their deep-sea ships and bivouacked during the war?" I wonder, as I imagine the time that "Achilles wept, and sat apart by the grey wave, scanning the endless sea."

The next day I pass the chic island of Bozcaada and a few hours later reach the Temple of Athena atop a crag in Assos. Built on the highest point of the city, it is the first and only Doric temple in Anatolia and a tribute to Athena's role as city protector. I'm delighted, as though stumbling upon a long-lost girlfriend, to see the island of Lesbos glimmering in the Aegean Sea. The view accentuates the beauty and tranquility of this serene hilltop tribute to my goddess guide, and I spend a couple of hours in calm and contented contemplation.

A brochure (yes, I read brochures) informs me that "the buildings in the ancient city of Assos, founded in the sixth century BC on a dormant volcano, were made of andesite, which is a volcanic rock difficult to process but very stable. The sarcophagi made in this city were very famous in the ancient world and became a top export because they were called 'flesh-eating sarcophagi' since they rapidly consumed the bodies placed into them."

Flesh-eating sarcophagi (plural of the Greek word *sarcophagus,* which actually means "flesh-eating")? Now that's what I want to get as a lasting MedTrek souvenir!

I wonder why Alexander didn't make a side-trip here. After all, Aristotle lived here from 347 to 344 BC and established a school of philosophy, though I'm unable to find any notable commentary by him about flesh-eating sarcophagi.

Author Eric Newby made another pertinent observation while visiting Assos, which was founded during the Trojan War on the southern shores of the Troad. During his long tour of the Mediterranean with his wife, they saw so much that "we ceased to care what epoch any particular remain dated from." This is easy to understand in Assos which has been occupied, liberated or inhabited by Lydians, Persians, Greeks, Alexander the Great, Romans, Byzantines, Muslims, Crusaders and Turks.

After I explore Assos and calmly continue my walk down the coast towards İzmir, it occurs to me that Troy was the first milestone on Alexander's journey into Asia. From Troy he marched through Lampsacus and Priapus to the east. There he reunited with the forces his father dispatched two years earlier and was soon ready to face a Persian army, thought to consist of 100,000 soldiers, led by King Darius III.

Before we parted, I asked Alexander how he imagined spending a typical day once he began fighting the Persians, though I already knew that he preferred to stay up late and rise early.

"After I'm awake and make sacrifices to the gods, I'll sit down to a moderate breakfast and spend the rest of the day administering justice, managing army business, making military decisions, meeting with my commanders, writing memoirs, reading history, civics, classical tragedy and modern poetry, and maybe, depending where we are, go hunting," said Alexander, who ran his army from a royal tent that included a war chamber, not unlike the war room in the White House, located near his private apartments.

He made it sound like a vacation instead of a war.

I'd heard that on marches that required a moderate pace, Alexander's favorite pastime was to step onto a chariot, stir the horses into a gallop and alight from it at full speed. He enjoyed vigorous exercise and considered himself a runner of Olympic standard, though he wouldn't compete "unless I had kings to run against."

His cavalry usually marched on foot to spare the horses and each soldier carried his own bedroll, weapons and armor, including spears, swords and shields. Baggage animals and wagons transported tents, water and food for chamberlains, bodyguards, an elite infantry and mercenaries, who somehow functioned together on the battlefield despite different languages and training.

The troops wore tunics, helmets and cuirasses and trumpeters attached to each unit conveyed orders. Most soldiers were bearded, despite Alexander's preference that they shave (he thought beards gave the enemy something to clutch at close range). Perhaps even Alexander realized that it's hard to shave every day on the trail when you're lugging 50 pounds of heavy gear. Alexander, of course, had courtiers, groomers, barbers and miscellaneous slaves to keep his beautiful face smooth and clean and his golden locks golden. The marching, sweating, foot-dragging, armor-carrying troops had none of that.

Alexander traveled with a personal court of about a hundred courtiers known as "Alexander's Friends" or "Companions," who were his confidants and most trusted advisers. He'd first known many members of this cliquish group when he was a teenager.

"I'll occasionally nap in the afternoon and in the early evening, after I'm bathed and anointed, I'll call for my bakers and chief cooks, to confirm the dinner menu," continued Alexander who, like me, loved taking baths after a hard day's walk. "I really never care to eat until it's very late and very dark. That's the time I get important reports from my Companions on the state of the campaign."

Although his drinking will merit a separate discussion when we meet down the road, Alexander was actually very temperate in his choice of food and any rare delicacies sent to him would be distributed among his Companions.

Alexander first engaged the Persians in combat and, according to Plutarch, lost a number of men and was almost killed himself in the bloody battle at the Granicus River, where he "advanced against whole showers of darts thrown from the steep opposite side, which was covered with armed multitudes of the enemy's horse and foot soldiers."

That battle in 334 BC was the first of his three major victories over the Persian army and Alexander gave thanks and paid proper respect to his patroness, Athena. After he defeated the Persians for the first time, he sent 300 sets of Persian armor dedicated to Athena to the Acropolis in Athens. That was payback for the time the Persians had burned Athens to the ground in 480 BC.

Following every battle, Alexander personally visited each of the wounded and granted the parents and children of his fallen troops exemption from taxes.

"Alexander, though suffering from a wound which he had received in the thigh from a sword, visited the wounded, and having collected the bodies of the slain, he gave them a splendid burial with all his forces most brilliantly marshaled in order of battle," writes Arrian.

He also buried the Persian commanders and the Greek mercenaries who were killed fighting on the side of the enemy and sent prisoners back to Macedon as slaves in the fields. At one point, he let some of his married troops return home and their glowing reports of Alexander's leadership and victories encouraged an infusion of fresh troops.

Alexander won't rejoin me on the coast until I MedTrek further south when he cuts back to Ephesus (he's now in Biga en route to Kalkim where a bridge is still named after him), where we'll connect with each other again. Here are some of the things he missed as I continued my walk – with no Companions, no baggage animals, no chefs, no beard and no bathtub – down the seaside along the Olive Riviera to where I set up a base camp in Küçükkuyu, perhaps the most rhythmically named town on the entire MedTrek, which is located on the Gulf of Edremit at the base of Mount Ida.

As Athena instructed me, I spend another productive day with my guide named Usher (a corruption of his true Turkish name Asir) in the *Kazdaği Milli Parki*, or the Kazdağı National Park (KDNP). We again climb to the highest peak on the western side of the Mount Ida range, where I look down on distant Troy, just as Zeus and company did during the Trojan War.

Again, I am excited about getting to the top of Mount Ida because of an enticing paragraph in the *Iliad:* "At full stretch midway between the earth and starry heaven they ran toward Ida, sparkling with cool streams, mother of wild things, and the peak of Mount Gargaron where are his holy plot and fragrant altar. There Zeus, father of gods and men, reined in and freed his team, diffusing cloud about them, while glorying upon the crest he sat to view the far-off scene below – Achaean ships and the Trojan city."

In fact, Mount Ida is right up there with Mount Olympus, and I again give the gods my thanks for locating their earthly homes in such heavenly spots.

Usher, who insists that he's not Athena in disguise but just a regular-guy guide, is once again a fountain of information during our six-hour hike up Mount Ida, where the Olympian gods watched the progress of the epic battle around Troy and where several mythic events in the works of Homer occur.

As I recounted earlier, it was here, in my favorite book of the *Iliad,* that Hera seduced and distracted Zeus long enough to enable the Greeks to temporarily take the initiative in the war. The delightful passages describe how Hera contrived, executed and succeeded in her plan to overpower the god of all gods, using one of the oldest weapons on earth: sex.

After I sent a GPS signal from the summit and felt I had spent enough time admiring the view of Troy and the Hellespont from magical, mystical, mythical, and holy Mount Ida, I take a SideTrek to the ancient Greek city-state of Pergamon, where the use of parchment was invented (parchment, in late Latin, was known as *pergamina*). Now known as Bergama, I explore another Sanctuary of Athena at the hilltop Acropolis there. Then I MedTrek for a few days in the direction of İzmir, along the Mediterranean seashore through the towns of Ayvalik, Dikili, Candarli and Denzikoy. When I make it to İzmir, which was called Smyrna in antiquity, I visit Homeros where the Turks claim Homer was born.

By the time I reach the buzzing and busy İzmir seafront, I have walked exactly 8,802 kilometers since the MedTrek began in France in 1998. I then follow the final instruction given to me by the cunning and crafty Athena: "Don't return to the Mediterranean until you've written the last word of *The Idiot and the Odyssey II: Myth, Madness and Magic on the Mediterranean*," said the spear-carrying wily and wise goddess. *

* Portions of this chapter appeared in *The Idiot and the Odyssey II: Myth, Madness and Magic on the Mediterranean.*

# FOLLOW THE IDIOT

## CHAPTER PHOTOS

## CHAPTER MAP

# PART TWO

## TALKING TURKEY

*Edging into Ephesus*

*Meeting Alexander the Great in Bodrum*

*Walking the Lycian Way*

*Talking to Alexander in Antalya*

*Confronting ISIS at the Syrian Border*

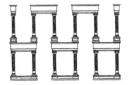

# Edging into Ephesus

"We of Macedon for generations past have been trained in
the hard school of danger and war."
– Alexander the Great

"A personality of quite unique genius, a marvelous mixture
of demonic passion and sober clearness of judgment."
– Ulrich Wilcken, *Alexander the Great*

---

I came to İzmir at the behest of the goddess Athena, who wanted me to walk precisely 4,401 kilometers for each of my first two books. I reached that exact milestone (I actually call it a kilometerstone) requested by my wily goddess guide after I paid a visit to nearby Homeros, where the Turks claim Homer was born. I'm now in Anatolia, or the Asian part of Turkey, which accounts for 97 percent of the country's area, continuing my walk down the Mediterranean coast to Egypt.

That's not quite as easy as it sounds. The Turkish coast features a wild, jagged, oft-impassable shoreline with dense forests, myriad promontories, thousands of coves and hundreds of inviting beaches in Pamucak, Oludeniz, Bodrum, Patara, Antalya, Sidon, Alanya and some other special spots that I'm keeping to myself. It's rugged and spectacularly beautiful.

Although Alexander the Great occasionally took inland routes through large swaths of Turkey, his primary goal was to control the entire coastline and, by doing so, rending the Persians highly regarded navy useless by depriving them of their harboring places to land. The path I'm strolling along now is the one he would have taken had he been able to simply walk and enjoy the Mediterranean rather than fight King Darius III and ultimately head east on his conquering spree.

Alexander's successors moved İzmir from its isolated location at the tip of the gulf to its current, more-protected location in the back bay. They credited the relocation of the city known as Smyrna in antiquity to Alexander who, they claimed, was told to make the move in a dream.

It's conceivable that Alexander walked along the seaside here through a suburb of İzmir called Güzelbahçe and continued 41 kilometers on to the resort city and port of Çeşme. He may have wanted to see the Bağlararasi Bronze Age harbor settlement, first inhabited in the third millennium BC and rediscovered, and uncovered, in 2001.

Whether he did or not, Çeşme is an ideal location for my next base camp.

Once I drop off my gear, I resume the Turkish part of my MedTrek at the Üçkuyular ferry on the western side of İzmir and again imagine that Alexander is with me, in spirit if not reality. I also imagine, for a fleeting moment, that I am one of his scouts slipping in and out of enemy territory to bring back vital information about the enemy's position, troop strength and weaponry.

Getting from Çeşme to Üçkuyular to start the MedTrek involves a 90-minute bus ride that goes quickly due to an ongoing conversation with a Turk who lived in Germany from 1968 to 2004. We discuss the two countries, their respective difficulties and, most importantly, the teeth he was going to have repaired in Konac, or downtown İzmir. Like everyone else, my mustachioed acquaintance has an opinion about whether Turkey should join the European Community ("Who wants it? Who wants the euro?" he asks me in 2013. "It's going to fall apart!"). We also discuss the difficulties his daughters are having in Germany due to the tight economy and the influx of refugees from neighboring Syria.

When I get off the bus I feel as happy as Alex in Wonderland to be back on the path. I even disguise my slight discontent when a café at the *otogar,* or bus stop, charges me four Turkish Lira for a grainy, thick coffee. That's about double what I figure it should cost and reminds me to constantly be on the lookout for the price gouging and overcharging that frequently occur in Turkish seaside restaurants. This was a scam that I detected when I was first in Istanbul in 1968 – the memorable phrase I learned on that trip as a college student was "No money, no honey" – and the truth of those words has been confirmed during many touring and working visits since then. Incidentally, the symbol for Turkey's currency changed from the bland letters TL to the more expressive, but costly and controversial, ₺ symbol in March 2012.

The İzmir promenade is blossoming with flowers, sculptures, benches, trees and other treats on a sunny spring morning. It's a breeze to walk an hour from the ferry to the Crowne Plaza Agamemnon Hotel (why not the Crowne Plaza Alexander Hotel, I wonder? Heck, let's name everything in the eastern Mediterranean after the man) where I have a discussion with the concierge about the rising price of a Turkish coffee, use the Wi-Fi and make another attempt to master the somewhat difficult (for me anyway) Turkish phrase for "I thank you" – teşekkür ederim. I must have a mental block because I have to keep asking people throughout the day how to say it. "Tea, sugar and cream" is the way I finally remember it. Close enough.

I continue on the pleasant promenade until I run into the first of a long string of military installations that block access to the sea with menacing graphics that include a soldier with a gun informing me that this is a "Military Security Zone – Entrance Forbidden."

After taking a few photos of the intimidating sign (another warning proclaims "Photos Forbidden," but I ignore it), I walk along the fence encircling the base. It doesn't take me to long to get in a verbal tussle with soldiers who want me to backtrack, until I convince them that I won't and they reluctantly and resignedly let me trespass through a neighboring farmer's fields. The farmer, when I meet him, as I trespass on his land, is so polite that he unlocks a gate and permits me to trespass through another neighbor's fields down to the sea.

The most challenging segment of my walk today is on a narrow, 18 inch wide seawall directly above the rocky seashore abutting the autoroute. I delicately balance on it for three kilometers (I smile as I imagine Alexander and his troops tottering single file on the narrow seawall) and, although vigilance and great agility are required, I calmly make it to Güzelbahçe where, after 17 kilometers, I have a simple but satisfying seaside lunch of eggplant salad, beans and sparkling water.

I usually stop for lunch at places with Wi-Fi and when there's a problem connecting to this one, I'm introduced to the charming, young "technology administrator" who reboots the system and is amazed at my peripatetic project. She's taken aback when I mention that she's more skilled than many of her male geek squad contemporaries. In Turkey, that comment is considered enlightened rather than sexist.

I'm wearing a lime-green T-shirt with "MOROCCO" written on it in English and Arabic and a waiter freaks out because he mistakes the drawing of Morocco's state ensign, a green pentagram representing the seal of Solomon, for the Jewish Star of David. It takes a few of his colleagues to quiet him down after he confronts me in an era when relations between Turkey and Israel are strained and tense. My choice of the right T-shirt is, as it's always been, a big decision at the beginning of every MedTrek day and once again I'm reminded of the sometimes dangerous misinterpretation of symbols.

The restaurant's maitre d' claims it's only ten kilometers to Urla but by the time I arrive in the seaside village and cozy picturesque port of Çeşmealti, where I relish seeing fishermen patiently repairing their nets in mid-afternoon, I've walked 33 kilometers. I call it a day and decide to take a minibus to the *otogar* in still-distant Urla to return to my base camp by bus. A Turk who lived in Chicago for 17 years tells me that I can walk on a local road to Çeşme from the next town if I take a short ride on a minibus that will cost me 2₺.

I jump on the minibus and am amazed to see a very blond Alicia Silverstone, or is it Reese Witherspoon, lookalike who, it turns out once we start chatting, is working on her PhD in Istanbul after graduating from Harvard.

My stilted conversation, as an American amid the usual array of working Turks found in a minibus late in the afternoon, makes me feel like I am an incompetent male character in *Clueless VII*, especially when I make such stupid comments to Alicia/Reese as "I've got to get to Çeşme ASAP to charge my iPhone."

Alicia/Reese tells me that she's getting a PhD in Turkish literature after majoring in English at Harvard; I tell her that I majored in English at Stanford and am writing books about my walk around the Mediterranean.

"What's a graduate of Harvard doing in this minibus?" I ask her.

"What's a graduate of Stanford doing in this minibus if he's supposed to be walking around the Mediterranean Sea and writing a book about it?" she responds.

We crack up.

Alicia/Reese is going to Karaburun, located at the end of the long, wide peninsula of the same name, and stays on the bus when it lets me off at a crossroad in the middle of nowhere to continue MedTrekking on the long, lonely, trafficless and very rural two-lane blacktop to Çeşme. But OMG I did meet Alicia Silverstone or Reese Witherspoon on a *dolmuş* (*dolmuş*, the word for "minibus," is pronounced *dolmush* not *dolmuss*, which means "pig") in Turkey! One more for the record books.

I contentedly smile to myself about the complete unpredictability and wondrous surprises of the MedTrek. The gods are indeed throwing me glorious sights, sounds and experiences. I say thanks to Athena, Zeus and the rest of them, and push on.

I pass the hillside campus of the İzmir Institute of Technology, which abuts the İzmir Technology Development Zone, and walk another eight kilometers up the steep road admiring the hills and the sunset when a man stops and insists, really insists, that he take me to Çeşme.

"It's getting too dark to walk here and it could be dangerous," he says without letting me say a thing. "Get in!"

I instinctively know he's a cop, get in the car and crisply answer the questions he asks me:

"What's the name of your hotel?"

"The Çilek Marina."

"How did you get to Çeşme?

"By ferry."

"How long are you staying?"

"Just a couple days."

I learn that he's an important cop when he shows his ID at a military checkpoint and they greet him like he's Alexander the Great.

By the time I get back to my hotel, having lingered (I rarely linger) while walking through the town in the early evening to buy (I rarely buy) a sexy red swimming suit for Liz that I spotted on a mannequin, I've walked 41 kilometers – another marathon.

One of the treats of traveling and staying almost anywhere in Turkey are the artistic creations decorating beds that are formed out of bath towels and, usually, surrounded with rose petals. I decide, when I finally return very tired to my base camp that night to find a camel-shaped towel on my bed, that these flourishes are actually presents from either my mentor goddess Athena or, maybe, Alexander himself. True or false, I give the impermanent art works credit for the pleasant dreams I often have in Turkey.

I'm so tired after the long day that I postpone writing my usual nightly notes about my walk, delay dealing with email and don't even play a few moves of online Scrabble, an obsession even when I'm MedTrekking. I put off all non-essential activities until the next morning and vow to stay at the hotel late enough to enjoy the 8:30 a.m. breakfast.

That's another treat in Turkey. Almost everywhere, even in the most inexpensive hotels, there's a copious Turkish breakfast! The one here includes *beyaz peynir* (white cheese), honey and jam, black olives, fresh tomatoes, cucumbers, *kaymak* (clotted water buffalo cream), a soft-boiled egg, lots of warm bread just out of the oven and, for me, black coffee with milk instead of the traditional black tea.

I return by *dolmuş* to the place the undercover cop picked me up to continue exploring the Karaburun Peninsula. I admit that I'm amazed to find such a steep and sprawling mountainous promontory at the extreme western end of Turkey. The cape includes İzmir's Karaburun, Urla and

Çeşme districts and is surrounded by the ever-inviting Aegean Sea. An ideal spot to walkabout for a few days.

It is also, I write, "confusingly covey and curvaceous." (I perhaps just created the word "covey," which means "full of coves") The walk here is particularly challenging because the coves are deceptively large, the hills and mountains are surpassingly steep and the beaches are often surfaced with hard-to-walk-on pebbles rather than smooth sand.

I am amused to find a benchmark (actually a bench in the middle of nowhere on a rare sandy beach) and an aphrodisiac (a sign near the bench warns "Danger: Sea Urchins," which the owner of my hotel in Çeşme says are a Turkish aphrodisiac). From the top of the next hill I have an excellent view of the Greek island of Chios, where the Greeks (and I) are certain Homer was born. Urchin-powered or otherwise, I am getting a grip on the landscape.

Along the way around the peninsula I meet a local Turk, whose wife and daughter are modestly sunbathing fully clothed on the pebbles. He offers me a honeyed dessert pastry. This pleasant family, and the farmer who lets me "trespass" on his property, obviously don't see many hikers here.

It's April, the time of year when seasonal construction and rehabilitation are getting underway at numerous hotels and resorts preparing to open for the summer season. Restaurants and bar decks are being reinstalled, there's a mad rush to bring four-star hotels back to life and a number of swimming pools look like they might be full in time for a season that starts in June and begins to fade in September.

It's very clear, as I continue my peninsular walkabout, that I won't be able to MedTrek every centimeter of the Turkish coast like I did in France, Spain and Morocco. It's not that the Texas-sized country is too large or the 4,362-kilometer Mediterranean and Aegean seaside is too long, but that the coast is, in some parts, simply unwalkable due to the topography.

Right now though, I feel completely at ease walking on a generally vacant coastline amid empty resorts and rising hotel developments. But I'll have to begin sensibly evaluating the terrain and selectively choose where I'm going to go, where I can and cannot travel. I also decide to do some exploring and take tomorrow off to visit Çeşme's fort and jump on a ferry for an overnight trip to Chios.

I've been to Chios before and I decide to drop in again lured by a lingering line in my head written by Arrian: "Memnon, whom King Darius had appointed commander of the whole fleet and of the entire seacoast, with the design of moving the seat of war into Macedon and Greece, acquired possession of Chios, which was surrendered to him by treachery."

I also want to pay homage to Homer, the purported author of the *Iliad* and the *Odyssey,* on this visit on behalf of Alexander. I figure that

Alexander would have liked the island of Chios because he tended to have simple tastes.

How simple were Alexander's tastes?

"I went into the King's sleeping-place, to prepare his bed," recounts Alexander's Persian eunuch and servant Bagoas in Mary Renault's *The Persian Boy*. "It amazed me to find it not much more than a common captain's, with scarcely room for two. There were a few fine gold vessels, I daresay from Persepolis; but the furniture was just the bed and clothes-stool, the washstand, a writing-table and chair, a rack of scrolls and a fine bath of inlaid silver, which must have been Darius's. I never saw a king keep so little state; he lives worse than any general would with us."

Given his simple needs, Alexander probably would have liked my room in Chios at the Amalia Hotel where I stayed when I MedTrekked around the island in September 2009. The €30 per night price hasn't increased and there is a lovely view from my balcony beyond the green-and-red port lights to Turkey. In the morning I enjoy another *bougatsa crema* breakfast, check in on the archaeological dig now underway at Homer's birthplace, post a photograph of the local drink called Mast, show a few people the photos of Chios in the .pdf version of *The Idiot II*, lunch in the sun on the port and take a 5 p.m. ferry to return to Çeşme.

Alexander never made it to Chios but would learn in Egypt that Cyprus, Rhodes, Phoenicia and the Aegean islands of Tenedos, Lesbos, Kos and Chios had all abandoned the Persians and come over to his side.

The next day, back on the mainland, I head southwest and stop at a fish market on the outskirts of Çeşme, where local restaurant owners come to buy their fish and tell lies early every morning. Adjacent to it are lots of shops selling crops from this rich agricultural area, including artichokes, watermelons and tomatoes.

I have my first swim of this MedTrek outing later in the day when temperatures are so hot that they cause my iPhone, which is at the top of my backpack, to automatically message me that it's out of action due to the heat. To ensure that it's not destroyed, I wait in an air-conditioned hotel lobby until it cools down enough to permit me to take a photo.

That's a first, though it's hardly *really* hot; it's simply summer in April and I post a photo showing all my clothes and gear on the beach, that "I'm skinny dipping southwest of Çeşme, Turkey."

I imagine, as I enter the cool and refreshing sea, what the pile of clothes on the beach would look like if Alexander, who wore much more clothing than I do, had gone skinny dipping. It would have included his tunic made in Sicily, an ornate cloak and belt given to him by the city of Rhodes, his iron helmet polished as shiny as silver and his *gorget* decorated with precious stones. The sword given to him by the king of the Citieans would have been used to weigh down the pile.

When I arrive at Alaçati Beach, I start talking to anyone who speaks English looking for advice about the terrain. A windsurfing instructor, a waitress, a lifeguard, a hotel employee and some fishermen (in that order) all advise me not to continue walking beyond the next beach, the one below the wind farm on the mountainside, because of the thick foliage and cliffs.

"You might make it a little way but you'll have to turn back," says the lifeguard.

The overwhelming efforts to dissuade me from walking the mountain range after the next beach – especially by fishermen who know the coastal typography – convince me to move my base camp from Çeşme south to Sığacık, a town in a small gulf described by the 16th-century Turkish navigator and cartographer Piri Reis as "an anchorage with water like *yufka*," which is a paper-thin pastry.

When I'm waiting for a *dolmuş* I chat with a 24-year-old Canadian woman from Ottawa wearing short shorts who tells me how safe she feels teaching English in İzmir and mentions that, from her perspective, a low-cut blouse is more provocative than her short shorts in the eyes of Turkish men. Who knew?

I don't feel good about skipping a walk over the hazardous mountains but admit that the warnings make sense when I look back at the steep cliffs from the protective port of Sığacık. To compensate, I have a mixed sole/sardine/salad lunch that lasts four hours and walk through the Sunday market to feast my eyes on fresh artichoke hearts, spinach pies and other Turkish delights.

I bivouac at a family set-up whose owner runs an organic food shop in the town center and asks me to call her TJ. One advantage of the hillside Orion pension (the password for the Wi-Fi is "summerwind"), besides the view over the colorful Sığacık marina and a big turtle in the garden that is apparently the family pet, is that I don't have to wait until 8:30 a.m. for the usual Turkish breakfast, because I can make my own.

The next morning, the packs of neighborhood dogs bark in unison as the *muezzin* breaks the silence of night with the call to prayer at 5:11 a.m. I use this as an excuse to have my first coffee and eagerly get out the door at 6 a.m., twenty minutes before sunrise, with the intention of MedTrekking at least 33 kilometers today to reach the 9,000-kilometerstone on my walk around the Mediterranean Sea.

I again wonder how long it would have taken Alexander to walk the distances I walk.

Plutarch says Alexander, at one point while he was pursuing Darius across what is now Turkey, marched thirty-three hundred furlongs (a furlong is about an eighth of a mile), or over 412 miles, in eleven days. If true, that's 37 miles, or almost sixty kilometers, a day. Arrian says that

"The pace of his presumably rhythmical military march can be bewildering, once racing 70 miles in two days with a hand-picked force."

With everything they were carrying, and the large number of troops and logistics involved, I'm extremely impressed.

Incidentally, by the time Alexander died, his entire European and Asiatic campaigns from 336 to 323 BC had covered 20,870 miles or 33,587 kilometers – about 1,605 miles per year.

Far faster and further than I could go. Kudos for a remarkable achievement.

Sığacık – a magnet for windsurfers, sailors and rock climbers – is close to the ruins of Teos, which prospered from 1050 to 1000 BC. One of twelve Ionian cities, Teos was home to the magnificent Temple of Dionysus, the largest temple dedicated to the god of the grape harvest and ritual madness anywhere in Turkey, built at the beginning of the $2^{nd}$ century BC by Hermogenes of Priene.

Contemporary Teos has been intensively farmed, which makes it difficult to excavate or explore the site, though plowing has brought some pottery to the surface. As I walk through its crumbling remains at 7 a.m., while there's still dew on the grass, my imagination goes wild as I eye a column here, a water conduit there and other stone remnants of the ancient civilization.

The next few miles of coast are not the Aegean's finest, unless you like trudging through plastic that's washed ashore during the winter. Fortunately, the Turkish military has taken over a stretch of seaside here to conduct old school landing exercises (remember, that seriously threatening Greek island of Samos looms just off shore!) and as a result this is the only clean stretch of seaside in the area. It's slightly bizarre, from an aesthetic point of view, that a military presence would be preferable to civilian occupation, but that seems to be case.

The one thing the plastic doesn't seem to impact is the bountiful agricultural output. The previous day in the market I saw floating artichoke hearts for sale by the dozen and now I see where they're grown, along with olives, citrus and other crops. Another thing the plastic doesn't impact is, from a distance, the solitary beauty of a seaside mosque. It's definitely a lead candidate for my "Entering Ephesus" feature later in the week.

The coastal contours, the high hills and the warm weather must make me look pretty bedraggled because a number of Turks stop to offer me a lift. They probably wouldn't stop if I were hitch-hiking but I appreciate their gestures – which are typical examples of the national Turkish trait known as *misafir*, or hospitality.

The last eight kilometers of the walk are on generally-ignored beaches with in-need-of-repair promenades and not many sunbathers. All this could change (will April litter bring May glitter?), as it does almost overnight in the south of France once the season gets going. But I'm not expecting a Saint-Tropez-like clean up. This area reminds me more of the poorer parts of Spain, though I am impressed with the exercise equipment that the Turks have installed on many of their beaches, whether empty or crowded. In fact, I regularly use some of the machines to exercise some unused upper body muscles.

When I reach the 32-kilometer mark of the day, I celebrate my 9,000[th] kilometerstone (not to be confused with a milestone) on the MedTrek with a dance in the surf and a refreshing swim.

"Ah, I'm still having fun walking around the Mediterranean," I reflect. "What a treat!"

On return to my Sığacık base camp, I complain to TJ, the owner of my Airbnb squat, about the generally dismal state of the seaside and the fact that the military seems to control most of the coast. She tells me that it's seasonal and that everything will be picked up and cleaned up for the tourist season. Her husband adds that he won't be surprised if the military cedes some of their beach holdings in the future. He also remarks that agriculture, particularly artichokes, is still a big mainstay of the economy.

Base camp moves always lead to a discombobulated day and today is no exception. I leave the Sığacık squat at 6:56 a.m., miss the 7 a.m. bus (it came at 6:55) and it then takes me three buses and over three hours to get to Kuşadasi. Once there, I immediately ditch my duffle bag and take an hour-long bus back to Ürkmez to resume the MedTrek at noon at the exact spot I stopped yesterday.

I know, I know, sometimes I don't understand the logistics either. Still, it's good to have a base camp for four nights rather than trudge more than a few kilometers with all my gear. I adopted this method shortly after I began the MedTrek in France in 1998 and still find that it makes things much easier.

Although most of the beaches look pretty sad, the tide (actually there is no tide in the Mediterranean but it's a nice phrase) may be turning because throughout the day I see cleaning crews near the water. Could this be National Garbage Pickup and Beach Refurbishment Day? It's happening not only on the beaches but also in the mountains, where I meander when I have to walk around the military bases. People are cleaning up everywhere.

By the end of the day I realize that military installations aren't my only beach-blocking enemy. Gigantic tourist complexes, each resembling a mini-Disneyland, are more and more frequent as I approach Kuşadasi, an important port for tourist ships with passengers eager to visit ancient Ephesus. Until this point, I'd seen, with the dramatic and welcome exception of Alicia Silverstone/Reese Witherspoon, very few foreigners. Yet just this morning I spoke to some blonde and very white Danes tanning on the beach in front of one hotel and witnessed a loud-speaking French couple arguing at another.

When I run into the Paloma Club Sultan Resort built on 120 hectares with 434 bungalows/suites/rooms and enough Wi-Fi networks to handle a country, I realize that I ain't seen nothing yet. These resorts make Disneyland look modest and, though I enter the premises of one hotel from the seaside without too much problem and walk undetected to a bar near the pool, I soon get nabbed by security and have to talk myself out of the place.

I mention, somewhat mis-paraphrasing that great line in *Butch Cassidy and the Sundance Kid*, that "I'm not going to rob you leaving the resort. You shouldn't have any problem with me leaving the resort. I'm going to rob you if you let me in the resort. That's when you have a problem."

They didn't have a clue what I was talking about. And I'm not sure you do either.

I finally convince the security team to release me, return to the water and meet some picnickers who tell me that I'll be trespassing if I walk on, or even in, the sea.

"Nobody owns the sea," I say.

They didn't have a clue what I was talking about either.

Ignoring more irksome resorts throughout the afternoon, I ramble along the seaside through rice fields and over a few fences, up and down mountains and along the shoreline road, far above the sea, where I can see Kuşadasi in the distance. I can even make out a liner docked in the port beneath the Hotel Stella, where I'll be staying for a few days to visit Ephesus and walk further south.

Prior to catching the *dolmuş* from Kuşadasi the next morning back to Ahmetbeyli, where I ended yesterday's MedTrek, I have an extended conversation with the "manager" of the Kuşadasi-Seferihisar minibus *otogar*. I compliment him on snagging a job that basically involves orchestration of buses and passengers – and the little bribes and tips that come with it. It seems very Zen to me but, he explains, "it's neither good for body nor brain and I'm very stressed." I tell him MedTrekking is good for both the body and the brain and I'm not stressed. Maybe I can help him out.

"Want to join me?" I ask.

"Are you crazy?" he replies. "I've got to work."

From Ahmetbeyli I meander into the back country until I get to Ephesus. Like Troy, Ephesus impresses me and my imagination goes wild as I fantasize that I am standing in the same spot as did Alexander the Great. This doesn't happen often but I feel chills running up my entire body, from the tips of my toes to the top of my head.

Alexander was heralded as a welcomed liberator when he arrived in Ephesus because Ephesians detested the dictatorial Persian rulers who had destroyed their temples, toppled their statues, violated their cemeteries, ignored their voices and raised their taxes. Once liberated, the citizens went on a Persian killing spree, though Alexander is credited with both reducing the violence and restoring a democratic form of government.

I always look forward to walking downhill from the top to the bottom of Ephesus, which was a settlement during the Bronze Age and became an important city on the Ionian coast by the 10th century BC. I follow the cobblestoned Harbor Street past agoras, baths, temples, fountains and well-known monuments that include the Library of Celsus built by the Romans, the Temple of Artemis (which took 120 years to construct and, say the history books, dates from precisely 550 BC) and the amphitheater with seating for 25,000 spectators.

It was the Temple of Artemis, you might recall, that burned down on the day Alexander was born and it was still being restored when he entered the city. Alexander proposed to finance the reconstruction project and have his name inscribed on the front but his offer was refused because, the ancient historians tell us, "it is not fitting for one god to build a temple to another." Instead, he had a portrait painted by Apelles of Cos that illustrated him throwing a thunderbolt, as though he were Zeus.

After Alexander's death, Lysimachus, one of his generals, ruled Ephesus, but things began going downhill when the city was taken over by the Romans in 129 BC. It continued going down the tubes when the Goths destroyed it in AD 263, was hit by an earthquake in 614 and finally abandoned, largely because siltation distanced it from the sea, in the 15th century.

The guides who take visitors through Ephesus today have the timetable and layout down pat but very few of them concentrate, as I do when I guide people, on practical necessities during ancient times. I always start my personally-led tours of Ephesus with first-time visitors by describing the ancient city's comparatively advanced public services, including municipal toilets. My favorite public toilet consists of 36 holes, spaced a bit too close together for my comfort, on long marble benches with water flowing in a downhill channel underneath to "flush" the waste.

I know you're wondering about a number of things so let me make it clear that a sponge on a stick, rather than toilet paper, was used at the time. And if there was a water shortage, and no flowing water, slaves would have buckets of water handy. That's not all slaves did. In the winter they would walk down to the toilets, cross the mosaic floor and warm the marble seats for their masters by sitting on them.

Idiotic Tip: Try to get the first "toilet" instead of the 36th!

I also take my tours to the House of the Virgin Mary a few kilometers away where they can appreciate the view from the men's urinal.

# SEVEN WONDERS OF THE ANCIENT WORLD

The Temple of Artemis (Diana) at Ephesus was one of the Seven Wonders of the Ancient World, according to a list compiled by Philo of Byzantium in 250 BC.

The others were:

*The Great Pyramid of Giza.*
*The Hanging Gardens of Babylon.*
*The Statue of Zeus at Olympia.*
*The Mausoleum at Halicarnassus.*
*The Colossus of Rhodes.*
*The Lighthouse of Alexandria.*

I recall art historian and professor Constantine Christofides, a Greek born in Alexandria, Egypt, suggesting what iconic historical remnants I should see on my walk around the Mediterranean when I interviewed him a decade ago in Aix-en-Provence, France.

Christofides, who spent over three decades photographing various European and Middle Eastern pilgrimage routes, said "The Mediterranean is where it all started and there's a confederation of knowledge, culture and disciplines everywhere around the sea. Every human being, before dying, should see Marseille as well as the citadel in ancient Mycenae, the Knossos palace in Crete, Hagia Sophia in Istanbul, the Pyramids in Egypt, Carthage in Tunisia and Fez in Morocco."

Now, of course, there are the seven wonders of the Contemporary World that I've had the opportunity to visit. Been to these yet?

*The Great Wall of China.*
*The Taj Mahal in India.*
*Petra in Jordan.*
*The Colosseum in Italy.*
*Christ the Redeemer in Brazil.*
*Chichén Itzá in Mexico.*
*Machu Picchu in Peru.*

Forget whether Saint John actually took Mary, the mother of Jesus, to this modest stone chapel and shrine (the Catholic Church has never authenticated the event) but walk past the wishing wall, where pilgrims post their written prayers, into the men's room and enjoy the view you get from a standing position at the urinals. I urge women not to pass this up and recount that when I told a member of the House of Lords in London about the view, he visited Mary's johns, or WCs as he called them, and afterwards thanked me for the tip.

Alexander's actions in Ephesus made him extremely popular and public opinion was on his side when he continued his march to Miletus and Halicarnassus (now known as Bodrum), which, unlike most towns which simply surrendered to Alexander, he had to take by force in order to dominate the entire Turkish seacoast.

Arrian reports that "After stopping in Priene where he contributed to a temple of Athena Polias ('King Alexander set up this temple to Athena Polias,' reads the inscription) he moved south to Miletus where he excused Greek mercenaries who had fought against him and also decided to disband the Greek fleet and fight the Persians at sea by "overcoming the ships from dry land" and not allowing them access to any ports. It was a novel strategy, and it worked.

After Ephesus, I return to the coast and meet some Germans on a horse safari, nod to lots of fishermen along the way and use the Wi-Fi at the Ephesus Hotel, another luxury resort that I consider a blight, albeit a utilitarian blight, on the coast. Once I sneak in, I'm trapped inside the sprawling complex until I manage to untangle a patched hole in the security fence and descend through a water park on the opening day of the summer season. I'm caught again, but it's not an unpleasant experience. A delightful English-speaking young female Turkish security guard pleasantly escorts me to the entrance/exit and thanks me for bringing the flaw in the fence to their attention.

Compared to the up-and-down of the previous days, it's an easy hike into seaside Kuşadasi and around the bay to the Stella Hotel. I send a GPS marking the spot where I'm sitting on the promenade before I check out of my room.

Hasan, the London-educated hotel owner, turns out to be the fixer he claimed to be in his email to me when I reserved:

Dear Joel Stratte-McClure,

My name is Hasan from Hotel Stella Kuşadasi. I have taken a reservation in your name and would like to confirm it personally. Also I would like to tell you that I am always ready to help you while you are staying in our hotel. You can ask me questions and I would like to help you in everything. I can book tours to Ephesus, Virgin Mary's House,

Didyma, Priene, Miletus, daily trips, bus tickets all over the Turkey, Samos ferry tickets, and if you need any transfers from airport or anywhere around just let me know. I would like to help you as much as I can. I am here to make your holiday enjoyable. Please do not hesitate to ask me any questions. Thank You.

Best Regards,

Hasan

# *HASAN FROM HOTEL STELLA*

Among other things, Hasan upgrades me to a double room with a balcony that probably has the best view in town, gives me the April (€25) daily rate for my four-day stay that lasts into May, and offers to be the fixer for anything else I need. Of course, a typically healthy Turkish breakfast is always included.

The next morning, to reward myself for making it this far, I let Hasan set up a complete day off that includes a Turkish bath, facial and massage at the Rina Hammam.

Before I leave the hotel, I write a blog entry entitled "Coasting to Kuşadasi":

"The 162-kilometer MedTrek from İzmir to Kuşadasi is a piece of Turkish delight if you ignore the pathless mountains, off-limit seaside military zones, imposing luxury resorts, dangerous sea urchins and omnipresent barbed-and-razor wire fences.

The Turks love theoretically a impenetrable fence, a penchant that I believe is due to their testy relationship with Greece, Syria and other neighboring countries. When I enter one residential area from an open gate on the beach, I'm unable to find a way out at the other side due to serious razor wire on the top of the fence. Even The Idiot isn't stupid enough to tackle razor wire during an up-and-down-mountains-and-along-the-sea stroll.

But every time I am detained for trespassing (it's easy to find a way into private resorts and farmers' fields, not always easy to get out) I manage to avoid serious trouble with my "Nobody owns the sea" argument.

The seaside is making a winter-to-summer seasonal transition. The mosques look radiant in the sunshine, fishermen calmly patch their nets, clean-up crews are everywhere and the Turks are pitching tents in the sand.

I skinny dip in numerous coves, workout at free gyms on the promenade and sit on empty benches.

My three sweetest moments between İzmir and Kuşadasi are (1) exploring the ruins in Teos at dawn, (2) catching a sunset in Kuşadasi and (3) enjoying a recuperative Turkish bath, massage and facial at the Rina Hammam and Fitness Center in Kuşadasi."

 *COASTING TO KUŞADASI*

I'm in constant touch with Liz who will arrive in Bodrum in a few days and tell her to be aware of the touted low prices and deals on every street corner. Like every bazaar town, the Bodrum airport is full of fixers, arrangers and taxi drivers who always start a conversation with, "Where are you from? Where are you going? Can I help?"

My regular retort is that I'm walking through Turkey and then I speedily rattle off, trying to keep them in geographical order and pronounce them correctly, the names of the places I've been – Eceabat, Çanakkale, Truva, Küçükkuyu, Bergama, Ayvalik, Dikili, Candarli, Denzikoy, İzmir, Üçkuyula, Çeşme, Kuşadasi, Kazdağı...you get the idea – the names are about the only thing I can say in Turkish that sounds Turkish. That both shuts them up and earns me a bit of respect.

I'm not the only one who lists the places he's visited to impress people.

Alexander used to do the same thing, and he once, according to Arrian of Nicomedia, told his troops that "you hold possession of Ionia, the Hellespont, both the Phrygias, Cappadocia, Paphlagonia, Lydia, Caria, Lycia, Pamphylia, Phoenicia, Egypt together with Grecian Libya, as well as part of Arabia, Hollow Syria, Syria between the rivers, Babylon, the nation of the Susians, Persia, Media, besides all the nations which the Persians and the Medes ruled, and many of those which they did not rule, the land beyond the Caspian Gates, the country beyond the Caucasus, the Tanais, as well as the land beyond that river, Bactria, Hyrcania, and the Hyrcanian Sea...The wealth of the Lydians, the treasures of the Persians, and the riches of the Indians are yours; and so is the External Sea."

Whew!

He makes me look like an amateur list-maker.

# FOLLOW THE IDIOT

## CHAPTER PHOTOS

## CHAPTER MAP

# Meeting Alexander the Great in Bodrum

"You know there's not a part of me without a scar or a bone broken by sword, knife, stone, catapult, and club. I've shared every hardship with all of you."
– Alexander the Great

"His love of glory, and the pursuit of it, showed a solidity of high spirit and magnanimity far above his age."
– Arrian of Nicomedia

It's a slightly cloudy morning, which momentarily means a bit less sun and heat than usual, but Hasan tells me this is nothing compared to a *real* summer day in Kuşadasi when it's "35°C in the shade and 55°C in the sun." That, if you're thinking in Fahrenheit, is "95°F in the shade and 131°F in the sun."

Can't argue with that.

We're watching a cruise ship dock from Hasan's hotel's balcony at 6:23 a.m. before I take off from the Stella for a morning swim at a beach a few kilometers away. After breakfast I head south on the seaside promenade past Pigeon's Island and continue in high spirits along the coast, strolling sometimes on the hard sidewalk and sometimes on the soft sand, to the renowned Ladies Beach, where I'm the first visitor. I see no ladies but lots of *chez (sic) longue* (aka *chaises longues*) seemingly prepared for apparently awaited ladies.

After a twenty-minute swim, I continue on concrete sidewalks and wooden walkways through the grounds of numerous hotels and resorts that look much less posh and much more relaxed than the Disneyish ones north of town. A security officer at one resort tells me, as I wish all security guys would but don't, "We welcome you but please just stay on the beach and don't go inside." Now that's a helpful and informative attitude that could be replicated at some of the fancier joints that use a more threatening and ferocious approach.

Most of the neighborhoods south of Kuşadasi consist of apartments and I continue on beaches that run through increasingly egalitarian resorts with both local and foreign clients, who seem to be primarily Dutch. Not that there isn't a snag or two. I get cut going over a barbed wire fence into one resort where I'm both barked at by dogs and rudely stopped by security men who hear the dogs and don't try to practice their smiles while they brusquely escort me off the premises.

I'm amused by, and photograph, a massage table under some palm trees that is destined to be a post entitled: Where to get a massage between Kuşadasi and a mountainous national park." The sight is enough to encourage me to stop at the very friendly Silver Sand Beach café for coffee, a tuna sandwich and a Wi-Fi break at noon after I've walked 15 kilometers.

I tell the owner about my MedTrek and he actually apologizes about the filthy state of Turkish beaches. A friendly waitress points to the mountains in the distance and says that "the national park is only eight kilometers away and it's very clean once you get away from the sea." She shows me how close it is on a map and advises me to "be sure to check where you can walk and where you can't."

As I head further south, I enjoy watching the mountains become closer and clearer and it doesn't take me long to reach the town of Güzelçamli. I pass the port, learn that the entrance to the national park is a kilometer away and lay in the sun on a wooden pier debating whether I should get in the water again. I don't.

I ask around and get the scoop about the Dilek Peninsula and the Büyük Menderes River Delta National Park from a municipal tourist office, telling anyone I speak to that I plan to return in the morning to MedTrek to the other side. A city official tells me to "Be sure to take the left path that says 'Canyon' because the end of the peninsula, due to the proximity of the Greek island of Samos, is under military control." He scrawls directions on a map that will enable me to avoid a confrontation.

Then I head to the Zeus Cave (which the Turks call Zeus Magarasi) for a refreshing almost-dark swim in pleasantly cold fresh water and am told by a 24-year-old Turk, whom no one would describe as thin, that "You're too old to swim." I thought he probably presumed that I was in my 50s and was actually shocked when a few minutes later he shouts, "I'll bet you're 65!"

The fat (he's gone from being described as not thin to being fat) guy's German-speaking sister is also in the water and when I get in, she compliments my stroke. I probably should have challenged her obese (he's gone from not being un-thin to being fat to being appallingly overweight) brother to a race but he's with a group, which might even qualify as a gang, of six guys. As you may know, I've been wary of groups or gangs of guys like this since I was robbed by three Gypsies (they were all thin) south of Salerno, Italy. I figure this bunch will nab my knapsack, iPhone, money, glasses and everything else during the swimming race.

So I reply simply and politely, "You're right and it's a great age."

I return to the entrance of the national park the next morning, pay the 3₺ entrance fee and follow the directions given to me yesterday. It turns out "Canyon" is a certifiable misnomer! What I should have been told was "Go six kilometers along the coast and 15 kilometers across the mountains on a trail that is eight kilometers up, two kilometers along the crest of the mountain, five kilometers down and a last seven kilometers through the ghost town of Doğanbey." This is a full roller coaster of a mountain crossing!

Despite the poor directions, it's nonetheless a pretty, peaceful and pleasant day's walk on a hard-dirt path through the Dilek Peninsula National Park amidst myriad flora, fauna, birds and bugs as well as astounding views of the park's peaks, glimpses of the nearby (and apparently threatening) Greek island of Samos and the extraordinary Büyük Menderes River Delta.

After the national park, the morning walk on the beach is almost completely shoeless (barefoot or sandals) and necessitates fording the Büyük Menderes (aka Maeander) River. After chatting with some fisherman and gleaning a knowledge of the river from them, I cross the mouth of the river by wading 100 meters into the sea and finding, as they said I would, a sandbar that enables me to walk without meandering in waist-high water to the other side. River crossings are sometimes a tricky business, but I make the crossing without incident, grateful as always to the special gods whom I know are still watching over me.

The Maeander River really does meander through a vast delta that is swampy, reedy, marshy and muddy with an inland lake separated from the sea by a thin, broken string of sand. It's easy to understand that in classical Greece the name of the river had become a word synonymous with anything (from rivers or trails to speeches, road trips or long books) that is convoluted or winding. As the Greek geographer and historian Strabo correctly explained, "its course is so exceedingly winding that everything winding is called meandering." It's a joy when I come across a wonderful word like this that began in such a unique and specific way.

I send a GPS signal from seven kilometers into the "Canyon," which has very convenient stone markers every kilometer (true kilometerstones!). There are numerous waterholes, into which I frequently dip my hot head, and a fair amount of shade. At one point I'm shirtless and so Zenned out that I don't want the trail to end, which it does finally in Doğanbey, an eerily empty ghost town (one guidebook calls it "an open air museum") that's a silent testimony to its past Greek and Turkish residents, with a great assortment of cultural remnants and architectural styles. The village was known as Domatia when it was populated by Greeks and became Doğanbey after the Turks took it over during the unique and surreal population exchange in 1923.

Looking further back in time, I stop a bit inland to see the theater at Miletus, which, before the Persian invasion in the middle of the 6th century BC, was considered to be the greatest and wealthiest of Greek cities. Perhaps its formidable reputation is why Alexander relished taking it by a forceful siege using 4,000 troops to obtain "mastery over the Persian fleet by defeating their army on land." Because it was key to his military strategy, Alexander wisely decided that if he occupied Asia with a land force he would control the ports, prevent the Persian ships from replenishing their supplies and not need his own fleet.

The next day I decide, primarily due to the convergence of two major rivers which constitutes a major obstacle, to kick off the MedTrek on the dry road a few miles inland. I cross both rivers on bridges and then, discounting the advice of the residents of a tiny village who tell me I'm making a big mistake, return to the seaside and continue towards Didyma. I plan to pay my respects to the gods at the mysterious and magnificent Temple of Apollo.

I'm again aware of the wealth of sites, sights, soils, sounds (birds, frogs, everything alive, it seems, is making a noise) and smells (that particularly unique between-fresh-and-stagnant marshy scent) found only in a very fertile delta.

Once I head inland I realize that "big mistake" means that I am deterred by the vast fields of grain, a maze of canals, a plethora of swamps and marshes, puddles of mud and the very contour of the coast itself. The villagers' advice was sound; I should have listened. Indeed, as the hours pass, all of these factors present me with myriad difficulties that add detours and kilometers to the day's journey as I negotiate my way through cotton fields, wheat fields (the pollen turns my legs orange), MedTrekker-blocking canals, freshly plowed fields, thistle-filled fields, brush-covered hillsides and lots of mud.

After my shoes get wet, soaked really, I know they'll stay wet throughout the day so, glad that I always have two pairs of footwear, I revert to sandals. I frequently have to cut inland and finally, thirsty and slightly frustrated, reach a road indicating that Didyma is only ten kilometers away. Looking back on the mountainous peninsula that I emerged from a few hours earlier, I realize I've made a decent distance. I collapse on a beach near a bar in Yeşilköy where, after a 25-kilometer delightful delta-and-sea spanning slog, I immediately, to the open-mouthed astonishment of the owner, down a 1.5 liter bottle of water without taking a breath. Whew!

The conditions are reflected in a text I send Liz, who will be arriving the next day, when I settle into a new base camp in Akbük: "Shower needed but you'd love my gnarly swamp smell, though I tossed my socks. Awaiting a roasted chicken off the spit." Life is good: dry socks, chicken in the gullet, my loved one and best friend on the way.

That night in an email an Idiot-ic Reader asks about the expense of the MedTrek in Turkey and I let him know that, for a backpacker, walking in Turkey is one of the best deals in Mediterranean travel today.

"That's because I keep it simple," I write. "All I insist on is a room with a sea view and Wi-Fi for less than €25 ($32.50) with, usually, breakfast included. That's especially easy for The Idiot – any idiot actually – in Turkey before the switch to summer season and summer prices. Each of my four base camps – in Çeşme, Sığacık, Kuşadasi and Akbük – on my current MedTrek outing had a pleasant view of the sea and cost €25 or less."

Pretty-in-pink Liz and I kick off in Yeşilköy at the precise spot where I arrived sweaty, smelly, soggy and sunburned three days ago and our walk into Didim is a perfect start to her first-ever day of MedTrekking. We stroll along the sea on rocks, trails, clay or sand until, after five kilometers, we reach a resort called the Majestic, where a young lifeguard makes the mistake of pretending that he is the head of security.

Once I straighten him out, we move at a delightful, easy pace and visit the Didyma archaeological site, an alluring ancient Greek sanctuary that was home base for the Didymaion, aka the Oracle of Apollo. Next to Delphi, the Didymaion was the most renowned oracle of the Hellenic world and was, as so many of them were, first mentioned by Homer.

Back in the day there was a 17-kilometer Sacred Way to Didyma that featured ritual way stations and statues of members of the Branchidae family. Some of these statues, dating to the sixth century BC, were taken by one Charles Newton in the 19th century and are in the British Museum. We blame Charles Newton when we can't locate the Sacred Way and are forced to find our way to the sanctuary by walking through a maze of urban streets.

I don't want to pressure this particular oracle about where I might find Alexander's remains. I simply want to determine where Alexander the Great went next on his military campaign in Turkey. One can only ask so much of each oracle; they are a bit stingy about parceling out their wisdom sometimes. So my questions are simple and brief, and the Oracle graciously responds. I should, I'm told, continue the MedTrek in Güllük after taking "a much-needed spiritual break on Patmos, the Greek island."

We walk from Didyma back to the seaside through Alikentum and continue until we stumble upon the Liverpool Reds seaside cafe (the password for the Wi-Fi is "liverpool"). We stop for a coffee and are amused that the soccer-loving British customers haven't even heard about the nearby Temple of Apollo.

After passing the Caprice orthodox religious hotel, where the women on the beach are swimming fully clothed, and enjoying a new promenade with spiffy shower/bathroom facilities that takes us into Akbük, we arrive at our Patio Beach Club base camp just before total darkness after 29 kilometers. During the relaxing buffet dinner at a table looking out over the lights of the city and the lapping Mediterranean, I ask Liz about her reaction to her first day of MedTrekking

"There were so many different sights and terrains," she tells me in that light, easy, slightly rushed way she has that I so adore. "Beach, rock, bogs, thistles, thorns, hayfields, cities, ancient ruins – so many things to catch my eye and amaze me! And so many odd occurrences and sights. I loved the bleached white bones of cows' skeletons. And the shotgun shells in the path and the three wild youths who ran towards us screaming. That frightened me a bit, though they turned out to be harmless. It all made me realize how isolated we are and that how welcoming and helpful people are even though we can't speak Turkish. People stopping to offer us rides, people giving us advice on our journey. They were lovely.

"The best was that I was so aware," she continued, with wonder and amazement evident in her breathless tone. "I could feel each minute and each step go by, but the hours flew and I was amazed when we'd suddenly been walking three hours and had gone ten kilometers, then over nine hours later we'd gone 29 kilometers. I'm glad I'm in good shape because we're constantly moving.

"It's very spiritual," she went on. "Wonderfully spiritual, uplifting and enlightening. I felt my 'being' with nature throughout the whole day and I liked having an occasional mosque in the distance as an inspirational marker. I can't speak the language, I have no idea where I am, I've got to have faith and look for the best in every situation. The beauty and history are huge."

Liz follows my suggestion to take a day off (I always encourage first-time MedTrekkers to take a day off between long hikes) and I MedTrek alone for 18 kilometers the next day, along the coast from the eat-all-you-want-for-€17-a-night Patio Beach Club Resort (our spacious two-story room and the scarcity of other guests add to the allure). It is an instructive day and I learn two things:

1. It's impossible to walk any further along the coast due to cliffs that completely block access to the sea – and the inland road to Milas is too distant for any decent sea views.

2. There will be a new multibillion dollar development here called the Bodrum Sea Resort built under the auspices of Kazakhstan's YDA group.

In fact, the construction manager, who comes to meet me when I'm stopped by security as I approach the sales office at the top of a hill with a gorgeous 360° view, tells me that Ritz Carlton, Canyon Ranch and Louis Vuitton are all involved in a development that "will be far more up-market than anything Turkey's seen before and will include the country's last eight private beaches." I tell him that this is the most impressive sales office I've ever seen for a resort that doesn't exist.

He also informs me that if I find Turkish a difficult language I should try to learn Russian, which he still has trouble with after working for YDA for ten years in Kazakhstan. Now that's a difficult language, he avers. But I'm sure he can say "rubles" in Russian, Turkish or Kazakh. Or English, for that matter. He offers me a ride to Bodrum and tells me that the reason there are so many unfinished developments along the coast is "because the government passed a law prohibiting any buildings closer than 200 meters to the sea – no one is sure what will happen to the existing shells but now no one can take them over." He adds that "much of the coast is a mess and an embarrassment."

The construction manager is not the only one who notices lots of empty existing developments and even more to-be-or-not-to-be-finished housing projects. I take photographs of examples of both types of eyesore near the working and up-market Apollonium Spa & Beach Resort, where 70 percent of the clients are British, before I continue to the end of the tarmac road at the tiny village of Konut Yapi. I'm led into town by a doe goat and nanny twosome who wander past some grazing Angus cows on the last beach reachable by car. Beyond is a dense, thickly shrubbed hillside and the town of Güllük.

My best and longest lasting memory of the Patio Beach Club is returning to Liz, who looks like a model for the Mediterranean Diet, comfortably lazing on a *chaise longue* in the sexy red bathing suit I bought her off a mannequin a few days ago.

Unfortunately The Idiot and his MedTrekking partner don't leave the spacious, tranquil and inexpensive base camp in Akbük without a slight hitch. Here's the gist, from my point of view, of how we were delayed in reaching our next base camp in Bodrum:

Dear Altinkum Transfers,

I booked one of your buses from the Patio Beach Club in Akbük to the Bodrum Airport at 10:30 a.m. on Saturday, May 11, and paid reception the requested £20 fare for my partner and myself.

The bus that picked us up, we learned when we reached the main İzmir-Milas road, was going to the İzmir Airport and, after being taken to İzmir against our wishes (we were not allowed to get off despite numerous telephone conversations with a "Mr. Ali," whom our driver called "a crazy boss," in your offices), we were dumped by your driver at 2:45 p.m. at the Akbük exit on the İzmir-Milas road. We waited until 3:30 p.m., hoping that "Mr. Ali" would provide his promised alternative transport, but no one came. We were forced to take other buses, and pay additional fares, to get to Bodrum.

Please be advised that I have lodged a complaint with the *Jandarma* (police), will contact various Turkish Tourist authorities and will write a number of US/UK travel editors concerning your unprofessional and irresponsible, if not illegal, business practices.

Your inability to provide an alternative form of transport in the face of your own mistake (the Patio Beach Club will confirm that we were going to Bodrum) is unacceptable.

I will advise everyone I know, and everyone I don't, never to use your transport company or stay in your hotels.

You are an embarrassment to Turkey.

Inshallah and Best Regards,

## Joel Stratte-McClure, US Senator

In the end, the bus company admitted that the mix-up was their mistake and offered us a Turkish bath if we ever returned to Didyma. The offer was "good for life" but I gave it to a British acquaintance living locally and he used it the next day. He said they treated him like he was a member of parliament.

We follow the oracle's advice and catch a ferry to Patmos where we visit the Cave of the Apocalypse, where Saint John received the revelations, and meditate daily for a week.

I thought the oracle was suggesting that it was a good time for me to indulge in some self-examination and self-cultivation but instead I'm given this very random message:

"In Halicarnassus (now known as Bodrum), Alexander met the one-time queen Ada who he restored to power as the satrap of Caria and let her adopt him as her son. That shrewd move enabled him to assume her throne when she died. YOU must find a one-time queen to adopt you when you get to Carthage in Tunisia."

Queen? Tunisia? It didn't make much sense to me.

Another momentous occurrence on Patmos is a result of author Jeremy Thomas's critique that mackerel were not mentioned in my earlier books. I'm delighted to rectify that lapse.

## WORLD-FAMOUS AUTHOR CRITICIZES THE IDIOT

When we ferry from Patmos back to Turkey, Liz and I set up a new base camp at the just-opened spic-and-span Alamatra Marin Hotel on the marina in Bodrum where, despite a very small room, there's a gracious view of the sea and Wi-Fi. A Turkish guide we meet at breakfast tells us (in the first of many auspicious omens that day) that "It's a brand new hotel, just two weeks old, and very clean." That doesn't stop Liz from requesting new sheets for the bed.

The guide explains that when Alexander arrived in Bodrum, then called Halicarnassus, it seemed impregnable due to its walled citadel. In fact, it turned out that this was one of the few places that Alexander asked for a truce to remove his dead soldiers and it took years for his troops to completely secure the town.

The guide is so knowledgeable that I pass on to him a 1994 issue of *National Geographic*, which features Turkey and was given to me by a member of the UK House of Lords in Patmos.

The second omen, after a leisurely meditation session and Turkish breakfast, is finding a *dolmuş* on the verge of departing to Güllük just at the moment we arrived at the *otogar*. Güllük is the first of three inviting little towns we stroll through as we meander around another of Turkey's many densely forested peninsulas/inlets/coves.

Another omen occurs when we meet a young and heavily-gelled French-speaking Turk (I might say his thick hair came up in steep waxy points over his head like a wave about to break on the Turkish shore, but that would be a cliché, so I will skip it) who gives us instructions about which roads to take and mutters dark warnings of ominous obstacles ahead. He cautions us about "*chiens méchants et les surprises*" which we imagine will be wild dogs (*chiens* being French for "dogs") and evil-intending thieves but instead turn out to be roosters and a farmer plowing his field.

We round the peninsula and continue along the coast to the surprisingly delightful town of Gülinclik where we venture into the village market and find fresh artichoke hearts, dates, figs, candies and an inviting hotel on the sand where we have coffee and orange juice and avidly replenish our low electrolytes. Liz consumes hers like she's just survived a 100-day hike across the Sahara.

After a splendid seaside walk out of town for a few kilometers we are forced to climb up to the seaside speedway and gamely continue until Liz deems, and I agree, that, due to traffic, it is too dangerous. A *dolmuş* takes us on a road into the hills where we drink a miserable cup of coffee (the *National Geographic* story pointed out that there are lots of cafés in Turkey but no one drinks good coffee because Nescafé still rules) before returning to Bodrum for dinner at the Yacht Club, where we wind up most nights we are in town.

The good omens continue when we return to Torba the next morning and are immediately given Wi-Fi access and free bottled mineral water in the luscious lobby and plush chairs of the ornate Voyage Hotel. How often has this happened to me on my own? Never, is the answer. It's due to Liz, of course, the good omen maker and bringer of good fortune. Liz can charm the Fates, I'm convinced of it. Each day brings more proof.

We leave Torba hiking along the seaside, but after an hour our pleasant beach walk is interrupted by a dense forest passage with unfriendly dogs, brambles, a rocky coastline and enough adversity to make Liz exclaim that "MedTrekking is an exhilarating and exciting adventure."

Her appreciation is heightened as the dense forest forces us into the water ("Watching MedTrekker Liz Chapin hike in the sea after coping with the densely vegetated forest on the Turkish coast" is the caption of my photograph) until we arrive at a private estate and meet a visiting textile executive from Istanbul. His boat flies both the US and Turkish flags and he has a daughter living in Marina del Rey, California.

In typical Turkish fashion, he offers us cherries, breadsticks and cheese and, even better, the use of his boat as our water taxi. We leisurely motor back to Göltürbükü, stopping once in a paradisiacal bay for a dip in crystal clear turquoise water before he provides us with a salad and *mezes* lunch. Lunch on the deck of a private yacht on one the most beautiful coastlines in the world: priceless. Liz proclaims this another omen and again I'm bemused that this type of treatment doesn't usually occur when I'm alone. That I am gray-haired, late 60-ish and male, while Liz is blonde, female and lovely, has nothing to do with it, of course.

Now wait, don't start thinking these conveniences are the only reason I invited Liz to come along on the MedTrek!

Göltürbükü is the Saint-Tropez of the Bodrum Peninsula with an upscale Mandarin Oriental Hotel helping justify its self-proclaimed billing as the "top luxury vacation spot on the Mediterranean." A bold claim, considering "the Mediterranean" includes the French Rivera, the Amalfi

Coast and all the Greek isles, but let it be. We walk through one property and Liz sees a sign that she thinks indicates the name of the resort though, we find out later, it means "Do Not Litter." When we return to our Bodrum squat and the room has not been cleaned, Liz admits she is ready to move to the inviting Voyage Hotel in Torba or the plush Mandarin in Göltürbükü.

The impact of heavy-duty MedTrekking might be the reason Liz walks through fresh cement the next day. A Turk sitting nearby laughs uncontrollably as I scrape the cement off Liz's toes – her sandals, alas, will only make it to the end of the day.

We continue for another eight kilometers on a colorful up-and-down *corniche* walk that includes a photo session with Turkish women in Küçükbük ("Discussing the MedTrek with a fascinating group of infatuated and intrigued Turkish women near Küçükbük") and an unpleasant brush with a surly, stout fellow laughing at my fatigue as I walk uphill when we are escorted out of a private resort (The security guard shows me his phone with a translated text that reads "You are not permitted to enter here in") just before we get to Gündoğan (not to be confused with the Turkish football player of the same name).

While we wait for a *dolmuş* back to Bodrum I explain the degree of difficulty of the day's hike to a restaurant owner.

"There is enough variation in vegetation and vistas, including 32 islands and islets with dozens of quiet bays, to make the Bodrum Peninsula's 174-kilometers long coastline an ideal slice of easy-to-torturous MedTrekking," I say. "And the man-made contributions, from many farms to fashionable resorts and marinas, range from humble to ostentatious. And everyone, from women at a *dolmuş* station to the *dolmuş* drivers and school kids, wants to chat."

"That's nature and the impact of humans, or Turks anyway!" he replies.

If the past few days were dedicated to good omens and photographs, today is devoted to people, social engagements and networking. The steep hills (Liz says that going vertical should count for twice as many kilometers as going horizontal but I don't buy it) slow us down as we make our way through Gümüşlük to Turgutreis. In between, we stroll through Yalikavak where a gigantic, sleekly designed port is being built/renovated/improved to rival Turgutreis as the most beckoning marina for the boat-owning crowd at the western end of the mountainous, densely vegetated Bodrum peninsula.

Our social engagements begin when we meet a Turkish woman who lived in Germany, worked for Lufthansa, then returned to her home country. She speaks excellent English and discusses the global political scene with a jaded "it's too bad that there isn't communism vs. capitalism any more" *Weltanschauung*, or worldview. She's earnest and convincing.

By the time we're done, she and Liz are ready to buy a home together in Gündoğan.

We continue at a slow pace – only four kilometers in 2.5 hours – and manage to get through most resorts by showing everyone we meet a *Jandarma* keychain, given to me by a gendarme officer a week ago when he was investigating the mistaken bus scandal. The magic charm and gets us through most security and defensive barriers.

When private security officers see the word *Jandarma* on the key chain it immediately has an Open Sesame effect. It's wonderful. Who knew? We enter a private resort called Ola Mare (a locked-looking gate is actually open) and when I show an employee the key chain he tells us "Sure, feel free to swim in the infinity pool."

Things change when the big boss appears on the scene. His superior doesn't like us; we're ejected again. Our friend has to escort us to the door. But, as he shows us the exit he whispers, with sincerity I think, "I like you and I'm sorry but..."

To practice his English, a retired diplomat stops and offers us a two-minute ride into the town where the weekly bazaar is underway and a British couple explain how high the hill is between Gündoğan and Yalikavak.

"Look how we engage so many people and create happiness and smiles while we walk," Liz says as we enjoy a vegetarian pizza at Domino's in Turgutreis. I agree with her. Then I buy a new pair of cheap yellow swimming goggles that last about ten minutes in the seawater.

A delightful, breezy and refreshing coastal hike that we launch in the Turgutreis marina with a filter coffee ends at Joker's Beach in Ortakent-Yahşi with a friendly dog that follows us for an hour. In between, we enjoy one of the most user-friendly hikes of the Bodrum Peninsula with none of the harsh terrain, high hills, dense vegetation or irregular coastal contours that we'd encountered the past few days.

*MEDTREK MASH DANCE*

Not only is the hike along smooth urban promenades, or sometimes on sandy or pebbly beaches, and occasionally on lightly trafficked rural roads but we also manage to spend an hour at Solida Beach at the Termera Resort near Akyarlar swimming and tanning. I am so pleased that I do a MedTrek Mash dance in the middle of the resort, mooing at cows across the street, and win a dinner from Liz when I correctly bet that a low blip on the horizon is Kos, the Greek island, and not the coast of Turkey, as she gambled.

What makes the day even sweeter are the stark Arizona-like mountains and hills that contrast with the palm trees and beaches, including a beach called Camel Beach that actually has a few camels, and a break at a bakery for Turkish tea with milk. The concept of adding milk to tea freaks out the Turkish owner of the rural café but he still takes our money.

"Wonderful, beautiful, fairly easy walk on a jewel of a day and we put in the distance," says Liz.

The highlight of a pleasant beach walk into Bodrum – from Ortakent through hotel-resort-and-beach filled Yahşi, Bitez and Gumbet Bay – is definitely the presence of an old roan-colored homeless hound that we name Sparky.

We encounter enough animals on the 174-kilometer long coastline around the Bodrum Peninsula, which is part of the Turkish Riviera or Turquoise Coast, to start a zoo. And most of them – including three ducks, a colony of cats and several aging homeless hounds – want to adopt us.

But Sparky, who spends an entire day close to my heels, is the most persistent. It grieves me to think of him even now.

Sparky picks us up in Yahşi and follows us faithfully until we finally manage to lose him, after numerous unsuccessful attempts, in Gumbet Bay where we stop for lunch at Roy's Place. During his three hours with us he drinks two liters of water, which Liz and I pour in various containers en route. He trots nimbly behind us and moons at us with several lifetimes' worth of sad yearning and endless need. For communicating raw feelings and conveying desperation, I've never met anything like him, canine or human. He was exceptional, and we encounter one market owner who says he is "a gift from God." Liz thought so too.

"He was definitely our gift of the day," affirms stray dog-loving Liz. "He walked through walls and fences when we tried, for his own good, to leave him in a protected environment. He was humble in front of younger dogs and didn't ask a thing of us."

Old Sparky clings to us like glue as we admire hilltop views, climb rock walls, struggle through wire fences, cross rocky coasts and stumble down bramble-filled paths. We try to scare up an owner for him, but to no avail. Numerous people indicate that they aren't ready to take him on and when we last see him he seems finally to have despaired of making us his parents, all his dreams of a new life going up in smoke. He appeared to be very slowly making the DogTrek back to wherever he calls home. A sad dog disappearing into the sad distance. It is a heart-breaking sight, but there is little we can do. We can't take him with us; we can't provide the care he requires. Hopefully someone has taken him in and he now has a home and is being fed.

To try to forget Sparky, we explore the Bodrum Museum of Underwater Archaeology in the Castle of The Knights of Saint John. Then we have a dinner in Sparky's honor at the Bodrum Yacht Club where a young waiter called Murat takes care of us. He has no clue what's going on when we insist on another place setting for Sparky. We don't share our sadness about Sparky with him; why spoil his day? I'm sure he has enough miserable things of his own to mull over. We humans seem to never run out of trouble.

According to the historian Herodotus, there has been a castle-like structure on the same site here in Bodrum since 3000 BC. In 334 BC, the Caria region and its capital Halicarnassus (now Bodrum) were invaded by Alexander the Great and the Physkos castle was besieged. Although the siege lasted for a month before the city was finally overrun, the town's inhabitants outside the castle walls destroyed everything they owned and fled to the hills. The invaders, well aware of the strategic value of the castle, repaired the destroyed sections of the town to house a few hundred troops while the main army continued south.

The next day we head out from the Alamatra Hotel overlooking the mosque (I tell Liz that the volume of the *muezzin*'s call to prayer indicates the religiosity of a particular mosque or community – and this one is only medium loud), then proceed past the harbor, the marina and the castle in Bodrum and head east towards Oren. En route we have a memorable orange and apple smoothie at a shipbuilding facility five kilometers out of town and walk through the Bodrum Holiday Resort. Further on we get completely waylaid at the Ersan Resort's new *butik* hotel where Çan (pronounced "John") Erozden gives us a thirty-minute tour of the almost finished superlux suites with private hammams, pools and terraces. The twenty black-and-white suites are called Rook, Bishop and King and now go for €1600 a night.

Çan doesn't have enough clout to convince the security manager to let us walk through the adjacent Ersan Beach resort and we're forced to take a high mountain road to get around the properties. When we reach another boatyard and find the coast impassable, we sneak back into the Ersan property and have a private seaside terrace/deck/pier with all of the trimmings (hammocks, large *chaises longues* and beds) to ourselves for tanning and swimming for an hour.

"My kind of MedTrekking day," says Liz.

We walk six or so kilometers through the sedate and sterile Kempinski Hotel, the brash and boisterous Latanya resort and the topless and typical Club Med to the Hapimag Resort, which bills itself as "The Treasure of the Aegean Coast." I find a pearl of a blazed path that takes me, while Liz has some quiet time, a further five kilometers along the Aegean Sea.

The marked path, which offers a few panoramic views of the top of a mountain and the end of a peninsula, is, despite some rocky and overgrown parts, the first and best of its kind that I've experienced in Turkey. Although it's 5 p.m. when I start the walk, I don't pay any attention to a sign at the gate that says "when it is dark or close to darkness, it is highly recommended not to go out of the fences for tracking without having the necessary equipment with you...as in every natural area, the presence of wild animals is unavoidable."

Instead I speed up and nearly sprint to get to "The Bay" that, say all the maps, is the end of the line. I take some photos to document the extraordinary trail and go skinny dipping on a pebbled beach. The beach is human-free on a dusking evening that feels like the calm before tomorrow's projected storm, which here means heavy winds. I swim in the tender calm of this treasured spot, outracing the storm. The yin and yang of the weather, the punch and pull of the wind, the spin and tumble of the world...I feel it all, here, now, swimming in the half dark. That night, or at 2 a.m. the next morning, Liz and I are the last ones on the nightclub dance floor at the Hapimag Resort.

We have to hitchhike the next day from Ören to Çökertme (pronounced something like "chick-et-me") to reach our new base camp and Liz works the blonde magic when she gets four rides from only five cars. How often in the past has that happened to me? (Never.) She also has a way to convince Turkish hotels to give her the precise number of sheets she wants (the Turks rarely supply sheets, especially top sheets, for beds and obtaining them often requires complex negotiations) without causing too much protest. This never happens to me without a major argument or tedious discussion.

After the stark, steep and challenging mountainous terrain, it's a delicious change to walk the next day across the Ören plain formed by alluvium from the Kocaçay River, despite the presence of a thermal power plant with a towering flue and patchwork underway on the narrow tarmac seaside road.

Why delicious?

Because the road is usually deserted, the fields are agriculturally rich and throughout the walk there are sea views on one side, and views of the next range of mountains on the other side. In addition, rural Turks seem to be even friendlier than urban Turks. We see one family swimming, wave at them and, an hour later, when they pass us in their car they offer us a ride. Other drivers also stop and ask if we need a lift.

It's a playful day and we stop to sunbathe for half an hour, buy tomatoes/cheese/bread/drinks for lunch (7₺ or $3) and play on free exercise equipment as we MedTrek along still-empty beaches. Highlights of the day: a "tree house" that would make a great campsite and a fashion shoot with me introducing my Idiot-ic Yin-&-Yang fashion line which consists of a shirt with just one sleeve and pants with just one leg. Obviously a hot seller.

We arrive at Ören (the name means "ruin"), a comparatively sprawling town in a part of the country where mountains limit urban space. Once again, most of the residential vacation homes are still empty as we walk towards the Silvanus Hotel. And, at this time of year, things are still inexpensive. A dinner for two with pizza, mineral water, salad, more salad and fresh bread is under $10.

Yet the town's brochures show beaches (the 8.5 kilometer-long beach is one of the longest in Turkey) packed with vacationers enjoying the Gökova Gulf and the pamphlets tout the fact that Ören is built on the ancient city of Keramos (named for the father of pottery and son of Dionysus and Ariadne) dating from 3000 BC. Another plus, apparently due to the low humidity and dense forests, is the clean air.

The stark, steep and mountainous coast beyond Bodrum would intimidate even the most ardent would-be MedTrekker. The mostly pathless 100-kilometer long Gökova Gulf, which separates the Bodrum and Datça peninsulas, is punctuated with forests of pine and cedar trees, countless cliffs, dense vegetation and rocky shores.

We walk around the mountain behind Ören to another town named Akbük, past old aqueducts and new coalmines situated in the spring-green forest, before continuing on a seaside road above the Gökova Gulf that we both liken to Big Sur in California. At the same time the mountains eerily

## MEDITERRANEAN BOAT CAPTAIN

resemble the hills around Gourdon near my previous home in the south of France and the clear turquoise sea below frequently makes an appearance through towering pine trees. Across the vast bay I can dimly see Cleopatra's Beach where I'd spent the night when sailing with my South

African pal Gordon Kling two years ago.

Most of the action – sailing, surfing, fishing, tanning – is near, on, in or under the water. There are only a few paths, some luxury resort oases, occasional beaches and some amusing roadside attractions.

It is so cool and inviting that the much-quoted slogan, "See Rome and die, see Gökova and live longer," seems well deserved. Jacques Cousteau waxed that "I sailed on all the seas of the world but if you are looking for heaven on earth then it is Gökova Gulf." And a young man working for the power utility agrees and tells me "The Gökova Gulf is the most impressive in Turkey, better than Antalya."

It's rare that I lose my temper on the MedTrek but I have an amusing argument when there's a 2.50₺ charge to enter the beach near Akbük. Besides losing my temper, I lose the argument and we take the road and wind up at the family-owned Cardak fish restaurant where we eat two red mullets apiece. After a walk with superlative views on the spectacular little-used road, we spend the night at the Iskele Motel in Akyaka at the end of the indented bay.

I congratulate Liz on completing her first MedTrek outing, which she says "was a blessing," and we take a break from the MedTrek in Göcek where we join Gordon Kling and some South African friends for a day on the water. We sail from Göcek over unfortunately nauseous seas to a bay south of Fethiye where, among other things, I present my *Follow the Idiot* cap (I always give away my cap at the end of a MedTrek) to Osman who runs a seaside restaurant with a natural fish pond and soothing after-dinner mint tea.

There's great turmoil and unrest in Turkey right now. Riotous political protests and social turmoil have broken out in Istanbul but the ongoing unrest in Taksim Square isn't yet obvious during our 500-plus kilometer MedTrek during May 2013. Although the protests will ultimately spread and alter the socio-political complexion of contemporary Turkey, at the moment the clamor seems far from these shores of the Mediterranean Sea.

The next morning a group of us leave the boat and hike eight kilometers through orange groves and hills covered with olive trees into the "ghost town" known as Kayaköy, which is filled with old Turkish houses with carved timbers and latticed windows. The sail and walk give us an idea of what's ahead when the MedTrek resumes on August 30 on the Datça peninsula, where I'm scheduled to participate in the Peace Swim from Datça to the Greek island of Symi on the 1st of September.

# FOLLOW THE IDIOT

## CHAPTER PHOTOS

## CHAPTER MAP

# Walking the Lycian Way

"Every light is not the sun."
— *Alexander the Great*

I spend the next three months in Northern California reading everything I can about Alexander the Great and training both to resume the MedTrek and to participate in the annual Peace Swim when I return to Datça in late August.

My favorite hike that summer is a 16-mile roundtrip stroll on the Redwood Creek Trail on the Pacific Ocean in Humboldt County to a grove of some of the world's tallest trees. The swimming takes place at a US Masters Swimming National championship in southern California where, competing for the first time in the 65-70 year-old age group, I somehow manage to pick up a medal. And I frequently workout in Whiskeytown Lake where, though it isn't salt water, I also prepare for the open-water swim from Datça to the nearby Greek island of Symi.

This will not be my first time in Datça. I walked across the Datça Peninsula into the port town with Gordon and Anne Kling in 2011 when we were sailing on the Turkish coast. It was then that I met Ahmet Ozturk, a pony-tailed fixer who rents a lavish *gulet*, a two-masted wooden sailing vessel, to tourists and told us about the Peace Swim. When Liz and I arrive by ferry from Bodrum in late August in 2013, I call Ahmet and we meet at the local yacht club.

Unfortunately Ahmet has some bad news when we get together on a very windy day: the Peace Swim has been cancelled.

"Bad weather?" I ask. "The economy? The riots? Politics?"

"It wasn't due to the Greek economy or the Turkish political scene but just our lack of organization," Ahmet admits. "We just didn't get it together to do the swim."

That's probably not the whole truth. The Greek economy is still in the doldrums, the riotous Turkish political season and social unrest will heat up again when school starts and then there's the visa conundrum. Turks, even swimming Turks, can't visit Symi without a visa and obtaining one is a lengthy and laborious process.

The cancellation gives us an opportunity to relax on Ahmet's *gulet*, enjoy a seaside dinner in Datça and set up our local base camp. When Mehmet Kutay meets us at the town's mosque, he gives us a lift to the suburb of Eski Datça and the Dene Gardens, a hotel he bought in 2007 and now uses for select guests. That includes us because, he tells me, "I like that you're writing about Turkey and your walking project intrigues me."

Mehmet puts us in "The Stone House" with two gigantic rooms for only $20 a night, shows us around the spacious grounds and introduces us to his wife Yağmur (which means "rain"), his 3.5-year-old daughter Tamara and his neighbor Güler, the widow of Çan Yücel, a Turkish poet noted for his use of colloquial language. Yücel's nearby house is frequently encircled by fans.

We are told we have the run of the place, including the swimming pool and barbecue, and, after chatting around the dinner table for a few hours, we plan to follow a well-marked trail out of town the next morning. Or rather, Mehmet thinks "it might be well-marked."

It turns out that it might have been smarter to have attempted a solo swim in the dark to Symi.

A brand new trail sign does indicate that it's only 15 kilometers from Eski Datça to Domuz Çukuru and, inspired, we kick off with the familiar upbeat gusto I experience at the launch of every new MedTrekking outing. I take it in stride when we make a false start up the wrong mountain and am particularly patient when we stop to get photos of a woman baking bread in Hizirsah Koyu.

There's no problem during the first 11 kilometers but the last four (which become seven) are through trailless, bush-filled mountains and we foolishly continue to tolerate the heat and futilely negotiate the brambles, the slippery rocks and a lack of a path and water until we're delirious, disoriented and dehydrated.

Liz tries to call Turkey's 911 equivalent but there's no signal and as we discuss the possibility of dying of thirst, the best I can do is come up with an anecdote about Alexander the Great.

"Alexander was once in this situation," I tell Liz. "According to Plutarch, when he was dying of thirst some Macedonians, who had fetched water from a hidden river they had found, saw Alexander and offered him some water from a helmet. He asked them to whom they were carrying the water.

"'To our children,' one of the men replied. 'But if your life is saved, it is no matter to us that they all perish.'

"Alexander took the helmet into his hands but, without taking a drink, returned it with thanks.

"'If I alone should drink, the rest will die,' he said.

"'The soldiers no sooner took notice of his temperance and magnanimity upon this occasion, but they, one and all, cried out to him to lead them forward boldly, and began whipping on their horses,' wrote Plutarch. 'For whilst they had such a king, they said they defied both weariness and thirst, and looked upon themselves to be little less than immortal.'"

"Thanks," says Liz, "That's very comforting and makes me feel much better. Let's keep walking."

Fortunately she has a compass to lead us in the right direction towards the sea. In fifteen minutes I can see the sea in the distance and think I can also see, though it might be a mirage, a boat dock.

"Look, if there's a boat dock that means there's a market and that means there's a Coca-Cola machine and that means everything will be fine," I tell Liz.

We're both showing signs of dehydration. We're disoriented and have to fight to stay awake and walk on.

We finally arrive, our legs butchered by brambles and bushes and our throats parched, at a seaside resort called Pig's Bay Camp and we learn from Musa Unal, after seriously sucking down six liters of purified water (there is no Coca-Cola machine), that rain and wild boar knocked out the now-overgrown trail two years ago.

"You're hardly the first persons to be lost," he says. "But you should consider yourselves lucky to have found us."

His sidekick Eray adds that "Pig's Camp is closed, we're nomads, there's no time here, no day here."

Musa's welcome is another typically Turkish example of *misafir*, or hospitality.

"This is Turkey and you dine and stay with us," he says as he discusses the resort and the problems he has been having. The first problem is, of course, the bureaucracy. "I closed it because I couldn't get a permit this year due to the lack of a road," he says, his voice rising a bit in exasperation. "I told the bureaucrats that 'the sea is my road' but they wouldn't listen!" He also elaborates on his nomad-like attitude about money. "I prefer to do without it and live off the fish and the land," he confides. And he dips briefly into the dangerous politics of the moment. "I had two friends in a coma after the protests in Istanbul," he tells us, *sotto voce*. "But don't worry! You are my guests."

Musa and Eray serve us freshly barbecued chicken, grilled vegetables, rice, *tzatziki* and grape leaves on a picnic table before showing us to a beachside sleeping platform under an olive tree. There is a ferocious wind that night and olives keep dropping, wild boar keep snorting and Musa is up throughout the night to check on the "Nomad," the inflatable Zodiac boat he uses to transport guests when Pig's Bay is operational.

The next morning Musa, who refuses to charge us, gives us a 10-kilometer lift out of the Bay of Pigs in the "Nomad" to Mesudiye, where we gratefully buy him a morning coffee before we continue walking on well-marked TR hiking trails and the coast road to Palamutbükü.

Along the way, on an almost-too-hot-to-MedTrek day, we meet a man cutting branches off a mastic tree that he says he is going to use to barbecue kebabs at his restaurant near the marina. When we arrive at the Adamik Café, I have a gigantic portion of spaghetti with grilled shrimp that, I am told, "will keep you not hungry until breakfast." It's good to be not hungry.

I have almost forgotten the steep, mountainous, hostile, unforgiving countryside and impenetrable forest but I am grimly reminded on this hot, difficult day. A woman at a nearby table shrieks upon seeing the butchered state of Liz's legs, which she's treated with peroxide to disinfect and minimize scarring. Fortunately, the owner comes over and tells her he always has the same marks on his legs after the first day of hunting season.

"This countryside is for boars, not women," he says.

I post a "Where is the Idiot?" item with photos of our butchered legs that reads: "Rejoicing that we're not MedTrekking every centimeter of the impenetrable forest on the seaside of the unforgiving mountainous Datça Peninsula."

When I pass Pig's Bay on a ferry a year later and look at the peaceful stretch of sand between two seemingly impassable hillsides, I'm amazed that we were able to walk into it. I have to agree that the sea is the road. Don't forget it!

The next day, Liz and I spend an incredible amount of time walking a mere twelve kilometers, perhaps the slowest in the history of MedTrekking, along a seaside path east of Datça.

After just two kilometers, we stop for an hour-long nap on the green grass of an out-of-business hotel. Then we dawdle at the Knidos archaeological site. The long-and-grey-haired professor leading the dig is working with a team of American summer interns and we watch them diligently and delicately scoop through a layer of history. Four kilometers later, we stop for an hour-long lunch, do some skinny dipping and call it a day after we reach Billur Kent.

One reason for the lackadaisical pace is the aftermath of the challenging MedTrek in the heat to the Bay of Pigs; another is a bug I pick up that has unfortunately caused me to sample more Turkish toilets in less time than perhaps any other MedTrekker. I'm so hard hit, in fact, that I get into bed at 6 p.m. and take the next day off to recuperate.

When I've made a comeback from a serious bout of stomach something that erupted either after the dehydration drama at Pig's Camp or from the subsequent food I ate at the Adamik Café that was going to keep me "not hungry until breakfast," I intend to get in a serious day of MedTrekking.

The following morning we pass a sign that says "The Datça peninsula has been a popular summer place since the antique times for its beautiful and healing microclimate…Datça was blessed by the Gods with its high oxygen levels and a magic piranha (sic) which is known to heal the spirit as much as the body."

Thank goodness.

We take a cultural dip into the Archaic Sanctuary of Apollo and make a water stop at Ali's Restaurant (Ali's offers a combo of a glam restaurant, pools and a traditional restaurant with a well-tended beach) in Kiraincir/Ozil. Then, after some mountainous road walking, we visit the top-of-the line Aktur Resort with its Leo Beach. Prompted by the fresh water showers, we chill for an hour's swim that includes some sunbathing on a floating raft.

Another mountain road brings us to Aktur Kurucabuk beach where – after grazing throughout the day on grapes, figs, corn and bananas bought at local markets – we're served, in record time, a respite of olives, bread, green salad and cheese before catching a *dolmuş* back to Datça. The next day we'll move the base camp from Mehmet's lovely stone house and garden to Marmaris.

That night, Mehmet, a gracious, soft-spoken man of 63 who will soon head back to Istanbul for the start of his daughter's school, reminds me that the Datça Peninsula separates the Mediterranean Sea from the Aegean. An interesting fact, and I wonder if it affects the wind, the air, the color of the sea. Do we move from one spiritual or magical sphere to another, leaving the Med, touching the Aegean? He cautions me about doing any real estate deals in Turkey, tells me he hopes the current government will fall or at least be tempered by current protests, and predicts that Turkish lira will further decline.

The 90-minute bus ride from Datça, a town of about 10,000, to Marmaris, a town of 30,957 in the winter but 300,000 to 400,000 during

 *LOOKING BACK AT DATÇA*

the summer, indicates that, apart from a few isolated bays and one-boat towns, most of the coastline consists of impenetrable mountainous forest that would be impossible to MedTrek. It's easy to understand why Alexander the Great gave this then-remote tip of an 80-kilometer-long peninsula a pass.

We spend two nights in Marmaris, the Russian-and-British-frequented, party-time horseshoe-shaped beach resort that makes Datça look like a dacha. There are lots of pubs, lots of very white or very red foreign tourists, and scores of beachside hotels offering all sorts of water sports. Many tourists are decidedly oversized and I'm not surprised when we stumble on a fashion shoot with oversized models.

We get a room at the Amos Hotel where, aside from Hasan at the Stella Hotel in Kuşadasi, we meet one of the friendliest receptionists on the Turkish coast. Zehra ("I've loved my job since I started in 1995") and most of the staff treat us like celebrities just because we're American and give us a sea view room at a decent enough end-of-the-summer price.

The rush and rash of construction during the past thirty years has almost succeeded in camouflaging the fact that the Marmaris Bay is one of the most beautiful and historic bays on the Mediterranean. After all, the Marmarians were a courageous bunch; they defended their city against Alexander and in the face of defeat, like the Carians in Bodrum, set the place on fire and fled to the hills.

Our initial Marmaris walkabout begins at İçmeler, at one end of the bay, and we walk nearly 20 kilometers along the seaside promenade and forested coastline to the Yacht Marina to the south, where we have drinks, a swim and dinner at the Garden Restaurant. The glorious beauty of the bay, and the dawn-clean sunrise and sandy beaches, overpower the number of bodies on the beaches and a frenzied nightlife that rivals anything found anywhere on the Turkish coast. To get away from the unpathed, hostile and impenetrable coastline on Turkey's Datça peninsula, this almost romantic 20-kilometer urban/rural stroll might be the answer.

My photos show the bay at its best – glimmering, glassy water surrounded by stark but bramble-and-tree covered mountains, with lots of sailboats and every imaginable water sport, from banana boating to kite surfing.

# ALMOST DYING IN TURKEY

When we reach our destination of Dalyan, we decide to explore the area by taking a MedTrek-rare day-long $15 group boat tour. It's worth it, at least in a funky way. We get down and dirty at a mud bath (less vile-smelling than the one that had me tossing out all my clothes on the island of Vulcano in Sicily) and float out on Lake Köyceğiz, one of Turkey's largest coastal lakes, rich with reptile species like tortoises, terrapins, snakes and a wide assortment of insects, including a nice mix of dragonflies and damselflies.

During a day of pure old school tourism, we enjoy a refreshing swim and have lunch at the self-service Denizkizi Restaurant on the Dalyan River, which runs into the Mediterranean. We stop at the Iztuzu Beach for a five-kilometer walk that includes visits to The Kaptan June Sea Turtle Conservation Foundation and the Kaunos Archeological site.

During the day I learn about the 135-employee strong Dalyan Boat Coop that has organized a majority of the local boat drivers/owners/tourist companies on the lake and river. And I end the afternoon with my first barber shave of the MedTrek outing before recording an Idiot-ic Reaction by Liz in front of the mosque.

Like I said, pure old school tourism.

We get the earliest start of this MedTrek outing after "encouraging" the owners of the hotel to serve us breakfast an hour before the usual time. Taking off from Dalyan for Gökbel with energy and enthusiasm, we scoot out of town, cut up the hill and pass the turn to Iztuzu Beach with glee, gusto and guts. Once we climb to Gökbel we're rewarded, after talking to two discombobulated British bird watchers, with a stratospheric view of Dalyan, Iztuzu and the Mediterranean.

I expect a hard trudge across the mountains but instead we have a downhill stroll though a pomegranate-filled valley on a road frequented only by tractors and farmers. A pleasant breeze cuts the heat, and when we arrive in Sarigerme for salad, tea, Wi-Fi and an hour off, we've walked 17 kilometers.

That warm-up distance is followed by a splendid nine-kilometer, 5₺ stroll along the well-tended Sarigerme beach before crossing two rivers (we ford the first but have to bribe a boater to cross the deeper Dalaman

River) and enjoying a walking meditation foot massage on the alternatively sandy and gravelly beach with a complete absence of people.

Once we reach the end of the beach, along a fenced-in military zone, we're back to the mountainous, unwalkable coastline and a promontory that separates us from the town of Göcek.

## KISS YOUR POMEGRANATE

We move our base camp to Göcek and take off just before sunset to walk through the six marinas that make the town such a sailing haven: Club Marina, Skopea Marina, Municipality Marinas, Marinturk Göcek Village Port, Marinturk Göcek Exclusive and D-Marin Göcek. All of the marinas are up-market, led perhaps by the D-Marin that has a private beach, and there's no shortage of services, from restaurants to ship chandlers. The promenade begins at the port northwest of town and winds through a ship-building facility before wandering into completely urban territory. On both sides Göcek, though, the steep and impassable forested coastline takes over. On this coast the cliffs win.

Definitely a jewel of the Med, Göcek is a gem on the Turquoise Coast, as this part of Turkey's southwestern-most shore, celebrated for its beaches and scenery, is called. Göcek's islands, coves and secluded bay are so inviting that visitors have traditionally been referred to as "guests of God." Beyond the Baba, Akdağ and Bey mountains, which drop precipitously to the main coastal highway is ancient Lycia.

We again get our laundry done at Dolphin (25₺) then choose to eat at the Blue restaurant rather than the nicely named and popular Kebab Hospital. Due to Liz's dietary preferences I have more tomatoes and cucumbers on this outing than on the entire previous MedTrek.

As we begin the walk into Fethiye there's finally a break in the incessant cliffy coast side in Yaniklar, where the beaches blend into the pine forests. We're almost immediately assaulted by crowds in the heavily British populated coastal town of Calis Beach (çaliş is the Turkish word for "work," but "Work Beach" is now full of tanners and drinkers on a low-cost holiday).

Once again, as in Spain and parts of Crete, the British have exported their vacation culture and lugged their soggy British tastes with them – from traditional English breakfasts to bountiful quantities of beer and liquor. Beyond Calis Beach, a new road and expanded promenade lead into Fethiye, built on the ruins of Telmessos, which Alexander the Great visited well before the British put up all English signage.

I personally wouldn't choose Fethiye, as some 40,000 Brits have done, as a vacation spot, but we meet many English speakers who've opted to live here, or to pay a visit, because of the inexpensive lifestyle and the touted competitive prices for everything from an exported English breakfast to travel packages.

The high point of Fethiye for us is not the pleasant enough stroll on the promenade through the town, but rather the 12-kilometer walk around the promontory just south of town. An empty, carless road makes for an easy up-and-down beach/cliffside MedTrek in 38°C heat.

Ah, the heat. It wrecks men's minds and makes them do strange things. Maybe it's the heat that encourages me to challenge the three uniformed security guards at the Letoonia Club and Hotel when they demand €70 for a one-day entrance just to walk through their noisy posh resort.

Soon, for the heat or other reasons, I'm ranting and chastising the security officers for not allowing us to walk on the seaside and I tell them I plan to defiantly swim along the coast and they can arrest me when I come out of the water on the other side if they so choose. Liz films our argument, recording the actions of the forlorn security guards who follow us as we walk (unwillingly but resignedly) around the two-kilometer hotel barrier. At the next beach, I let it go and enjoy a salad with grilled chicken at a campsite picnic table.

The next day is spent boating to the 12 islands near Göcek and I'm again reminded of how steep and hostile the coast is while we swim at four different stops. More importantly, Liz points out that the captain (dressed in a spiffy uniform one moment, a cook's outfit the next, then a dishwasher's, truly a man for all shipside seasons) has a crush on me.

"He shook my hand, then completely ignored me, looked at you and said *Lokum, Lokum*," Liz said, pointing out that *Lokum* means "Turkish Delight, or you're my sweetie!"

Ah, the yin and yang of MedTrekking. Despised by security officials one minute, propositioned by a boat captain the next.

On our last morning in Göcek, Liz went out to purchase last-minute gifts for the family and instead came rushing back with a detailed map of Lycia and the Lycian Way that will prove invaluable further down the coast.

After a few weeks of MedTrekking, we bid *au revoir* to Turkey and fly to the French Riviera. To recover from MedTrek Madness, Liz and I take a week-long break at the Lerins Monastery on Île Saint Honorat off

Cannes – where I spent the first night of the MedTrek in January 1998 – described in the chapter entitled "Quick, Get Me to a Monastery!" in *The Idiot and the Odyssey: Walking the Mediterranean.*

Ah, how nice to be back with Cistercian monks and explore the island's fortified monastery, the chapels and the views of the church and sea from our rooms. Each morning at 5 a.m., I meet a nun as I surreptitiously squat in the tiny corner where Wi-Fi is available. I confess that I feel like a sinner using the Wi-Fi while on a spiritual retreat.

"If this is the worst thing you've done," the sister replies. "I wouldn't be too worried."

Before we head back to Liz's place in Geneva, Switzerland, we visit the refreshing new Museum of European and Mediterranean Civilizations (MuCEM) in Marseille and get further insight into the historical role of the sea and the peoples around it.

When Liz and I return to Turkey the next autumn, I can't resist, after seeing a large sign on the road, grabbing a room in the four-star Montana Pine Resort in Hisarönü simply because it abuts the beginning of the Lycian Way, the 509-kilometer seaside mountain path that we'll be following from here to Antalya.

Before embarking on the historical trail, we spend a day exploring the dramatically over-Britished town of Hisarönü, an away-from-the-sea waterless resort filled with tattoo parlors, hairdressers with names like "Curl Up and Dye" and enough competing souvenir stores to have T-shirts selling for a British pound a pop.

Although lunch at the Butterfly Restaurant (Butterfly Valley is a few kilometers down the road, hence the name) is decent, there's not much to recommend the town except for its location as a *dolmuş* hub and proximity to the Blue Lagoon beach resort of Ölüdeniz, a five-kilometer walk down the hill.

On our first afternoon, we head downhill to Ölüdeniz for a walk up and down the beach and have a coffee while watching paragliders land after they descend from Mount Babadağ, about 1,900 meters above the sea. We're not far from the ghost town of Kayaköy where we sailed with Gordon Kling a few months ago and, remembering Pig's Bay, we stock up on water to be ready to launch the first steps on the long Lycian Way the next morning.

To get Liz excited about this MedTrek, I cite a line from the day's entry in *365 Tao Daily Meditations*: "A butterfly lives for a day. It comes into the world with very little reason except to fly and mate. It does not question its destiny. It does not engage in any alchemy to extend its lifespan or to change its lot. It goes about its brief life happily."

"Are we capable of becoming butterflies?" I ask her.

We're being driven to such extremes of over-preparedness by the vivid accounts of the Lycian Way's rugged nature (as well as vivid memories of our waterless and dehydrating experience in Pig's Bay) that we're up two hours before the sunrise for the day's trek. We're carrying three liters of water each and are ready to do battle with goats, scorpions, giant butterflies and mythical beasties and monsters too when we leave the Montana Pine Resort on the nearby trailhead.

We've been forewarned that the Lycian Way, which includes some of the routes taken by Alexander the Great, will be a difficult uphill climb on goats' paths until we reach the village of Kirme.

In fact, our first day turns out to be, by MedTrek standards, a pleasant, albeit uphill ramble on a path clearly marked by white-and-red slashes with majestic views of the Blue Lagoon below and Mount Babadağ towering above. But although the degree of difficulty may have been exaggerated, the estimated distances are spot on. We arrive at Kirme after ten kilometers and reach Faralya in just under fourteen.

The highlight of the morning is definitely our descent into Butterfly Valley, a 45-minute cliffside exercise that involves rope climbing, a few scary steps and gorgeous views. There are no butterflies in Butterfly Valley (all of the posted signs say "Shshsh!") but lots of day trippers who come by boat from Ölüdeniz and take a stroll up to a barely existing waterfall (it's summer and dry). Because we make the treacherous climb down into the valley, rather than arriving by sea, we aren't charged the 5₺ entrance fee.

Liz balks at making the treacherous ascent to return to the Lycian Way and opts to take the easier, softer way and grabs a boat back to Ölüdeniz. I make the steep and sweaty 45-minute climb solo before continuing another seven kilometers on the Lycian Way to Kabak. Once again, the well-marked and easy-to-negotiate path ascends from the village of Faralya through a forest over the crest of the mountain into Kabak, an elevated seaside village beyond Ölüdeniz. Kabak is largely ignored by the tourist crowd who restrict their meanderings to the Butterfly Valley or the big Club Lykia World resort at the bottom of the Kidrak Valley.

While there may be a dearth of butterflies, there's no shortage of bees on the Lycian Way. Not only do they swarm above every cistern, spring and water source but they're also provided with well-regulated hives tended by one or two beekeepers who dress in the usual paraphernalia, carry smokers and also sleep on the site. To guard against honey thieves, I presume.

Most of the forested and mountainous walk is through a species called Montana pine (though most of the pine in the state of Montana is Ponderosa) and Mediterranean *maquis* and there's frequently evidence of avalanches and rock falls, most notably a mountain in Kirme visibly sliced in two by an earthquake in 1957.

Apropos of nothing, I probably sweat more on the afternoon part of this walk, which begins with a heated climb up the cliff from Butterfly Valley, than on any other MedTrek outing so far in Turkey. I have to wring out my shirt and let it dry on my pack; I take my shorts off and walk in my underwear on the unpeopled mountain crest, and my gloves are soaked with sweat as I negotiate rocky climbs.

In retrospect, the highlight of the current MedTrek outing in Turkey is not the sea view looking back at Dalyan, my pomegranate video, the sandy Sarigerme beach walk, the sunset in Göcek or the look over my shoulder at Fethiye. It is reaching the starting point and MedTrekking the first 57 kilometers of the Lycian Way trail (a real trail!) that stretches from Fethiye to Antalya on beaches, along coastal mountain ranges and through rural villages and seaside towns.

At 5:30 a.m. Liz and I awaken in a rustic tent at the Turan Hill Lounge overlooking Kabak Bay and I'm soon in the kitchen getting coffee before our six kilometer uphill hike to Alinca, a hilltop hamlet of a dozen houses.

As the Lycian Way has proven to be in its early stages, this is a generally well-marked uphill hike that's much less warm and sweaty before sunrise than after. We're followed by one of the Turan kittens but he wises up, and gives up, after half a kilometer.

We have breakfast – cucumbers and cheese with pita bread – at a hillside campsite at 8:30 a.m. but otherwise charge to the top, admiring views of Kabak on the way. Kabak is at the end of the seaside road and the climb takes us over a mountain range where the beginning of the road network leads towards Alinca, where the view from Bayram's Teahouse (which is a café in Bayram's private home) is my photo of the day. Beyond the teahouse are the villages of Yediburunlar and Gey, each consisting of a few houses that serve as informal *pensions*, a market, and signs for a restaurant at a nearby lighthouse. Half of the walk to Gey is on the almost carless mountainside road and the rest is through farmers' fields sprinkled with goats and olive trees.

We read that beyond Gey the "road is badly marked" but we're eagle-eyed enough not to miss any of the red/white slashes, some weathered, some fresh. The path above the majestic Med is slightly more difficult and Liz, who almost never swears, screams when she begins a slight slide down the steep hill after I tell her to "Stay on the path!"

"What fucking path, goddammit!?!"

While indeed slightly pebbly and crumbly, the path does take us to the mosque in Bel where we end the day's MedTrek outing faced with the dilemma of how to return to our Kabak base camp. Liz, ever resourceful, negotiates a motorcycle ride with Ahmet. That turns out to be a smart move due to the complete lack of traffic on one-lane country roads that, says Liz, are "desolate, without promise of a ride."

If my kids, or anyone else, were ever dumb enough to ride as a threesome without helmets on a motorcycle on a gravelly mountain road I would shoot them. But we edgily sit on the tiny seats, pray and gleefully pay 40₺ when we arrive near Esen to catch a *dolmuş* to Fethiye. There we catch another *dolmuş* to Kabak in time to make it back for the natural buffet dinner on the terrace.

We're relieved, as we end this round of MedTrekking, to see the Turan kitten back home for dinner.

Liz and I discuss how our relationship is tested and grows stronger while MedTrekking and I reflect on Alexander's lifelong friendship with Hephaestion, which he considered akin to the friendship between Achilles and Patroclus that is depicted by Homer in the *Iliad*. In both cases, the friends were also suspected of being lovers which in those days was common and accepted.

Hephaestion was Alexander's best, and longest, friend, and Alexander was so proud of their relationship that he told me one morning, "Hephaestion loves me *as* I am, not '*who*' and it is he whom I love, no other. I am nothing without him."

I amusingly recall, and relate to Liz, that the philosopher Diogenes of Sinope once wrote "Alexander was never defeated, except by Hephaestion's thighs" and Alexander's mother was concerned about their friendship from the get go. Plutarch wrote that "Alexander's greatest emotional attachment was to his companion and childhood friend, Hephaestion."

Liz and I are already friends and lovers, which gets that topic out of the way. And I tell her that you never really know someone until you walk together. It will be interesting to see how things evolve as we head down the coast of Turkey.

Incidentally, Hephaestion, as Alexander's personal bodyguard, later became the commander of the elite Companion cavalry in Alexander's army and, renowned for his organizational skills, was occupied with many of the logistics involved with the campaign. I presume Liz will be a similarly important companion, my wing woman.

But more importantly the two of them were tight confidants (Alexander even let Hephaestion read mail from his mother) and Alexander was shattered – and "lay either moaning or in a sorrowful silence" – when Hephaestion fell sick in Persia with a fever and died.

When that happened, Alexander crucified the attending physician, cut his own hair (as Achilles did when Patroclus was killed in Troy), had the manes and tails of all his horses and mules cut off, and prohibited any music in the camp. The Oracle of Ammon, through a messenger, instructed Alexander to honor Hephaestion and sacrifice to him as to a hero.

Alexander – who once told Hephaestion that "If you were to fall, Hephaestion, even if Macedon were to lose a king, I would avenge you, and follow you down to the house of death" – later destroyed the Cossaean nation as a sacrifice to Hephaestion's ghost.

"He lay prostrate on his companion's body for the greater part of that day, bewailing him and refusing to depart from him, until he was forcibly carried away by his Companions," wrote Arrian. "He prepared large and lavish chapels for the hero Hephaestion in the Egyptian Alexandria, one in the city itself and another in the island of Pharos, where the lighthouse is situated."

Hephaestion, just before he died, purportedly said, "My Alexander, I remember you as the young man who wanted to be Achilles, and then outdid him...I'll always think of you as the sun, Alexander. And I pray your dream will shine on all men. I wish you a son."

I return to the US from Geneva and receive a Mediterranean olive tree as a Christmas present from my kids as well as a plaque in French that says: "An Idiot Who Walks Goes Further Than An Intellectual Sitting Down." A week later, during a New Year's visit to South Africa, I see another MedTrek-apropos sign in the Johannesburg airport that says: "If you want to go fast go alone; if you want to go far go together."

In April, on my return to another round of MedTrekking, I speak to a high school class in Gainesville, Florida, and some book groups before I fly to Nice to meet Liz, who has just relocated to the US after 21 years in Geneva, and then we fly together to Istanbul (where Liz has never been) and we visit the Topkapi Gardens, the Blue Mosque, the souk and my favorite hammam. From Istanbul we grab a flight to Dalaman and spend a night in Göcek before returning to the MedTrek.

We get to Kalkan, south of Bel, after taking a bus ride that involves a woman who goes berserk because she's on the wrong bus and a young man who has an epileptic fit, perhaps because the woman has gone berserk. Both of them are taken off the bus at a military installation.

*WHY THE IDIOT CAN'T TALK AT A FLORIDA HIGH SCHOOL*

The trail from Bel meanders through a hilly countryside with striking views of the turquoise-colored Mediterranean until we descend to Patara Beach. This is reputed to be one of the best sandy beaches in Turkey and the site of the one-time capital of the Lycian nation. Not only did Homer mention Lycia and did Alexander the Great conquer it, but Saint Nicholas, aka Santa Claus, is said to have been born here.

On the beach, we meet a young German author, Melanie Heinle, who's camping with her family. She's written a book about archaeology on the Lycian Way and gives us helpful insights and interesting tidbits about "The Way." Armed with new info we are ready to walk barefoot on the beach for our visit to Letoon, once a major religious center that gets its name from the goddess Leto, the mother of Apollo and Artemis.

We have a salad/yoghurt/cookies lunch at Patara Greenpark restaurant before a 12-kilometer beach walk that kicks off a monumental MedTrekking day punctuated by visits to the ancient naval fortress of Pydnai and the history-rich cities of Letoon and Xanthos.

We discover, after we pay the token fee (5₺) to enter ancient Letoon, that everything is remarkably well-preserved. The historically important site is almost at the seaside and one of its main structures, the Assembly, has been reconstructed out of gleaming limestone and marble. I take photos of a handsome goat looking for a seat in the ancient amphitheater and a shot of Liz in front of the Mettius Modestus archway that is the symbol of Letoon.

Besides having lots of cows in the field with darling calves (it's spring) Letoon is a must-see not only because it remains intact but also because after the Lycian epoch, which began before 2000 BC, it was inhabited at different times by Greeks, Romans and Christians. It's thrilling to think that the Lycians sent troops to fight in Troy during the Trojan War in 1194 BC and surrendered to Alexander the Great in 333 BC. Necropoli from the different eras act as a timeline.

We cut east for another three kilometers, passing the M. Ufuk market where we buy an ice cream sandwich and another store called "The Harrods of Patara," to arrive at the ancient city of Xanthos.

Xanthos, at the top of a hill above Kinik, was, of course, missing the Nereids, which I recently photographed at the British Museum. Unlike the Elgin Marbles, which the Greeks want back, the remains of the 4th-century BC tomb taken by Charles Fellows in the 1840s seem to be unchallenged in their current home in London. Xanthos, I recall, was also noted by Homer, who mentions that the city's troops also fought with the Trojans. Though Liz and I arrive from the sea, Alexander chose a different route and crossed the Xanthus River to invade Lycia and its satellites. All three cities, and thirty smaller towns, surrendered to him.

We walk to greenhouse-infested Patara, which sits in an obviously soil-rich valley. The greenhouses aren't in business, however, because of the intense summer heat that kills tomatoes and other crops. Then we continue on a fairly new and very wide road with stupendous views of the seaside. Perhaps because it's Sunday, there's minimal traffic all the way to our portside base camp at the Pirat Hotel in Kalkan, which boasts a splendid fourth-floor view of the sea ($58 for two).

The next morning, on a walkabout through British-filled Kalkan we pass numerous for-sale or not-for-sale villas along the port, some of them quite nice and those on the market priced at either £295,000 or £395,000. We follow a red-earthed road that leads to a narrow red-earthed path that we hope will take us around the steep, heavily foliaged headland.

Along the path there are even a few red-and-white markers, but after an hour thrashing through sometimes thick brush Liz makes the choice, probably a wise one, not to risk her life on the first day back at MedTrekking and we turn around. It's never a waste of time to explore a particular route and the most memorable encounter on this pathless path is between Liz and a tortoise which leads to a "Where Is The Idiot Today?" post entitled: "MedCrawl: Observing a key rule in Patara, Turkey: MedCrawl before you MedTrek." We have our last fish dinner at the Marina restaurant in Kalkan before moving the base camp down the coast.

We leave Kalkan and coast for 27 kilometers along the waterfront in the direction of Kaş. After a kilometer, we find ourselves on the newly-cut road above the seaside and follow it – step-by-step, up-and-down – along the gorgeous Mediterranean seaside. With only minor interference from cars, and not a single café to distract us, we continue without a break until we're five kilometers from Kaş. Here we stop for some cheese toast at a beach filled with peacocks (including a lovely white male with magnificent plumage), rabbits, chickens and, yes, Turks. It's still not the summer season and the kitchen and beach facilities are operating at slow speed.

The hike along the mountainous, rocky coast does feature three small sandy beaches (the best is the Kaputas Beach at Mavi Magara) and the water color is remarkable, varying from bright turquoise (which is why they continue to call this the Turquoise Coast) to deep, dark blue. The small towns and apartment complexes on the way seem uninhabited (again, the season hasn't started) and it feels like we have the gorgeous stretch of sea to ourselves all the way to the marina in Kaş. Once past there, we find ourselves in a vibrant city that's a bit more upmarket than Kalkan with a spacious sports facility and lots of shops, hotels and restaurants.

I tweet about the Turkish ATM ripoff (some banks are charging 3.5-5.5 percent commission and, though they warn customers on the screen, I point it out and suggest that tourists stick to PTT and HSBC ATMs) and feel I've done my good public service deed for the day.

Our Kaş base camp is at the modernized Linda Hotel (€42.50) where our third floor room and balcony afford another blissful view of the Mediterranean. It's cloudy and sprinkly and we take an urban walkabout to meet some local villagers – the owner of the soon-to-be-open Sea View Hotel who's imported wood from Russia to create a fresh smelling deck above the sea, the owner of the Tante Rosa restaurant who says I "hate Erdoğan (Turkish president Recep Tayyip Erdoğan) and am a communist" while serving us a delicious salad-with-stuffed peppers lunch. We talk to the owners of numerous travel agencies who supply us with information regarding the underwater village at Kekova and ferries to Kastellorizo, the nearby Greek island that Liz and I hope to use as a launch pad for our annual Patmos retreat). We also meet the owner of a restaurant where we're served apple tea and a bank officer with whom I discuss the ATM commission conundrum.

Then we visit Antiphellos, the amphitheater just east of town, and catch a few zzzs on the top level before walking back to the Linda.

Still on the Lycian Way, we leave Kaş, pass the Büyük Çakıl Plaji and continue on the seaside until reaching Limanağzı, a pebble beach with restaurants that we could have reached with a water taxi for 12.5₺. From there, the seaside walk continues uphill to the ruins of Apollonia and the villages of Boğazcık and Kılınç. The first highlight of the day occurs in Ufakdere, where two welcoming brothers, one who lived in the UK for fifteen years, are revamping a resort facility with solar panels, comfy couches, Ottoman tents and other nice touches. Then, two hours later, we arrive at the beach at Üzümlü where there are cars, fishermen and picnickers. I get in the first swim of the year before we head uphill for another two hours towards Apollonia.

We run into lots of people who are walking a segment of the Lycian Way (indeed, it's worth mentioning that the popularity of the path is largely due to Kate Clow, whose book, *The Lycian Way*, published in 2000, is still the Bible for walkers) and meet a Dutch family at Ufakdere who are down hiking for a week.

Isabelle and Ipec, a French/Turkish friend/business partnership selling textiles throughout Europe, who have come from Istanbul for four days, walk the last stint uphill with us and pose for a photo with Liz. Another couple, Wolfram and Petra Lobnitz from Berlin, offer us a ride back to Kaş and on the way we take a side trip to Phellos in the hinterland.

After a day off in Kaş (to get laundry done, which is always a luxury when MedTrekking; enjoy a mouth-watering fish lunch at Smiley's on the port; and join some friends from Paris for drinks on the terrace of the Narr Hotel), we take another inexpensive Turkish tour that includes a mini-bus from Kaş to Üçağız and a boat ride around the sunken city of Kekova and the Pirate's Cave to an impressive castle, built in the Middle Ages by the Knights of Rhodes to fight pirates. The day ends at the tombs in the fishing village of Kaleköy (the name means "castle village") where we meet an interesting British/Chinese couple from London/Hong Kong who tell us intriguing stories about investing in Turkey.

I must be aging, or maybe it's Liz's presence, but a few years ago I would have scorned anyone who took a packaged day tour like this. Such travel would have been an anathema to me and a violation of MedTrek ethics. But now, well, here we go again.

It's the boat trip to, and swim in, the ancient sunken city of Simena, located in a Specially Protected Area just offshore, that intrigue me. The only sensible way to get to the half-submerged ruins of the residential part of Simena, caused by the downward shift of land due to an earthquake in AD 140, is by boat. Thus the tour.

As we swim and sunbathe during the water outing, I figure this is also a decent way to move our base camp down the seaside through a mélange of ancient, medieval and modern Turkey. This turns out to be another social day on the MedTrek. We snap iPhotos, swim and lunch (a pretty decent onboard lunch that's a mix of chicken, salad, vegetables) while talking to our German, British, Turk, French and Chinese fellow travelers. We make water stops throughout the afternoon while joking about Liz's fascination with a young handsome Turkish guide on the boat whom we nickname Marshmallow because he has a large pack of her favorite marshmallow cookies when he comes on board and she makes an immediate connection.

Liz loves the social aspects of MedTrekking 24/7; I like it only in brief doses. For example, she says she wants to walk for weeks with the enjoyable and entrepreneurial British/Chinese couple, to which I respond, "It was very nice meeting them."

The Lycian Way continues from just outside the front door of our seaside Theimussa Pension and our walk to the ancient port of Andriake begins by following a sign that says: "Way to Castle and Tombs."

It turns out, after we walk awhile, that the "Way to Castle and Tombs" is not a signpost for the castles and tombs in Kaleköy but instead for the castles and tombs in Üçağız, or Kekova, where we were yesterday. Liz somehow guides us out of Üçağız (where I notice that there's a sparkling new WC in the center of town that merits a mention) to the well-marked Lycian Way where a detailed sign informs us that we're three kilometers from Kaleköy and that it's seven kilometers to Kapakli and about 15 to Andriake.

Throughout the day, signs and white-above-red vertical slashes guide us along the seaside on rocky hillside paths with frequent pastoral interruptions and exceptional views of bays with anchored boats. We meet a trio of Ukrainians, a German and lots of big friendly Turkish hiking groups out for their Sunday stroll. When we get to Andriake there's a mysterious sign that says "Welcome to the other side" just before we cross a very unstable bridge across a river.

I spend the day adding tiny rocks to already-established rock markers on the rocky path and take a minor fall when I begin fantasizing about Xanthos (the ancient city, not the Greek model) before we have a salad lunch in Andriake. There is no transport back to the Theimussa Pension, which inspires us to walk/hitch/taxi inland to Demre and visit the iconic rock-cut tombs at Myra. Besides investigating the impressive catacombs and theater, we encounter a group of Italian monks traveling in the footsteps of Saint Paul and black-clad Romanian Orthodox nuns whose somber tones make Liz look especially colorful in her pink-themed MedTrekking outfit.

Demre, were it not for the Myra Tombs and the Saint Nicholas Church (yes, this is where Santa Claus was purportedly born), is such a forgettable town that we don't even consider making it a base camp. Instead, after a Turkish Village Breakfast with plentiful kebabs at a gas station on the outskirts of town, we continue on the narrow seaside road to Finike.

The first ten kilometers outside Demre are along a large lagoon (it's impossible to walk on the beach because the inlet is too deep to cross) through the town of Beymelek. Then, 17 kilometers of windy, narrow and twisty road that make this as good a place as any to worry, if you are inclined to worry, about being hit by a truck while MedTrekking. In fact, we see one truck graze the roadside rail and a couple of cars treat the stretch like Le Mans-sur-Mer. There are a few pebble beaches and one nifty cave but the main reason for taking this road is to avoid the three days it would take to get from Demre to Finike on the now-inland Lycian Way trail.

One guidebook to the Lycian Way says the 21-kilometer walk from Finike to Mavikent is "boring, flat, through rows of greenhouses and a good place to take a cab" while another says "taking public transport (or even hitchhiking) is the obvious sensible choice to cross this uninteresting coastal plain, covered by nothing else but greenhouse plastics."

But not us. We again decide to risk the boredom, accept the exposure to plastic, cheat death and walk.

Liz spends the next day relaxing in Finike while I welcome kicking off the next stretch of the MedTrek, despite the guidebooks' admonitions, with a flat hike that mixes a wide promenade, seaside sidewalks and sandy beaches – a pleasant change after the past two days of rocky paths and narrow roads.

Except for lots of pyramid-like sculptures at roundabouts that all feature oranges, the big crop here, the only thing out of the ordinary are lots of picnickers. I wonder if it isn't some type of holiday. In fact, I later learn, May 6 is the day the Turks celebrate the arrival of Spring but I'll always call it National Picnic on the Beach Day, though some German hikers tell me they think it's National Walking Day.

I'm walking meditatively without Liz for the first time on this outing and, while I miss her (and definitely miss luxuriating with her at an hammam in Finike where all the women thought she was German when she sat completely naked in the steam room), I once again cherish how fortunate I am to be indulging in this type of project and how excited I always am to be back on the Mediterranean. I've been doing this for fifteen years and I still have "a kid in a candy store" feeling about the whole thing.

I stop at a market as I enter Kumluca and, after I buy some water and Noggers (my favorite ice cream bars), I'm offered a fresh vegetable sandwich and tea by the owner who invites me to sit down and check the Wi-Fi. Then I walk along the beach past a community of homes on stilts (a Med rarity) and into Mavikent, where I'd initially intended to end the day. I learn, however, that trails and roads continue to Karaöz and Çavuşköy and get very jazzed when I see a Lycian Way trail sign indicating that it's only eight kilometers to Karaöz.

The picnickers are especially evident near Karaöz, at the end of my 28-kilometer MedTrek, where hundreds of cars block traffic and thousands of Turks are gathered in family units on carpets and mats. As I near town, the number of picnickers increases even more due to roadside marketers selling lots of grilling equipment, as well as shoes and textiles.

No one pays too much attention to me but when I am greeted I adopt the Turkish habit of putting my right hand on my heart before speaking and occasionally tap my forehead to theirs when meeting someone who looks like they might become a lifelong friend.

In a couple more days, we move our base camp from no-frills Finike to bucolic Çirali where we install ourselves and our gear at the on-the-beach Ogile Hotel complete with two swimming pools. About two walking days from Karaöz and two more towards Kemer, it should be the perfect MedTrek base camp. *Inshallah* and *mashallah*, I say to myself. Incidentally, *mashallah*, also spelled *masha'allah*, is an Arabic phrase that means, "God has willed it" and expresses appreciation, joy, praise, or thankfulness for an event or person. It contrasts with the more commonly used *inshallah*, which means, "As God wills it."

The thought of another long day on the MedTrek has me up at dawn (4:45 a.m.) listening to the cacophony of the roosters, the *muezzin* (5 a.m.) and the birds that inhabit the pine and cedar forests in Çirali. It's brisk when I have my morning coffee and meditation at the pools near a score of wooden log cabin bungalows. Beyond them is the mosque and, to the north, Turkey's Mount Olympus.

Whichever way you decide to MedTrek, from Adrasan to Çirali or Çirali to Adrasan, you'll go up-and-down the 937-meter (3,074 feet) Mount Musa on vertical cut back trails through pine, cedar and strawberry tree forests. Head from Adrasan to Çirali and you'll walk through the ruins at Olympus at the end of the hike, head from Çirali to Adrasan and you'll see the ruins first. The six-hour hike is equally well-marked in either direction and the beach restaurant in Adrasan, where power is out due to a storm when we arrive, has a roaring fire going when we arrive at the end of our hike and serves excellent cheese salads and Turkish teas.

This stretch is the most popular Medside hiking path that I've encountered since Cinque Terre in Italy, and easily the most popular segment on the Lycian Way. We meet, and in many cases chat with, hikers from Canada, Germany (by far the majority), Ukraine, England (a tall thin male Brit bellows when he sees us and protests that his smallish, somewhat fragile-looking girlfriend is fine wearing only a T-shirt, shorts and flip-flops on what will be a very rainy afternoon), Turkey, the Netherlands and France.

I again run into a French hiker whom I met a few days earlier who's hiking every bit of the Lycian Way and is going to take a day off in Çirali to let a blister heal. He tells me "*À chacun son propre chemin*" or "To each his own path" when we discuss the different approaches hikers have to the Lycian Way, though, being French, he makes sure that I understand that this is also a respectable philosophy for everything in life.

About half the hikers we see are carrying heavy packs. The other half are carrying light day packs and, in many cases, a travel company transports their baggage from pension to pension on a daily basis. That's not our case, of course. We carry light packs and at the end of the day find transport back to our base camp. Today, it takes us four hitched rides and one *dolmuş* to make it back to Çirali. It is a delight to give the cleaning lady from the Ogile Hotel, who gave us our final lift to the front door, a 10₺ tip that she attempts to refuse.

Although the rain and cloud cover obscure decent views of Turkey's Mount Olympus, highlights of the day include a sand crab we find at least five kilometers up the mountain from the beach, the bleating calls of a baby lamb separated from its mother, a dog refusing to eat our cookies and a major shipwreck in the American Bay near Adrasan.

Rain washes out the possibility of a long hike the following day and we're not even able to walk a few kilometers to visit Chimera, the hillside in Yantaraş near Çirali where, according to Greek mythology, flames produced by a fire-breathing monster emanate 24/7. The fires, presumably fueled by natural gas on a hillside of limestone, overlook the sea and provide the same spectacle during The Idiot's era as they did during the days of both Homer and Alexander.

The sky clears the next day, and we hike south along the Çirali beach and, after two kilometers, again join the Lycian Way through the mountains to Tekirova. Unlike the hike from Adrasan, this one is a more tranquil up-and-down romp along mountains that along the way descend to four or five beaches, including the well-known Maden Beach. When we reach the first beach I see a *gulet* preparing to bring passengers ashore and quickly gather a lot of beach garbage into an already half-full plastic bag.

I'm thrilled when, after introducing myself to a group of hikers from California, they take it on board.

Hiking by *gulet* along the coast is probably easier than having luggage moved from pension to pension each day. Besides the Americans, we meet some Australians from Melbourne and some Russians during the day. But the most delightful people we run into are nine Germans who are going to spend a few days re-marking and refurbishing the red-and-white signage on the Lycian Way. We thank them for their service.

Liz and I are among the first hikers on a well-marked path that has been washed clean by yesterday's storms. It's smooth and easy-going except where wild boars have uprooted a number of plants foraging for food. The mountain path and beaches end after about ten kilometers and the rest of the "trail" is a wide dirt road – a splendid walking surface because the only vehicle we see is delivering the paint for making the trail and the Germans' camping gear to Maden Beach. There are delightful views around every corner – Liz says it is "one of the most pleasantly challenging uphill hikes on the Lycian Way" – until we get to Tekirova and see the ostentatious Russian-built Amara Dolce Vita Hotel which, among too many other egregious things to list, has its own zoo.

We get the impression that it's a "Russian only" establishment, or so says a Turkish guard at the back door who apologizes for offering us only water instead of Fanta or Coke. But then we meet a young German woman who says she booked through a travel agent and was amused to find that all the Russians she met immediately apologize for having defeated the Germans in World War II. It is the anniversary of the defeat of the Nazis in World War II and Vladimir Putin had just made a big spectacle and speech about it in Moscow.

"Oh my God that was 60 years ago and I just had to laugh," the blonde German tells us.

As we walk down the beach into central Tekirova, I bump into a bona-fide Russian and he immediately points to my hair and indicates, from what I can tell, that we're both graying and getting old. Ah, solidarity between aging men from angry countries. Is it a good thing? Not sure. He doesn't apologize to me, at least, for defeating Germany in World War II.

We hitch a ride back to Çirali with a delightful English-speaking Russian from Moscow and that night finally visit Chimera, one of the brightest highlights of the Lycian Way. The hillside in Yantaraş, just a few kilometers from the Odile Hotel, is associated with Greek mythology and I tell Liz that "this is the home of a monstrous fire-breathing monsteress called the Chimera. She has the head of a lion, the tail of a snake and the body of a goat, and is described in the *Iliad* as 'a thing of immortal make, not human, lion-fronted and snake behind, a goat in the middle and snorting out the breath of the terrible flame of bright fire.'"

It's still not known exactly what produces the flames emitting from cracks in the hillside, though traces of methane gas can be detected. Whatever the scientific explanations for the flames, I enjoy the many myths associated with fire that has been burning since antiquity. Did, as Homer conveyed, Bellerophon arrive on the winged horse Pegasus and kill the Chimera in atonement for the supposed rape of a Lycian king's daughter? Or is the fire due to the god Hephaestus? Whatever the origin, the Olympic Flame was lit here for hundreds of years.

Although Tekirova heralds the much more touristic, built-up and social Mediterranean seaside near the Lycian Way, the Phaselis ruins just beyond it, still tucked safely away in a protected bay, are a gem of antiquity. The three ports – ruled since 690 BC by Lycians, Persians, Carians and Limyrans before Alexander the Great arrived – have been heavily damaged by earthquakes but it's easy to imagine earlier life there as we walk in the agora, the baths, former houses and a temple to Athena (who was the main goddess of the city). And it's an absolute delight, a very MedTrek moment, to catch a contemporary ballerina posing for pictures amid the ruins with the Mediterranean as a backdrop.

Some way inland is Turkey's Mount Olympus (the Turks call it Mount Tahtali), which was visible, clearly or often under cloud, from Çirali. From the Lycian Way in Beycik, it's a six-hour climb up the 2,365-meter (7,760 feet) mountain in the Beydağ National Park but conditions the day we were there were too dicey to either make the climb or take the Turkish-Swiss Olympos Teleferik, known as "Sea to Sky," to the top.

We continue through Kiriş on pebbly beaches through Russian-dominated hotels (it's here, incidentally, that for the first time in years, perhaps since the introduction of the euro in 2002, that I see all the prices listed in $, € and ₺). But we are dead-ended when we run into the buttoned-up-tight construction zone for another hotel. Instead, we walk on a road through orange groves and a forest and move our base camp from hippieish Çirali to the Forest Park Hotel, on the edge of a forest in urban (more marina than Russian) Kemer.

Kemer is a comparatively upmarket town with nice neighborhoods for locals living here and a town-long seaside promenade. But it's not as cosmopolitan as I think. A waiter at the Lotus Beach Hotel tells us "I've been working here four years and you're the first Americans I've seen – Russians, Germans, Swedish and everything else but no Americans."

Indeed, Russians are now Turkey's second most important tourists after the Germans, and Americans are low on the list. The tourism numbers illustrate why so many Turks speak German and Russian, a good way to gauge the dominant nationality of visitors.

"First they had to learn German, then they had to learn Russian, now they may have to learn English," says one German tourist. A hotel owner adds that the Russians love staying in this part of Turkey because they pay an all-inclusive rate, including booze.

"They're all about drinking and disco," says Cemal Altun, who's worked at numerous hotels in Kemer. "They drink a lot of our profit."

But we learn Kemer might not be ready for Americans when Liz asks for a manicure at the Forest Park Hotel. The trio who show up have primitive equipment and use a flashlight to illuminate her hands. She politely cancels.

We take off on the Kemer seaside promenade past what we agree is a pleasant, normal mid-sized town made more prosperous by a multinational tourism industry. I spot a hotel I would have preferred, location wise, to the Forest Park, and even some beaches where I can spend a few hours. Liz agrees there are far more Russian women than men. We run into an ethereal svelte blonde in a minuscule bikini and an alluring beach hat picking fire-red poppies in a field outside town and both feel like we're in a David Hamilton photo. Liz tells me not to stare but, like her cautionary comments that I should refrain from arguing with security guys and her desire that I not swim nude when there are people around, I can't resist. We're witnessing the true definition and example of pastoral beauty.

The first security encounter of the day occurs when we enter, unbeknownst to us, the Palmiye Club Med (there's another hotel in Kemer called the Camel Club Med) when a guard, who introduces himself to us as Ur, says it's impossible to get over the promontory at the other end of the club's sandy beach. We say we'll give it a shot and he insists on accompanying us on a twenty-minute walk, climbs with us over the rocks at the other end, helps us assess the situation and walks back with us when we agree we can't get around the point unless we swim. As we head past the entrance to the Club Med a sign says: "The beach is not private but an entrance fee is charged for the facilities." I'm a happy MedTrekker despite the fact that we were stymied by a promontory.

A bit later in the day, in Beldibi, a second security guard cautions us not to walk through his beach and I give him the usual "No one owns the sea" rap. He insists that we won't make it through and are wasting our time. But, as usual, I insist. And he insists on walking with us. Twenty minutes later we hit an impassable canal and, somewhat embarrassed by the results of my bravado, we're escorted back and out. Still, I made the point that no beach is private despite the fact that we were stymied by a canal.

When we're in the middle of Göynük (I tell Liz on the way in, as we witness a number of hotels under construction, that "this town is a Tekirova-to-be" but it turns out that I'm wrong because it already is) I have an unstoppable desire for Turkish delights with coconut and pistachio and plop down 4₺ for a big chunk. We then drop into a place for tea and, though we don't have the necessary wristband to eat at a restaurant associated with a hotel, nobody stops us, and we leave a 15₺ tip for tea, coffee and salad.

It's hard to get access to the beaches in Göynük and Beldibi without an armband because the hotels and resorts are built so closely together that entry between buildings is almost impossible. However, wherever we walk, we can't help admiring the majestic mountains to our left, even when we're confronted with modern hotels like the Nirvana that are barriers to the sea.

A taxi driver in Beldibi has a chart that indicates we've walked 18 kilometers from Kemer but have 30 to go to reach Antalya. That keeps us chugging for another seven kilometers until we reach the end of Beldibi and another promontory that is so prominent a tunnel goes through it on the D400 highway, which locals refer to as the autobahn. While we walk through town, a number of shop owners beckon us in German and French (my "TEENAGE MILLIONAIRE" T-shirt informs everyone that I'm not Russian). When we ask one group to guess our nationality they run through ten different guesses (European mainly) before someone shouts out New York. That's how rare Americans are here.

On the bus ride from the end of Beldibi to the center of Kemer a Russian woman with a three-year-old sits by me and starts a harmless conversation. How far to Kemer? How much is a ticket? This is one of the rare interactions I've had with a Russian since we got here. They keep, like their hotels, to themselves.

Departing Kemer on foot, we negotiate steep mountains, high cliffs and long tunnels on the "autobahn" to arrive at the Antalya port where we have what Liz calls another social experience when we're dead-ended in the port. A workman tries to explain the way into the city while walking with us for fifteen minutes but, frustrated by my non-existent Turkish, calls his daughter and we have a hilarious discussion in English that starts politely enough when I say "Please thank your boyfriend for leading us out of here..." and she laughs in reply that "He's my father!" So much for my Turkish.

We begin a relaxed walk on the Antalya promenade and have a splendid Greek salad at Aydin Beach accompanied by *ayran*, Turkey's non-alcoholic national drink made of yogurt, cold water and salt.

I'll always remember this as the place where I equate the Turkish words for thank you – *teşekkür ederim* – with "the check please." We pop into a Starbucks, where barista Selin Akpinar, a Turkish 20-something born in New York and just brought back from the US by her parents, was complaining that "it takes me a month here to earn what I made in a week in New York and I don't like the Turkish mentality or that they're so unsophisticated."

The beaches – unlike those we've seen in the past few days in Beldibi, Göynük and Tekirova – are free of tourists because the season, in mid-May, still hasn't begun. That, plus the cliff top location of this town, makes me agree, from the seaside anyway, with Kamal Ataturk, who said "Undoubtedly Antalya is the most beautiful place of the world." However, he wasn't alive to see the expansion and population explosion of the smaller town he knew. We end the walk in the old town, where there's a splendid natural swimming hole, and are pleased that we've completed the Lycian Way.

My big social moment of the day occurs when we're bussing back to Kemer and a young man offers me, not Liz but me, his seat. Liz says it's because I look especially tired. Perhaps it is time to take a two-week break from MedTrekking on Patmos.

We hoof it back to Kaş, again spend the night at the lovely Linda Hotel and ferry to Kastellorizo (I file my first "Save The Greek Coast" item, which is billed as "The Idiot Reveals his Private Parts to Save the Greek Seaside from Privatization," featuring "The Private Eye" with a photo of my eye against the seaside). After lunch we catch a Blue Star ferry to Rhodes. The ferry route traces our walk along the Turkish seaside and we see Kalkan, the Patara beach and the path we followed on the Lycian Way from Fethiye. We're close enough to the coast that we can identify specifics on the path.

In Kaş, while eating my last Turkish *meze* and fish before ferrying to Greece for ten days, I send out a press release:

"The Idiot is again on a meditative spiritual retreat called 'The Patmos Experience' in Patmos, Greece, until he resumes the MedTrek in Antalya on May 28 where, alas, he'll bid adieu to the Lycian Way. The 500-plus kilometer blazed mountain-and-seaside hiking path that meanders from Fethiye to Antalya, Turkey, is a highly recommended delight.

The Idiot is now participating in a campaign entitled "Save the Greek Coast – Don't Privatize It, Clean It Up!"

As a MedTrekker who has hiked thousands of kilometers of the Greek mainland and island coasts without too much hindrance from security officers, the military and private resorts, I plan to actively protest the proposed bill to privatize Greek coasts and end free public access to the beaches.

I'll accomplish my goal by showing and photographing my private parts on Greek beaches in Kastellorizo, Rhodes, Kos and Patmos from May 16-25. Watch for photos and captions from Kastellorizo, Rhodes, Kos, Crete ('Don't Turn Crete to Concrete') and Patmos."

In Kastellorizo, to say goodbye to the Lycian Way, I hike to a hillside Lycian tomb, explore the hilltop castle (with the lovely Greek blue-and-white flag waving above it) and find a swimming hole (my suit is on the ferry so I swim in hole-filled underwear that I can dispose of after they're salted in the sea).

A few days later, on a high-speed catamaran called the Pride Dokekanisos, we're further from the coast and the high mountains with steep cliffs cascading into the Mediterranean look foreboding. In fact, the terrain appears so inhospitable that it's impossible to believe anyone, especially us, could walk it. It's hard to pick out Fethiye, Göcek, Dalaman, Marmaris and other sites and cities that would seemingly loom large.

# THE LYCIAN WAY

The 509-kilometer Lycian Way hiking path in southern Turkey is so aesthetically, culturally, historically, natur(e)ally, physically, socially and spiritually intriguing that even hundreds of photographs fail to capture its essence.

## LYCIAN SNAPSHOTS

## LYCIAN SIGNS

# FOLLOW THE IDIOT

## CHAPTER PHOTOS

## CHAPTER MAP

# Talking to Alexander in Antalya

"I am not afraid of an army of lions led by a sheep; I am afraid of an army of sheep led by a lion."
– Alexander the Great

"On their side more men are standing, on ours more will fight!" – Alexander the Great

---

Liz returns to the United States and I return to Turkey, riding shotgun for four hours in a *dolmuş* from Kaş that passes the Lycian Way and everywhere else that we had recently MedTrekked. When I arrive in the center of Antalya's *kaleiçi*, or old town, I find myself at the Sibel Pension run by a French woman from Blois who had married a now-deceased Turk.

After dumping my gear, I excitedly blitz on foot through the iconic highlights of downtown Antalya, ranging from Hadrian's Gate and the Broken Minaret (or the *Kesik Minare* in Turkish) to the alleyways of the *kaleiçi* and the Antalya Museum. I admit that I didn't make it to the Antalya Aquarium, rumored to be the world's longest tunnel aquarium, or the much-touted Aqua Park. You can't do it all.

I'm wandering in the Antalya Museum, steeped in southern Turkey archaeology and history, when a statue of Alexander the Great appears in front of me, as if the gods ordained it. Not far away is a statue of Hercules and the Sarcophagus of Hercules, which depicts his Twelve Labors carved in stone.

The statues that gave the best representation of Alexander were those forged by Lysippus, one of the best-known 4th century BC bronze sculptors, "by whom alone he would suffer his image to be made," according to Plutarch. Astute observers constantly comment on the inclination of Alexander's head "a little on one side towards his left shoulder" and his "melting eyes" ("He looks like a boy, till you see his eyes," said his Persian servant Bagoas).

"Lysippus of Sicyon was one of the most famous of Greek sculptors and Alexander made it clear that no one should make a statue of him but Lysippus," asserted Arrian.

Besides underlining Alexander's military might and prowess, the museum illustrates that his patronage of the arts is an important legacy of his reign. Alexander's other chosen artists included the painter Apelles, the gem cutter Pyrgoteles, and the architect Deinocrates of Rhodes, who planned Alexandria in Egypt.

One critic contends that Alexander's "personal, civic, and religious commissions reveal his taste in monuments, which tended toward ingenuity, boldness, and magnificence."

I stay in the museum after it closes (I hide in a utility closet on the second floor) to have a serious chat with Alexander, who gives me suggestions about MedTrekking beyond Antalya ("Don't miss Sidon, Tyre and Gaza," he insisted). Then we have a long discussion about his consumption of alcohol – and I inform him that the contemporary buzz is that Alexander might have been a full-blown alcoholic.

Certainly, as I mentioned earlier, we have a few traits in common and there's no question that drinking played a significant role during Alexander's era, in his life and, perhaps, in his death. The historian Aristobulus reported that "in the rage of his fever and a violent thirst, he took a draught of wine, upon which he fell into delirium, and died." Even the Oracle of Ammon in Siwa, whom you'll meet in Egypt when we get there, told Alexander that he might temper his drinking "in moments of tension."

One excellently researched book – John Maxwell O'Brien's *Alexander the Great: The Invisible Enemy* – explores Alexander's alcoholism and lists "the positive and negative attributes of wine in Alexander the Great's day." In fact, O'Brien produced a chart that illustrates the 603 positive attributes of wine and drinking alongside 117 negative effects. Doesn't seem like much of a contest.

"A wine-flushed Alexander didn't like to be criticized and had a cruel, self-pitying and darker megalomaniacal side that would emerge and be exaggerated with drink," wrote O'Brien. "His temper could become so ferocious that he was capable of killing friends and advisers or slaughtering innocent people who got in his way."

Indeed Alexander once, when very drunk, angry and quarrelling, struck his friend Cleitus the Black, the officer I mentioned earlier who saved Alexander's life at the Battle of the Granicus, with a spear and killed him. Afterwards, it's said that, in the typical style of a repentant alcoholic, Alexander abstained from food, drink and a bath for three sulking days and confessed that he had committed a crime. O'Brien calls this moody behavior "Achillean posturing or Achillean withdrawal."

And I've got to presume he was drunk when he set fire to Persepolis which must have seemed like a smart move when Thais, the Athenian mistress of Ptolemy, proposed it after a round of drinking in order repay Xerxes, who had reduced Athens to ashes. Alexander is said to have carried a torch and lit the royal palace afire himself, though he soon ordered that it be extinguished.

Alexander certainly loved drinking contests and was always proposing multiple toasts to applaud courage, mourn fallen comrades, celebrate the gods or encourage victory on the battlefield. He expertly kept everyone lifting their glasses and at one drinking contest he gave away his crown. In Susa, an important city in the ancient Near East, he hosted a wedding in 324 BC with 10,000 guests that continued until "fatigue, boredom, drunkenness and violence or sleep intervened."

"Look, I think that deep insecurity traced to my childhood both inspired my greatest achievements and also created a need for self-assurance," Alexander tells me during my night in the museum, sounding a bit too much like someone who's had therapy for a couple thousand years. "And maybe the relationship with my father made me want to prove that I was superior to him."

"Also I agree that, just like you, I was obsessive and compulsive about almost everything, but I don't think I needed anger management classes or a twelve-step program," he continues. "Everybody overdid it back then and I was in a high-pressure position, but I was a beacon of sobriety compared to my father. Anyway there is something noble in being accused of having a drinking problem when I was doing so well conquering the world."

I had to agree that he certainly didn't drink as much as his father.

Indeed, according to O'Brien, "Demosthenes compared King Philip, who is said to have slept with a gold cup under his pillow, to a sponge. Theopompus called him a *philopotes* (a lover of drink) getting drunk on a daily basis, going into battle drunk and throwing legendary banquets and parties. Both he and Alexander were reputed as much for their drinking as their heroics.

"Philip, typical of how Athenians regarded barbaric and hard-drinking Macedonians, was scarred, gnarled, abrasive, limping and lacked an eye while Alexander was good looking, intelligent and polite and had been tutored by the Athens pillar Aristotle and revered Athena, the patron goddess of Athens," continued O'Brien. "Fair skinned, his blond hair, rapid speech and penetrating gaze gave him a sense of excited gravitas."

I listen carefully until Alexander has nothing more to say. Then I tell him about my own overindulgence and, after sharing my own experience, describe how I finally realized that alcohol had me beat and asked for help.

"Actually, I'm a recovering alcoholic and I completely identify with your obsessive drinking and overindulgence because I did exactly the same thing," I say as I begin describing my own excesses and addiction. "It was a real weight off my shoulders when I admitted my problem and asked for help. A miracle, really, that gave me strength and hope."

"Well, I don't ask for help," Alexander replies. "I'd die first."

He did. At 32 years old.

Despite literature and rumor mentioning or focusing on Alexander's drinking, I have no clue whether or not he was an alcoholic. It's up to him to admit that. I will say that, during our late-night discussion, he did not admit that he was completely powerless over alcohol or that it had made his life totally unmanageable, though many observers, both back in the day and more recently, have pegged him as a functioning, or not-always-functioning, drunk.

When the sun begins to rise over Antalya and I am about to leave the museum, Alexander confesses: "My father drank too much and, although I criticized his drinking and behavior, I'm afraid I became much like him. I would drink when I was happy and I would drink when I was sad and it became difficult to stop. One was too many and a thousand were never enough. But I still was very high functioning, rarely shirked my responsibilities and when I did go too far…I felt pretty bad."

"Did you ever try to quit?" I ask.

"Every time I felt pretty bad, like the time I killed Cleitus; I'd feel so much guilt that I wouldn't drink for a few days," he replies. "But then…"

Although maybe Alexander is in denial, it's possible that O'Brien and others exaggerate the problem.

Plutarch wrote that "he was much less addicted to wine than was generally believed…and he loved to sit long and talk, rather than drink, and over every cup hold a long conversation.

"He would not be detained, as other generals often were, either by wine, or sleep, nuptial solemnities, spectacles, or any other diversion whatsoever; a convincing argument of which is, that in the short time he lived, he accomplished so many and so great actions."

Gossip columnists have been pretty active since the Macedonian king's death and alcohol is one of many issues of debate. Some say he liked to show himself a man of iron, above pleasure, to conceal any weaknesses; some claim he was impotent; some say he liked only boys; others contend that he was "one of the vainest men in human history."

Before I leave the Antalya Museum, Alexander gives me a few details about the next stage of the MedTrek.

"If you want to learn more about me, you must go beyond Alexandria and visit the Oracle of Ammon in Siwa," Alexander says. "But right now, pick up the pace and spend some time in Sidon. Say have you heard of Marco Polo? He may have some things to tell you."

Inspired by my discussion with Alexander, I want to reach the 10,000-kilometer milestone on this just-begun MedTrek outing. I'm so ready and raring to go that I start the pursuit at 5:30 a.m. when I step back to the seaside.

I have an "Ah, ain't this nice" fresh morning attitude and my steps are springy after the ten-day meditative spiritual break in Patmos and the night in the museum. The views along the cliffs as I head out of Antalya are stunning. I look back on the town through a telescope, admire early morning swimmers in the sea below, photograph a few sculptures on the boardwalk (none, I must add, of Alexander or Hercules), walk through a new hotel under construction and enjoy the almost vacant promenade as I stroll through parks and properties that abut the cliffside.

The Turks are morning walkers and a few of them pass me in the midst of their speedy hour's walk, perhaps not realizing that I am in full-day, twenty-year walk mode and pace. I stop to exercise on the omnipresent exercise machines, spend quite a while admiring the impressive Duden Waterfall, contemplate the touristic significance of lots of landing planes (the Antalya airport is about ten kilometers out of town) and realize that the many 10-15 story buildings, hotels and residential apartments are a tangible sign of the city's rapid growth.

I stop at the terrace of one hotel, where the restaurant has begun serving breakfast just after 7 a.m., and inquire if I might buy a meal. I'm told that the restaurant doesn't officially open until 7:30 but a waiter urges me to take some pastries. I pass a Starbucks a few minutes later, and a McDonald's shortly after that, and would love a coffee, but neither opens until 8 a.m. I walk on.

It seems to be a day for free food. I stop at the Nazar Beach hotel in Lara and when I tell the *maître d'hotel* that I'm not a guest but would like to buy a cup of tea, he gives me one (I thank him profusely). Later, when I'm allowed (well, not really allowed, but the security staff don't notice that I lack the red wristband required for guests) into the Fame

156

Hotel just before arriving in Kundu, I have two sandwiches, four cookies and a cup of tea. A bit later I enter a small café to buy a coffee but can't remember the word for milk (it's *sut*) and am so befuddled that I foolishly ask the woman behind the counter "Is there a Starbucks or McDonald's around?" She has no clue.

In fact, this is a Sheratonized coast (meaning it's chock-a-block with modern hotels) but I have no problem with security today, though I'd fantasized about being imprisoned and making world headlines with my "No one owns the sea" argument ("No country, national institution, hotel, restaurant or even you or I can pretend to have a claim on the Mediterrancan," I usually begin my well-practiced soliloquy). I don't try to get into a military installation where, in keeping with the holiday mode, the barracks are named J, K, L and M Motels, though the troops don't look like they're on vacation.

I now have a tried and tested way of ignoring security officials by greeting them with a nonchalant nod that, I think, makes it look like I'm just walking through their property and don't need to be bothered. Sometimes it works.

All of these hotels – which tend to have signage in Turkish, German, English and Russian – have a Disneyland feel with the usual music, dancing, water sports, volleyball, water slides, pools and other attractions. And they are uniformly gigantic with, I'd guess, an average of a thousand rooms each. Again, their proximity to each other means that the public can only access the beach at rare entry points between two hotels.

I take a few pictures of hotels because I don't want to forget that the dominant architectural modes are "built like a ship" or "built like the Kremlin." Kremlinization or Kremlinesque or Kremlinof, I call it. And though the first few beaches after my tea in Lara were empty, they're now over half full and dominated by Russians.

It's May 28 and the summer season is closer everyday.

After half an hour at the Fame Hotel, and just before I reach the Aksu River, I have a Wi-Fi break and tea with my new BFF (Best Friend Forever) Nazli who tends bar. She's 20 and immediately checks out my website and asks to be a member of my Facebook group. When I cut down to the sea and the Modern Palace Hotel, after a three-kilometer walk through Aksu, I reach my first river and find a boatman who will take me across for 2₺. He also tells me that in three more kilometers I'll hit another river and have to find another boat.

Finding the second boat, after a walk along an unbuilt smidgen of sea, is a bit more difficult but I bribe some young Turks, who indeed have "borrowed" a boat and are using kindling as paddles, to take me across for 5₺. The crossing's a success but one of them inadvertently trips me up when I'm jumping from the boat and I have a cut shin to show for it.

After five more kilometers I run into the Asteria Belek Hotel in

Kadriye and figure I might make it to Belek, another six kilometers away. I don't return to my Antalya base camp until I enter the first "golf & spa" combo in Belek. A taxi driver tells me that it's 40 kilometers back to Antalya (I've walked 37 kilometers today, according to my pedometer). On the *dolmuş* back, even I'm impressed with how far I've come.

I'm doing what Alexander suggested: "Pick up the pace and spend some time in Side, or Sidon as you call it today. It was one of my favorite base camps in 334 BC."

Arrian wrote that "Alexander then marched to Side, the inhabitants of which were Cymaeans from Cyme, in Aeolis. Then, having left a garrison in Side, Alexander advanced to Syllium, a strong place, containing a garrison of Grecian mercenaries as well as native barbarians themselves."

I kick off the next day MedTrekking into central Belek that, in my mind, has assumed the status of myth, though not a particularly positive one. Richard Barnes, a New Zealand journalist, asked me whether "you've walked through that scar called Belek."

Richard is referring to the fact that, except for the very few public beaches like the Belek Beach Park (where I meet the first Syrian evacuees on this outing), this stretch has the sea on one side and monstrously garish cheek-to-cheek hotels – with names like Magic Life, Caesars Palace (there's a rip-off Disneyland inside), Arcadia and Letounia with Kremlinesque and naval motifs – on the other.

The sand is uniformly covered with beach chairs and this is definitely a golf course strip. I have to remind myself that, while this type of travel isn't my cup of chai, thousands of tourists love this monstrous, garish, entertaining type of all-inclusive vacation and thousands of Turks are employed as a result. Russians had just outnumbered Germans at the Antalya Airport for the first time in history, according to the local paper.

But in tried-and-true, yin-and-yang MedTrekking fashion there's a hotel-free walk between Belek and Boğazkent that I prepare for by buying tea, *brot mit käse* and a bottle of cold water from an entrepreneurial Turk with an informal food stand, who tells me where to ford the first river but says I might have to take a boat across the second.

The 12-kilometer stretch of coast (there are presumably no hotels due to the rivers at either end, lots of marshes in between and comparatively poor beaches) is a delight to walk. The vendor's instructions prove correct and I ford the first river but pay 10₺ to get across the wider Boğazkent River.

There is one calamity however. A former Club Med on the outskirts of the Boğazkent beach, where I have a banana waffle for dessert and notice flocks of people leaving the town's mosque after the Friday noon prayer, looks like it bit the dust, though the golf course looks fine to me. Not that I care. In fact, you may recall that I mentioned why I quit golf in my first *Idiot* book.

Another high point of the day is that while it's a sand walk most of the way, the stroll into Sidon through the municipalities of Gündoğu, Colaki, Evrenseki and Ilica ends with a wide and pleasant paved coastal trail that separates the well-tended hotels from their manicured beaches. That's almost as exciting as the amazement expressed by every Turk, from a lifeguard at one hotel to a bus driver, when I mention that I walked from Belek (one thought I was 54, not 65).

Sidon is a marvelous archaeological site, but filled with irritating shops that have stolen the names of the gods – including Olympia, Aphrodite and Apollo – and there's enough club noise at night, much of it coming from a bar called "Stones," to make me glad that I have a garden room at the somewhat off-the-beaten-track Lale (Tulip) Hotel.

Nothing is better than kicking off a MedTrek day with a walk south from the Lale Hotel through a slice of the Sidon's ruins and past the "No Name Restaurant." I'm the only person on the path when I set out on the public beach, where there's absolutely no activity, but by 7 a.m. the Russians and Germans at the tourist hotels I pass are staking out the best *chaises longues* for the day. There's such an informality in the hotels, though it could be the early hour, that I enter one and have some fruit, a roll and a few cups of tea. Nobody notices, or seems to care, about my presence.

It's the kind of day that inspires me to take a deep inhale (I just posted a photo of "Stoned Participants," that would be stone sculptures, meditating on the beach) and relish the fact that I'm still able to get in some 30-plus kilometer MedTrekking days on the inviting sea. I reflect on how much happier I am to be walking than staking out a place to tan and figure that I'd tire of any of these places, even (or especially) with their all-inclusive philosophy, in less than a day.

There's not as much construction here as there was in pre-crash Spain in the early days of the MedTrek, but there is enough crane activity to draw a parallel. The unending number of hotels is obviously going to face a crunch of some sort at some time. There are just too many, the increase in tourists has to end sometime. Not today, though, as I exchange twice as many "Good Mornings" as on a usual day.

The real treat of the day occurs between the last hotel and the wide Manavgat River, a beauty of a river with abundant riverside growth and uniformly calm fishermen. It's a hearty river, and explains why the town of Manavgat, a dozen kilometers inland, has attracted more than 200,000 residents. The first fisherman I speak to says I'll have to walk inland to find a bridge to get across, but the next person I meet offers to take me across on his Jet Ski for free and I gladly give him 10₺ "so that we'll both feel good about the day."

I run into a camp of Gypsies on the edge of the river and, for the second time on this trip, I'm called "Baba" by some kids trying to scam some coins from me. It turns out that "Baba," meaning "father" or "older one," is a term of endearment and respect, and not a slur, which is how I initially interpreted it.

As I march through much less plush resorts with lots of space between each of them, I remind myself that it's easy to spot the Russians because of the way all of the women tie their head wraps. When I get to Kizilğaiç, I stop at a Vitamin Bar in a shopping mall, both ridiculously over the top for a rural area like this, to refuel and check email (it's 11:11 and I've gone 18.33 K). I'm told that it's 14 kilometers to Okurcalar, which is where the Alanya province begins. A sign says it's 37 kilometers to the city of Alanya.

As I continue on the beach the resorts get a little odder – though I love looking into the Zen Garden at the Flora Garden Hotel and I probably should have stopped in Kizilot to see if, indeed, they do kiss a lot – when I reach the coastal road. The proximity of the road to the sea forces many hotels to be on the un-seaside side and guests must go over or under the road, on over-or-under passes, to get to the sand.

One of the more delightful sights of the day is watching a woman bathe her entire body, quite intimately, with her swimming suit on near the Barbaroosa Pasha Hotel, where I'm invited to have a tea at the hotel café. I'm becoming convinced that either the security guards are kinder and softer the further south I go or that I've perfected a permanent expression that determinedly says "DO NOT bother me!" that keeps them away. When I return to Sidon, I go for an early evening swim in comparatively wild waves before dining on my usual 6₺ *doner kebab* at a hole-in-the-wall one-man resto, which reminds me of the place I used to buy *frites* in Paris in the early 70s near Place de l'Odéon.

The next morning, before moving my base camp to Alanya, I spend an hour drinking tea at a seaside hotel/restaurant downtown and again reflect on how fortunate I am to be MedTrekking. Perhaps that's because yesterday I saw half a dozen people either in wheelchairs, including one Russian I helped get down a ramp on the beach, or otherwise unable to do something as simple as walk barefoot on the sand. I think about this as I enjoy a Sidon sunrise and take photographs of the Apollo temple and an amusing Viagra-based drinks menu. Then I meet a Russian in such a frenzied fury, perhaps brought on by too much Viagra drink, over the imperfections in a leather jacket that he bought that I had no desire to be the Turk who sold it to him.

He reminds me that I'm irritated that the prices in many parts of Turkey are in € rather than ₺. Not because it gives local merchants more money (they always round up the exchange rate in their favor), but because I consider it unpatriotic behavior for a large country with its own currency. The only rival, in Russian-frequented areas only, is the $, but that's because Russians still aren't familiar with the euro.

When I walk by the now-in-ruins Great Bath in Sidon, a panel explains the various rooms for a traditional hammam: "Because of it being the largest bath house in Side, this building is called 'The Great Bath.' This building has Apodyterium (undressing room), Frigidarium (cold room), Tepidarium (semi-heated room) and Caldarium (hot room). The bath, built in the second century AD, was repaired in fifth century AD."

Too bad it wasn't restored for today's tourists, I thought, as I recalled the many scraping, massaging and oiling baths I've had in Turkey.

Then I begin to wonder if there are any names left for the thousands of hotels on the Turkish coast that already run the alphabet from A (Ada) to Z (Zen) and include everything from Aqua, Arabella, Arcadia, Aspendos, Banana, Blue Fish, Cesars, Cleopatra, Dreams Beach, Elvis, Fame, Green Hill, Jasmine, Leodikya, Letounia, Long Beach, Magnolia, Merhaba, Merlin Beach, Mermaid, Monte Carlo, My Home, Pegasos, Saphir, Sea Bird, Sea Port, Titan, Tivoli, Top, Viking and Washington to Uygula.

What names grab me after all this exposure? I love a place called the "Cleopatra Shakespeare Cafe" and the "No Name Restaurant" in Sidon.

## THE POET LAUREATE

The MedTrek into Alanya from Okurcalar passes through the communities of Incekum, Avsallar, Türkler, Payallar and Konakli before I arrive at the Alanya Marina just west of town and stroll to my hotel on the well-known Cleopatra Beach, where there are thirteen hotels named Cleopatra something.

First, though, I cross the Alara River and pass the Alara Grand Bazaar through the lovely named Justiniapolis and then enter the Incekum Natural Park where a sign indicates that it's 37 kilometers to Alanya.

I continue on the tarmac to get ten kilometers under my belt and slyly slip into the Saphir Resort. Again, I don't put this type of subterfuge high on the list of my ten best scams because it's so easy to slip into places like this, especially in the early morning or late afternoon, when a guard has turned his back or left his post. And, quite frankly, the free food, except for the fresh fruit and hard-boiled eggs, isn't very healthy or good: oily sausages, tasteless pastries, synthetic fruit juice. Despite my *The Idiot and the Odyssey II* cap and backpack, I slip out as easily as I slipped in and repeat the performance for lunch and ice cream at the Sentido resort, an alluring round-shaped hotel.

The next ten kilometers are spent on the seaside when I descend to the Nazir Family Resorts beach. After the sand, I walk through a construction zone, and a forested campground with very few people, and then proceed along another round of hotels and family resorts with lots of Russian and German families enjoying the sun and sea.

Things are going uneventfully – not one security guard or hotel employee bothers me when I walk on hotel property and serve myself, and one even apologizes when I drop a towering ice cream cone and create a big mess – until I get to the Adenya Hotel, which has a wall that almost completely blocks access on the seaside. I climb over the wall to get in and am quickly beckoned by a security guard who informs me that this is a special hotel, a Muslim-only hotel, and that I shouldn't be here.

I go through my rap about the open seaside and defiantly walk to the other side of the resort and attempt to get around or over another high wall. Two guards grab me and tell me that I am about to enter the "Woman's Beach," which I hadn't realized. I abjectly apologize (Alexander also often apologized and made amends when he was wrong) but ask to see the manager.

"We've had this hotel without public access for thirty years and we'll have it for thirty more," says the head security guard. "This isn't like the other resort hotels and you shouldn't be here. Don't even think of arguing with me."

I let them escort me off the property through the front door.

A bit further down the coast, while singing to the very popular tune by Avicii called "Hey Brother" in every resort, I pass Sealanya, a shark and dolphin park that costs a whopping €55 to enter. Too much for me, but I do have a tea break in Türkler when the friendly owner of a hole-in-the-wall Turkish café, which is a rare find amid all these fancy resorts, charges me only 1₺ for a chai and says I'm at the midpoint between Okurcalar and Alanya.

"It's another 19 kilometers," he says.

Indeed my pedometer is correct and is at 39 kilometers when I arrive.

I soon see Alanya's castle-topped mountain, with 93 towers and walls that stretch 6.5 kilometers in circumference. It was built by Aladdin Keykubat, the Sultan of the Seljuks in the 13th century. The Seljuks were rightly reputed as builders of mosques, tombs, roads and shipyards, and the impregnable-appearing fortress of Alanya that sits majestically 800 feet above the sea. From here, and other ports, they traded throughout the Mediterranean.

I'm so stiff the next morning that I decide to enjoy breakfast at the

Park Hotel and have my laundry done before taking any more steps, though I hope to reach the 10,000-kilometer mark before I end this outing. I have coffee with two friends, Russell and Kenan, who are constructing an Aqua Fun Sea Park on Cleopatra Beach. Russell points out that there are so many Russians in Turkey this year because they're so unpopular elsewhere in Europe due to the situation in the Ukraine.

"Turkey welcomes them," he says as he suggests I climb the octagonal 33-meter high Red Tower, built to defend the town's shipyard, cut from rock in 1228. After I walk around the Castle of Alanya and climb the tower, I swim to the shipyard also built by the industrious Aladdin Keykubat.

The next day's MedTrek out of Alanya kicks off an hour after the 4:30 a.m. call to prayer by a *muezzin* at a mosque near my fourth floor (with a view), $25-a-night squat.

I always love an early start and take off from the Park Hotel towards Gazipaşa where, among other things, there's a comparatively new international airport. So new that it's not on the 2011 (it opened in mid-2011) map of Turkey that I use to track my MedTrek steps.

The day's walk begins on numerous Alanya beaches – Keykubat Beach and Orange Beach among them – and the coast looks clear through the municipalities (or one-time municipalities since the new mayor of Alanya is apparently annexing many of them) of Oba, Tosmur, Kestel, Mahmutal, and Kargicak until I reach Demirtaş. I enter the province of Cilicia where homes are cut into the cliff sides and terraces have been carved on every hillside to grow bananas, grapes and other produce.

Although two guys coming out of a nightclub on the port make spitting noises at me, the only other people out at this dawn hour are street cleaners, other walkers and people using the exercise stations (including three Muslim women in full garb). I set a quick pace along the port – where I notice an array of garish pirate ships that take tourists on outings – until I have a tea at Mehmet's Bar which comes into view after walking twelve kilometers.

The walk is all along public beaches and there are none of the snazzy resorts that I've become overused to. This stretch, combined with Cleopatra's Beach, make Alanya an ideal location for anyone looking for different bits of sand and different styles of lodging during a long holiday. A travel brochure claims there are 70 kilometers of beaches (which seems a stretch, even for a travel brochure) and the few hotels, like the Happy Elephant and Green Peace, seem laid back and unabashedly cater to the Russian middle class. It isn't until I get to Kargicak at the end of the stretch of sand that a number of hotels, like the Dinler and Gold City, pretentiously decorate their facades with ***** stars. This has to be one of the biggest jokes in hotel rating history.

Atop a hill at the end of town is a contemporary castle called Utopia World that, an employee tells me, has "1,200 rooms and only Russian clients." I don't bother trying to visit the hotel, but I like its beach, which abuts a banana plantation.

I stop for a *gözleme* – a pancake filled with cheese, spinach and one too many hot peppers that I order by translating English on a Turk's cell phone after taking a photograph – at 11 a.m. near Demirtaş. By the time I end the day in Yeşilöz, I wonder if I might have entered a part of southern Turkey that is beyond tourism. It's June and the only hotel, the Hare, still hasn't opened and a dilapidated one across the street is closed and for sale.

I'm again pleased that I have a base camp in Alanya.

I return to Yeşilöz the next morning knowing that the 10,000 kilometerstone on my MedTrek is only 21 kilometers down the coast.

The day begins on a glorious two-lane coastal road that takes me through the ancient village of Iotape. Due to a new four-lane freeway through the mountains, it is virtually carless. The seaside at times resembles a mini-Big Sur and the weather has turned wet, windy and wild. Zeus, the god of thunder among his other jobs, seems to be throwing multiple thunderbolts and unleashing sporadic torrents. It isn't clear if The Idiot, who is either constantly drenched or ducking out of the rain, is being applauded by the gods or simply being made to look like, well, an idiot.

During the intermittent downpours, I seek refuge under a tarp covering a pile of fertilizer in a banana plantation, in a seaside ruin, in a cave, under trees, and in four different cafés until I finally MedTrek through the Gazipaşa suburb of Kahyalar, past the airport and onto Nanu Beach. By the time I reach Selinus, where Emperor Trajan died in AD 117 during his attempted return to Rome, I have two sets of wet shirts, socks and shoes.

All this gives me inspiration to write a press release:

"The 147-kilometer MedTrek from Antalya to Alanya in southern Turkey is a colorful walk in the sand compared to the rigors of the mountainous Lycian Way that preceded it.

Once beyond Antalya's cliffs and dramatic waterfall, the only problems for a long-distance MedTrekker are a few rivers, including the majestic Manavgat, that require creativity – a bathing suit, some kids willing to "borrow" a rowboat, a fisherman/ferryman needing a few lira and a lifeguard with a Jet-Ski – to ford or cross.

The only blight on the generally flat walk are the scores of upmarket resorts packed with German and Russian tourists that rigorously attempt to discourage MedTrekkers from trespassing on "private" property. The Idiot's most trying encounter was with security guards at the Muslim-friendly Adenya Hotel when he inadvertently walked onto the 'Woman's

Beach."

But sometimes it's worth it all when it means acknowledging a kilometerstone. On June 5th, The Idiot reached the 10,000-kilometer (6,214 miles) mark on Nanu Beach near the village of Gazipaşa in southern Turkey. It wasn't until he was atop Alanya Castle a few days earlier that he realized he could reach 10,000 kilometers on his current MedTrek outing.

How did The Idiot celebrate the 10,000th? With a day off in Alanya that began with a shave, haircut and massage followed by a visit to the city's archaeological museum."

My next fairly social MedTrekking day begins with an angelic shoeshine man and ends with a devilish handyman.

The shoeshine man is on the *dolmuş* that I pick up in Alanya at 7 a.m. to return to the 10,000 kilometerstone in Gazipaşa. He not only helps me find the right connecting *dolmuş* in Oba but also is so enthusiastic and calm about his profession, and so nonchalant and content about money, that I might start shining shoes myself.

"It's a difficult job shining shoes but I'm good at it and I like doing it," he says in self-described "street English that's just as good as my street German." He continues, "I probably average 20-30 customers a day at 2₺ a shine and that gives me the right amount of money to live on. Too much money can be a bad thing."

My next encounter, also on the *dolmuş*, is a blond woman in a red dress with very high heels (I don't inquire why she's wearing this attire at this time of day) who looks as fresh as a daisy. Any animosity between the USA and Russia pales while we discuss what she's doing here ("staying with my sister") and what I'm doing here ("just walked 10,000 kilometers"). We wish each other "Good Luck" when she gets off, leaving me in the company of employees working at hotels on the promenade south of Alanya, a fisherman, and a young woman with an arm in a sling who looks like she has just dislocated her shoulder. I was going to describe the pain I was in when that happened to me (I was showing my son how to execute a "perfect" ski jump in Courchevel in the French Alps) but she looked in too much agony to have a chat.

Next, I have a brief interaction with some guys constructing a new mosque near the *otogar* in Gazipaşa and during the next 22 kilometers, along a road through the mountains because the seaside is impassable, I meet lots of friendly market people, including one in Muzkent who gives me four free bananas. It's clear from the outset that I've left touristic Turkey for agricultural Turkey and that I can enjoy – and eat – tomatoes, bananas, strawberries and other fruits and vegetables being grown in nearby fields and greenhouses.

When the road through the Taurus mountains, that I've been walking on for four hours, finally reaches the seaside, where it begins its windy up-and-down stretch to Anamur, I run into a German on a moped who tells me about the Melody Beach Camp that's two kilometers down the hill from the cliff top.

Who could resist?

At Melody, I meet a devilish German-speaking Turkish handyman who convinces me that despite the camp's ideal location and nice beach I will never return. Irascible? Cantankerous? Contentious? Take your pick. He does everything from criticize my German and telling me I am asking too many questions to being the first Turk to ever invite me to sit down without offering me a cup of tea. He immediately squashes the fantasies I'd hatched about Melody being the ideal earth mother while walking down the hill past banana plantations.

"Melody is this location and a state of being, not a woman," the devilish handyman contends.

Then, looking completely befuddled, he asks me, "What is it you want?"

"I want nothing."

"How can you not want something?" he asks.

Then he accuses me of asking too many questions. Simple questions like "Can I buy lunch in the Café Istanbul (the hotel café)?" and "Do you have an available room?"

"The food and café are only for guests," he said, indicating that I wasn't one.

The fact that he constantly critiques my German makes me mangle it even more and, of course, I begin asking even more questions.

Maybe we just aren't getting along philosophically. I am telling him about the *raison d'etre* for the MedTrek, after he asks why I was *zu fuss,* or "on foot," and he says "I'm not interested," when I mention Homer and Odysseus. "That's way in the past. Only the future is important."

"*Ich bin nicht* in agreement," I reply. "Only today is important. Can you show me a room?"

After claiming that 65, my age, was nothing in the old-age bracket, I tell him he looks 55, though we both knew he is well over 70. He takes me into one of the ten bungalows, which he says will "guarantee a private, exclusive stay at our resort...with a 'nightlife' arranged by Mother Nature and not by noisy discos and bars." The rooms are pretty bad even by my tolerant MedTrek standards.

"It's simple rather than comfortable," he admits, pretty much sending me on my way and not even offering to be a Facebook friend.

My faith in mankind is quickly restored, however, when a worker in one of the banana plantations offers me a lift up the hill on his motorcycle, which I refuse. I am completely back to normal when a bus heading to Alanya comes up the hill from Anamur, Turkey's most southeastern point, the second I hit the tarmac (the devilish guy insisted that "you'll be waiting at least an hour at this time of day") to take me back to my base camp.


The next morning, torrential storms delay most of the buses heading back to Güneyköy where I'll resume the MedTrek.

I react to the delay with typical MedTrek equanimity, getting a tea and a roll while playing Scrabble against my iPhone, and patiently waiting until I finally get out of the station at 8:15 a.m. It's 9:30 by the time I get back to the road above Melody's, and kick off the day on the two-lane, windy, up-and-down mountain road.

There's very little traffic on a Sunday morning and my hillside road has wonderful vistas of the Mediterranean from every angle. I maintain a four-kilometer-per-hour pace and stop for some bananas (banana plantations are the rage everywhere) and eat them while watching a plantation owner weigh nuts. I later breeze through two cliffside restaurants to take in the view (there's now a calm-after-the-thunderstorms sedate look to the water) but keep going with only a few roadside stops to admire the glowing turquoise water until I get to Yakacik.

The village with two mosques is not only near the water (there's a sandy beach with no one on it and I'm the only tourist in sight) but also signifies that I'm leaving Antalya province and entering Mersin province. One thing I know about Mersin is that this is where Alexander plunged into the Cydnus River and was hit with a chill and fever that sidelined him for three months and worried everyone around him.

"Alexander was seized with convulsions, accompanied with high fever and continuous sleeplessness," wrote Arrian. "None of the physicians thought he was likely to survive." "His limbs stiffened, and he lost his color and the warmth of his body, making him look more dead than alive," added Curtius.

As bad as it might have been, Alexander survived.

I decided not to swim in the Cydnus, but rather to enjoy a formidable country sandwich (lot of onions, greens and meat straight from a skewer) in Yakacik before I continue an uphill climb on melting asphalt to Uçari.

I've walked 47 kilometers from Gazipaşa and the sign on the road says it's 38 kilometers to Anamur. Although it's only 4 p.m. I call it a day because it could be a long wait and bus ride back to Alanya.

I have a tea at a roadside café and apparently appear so stressed that the woman who runs the place (women seem to run all these places) keeps shouting "Challish, challish," which I take to mean "Relax, relax." In fact, the concierge at the Park Hotel later tells me it means "Quit working, quit working. *Çaliş* means working and *çalişma* means don't work," he explains.

I have just changed T-shirts, removing my sweaty MedTrek T and replacing it with the one that says "TEENAGE MILLIONAIRE," when a Porsche pulls up and, to my surprise, the driver waves at me to get in.

The 30-year-old constantly texting driver, whose name I never really comprehend (Hadroun, I think), is a laid back, friendly guy driving back to Istanbul from Mersin where he goes monthly to visit his wife, who's working there. He doesn't fly because "I'm not in control" and explains that he drives over 300,000 kilometers a year in his two cars (the Porsche, completely fitted out in the US, cost €250,000 in Turkey, where gas and insurance are also expensive) "because it's fun, I love it." He says he's the head of a holding company in Istanbul and works ten days a month.

We start talking about the value of money, or how to spend money, and I tell him that when Alexander the Great arrived in what's now Turkey, he was broke.

"But as he won battles against the Persians his fortune increased and he frequently gave it away instead of hoarding it, often with a message," I explain.

Then I share an anecdote.

Plutarch tells about a common soldier who was driving a mule laden with some of the king's treasure. When the mule grew tired, the soldier put the load on his own back and marched until he ran into Alexander, who saw that he was about to faint.

"Do not faint now," Alexander said to the soldier, "but finish the journey, and carry what you have there to your own tent for yourself."

His mother Olympias complained he should offer more moderate rewards in situations like this.

"You make them all equal to kings and in the meantime you leave yourself destitute," she counseled.

Not only is the Porsche driver, as Liz later says, my "Sunday angel" but he gets me back to Alanya in a third of the time of the fastest bus and goes out of his way to drop me on the seaside near the Park Hotel.

I spend my last night on this MedTrek outing at the hotel and leave bidding everyone – the night porter who brought me coffee when I came downstairs after the call to prayer every morning; the day porter who gave me the €20 rate and a decent corner room with two views that kept me here; the waiter at the pool – goodbye.

I take a taxi to the *otogar* and the driver honks at a bus pulling out towards Antalya, where I'm catching a plane to Nice where I'll lead some walking tours on the French Riviera. I spend the night at the Antalya Farmhouse near the airport (I don't think any reviews mention it is on the direct flight path) near Perge, an ancient city that Alexander the Great conquered with little problem because there were no city walls for defense.

I walk from the Farmhouse through fields and village streets to Perge, about five kilometers away, and am enthralled with the stadium, acropolis, closed theater and even the two living Roman soldiers who pose with tourists. The next morning my "last breakfast" is a great spread prepared by Ayfer and Ergun Turan with the best watermelon juice (a mix of melon, lemon, honey and mint) that I've ever tasted.

In Nice, I've been asked to speak about "Successful, Serious & Sexy Shameless Self-Promotion" – aka SSSSSP or "Five S's and a P" – to promote my books at a "Freelance Café" event on the rooftop terrace of a swish hotel.

Surrounded by an audience that includes some of my successful Riviera artist friends – including Nall and Jeff Hessing whom I met when I began living here in the mid-80s – two people who are very used to promoting themselves, I describe how there's been absolutely "no shame about shameless self-promotion" since Andy Warhol declared "everyone would have fifteen minutes of fame."

I tell my audience that "there are 24 key elements to SSSSSP" but restrict my hour-long talk to the importance of the P: "Passion, Practice, Perseverance, Phaked Patience, Perspective & Perverse Psychology."

When I return to California I begin training for the 38[th]Annual Trans Tahoe Relay open water swimming competition as a member of Team Tango, consisting of three women and three men. We wear sleek gold suits for the competition in the chilly freshwater Lake Tahoe that straddles the California-Nevada border at a challenging elevation of 6,225 feet (1,897 meters).

Then I prepare for the next lengthy stint of MedTrekking across southern Turkey to Syria with regular rounds of hiking, swimming and workouts until I resume the Zenny MedTrek a few months from now in the Turkish village of Uçari, about 350 kilometers from the Syrian border.

# ONCE AN IDIOT, ALWAYS AN IDIOT

Everywhere The Idiot goes he reminds people, or he's reminded, that he's The Idiot.

# FOLLOW THE IDIOT

## CHAPTER PHOTOS

## CHAPTER MAP

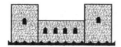

# Confronting ISIS at the Syrian Border

"Are you still to learn that the end and perfection of our victories is to avoid the vices and infirmities of those whom we subdue?" – *Alexander the Great*

"There is nothing impossible to him who will try." – *Alexander the Great*

Before leaving London to return for my last round of MedTrekking in Turkey I feel compelled to issue the following press release:

"London – The Idiot, who has walked over 10,000 kilometers (6,214 miles) around the Mediterranean Sea, resumes his hike across southern Turkey to Syria tomorrow after a visit to the House of Lords.

The American adventurer and author – who is walking in the footsteps of Homer, Odysseus and Alexander the Great – launches this segment of his ongoing MedTrek near the Turkish village of Uçari, which is about 350 kilometers (218 miles) from Syria. He expects to reach the

173

Turkey-Syria border on the Mediterranean Sea to conclude this MedTrekking stint on October 15.

Naturally, after this week's briefings in London, The Idiot is aware of the potential danger of entering Syria and discussed the plight of the country, including the recent spate of horrifying and obscene beheadings, while holding forth at Speakers' Corner in London on Sunday.

He mentioned that a recent travel warning from the US State Department stated that: "No part of Syria should be considered immune from violence, and throughout the country the potential exists for unpredictable and hostile acts, including kidnappings, sniper assaults, large and small-scale bombings, and chemical attacks, as well as arbitrary arrest, detention, and torture."

He added that Syria's coast, where he'll MedTrek just over 200 kilometers, is ostensibly still controlled by the government of Syria President Bashar al-Assad. Although it's difficult to accurately assess the situation in various parts of Syria, he produced a map created by *The Wall Street Journal* to illustrate the current territorial partitions within the country.

The Idiot indicated that he will evaluate the wisdom/stupidity of walking on Syria's Mediterranean coast when he arrives at the border. His long-time followers and readers will recall that in 2003, after meeting with the Algerian Embassy, which refused to issue him a journalist's visa, and the US State Department in Washington D.C., he decided not to illegally enter war-torn Algeria.

He may be an Idiot but he's not stupid."

I fly to Gazipaşa from Istanbul, take a *dolmuş* from the airport to the coastal town of Anamur, and notice on the way that multiple tunnels, high-tech terracing and a new four-lane road will soon complement, or perhaps eliminate, the narrow, twisty, curvy road I've been hiking on with its lovely sea view – along with lots of roadside family shops selling honey, pomegranates and nuts.

I set up a base camp on the Anamur Beach at the Ünlüselek Hotel and immediately walk towards Ören, which means ruins. Ören is the location of the former Anamur, called Anamurium, which was founded by Phoenicians before being occupied by Hittites. In the 12th century BC, Anamurium was the capital of the Anamurium kingdom, in the 6th century BC it was a part of Achaemenid Empire of Persia, and in 333 BC Alexander the Great annexed it.

On the way to these historically rich and wondrous ruins, I realize that I'm not in London anymore when I hear the call to prayer, smell the sheep and feel the heat emanating from the greenhouses. It's all very good, fresh and new. I welcomingly soak in the rural scenes and scents and enjoy a couple hours of solitude in Anamurium (such a pleasant roll-off-the-tongue poetic name) where there is no one else in sight. I bask under the hot sun and in the constant wind as I walk through the ruins, some dating from the fairly recent 4th century AD, in the southernmost spot on the Anatolian peninsula.

The day's first downside are the numerous rivers between the old Anamurium and the new Anamur, which, despite the small size of bananas grown here, is renowned as the banana capital of Turkey. Crossing the rivers involves frequent inland detours to upriver bridges.

Another downside appears in the evening when I try to sleep at my seaside hotel in Anamur (perhaps I should have anticipated this when I noticed the romantic multi-colored lighting and plastic-covered furniture in my garden-level cheapo room). A gathering of Turkish men, often reputed for dancing abilities that range from male belly dancing to social folkloric dancing to Sufi spinning, keeps me awake far too late. About the only decent aspect of their noisy presence is a quick video that I shoot and put on YouTube as a Reader Reaction from "Turkish men happy that The Idiot is back on the MedTrek."

## *THE DANCING TURKS*

The next day, when I mention the dancing and the morning heat to Halil Ünlüselek, the owner of the beachside Ünlüselek Hotel, he puts me in my place: "It was 40°C three weeks ago; it's barely over 30°C now. It's like California. It's almost winter. Enjoy it."

I leave my room, barefoot, and walk three kilometers on the beach towards Syria before I reach another river, though I realize later that by not sticking to the paved promenade, I miss seeing Anamur's seaside Jurassic Park and an apparently animated section of the Iskele beachfront. I do see, however, lots of Turks using flotation devices in the smooth-surfaced sea and more pious than usual Muslim women, all of them with headscarves and wearing full-bodied swimming costumes.

I have to put my shoes on when I encounter another wide river (which helps explain the area's fertile plain) and learn that there's a bridge just two hundred meters upstream. When I thank the boatman who gives me this information, he says with a burly laugh "*Günaydın,* Baba, good morning!"

I reach the impressive 4[th]century Mamure (*mamure* means prosperous) Castle on the beach and, not knowing it is closed for a year due to a $1 million-a-year renovation, "sneak" in the back door and get a few photos before the not unpleasant representative from the Turkish Ministry of Culture informs me that "we don't allow photos because people put them on the Internet and say our workers aren't qualified."

I, however, am impressed that the renovation of the moat-surrounded (except on the seaside) castle that once had 39 towers is taking place at all.

I buzz along the coastal road past the Turtle Campsite (did I mention that there were turtles in the Mamure moat?), cut into Bozyazi and continue on the waterfront for more than ten kilometers – hiking on fire roads in forests, climbing cliffs, meandering through housing units – until I reach the far side of town. When I look away from the sea, I spot the majestic Softa Castle on a hill above town that was built by the Armenian kings who ruled Cilicia during the Crusades when the area was known to some as "Lesser Armenia."

I feel the need for a chai and drop into a cafe on the beach. There I meet Suzan Denis Mason, a woman in her 50s from Lake Tahoe, one of the few Americans I will see in this part of Turkey. She's visiting her father who lived in the US for thirty years and worked as a chauffeur at Wells Fargo Bank in San Francisco. I talk to them about my recent swim in Lake Tahoe and my current hike during a long (for me) twenty-minute break.

"Walking will keep you young!" Suzan's 88-year-old father tells me, though his daughter guesses I'm 64, which is not far from my real age, indicating that walking doesn't seem to keep me looking too young. Alas! I had hoped it would.

I continue on the coast to the sandy, wavy, windy beach in Tekmen where I take my first dip of this MedTrek outing and let myself be pleasantly buffered and beaten by the breaking waves. I walk a few more kilometers (31 for the day) on the road before hailing a *dolmuş* back to Anamur where I stroll through the comparatively primitive hillside town center back to the sea.

I'm not sure if even Anamur's animated Jurassic Park attraction would have changed my opinion that the extreme south of Turkey, like the extreme south of many European countries, is much less wealthy than the north, though it could be the striking lack of a tourism infrastructure (there are no Russians here, but I do see a few Germans at my hotel). Fewer streets are paved, there's lots of litter and garbage, and I don't see any ATMs in either Anamur or Bozyazi, though the uniformed school children and greenhouses producing bananas and other agricultural goodies provide a spark of hope.

The next morning, I kick things off on the nine-kilometer bay through Tekmen and Tekeli, another stretch of the rich alluvial plain dedicated to greenhouse agriculture, and it's again clear that there's no tourism on this stretch of coast. The only motel on the stretch, the Sydney, looks so sinister and shabby that I'm glad I just set up a new base camp at the Hotel Dudum in Aydincik, where my wave-lapped $22.50 room (breakfast included) has a stellar view of the sea.

The big event of the day is tackling and enjoying the high cliffy road, aka the Turan Cemal Beriker Bulvari, that runs for 20 kilometers above the sea. It's a fatiguing walk not only because it is uphill and the road is narrow, which demands constant caution, but also because I insist on taking dirt roads that traverse the cliffs. Each time, as the dirt roads evaporate at a dead end, I'm forced to backtrack or, worse, get cut up fighting through brambles. When I take a break at the Aydincik city limit, near the well-known spring in Soguksu, I clean up my slashed legs with seawater and take a photo of the damage. You'd think I would have given up these side treks after the first futile off-road effort, but no, I try three times to find an off-the-tarmac hiking path. And I have to backtrack and deal with brambles on each occasion. If at first you don't...don't.

Despite the cars and trucks, which are forced to go slow due to the curvy road between Antalya and Adana, there is not much noise and I appreciate a serene and silent end-to-the-afternoon on the Mediterranean, typified by a before-the-storm-that-didn't-quite-hit climate. When I look towards Aydincik, known as Kelenderis in ancient Greek, there's a rainbow, and I see new tunnels being drilled for a speedier road. I look out at the Yilanli Ada island where the remains of a 2400-year-old port were discovered in 2002.

It's time for a day off to frolic in the sea below my "Rm w/a Vu" at the Hotel Dudum in Aydincik; visit nearby ruins where a fifth-century mosaic discovered in 1992 is being restored; help hotel owner Mustafa promote my photo and books on his Facebook page; and admire night lights on a row of vaulted rock graves, spanning a period from the sixth century to the 4th century BC, on the main road through town.

I have a fish dinner at the hotel-top restaurant with an interesting guest who might be more of an Idiot than I am.

Paul Wilma, 63 and Belgian, is currently on a solo cycling trip from Athens to Jerusalem (minus Syria and Lebanon) and has already visited Mount Athos and the seven churches of Asia Minor on this outing. He's been working for IBM in San Jose, California, for 25 years and has climbed Mount Shasta and Mount Whitney and has hiked the Camino in Spain.

"This is what will keep us young," he tells me as we swap outdoor adventure stories, adding that he walks about 30 kilometers or bikes about 130 kilometers a day when he's out and about. "It's addictive and I take time off from work without pay to do it. How lucky we are!"

I resume the MedTrek the next day after an 8 a.m. breakfast by taking a right out of the Dudum's front door through the as-yet-unexplored remainder of Aydincik. I stroll along a sandy beach, head up a hill and in a few kilometers turn right until I reach the cliffside entrance to the seaside Gilindire cave discovered by a shepherd in 1999.

As I explore the 555-meter long ice age cave, which opened to the public in 2013 and hasn't had too many American visitors based on the generally excited reaction from a group of people when I buy a ticket, I meet the founding shepherd, who now works as one of the guides. We spend an hour investigating dripstone formations, including stalagmites, stalactites, pillars, wall and drapery dripstones, leakage stone and cave needles. He tells me that the glorious, massive and womb-like cave is sometimes called Aynalıgöl, or Mirror Lake, in reference to the lake found at the end.

When I leave, I continue on a somewhat seaside road – a mix of the old road, the new road, promenades, beaches and even foundations for the yet-unbuilt stretches of the Turkish version of an autoroute – and restrain my off-track hiking penchant. This temperate behavior pays off and I have no new scratches at noon when, after 17 kilometers, I arrive in Karatepe and have a picnic (fruit nectars, biscuits and a Nogger) above an empty beach. I nod to some Russian workers staying at the Moda Motel in town who, I learn, are working on the construction of the Akkuyu nuclear plant near Büyükeceli. I continue through Sipahili and Yanişli and finally see the much-advertised Ulu Resort that, according to my count, has more billboards on a shorter stretch of road than any hotel in Turkey.

The big events of the day, besides the alluring azure sea itself and the walk through the undeveloped forested and mountainous countryside, is that I spot the island of Cyprus across the sea for the first time and, recalling the Chernobyl disaster, decide not to visit the Akkuyu Nükleer Santrali.

At sunset I find myself having a coffee at the Budakoğlu Bar on Büyükeceli Beach owned by Emrah Budak, who tells me that "I'm the very, very fat one" when he asks me to friend him on Facebook. My pedometer tells me that I MedTrekked 34 kilometers, walked for 7:15 of the eight hours I've been on road, and averaged 4.8 kilometers per walking hour. A satisfying pace and day.

There's no way over or around the mountains from Büyükeceli Beach to Yeşilovacik, so I grab a ride from Aydincik to Yeşilovacik (the driver "asks" me to pay 10₺ for it) and start the hike there. As I walk through town, I have an urge to binge on ice cream and buy three Noggers at different hole-in-the-wall shops as I continue to the under-construction autoroute and beach on the other side.

The Hellenistic Gözleğentepe Necropolis is on the old road out of town, but a sign warns that the tombs were pillaged centuries ago, so I skip it and follow another sign which proclaims that the lovely sounding Aphrodisias is eight kilometers away in the mountains. Many hours later, I wind up at the Akçakil campsite, a mini-Holland on the Med with almost exclusively Dutch-licensed camping vans and RVs. When I leave there and enter Taşucu, I see a ferry from Cyprus docking at the port.

I check the prices of a full-body swimsuit that I consider buying for Liz, who will meet me in a week, before hitchhiking back to my Aydincik base camp. I get some additional insight into Turkish *misafir*, or hospitality, when the businessman who picks me up stops at a café for the usual tea and peanuts and, in his hometown of Yeşilovacik, hands me over to some of his pals who continue to ply me with excellent tea and more peanuts.

This is called the Turkish tea handoff (it's a good thing) and I'm kept occupied and talking until a bus arrives.

The next day is spent walking through the agriculturally rich, bird-populated and almost uninhabited Göksu river delta between Taşucu and Atakent. It's a delight to be away from the mountains and to hike barefoot, often just wearing red Jockey underwear, for over 30 of the 39 kilometers I MedTrek today.

This nearly nude behavior began after I walked past two ports in Taşucu (noting that there are also ferries to Tripoli in Libya), the chic Hotel Zeus and the still-closed Calypso Bar on the longest stretch of beach since Alanya. There are no tourist resorts (the Göksu river delta is a bird-watchers paradise with over 300 species in the two lakes formed by the 260-mile long river that winds down in two branches from the Taurus Mountains) but lots of walkers for the first five kilometers on the west side of the delta. Then no one from there on (with one exception – that would be me).

I'm the only walker on the beaches, dunes and salt flats and I see only a few tracks – and most of those are from horses. I run into a lone fisherman who tells me where to cross one lake and one river. He's living in a tiny motor home and is more open, friendly and helpful than anyone else I'll meet today. He doesn't seem to care that I'm wearing only red bikini underwear.

After I ford the Göksu River, I'm looking forward to walking up the eastern side of the delta when I run into a channel with the brownest water entering the Med that I've seen on the entire MedTrek. The sediment-rich stream is not just entering the Mediterranean; it's sprawling, spreading and turning the sea brown. With the wind and sand, it's too broad to even consider attempting to cross.

Backtracking a few kilometers, I head north through the river delta – noticing pomegranates, peppers, olives, strawberries and dozens of other crops in the rich-soil alluvial plain – to finally arrive in Atayurt. I proceed to my new base camp on the fourth floor of the Inka Hotel, just across from the magical Maiden's Castle on an island offshore, in Kizkalesi (the password for the Wi-Fi is "misafir," which means hospitality).

I'm not the only guest, of course, and I'm not sure if my 75₺ rate with breakfast is good, bad or extortionate.

"There are 27 different guests at 27 different rates," smiles manager Mehmet Seyran.

"Heard of Trivago?" I ask.

Instead of continuing as a solitary MedTrekker meditating on the sand, the next day, I walk on beaches peopled mostly by Turks with restaurants and other treats in Atakent (lots of sand, comfortable and clean with swimming holes and *chaises longues* in the rocky coves) and Narlikuyu (rocky seaside with lots of picturesque restaurants for seaside dining that are waiting for clients when I walk through just before noon) to busy and buzzy Kizkalesi.

I resist the temptation to dive into the clear water in the coves in Atakent or eat at one of the many restaurants in Narlikuyu in order to leave enough time to swim around (or out to, anyway) the Magic Maiden's Castle when I get back to Kizkalesi.

Once there, I not only swim out to the Maiden's Castle from the beach closest to the Inka Hotel, but also take a walking tour of the interior of the island wearing just my Speedo swimsuit and goggles. Fortunately, the teens partying on the castle walls are too preoccupied with drinking and schmoozing to notice or remark on my lack of clothing.

When I head east the next morning my first stop is at the Korykos Castle just out of town. I learn that Korykos was one of the most important harbor towns of ancient Cilicia; it was rich in natural resources, manufactured everything related to seafaring and produced exceptional olive oil.

Shortly after visiting the castle, I find a Turkish lira on the dusty roadside and take this as an omen that it's okay to follow the D400, the road that abuts the coast to Mersin. That's not the only message I get from the street. There is also ample illustration that this part of Turkey is becoming noticeably more urban. The proof is in the litter and I'm pleasantly surprised to see a number of people hauling crates on their motorcycles to pick up plastic that's on the streets and in the bins.

There are some fourth-century Roman ruins at the entry to Ayaş, where I stumble into the first hotel with a security guard since the one in Alanya. The short and sweet black-haired female guard walks me down to the water at the boundary of the Neopolis Hotel to prove that I can't get around or over their fence. Then she lets me walk myself out the front door.

I pass through Kumkuyu and Limonlu and note that Limonlu is an apt name because everyone on the roadside is selling limes, lemons or pomegranates. In fact, the fruit grown here must be very special because heavy-duty fencing protects the trees from invading illicit fruit pickers. A bit later, in Erdemli, a giant lemon sculpture decorates the entry to the town.

About three-quarters of the day's walk is not on the D400. There's a national park just before Erdemli and a spiffy promenade on the seaside through the town of 115,000 people. It seems that Erdemli hosted the weightlifting competition during the 2013 Mediterranean Games (Mersin, where I'm heading, was the host city and the beach volleyball was in Kizkalesi) and I presume the promenade, and maybe some other more or less eye-pleasing things in a town overloaded with forgettable high-rise apartment buildings, exist because of the games. Though not everything was completed on time. I am amused by a sign for a €4 million waste-water collection and storm water drainage project due to start on 23.01.2012 and finish on 26.07.2013. For the record, it still hadn't started on 26.09.2014.

I run into the Alata Horticultural Research Station and am told by their security guard to forget about getting inside and keep walking on the D400. I follow orders for another five kilometers until I get to the deliciously named town of Arpaçbahşiş, where I cut down to the beach. Then I MedTrek for six more kilometers along a high-rise congested beach (a typical complex is called Flamengo 1, 2, 3 and 4) and give up, after a 40-kilometer day, in a place called Tömük, because I'm over high-rises.

The next day, I hope to make it from Tömük into Mersin to have an urban base camp and give Liz an easy first day back on the MedTrek. I'm not worried about the cloudy morning sky because my buddy at the Inka Hotel, Mehmet Seyran, assured me with a voice that precluded contradiction that "it will be partly cloudy, no rain."

Within half a kilometer, I have meandered through another maze of seaside high-rise buildings (high rise here means up to 20 floors) and am walking on a path between the sea and a complex of more tolerable two-story condos. I know I've left rural Turkey behind when I overhear three Turks on a morning walk having a serious discussion in English about "franchises" and see a Turkish couple taking a morning dip with the pompous air and aplomb of an English couple at their country estate. The restaurant owners are in a great mood and one even lets me pay for a tea, which only costs a lira (less than fifty cents), with some loose change that probably didn't total more than seventy kuruş (much less than fifty cents).

For some reason, I grow to like some of the taller apartment complexes, figuring that for middle-to-lower income Turks they are a vast improvement over some of the dilapidated squats I've seen near the sea. Often, at the squats, the living room furniture, usually a couch and a few tossed-away-by-wealthier-neighbors comfy chairs, are on the outside "porch." At one place, a hammock served as the bed and a campfire served as the stove. I also presume that more high rises are going up because people must be able to afford to buy them.

Anyway, that's what I tell a man I meet who lives in nearby Silifke, a town founded by Seleucus I Nicator, one of Alexander's generals. The young adult had gone to college as an undergrad in the US and was now going through the application process for a master's program in civil engineering at the University of Maryland.

The hard rain hits at noon, after only 12 kilometers, and I jump on a city bus (because I don't have a card, a man pays my way and I have an hour-long ride into Mersin for free) and get off in the middle of the town on the beach road. Then, in order to stay in a room with a view of the sea, I *dolmuş* back to a Hilton I saw to check on airport shuttles and room rates in view of Liz's arrival.

There are three more torrential downpours during the afternoon that make me glad I quit walking. I really know I've hit new MedTrek territory when I actually book a room, using a fraudulent corporate discount code, at the Hilton, one of the few hotels on the sea in Mersin. I always joke that "It's not the Hilton" when people ask me about my choice of accommodation on the MedTrek, but now (and I would have considered this against my religion a few years ago), "It IS the Hilton."

The Hilton turns out to be very practical, accommodating and romantic. The bus station is steps away and we'll be able hear the pleasant lapping of the waves and look out over the sea in our view-rich west-facing room on the 6th floor. I take the Turkish Air bus from the stadium near the Hilton to pick Liz up at the Adana airport. The next day we'll get a *dolmuş* back to Tece, where the rain had stopped me in my tracks, and walk into Mersin.

My *Follow The Idiot* item this week is entitled "Why Doesn't The Idiot Swim to Syria" and includes shots of me swimming on my current MedTrek outing. But Liz and I don't get in the water, even though it's her first day back on the MedTrek since we stumbled together into Antalya and its labyrinthine port a few months ago.

Our walk from Tece into Mersin is more pleasant, despite the apartments, than what I've seen the past couple days. There's a paved seaside sidewalk/promenade for ten kilometers and the apartment complexes are more spacious and less offensive than before. We also are exposed to enough local color – a bountiful Turkish breakfast, women kneading dough and cooking *gözleme*, women dressed in full-length black or in full-body swimsuits to walk their children in the water, women working in the fields, men playing backgammon in cafes, stray cats and dogs – to make Liz delighted to be back in Turkey.

We run into Pompeiopolis/Soli, a wonderful ruin that dates back to 700 BC and was visited by Alexander the Great before the Romans constructed over 200 colonnades. I take a photo contrasting the remaining

29 columns with the apartment buildings and Liz says, "You obviously have a thing about Turkish apartment buildings."

We sit on a bench and look ahead to Mersin, a town that includes what was once Turkey's tallest (55 floors) building, a mosque with six minarets (I get a shot with the minarets contrasting with palm trees) and over 20 ships awaiting a berth in the harbor.

We walk 21 kilometers on the 150-meter wide promenade that abuts the four-lane road. It features a central area planted with palms, a wide jogging path, exercise stations with the typical Turkish workout equipment, cafés, thousands of black cats/kittens (this is not the place to be superstitious about a black cat crossing your path), a seafront of gigantic rocks and a pleasure boat marina with a Migros supermarket where we buy a few Noggers. The reason the seaside walk is so spacious and there are – with the exception of the Hilton – so few buildings is because this is all reclaimed land. This is one of the saving graces, if not THE saving grace, of the town.

I learn about the reclamation project and pick up other news about Mersin from Onur Aygül, a 30-something Turk who has visited the US and is now working in Vienna, when we met on the shuttle to the Adana airport. In fact, Onur was staying with his family at the Dudum Hotel in Aydincik but, though we saw each other there, we didn't speak. During the bus ride we discuss the situation in Syria and other global topics but the most valuable information he gives me is a list of restaurants with the best fish, meat and liver in town – all within walking distance of the Hilton.

## SWEET SIXTEEN

It's a delightful MedTrek kickoff the next morning and I again fall in love with the spacious, buildingless promenade in Mersin as we walk east of the Hilton to arrive at the barrier to the town's gigantic and impenetrable (think high fences, razor wire, security guards) port complex about six kilometers away.

This walkway is everything a seaside promenade should be, with a spacious road for cars, a truly capacious area for everyone else, a spot reserved for the military with the usual warnings and fences, and no ugly buildings on the sea except for a pleasure boat marina, some Disneylandish carnival rides and a subdued modern conference center.

The promenade is also a complete contrast to the buzzy port that is filled with ships stacked with containers from every conceivable company from everywhere. The dozens of ships waiting for a berth indicate that Mersin never sleeps and we walk another six kilometers to get past the port. Then another eight kilometers take us along the sea and on roads past lots of chemical and petroleum plants emitting various noxious smells as lines of trucks wait to load or unload in front of every facility.

The only contact with humanity, or inhumanity, is a goat herder who illustrates to Liz with a cutting movement across his throat that his goats will "soon be for Allah" because of Kurban Bayrami, or the four Sacrifice Feast Days in early October. In fact, we begin noticing lots of sheep and goats for sale in local markets. It turns out that Kurban Bayrami is a very big deal.

Kazanli, where we arrive after twenty kilometers, is a modest but very friendly town (a young boy brings us chairs and tea when we sit down to change our shoes) with more policemen and *dolmuşes* than any place this small merits.

After the trudge through the industrial zone, we arrive at a hard-sanded beach abutting agricultural land next to a smooth, gentle sea that's a dramatic contrast to the recent stormy waters. No other hikers, just a few fishermen and lots of farm laborers tilling and tractoring. There are three rivers – the first one we cross on an upriver bridge, the second we cross by boat (after having tea with the two backgammon-playing village chieftains who secure us an oarsman), and the third we cross by foot (stupidly wearing only sandals; I endure a few cuts and scrapes because I can't see the bottom of the river). There are also a few dozen beach shacks – all of them abandoned. I get a photo of one shack and advertise it online as an airy B&B for $10 a night while Liz finds scores of sea shells by the seashore. One, she says, is destined for the Smithsonian.

Everyone tells us we're crazy to try to hike to Tuzla because of the multi-mouthed Seyhan (it separates Mersin and Adana provinces) and Ceyhan Nehri Rivers, which reach the sea west and east of Adana. We're forced to give up even before we reach Tuzla because of the swampy and remote conditions. But before we head inland we spend an hour having tea in one of the dirtiest, unhealthiest tents ever pitched on the Mediterranean. It houses a construction crew of four (the single "bed" for the workers and the rest of the mosquito-filled accommodation are not just a mess but a bug-infested pig-sty mess). We listen, without understanding more than a few words, to Nazim Bulut talk about a new luxury hotel that will be constructed precisely where we're sitting. Please hurry. It can only be an improvement.

Getting back to Mersin takes well over two hours, but we get a lift from two men, one of them an English-speaking electrical engineer named Serken who went to school in Cyprus and works in Adana. That ride takes us north from the sea to the D400 where we catch a bus back to town.

We rebase ourselves in Karataş, a small city 47 kilometers south of Adana with one of the most bustling small commercial ports I've seen in Turkey and also lots of *sitesi*, or residences, that aren't as bustling as the port, though it's now out of season and that may be the reason that they look emptier than empty.

The beach walk into Karataş is on more of the hard sand that we MedTrekked a few days ago. There are several small restos on the beach cooking fish (I see kids with a net bring in five good-sized fish), though the one I walk into tells me there's *yok* (no) chai, which is an odd social experience.

"Seriously?" I ask. "No chai in a Turkish café?"

"*Yok*," says the barman.

When we walk into town we pass an archaeological dig at the Magarsus theater, where we can see the beach back to Mersin in one direction and the mountains just north of Syria in the other.

I try to flag down a *dolmuş* that has "Karataş" written on the front as I edge back towards town but he buzzes right by me (after the inexplicable absence of tea, I almost take this personally) and we're escorted back to the Oykum Butik Hotel in a police car. The cops had seen our attempt to stop the *dolmuş* and obviously felt we were in need of professional help or some TLC (Turkish Loving Care).

The next morning we're eager to walk north towards the Ceyhan River, which was called the Pyramus in ancient times when the area was known as Cilicia. It doesn't take a map-reader to realize that there will be a lot of water between Karataş and Yumurtalik. Not just the majestic Ceyhan River, but also many smaller rivers, canals, lakes (they call them *dalyan*), lagoons and even genuine seas, like the Avciali Gölü lies in our path.

Once we get going we admire numerous new apartment complexes and visit the Ciz Magarsa Park Hotel, which also houses a tourism university. Then we cut inland close to villages like Bahçe, Bebeli and Yeşiköy. On the way, we discover sand dunes and peanuts, which apparently grow well in a sandy soil. That alone, this fortuitous blending of sand and nut, probably would have made this ex-President Jimmy Carter's favorite part of Turkey. We also see sheep being butchered and cut up for the Sacrifice Feast Day meals, one of the many Jewish/Christian/Muslim holidays occurring on this autumn weekend. In fact, when we walk through Bebeli we are invited to two feasts and every car on the road seems to be full of families going to join relatives for lunch.

We again learn the power of hitchhiking by not hitchhiking. A number of people, obviously in a merry holiday mood, offer us rides.

I mention to two Turks how happy I am to be crossing the Ceyhan River (they are amazed that I know it by name) and meet a family of four, led by father Nevzat Altunay, who asks us to pose with his kids for a photograph. An aquaculture engineer studying fish in the local rivers, Nevzat speaks English, like Serken the other day, because he went to a university in Cyprus. He thoroughly enjoys telling me about his job and the local wildlife and the flora – in fact, he takes a detour off the road to point out a unique tree, the *halep çamliği*, and invites me to watch him research fish.

A while later Liz and I see a large grouper on the beach and think its gills are moving enough that, in contrast to the many sheep and goats being slaughtered, it might have chance at a second life. We tenderly and carefully get it back in the sea and in unison say "Inshallah."

At one point, Liz and I are separated due to our respective walking paces and her time-consuming fixation to photograph sheep. When she sees me take a turn off the main road far ahead of her, she gets into a car with a respectable looking Turk to catch up. He turns out to be not respectable at all and makes a pass at her, forcing her to almost jump out of the moving vehicle. She's not very pleased with me. Note to self: Don't let that happen again and remember to walk at the pace of the slowest walker. Stay close and keep a better eye on my beloved walking companion.

Throughout the day, we're struck by the numerous shabby shanty camps of nomadic Turkish, Kurdish and foreign cotton pickers and agricultural workers in towns like Kaldirim. Although not quite down to the level of refugee camps, they're definitely the yang to the apartment building yin.

When we return to Karataş from Yumurtalik at the end of a 30-kilometer day, a passenger on the *dolmuş* asks where we're from and I perfunctorily respond "California."

He looks us over, from head to toe, slowly, and says in perfect English: "What the hell happened?"

We meet two Syrian evacuees at the hotel and I give them a brief course on how to be welcomed as a refugee in Germany, Sweden or the US.

"Doing a cutting hand movement to your neck to illustrate what will happen if you return to Syria is the best explanation," I suggest, thinking of the shepherd we saw a few days earlier.

The most memorable event in Karataş occurs the next morning when I look out to sea and spot the most extraordinary sea tornado, or waterspout, that I've ever seen on the Mediterranean. Wondrous. For the record, it appeared and disappeared shortly after 8 a.m. on Sunday, October 5, 2014.

In Yumurtalik, which seems like a buzzing metropolis after Karataş, we have a fish-and-salad lunch at Sabahattin Eskindağ's hole-in-the-wall harbor restaurant called Sabonun Yeri. A masseuse/reflexologist from Adana helps us order a meal that starts at two and lasts until five when we finally discover that Eskindağ is the town's poet laureate and the author of a book of poems about the Mediterranean.

Liz adopts some dogs on the beach and we stroll back through Ayas Castle (which includes an offshore island adjunct that's billed as another "Maiden's Castle") to the BCT Hotel where we enjoy a local concert from chairs on our fourth floor balcony before going out for some baklava at the café down the street.

The next morning starts off badly when the promised breakfast isn't ready at 7 a.m. and still isn't ready at 7:30. But I rebound by the time we head out of town and run into Gold City, three 16-floor apartment complexes that are so elaborate and ornate they remind many of Emerald City in *The Wizard of Oz*. From there it's a pleasant ten-kilometer walk on the cliffy, sometimes-rocky-sometimes-sandy beach (Liz, who's worried about her best friend who is very ill, surreptitiously collects enough stones and shells, perhaps fifteen pounds' worth, to weigh down her pack for the rest of the day) until a razor wire fence at a tight-security thermal power complex blocks us.

We cut inland along the perimeter of the impenetrable fence and are approached by one of the many guards who, after negotiation by telephone with someone speaking English, takes us to the east entrance of the complex. Without the ride (and pleasant treatment that included tea and directions out of the place as well as a strict "No photos!" admonition), we would have had to cut far inland and away from the sea.

A bit further on is the Botaş oil and natural gas terminal that has an equally tight security policy – including armed guards and surveillance stations on the seaside – that normally would have led to the expulsion of MedTrekkers long before they rang the doorbell. Botaş is the end of the Kirkuk–Ceyhan Oil Pipeline that has been transporting oil to the Mediterranean from Northern Iraq since the 1970s. Nearby is the oil terminal for crude oil pipeline from Baku that opened in 2006 and a recently built coal-fired power plant.

Fortunately we get the same treatment at Botaş as we did at the thermal power plant. A manager, who looks much further up the food chain than the guards, takes us in his pickup to the Iskenderun side of the facility (Liz scores some chocolate from him on the way) and we resume our walk after the guards at that end give us some tea and pomegranates.

The industrialization continues in the town of Toros, where there are coal and cement factories, and beyond that into Erzin where General Electric has just completed a natural gas power plant that supplies the Turkish grid with three percent of its power, according to 30-year-old Fatih Yaktubay, who works for GE and gives us a long lift from Erzin Beach, where we end the 34-kilometer MedTrekking day in the shadow of the GE plant, back to Yumurtalik.

During the ride we discuss Turkish sacrificial feast days, dogs and the US political scene. He tells us that the area from Mersin to Hatay is called Cukurova and when he drops off says, "You're very lucky to have your MedTrek project."

Liz, still weighed down with seashells, amuses Fatih when she offers him a shell as a gift that he accepts with a smile.

We're at the location where Alexander and his Hellenic League fought the key and much-studied Battle of Issus against Darius III and his Achaemenid Empire on both sides of the Pinarus River in November 333 BC. After Granicus in the north, this was the second major victory of Alexander's Asian campaign.

Some 30,000 Macedonian troops faced 100,000 (some historians put the figure as high as 300,000) Persians near what is now Iskenderun and books have been written about how and why the battle illustrated Alexander's tactical brilliance.

"In marshalling, arming and ruling an army, he was exceedingly skillful and very renowned for rousing the courage of his soldiers, filling them with hopes of success, and dispelling their fear in the midst of danger by his own freedom from fear," wrote Arrian of Nicomedia in the second century AD.

Alexander prayed to a rainbow of gods before the battle and afterwards built temples to Zeus, Hercules and Athena and changed the name of the nearby city from Issue to Iskenderun, the equivalent of "Alexandria" in Turkish.

The important victory enabled Alexander to open the *Pylae Syriae*, or Syrian Gates, and then head south to take control of Phoenicia, Palestine, and Egypt. It expanded his control on the Mediterranean and further prevented any incursion from the Persian navy. He continued to reject the creation of a Macedonian navy until seven years later.

The spoils of the battle included 3,400 pounds of bejeweled drinking cups and "seventeen bartenders in service of the Great King."

Arrian recounts that "When he beheld the bathing vessels, the water-pots, the pans, and the ointment boxes, all of gold, curiously wrought...and passed into a pavilion of great size and height, where the couches and tables and preparations for an entertainment were perfectly magnificent, Alexander turned to those about him and said, 'This, it seems, is royalty.'"

But he also had critics in his midst.

One fairly constant critic was Cleitus the Black, the officer who had saved Alexander's life at the Battle of the Granicus and was later killed by him in a drunken fight.

"Did you conquer Asia by yourself, Alexander? I mean, who planned the Asian invasion? Was it not your father? Or is *his* blood no longer good enough?" Cleitus says in Arrian's account. "Evil tyrant you are! Evil tyrant you've become Alexander. Pay attention lad; your father's still watching over you!"

"I am not my father," Alexander replied. "I've taken you farther than my father ever dreamed!"

The domestic situation in Syria didn't deter Alexander when he was here. Plutarch describes how, after the battle of Issus, he sent troops to Damascus "to seize upon the money and baggage, the wives and children of the Persians." This, said Plutarch, "gave the Macedonians such a taste of the Persian wealth and women and barbaric splendor of living, that they were ready to pursue and follow upon it with all the eagerness of hounds upon a scent."

I'm sure that Alexander would be happy to know that Iskenderun is now a thriving town, though it would be nice if he returned to destroy some of the industrial installations on the seaside.

When ferrying the MedTrek base camp to Iskenderun, we're so offended by the sight/site of the industrial complexes, including Iskender Iron and Steel Works, which blocks access to the sea for 15 kilometers, that I finally succumb to Alexander's advice to "take the chariot" and skip a walk on that blemished part of the Turkish coast to get into town.

The next morning we take off along Iskenderun's wide, grassy and sculpture-filled promenade (like in Mersin, there are few buildings on the seaside itself) and see an innovative machine that feeds stray dogs and is triggered when a benefactor recycles a plastic bottle. Beyond that is a remarkable sculpture of a man pulling in a fish net, then a military installation that looks like a barracks for officers and their families.

The walk is pleasant enough until we see a rare sign that reads "Forbidden To Swim" in English, Arabic and Turkish and that gets me thinking about all of the factories that have not only barred access to the sea but are probably among the likely polluters. Not that these factories are the only things separating us from the sea – the Iskenderun Navy base and many other military facilities are also to blame. And the sea isn't the only thing that's polluted here. There's very noticeable smog consisting of lots of exhaust spewed out by trucks, buses and cars and contained by the mountains.

Once rocky beaches replace the promenade, fences separate every bit of property from every other bit of property. Between the fences, we see a restaurant with a balcony over the sea, a municipal beach with a caretaker who likes the rock group Aerosmith, a Turkish woman living in Germany who joins us in bemoaning the litter on the beaches (and there's a lot from start to finish today) and three Turkish women – Felice, Semra and Cennet – who invite us for tea. The topic of discussion: weight and marriage.

We continue on a combination of seaside (often rocky) and road (often busy and narrow) and, after tea and baklava at the Sindirella

Pastansi pastry shop, finally wind up on hard sand beaches, clay beaches and rocky beaches that take us to Arsuz just in time for sunset. "An easy and calm day," says Liz who initially felt unsafe about the walk and was afraid we'd get fenced in.

One positive note, especially after the Mersin apartments, is that in Iskenderun there are very few high apartment buildings but many *sitesis* and *kents* with comfortable two-story condos and homes.

When we get a lift back from the beach to the bus station in Arsuz the driver invites us to come "shower, sleep and anything else you want" at his place and three women on the bus invite us for tea. Hospitable Turks!

When we are the last ones remaining on the bus, the driver blasts the music (Turkish music excites Liz and it is, of course, everywhere – though turned down during the calls to prayer) just as we pass the PrimeMall where there's a Robert's Coffee Shop. Roberts isn't the only English name I see here – there's the My House Restaurant and the No Excuse Kebab.

"What made Alexander tick?" asks Liz, after I describe the Battle of Issus over coffee on a terrace in Iskenderun.

"Glory, honor, loyalty, courage, valor, love and fame all got him here and kept him going," I say, probably paraphrasing many historians who've written about Alexander. "He was noble in war, endured the same hardships as his troops and introduced new military maneuvers that confused the Persians. He not only fought alongside his troops but usually treated them well, knowing the names of thousands, always visiting the wounded and giving the dead funerals and honors.

"There are descriptions of him 'appearing everywhere' during a battle and when two soldiers had abused the wives of some strangers, he told their commander to sentence them to death if they were guilty. Alexander never showed great enthusiasm for women and apparently refused to take sexual advantage of any of the thousands of women captured in battle. In Ecbatana, an ancient city in Media in western Iran, he was offered 100 armed 'Amazon' horsewomen but declined them because he worried that his troops would abuse them."

"My two favorite anecdotes about Alexander at war are when he refused to attack at night because it would be unfair to the enemy ("I don't want to steal a victory"), and when he refused a peace offer from Darius to obtain "in exchange for his amity and alliance, all the countries on this side the river Euphrates, together with one of his daughters in marriage."

Liz takes a day off and I leave Arsuz in the direction of Kale, 30 kilometers away. I'm immediately impressed by the Ulucinar River and the fact that Christian-ruled Arsuz has the only non-Muslim mayor in Turkey. As I head south, I pass the River Tenis (sic) Club, then the Arsuz Palm

Hotel and am given four heavy pomegranates by a farmer who tells me to keep an eye open for Fergin, who owns the Orient Camping site in Konaçik. He says Fergin "knows everything."

In fact, Fergin happens to be waiting for a *dolmuş* in front of the Orient when I walk by and does not seem at all surprised that I know his name. Although he's in noticeable pain and says he's on the way to a dentist's appointment in Iskenderun, I pump him for his reputed wealth of information. And he shows some respect when I tell him I walked much of Turkey's coast and that some of my favorite beaches included Turgutreis, Gumusluk, Yalikavak, Bardakci, Gumbet, Icmeler, Bitez, Aktur, Ortakent Yalisi, Karaincir, Aspat, Bagla and Akyarlar.

"This used to be a key route for all the Europeans who would drive through Turkey, Syria and Jordan to Africa but that, of course, is all over now," Fergin says. "You can keep walking all the way to Samandağ, but be sure you have enough food and water because there's nothing between here and there. The end of the *dolmuş* line is nine kilometers away in Işikli."

I cut down to the beach, rather than take the inland road to Işikli, and, after negotiating my way through olive and lemon groves, walk on the rocky, cliffy, difficult-to-negotiate beach for the next ten kilometers. It's a dramatic up-and-down slow-mode walk with exceptional views and terrain that requires some rock climbing (I'm wearing special shoes and gloves) to negotiate the cliffs.

When I'm finally blocked and can't keep going on the beach, I climb a cliff with lots of loose rocks and recite the usual note-to-self about how stupid it is to do a climb like this when I'm on my own (if there's one thing I haven't learned after eighteen years of MedTrekking, this is it). I am sweaty, breathless, exhausted and relieved when I finally reach the top. My heart's beating faster than it ever has and, between us, I'm slightly concerned.

"I'll never do that again!" I again tell myself.

I decide it's time to walk on the road – which is one of those very narrow, very little-traveled curvy seaside roads with delightful views – and realize that I'm out of water. I get some residue from tossed away bottles and buy two liters, and a bag of potato chips for the salt, when I reach Kale. The market owner invites me to have dinner with his family and I sit down for *ayran*, pita bread, a salad, rice and a dish of fried meat with peppers (which I can still taste as I write this years later).

I get a lift back to Arsuz with a fisherman, who stops his car at various places to drop off his catch to private customers, and then take a *dolmuş* back to Iskenderun for our last night. The next morning we plan to move the base camp south past Hatay, which was biblically known as Antioch, to Samandağ.

Liz and I return to Kale and, on one of those blissful, beautiful days of MedTrekking, walk to Samandağ on a nearly carless road that continuously abuts the sea. The air, fishermen, views, mountains and everything else are meditatively perfect. It's Big Sur and green Swiss hills on a placid Mediterranean.

The only thing bigger than the beach, which stretches for almost 20 kilometers, are the gigantic restaurants that apparently fill to capacity in August but are empty tonight. We meet a young couple and their uncle just outside Cevlik, a spot famous for its nesting sea turtles. They are from Antakya, but live in Istanbul and we all celebrate the day with a sunset-to-dark *balik ekmek*, a popular street food sandwich with grilled fish and various vegetables.

As we look south, we can see the lights of the Syrian port of Latakia down the coast.

The next day we hike into Samandağ, which gets its name from Jebel Sem'an, or Saint Symeon Mountain, in Syria and was founded in 300 BC by Seleucus Nicator, one of Alexander the Great's generals. Samandağ still has lots of Arabic speakers (Turkey annexed it from Syria in 1939) and, despite its reputation as a recruiting location for ISIS, is an ideal spot for the final base camp at the end of my last segment of MedTrekking in Turkey.

The following morning, we take off on the town's famous sandy beaches, aware that we'll hit the Orontes (aka Asi) River, on a day that's already sent us one downpour. In the distance is Mount Aqraa, a sacred mountain that has been called the Mount Olympus of the Near East and has a past filled with tales of Baal, the god of thunderstorms.

True to the map, we hit the river after six kilometers and are the only people there who are not interested in fishing. The preferred method of fishing is to attach a line to a balloon-like inflatable, let the wind pull it out and catch fish on the multiple lures (I call it "bubble fishing").

Everyone tells us the river is too deep to cross and rather than embarrassing ourselves in front of all the fishermen we walk four kilometers upstream, passing rich and fertile fields and lots of people walking, or riding on horse-drawn carts, towards the beach.

Once across the bridge, we continue through dusty, dirty-despite-the-rain villages, much to the amusement of baffled locals, until we finally reach the base of Mount Aqraa, where we meet two gay Christians, George and Arnold, who keep crossing themselves and are pleased to meet some non-Muslims. We consider following the one-way road that goes up the mountain to Yayikdamlar, and from there to Yeditepe, but are told by everyone we meet, including *dolmuş* drivers and the young guard at the local *Jandarma*, that it's very dangerous.

"Syria is only a few kilometers away," say George and Arnold in unison as I send a GPS to indicate where I'm ending the MedTrek on the Turkish coast.

The moment the message is sent, dark clouds enshroud the mountain, there are flashes of lightening and bursts of thunder, and a hard rain begins to fall.

Although we go as far as we can on the Turkish coast, I still want to see Syria and what lies ahead on the MedTrek before I throw in the headscarf and leave Turkey. This desire leads to a wildly serendipitous day that takes us beyond Yeditepe to the Syrian border in truly rural Turkey. Although far from the sea, I figure on the next MedTrek outing we can presumably get a ride back to the coast once we cross the border into Syria.

We accompany three Turks in the back of their truck as they make various calls on clients in the hinterland for their window installation and repair business. The high points of the day include the lengthy drive in stark mountains on narrow roads abutting Mount Aqraa; a few encounters with the Turkish military; numerous stops for clients, tea and the consumption of purely natural products (pomegranates, grapes, homemade bread, olives, peppers, figs, tangerines) and a look at farm animals (lambs, puppies, chicks); wondrous views into Syria and back towards and beyond Samandağ; and the company of the aforementioned Turks who argue like The Three Stooges, although at one point I think that they might sell us to the top bidder in Syria.

Our initial encounter was completely random (I mentioned at a café that Liz and I were looking for a lift to Yeditepe and one of the truck passengers responded that they were heading in that direction), but as the day progresses it seems to be destiny. At the end of the afternoon, we go back to the home of the big boss, meet his kids and grandkids, have a fish sandwich dinner on the seaside, and agree to meet at their home the next evening for dinner.

This is yet another example of *misafir*, or hospitality. It's one of the key concepts/truths that has been demonstrated to me throughout Turkey and that will keep us in Samandağ for another day.

The Turks, who I thought would be conniving and bargaining and scamming, turn out to be inviting, accommodating and trustworthy.

Another example occurs later that night when a silk merchant in Samandağ takes me to his shop and gives me a scarf that, he says, "shouts out intellectual like you are."

He wants nothing in return but a soft head butt, which is the way male Turkish friends frequently greet and say goodbye to each other.

After our tour to the border, it seems feasible to walk across the border at the first inland route, return to the coast in Syria, and stroll south to Lebanon in just a few days.

Really, who would notice?

The US State Department, of course, doesn't encourage American citizens to travel anywhere there's whiff of trouble, and I usually discount their advice. They are unequivocal, however, when it comes to Syria. Here are just a few excerpts from a lengthy travel warning in 2014:

"The Department of State continues to warn US citizens against all travel to Syria and strongly recommends that US citizens remaining in Syria depart immediately...The security situation remains dangerous and unpredictable as a violent conflict between government and armed anti-government groups continues throughout the country, along with an increased risk of kidnappings, bombings, murder, and terrorism...No part of Syria should be considered safe from violence...There is a terrorist threat from violent extremist groups including the Islamic State of Iraq and the Levant, (ISIL), formerly known as al-Qa'ida in Iraq (AQ), the al-Nusrah Front, and others...US citizens have been specifically targeted for kidnapping, both for ransom and political purposes, and murdered by members of terrorist and violent extremist groups in Syria....Due to the security situation in Syria, the US government's ability to help US citizens kidnapped or taken hostage is very limited..." It goes on.

People I meet on the ground also aren't too hot on the idea of walking into Syria, which today is the Mediterranean's most violent country.

"You have nothing to worry about anywhere in Turkey but cross the border and you're like a sacrificial lamb," says Mehmet Seyran in Kizkalesi. "Damascus was a joy five years ago but I have no interest in going there today. Nor should you!"

"Bomb, bomb!" says Karataş taxi driver Thin Kanga when I mention Syria.

"I'm solo cycling from Athens to Jerusalem but have just decided to fly over Syria to Tel Aviv," says cyclist Paul Wilma, the Belgian who works for IBM in San Jose. "Why play with fire?"

I remind Liz that the first country I was unable to enter was Algeria when I arrived at the border with Luke after MedTrekking 531 kilometers across northern Morocco. That country had been in turmoil since 1990 when the Islamic party, which had won a fair election, was not allowed to assume office. The Algerian Civil War with the Armed Islamic Group of Algeria may have officially ended in 2002, but the counter insurgency continues and I don't think I'd walk in Algeria even today.

At that time, I returned to my starting point in Antibes and headed the other way around the Med through less-dangerous Italy.

"I didn't set out on the MedTrek to get killed," I remember telling Elisa, an American journalist, as we discussed the logistics of the walk from Antibes to Nice. "It would have been vainglorious, if not suicidal, to enter war-torn Algeria. I'll tackle it from the other side after I walk through Monaco, Italy, Albania, Greece, Turkey, Syria, Lebanon, Israel, Egypt, Libya, Tunisia and a few other countries."

But where will I go now?

# TO SYRIA OR NOT TO SYRIA?

We're staying at the pretentiously named Grand Anadalou Palace, which is within spitting distance of the sea in Samandağ Deniz, a ten-minute *dolmuş* ride from the inland "downtown." There's a circular mosque on the main drag and a friendly local population that makes us feel distant from nearby Syria until...

...I'm sitting in the lobby playing online Scrabble (the Wi-Fi connection in our room is dicey) around 9 p.m. when a 30-something business type in a suit, who appears to be a Turk, gets up from his seat in the gargantuan dining room and addresses me in the best English I've heard since I got into town.

"What room are you in?"

I say, "I can't remember."

"What are you doing here?"

I say, "Trying to play Scrabble."

"What is your occupation?"

I say, "I play Scrabble."

"Where is your wife?"

I say, "Shopping."

"In the bazaar? Now?"

I say, "No, she's not bizarre."

"Where'd you get that ugly tie?" I ask. "Are you a car salesman? Or just a low-level government agent?"

"I'm going outside for a cigarette," he says.

I never see him again.

It doesn't take a super sleuth to figure out that this guy is either a government agent, a foreign agent, an ISIS recruiter or, maybe, a badly dressed, overly curious car salesman.

But when I tell Liz about the conversation, then get in bed, then hear noises on the ceiling from the room above, I think the mystery man could be a kidnapper for ISIS and immediately imagine that we'll be taken away in the middle of the night. When I'm still awake at two a.m., I think it might be time to get out of Dodge.

After all, we've come as close to Syria (just a few kilometers as the bird flies) as I want to get.

Paranoid?

It reminds me of a situation in Morocco in the summer of 1970 when I'd scored some hash and there was a pounding, middle-of-the-night knock on the door of my cheap hotel room in Tangier. I imagined it was either the police or the drug dealer and instinctively flushed my entire stash down the toilet. They, whoever they were, left without breaking down the door and I'll never know whether it was the police, the drug dealer or a car salesman.

The next morning, we decide to stay and have dinner with our border-visiting Turkish friends and enjoy the fresh fish that they barbecue on the roof of the family apartment building downtown.

I send Idiot-ic followers my first MEDTREK MILESTONE since my last book ended in İzmir.

# MEDTREK MILESTONE #11

We've made it to the Syrian border after five separate MedTrek outings in Turkey and now I've got to decide whether to walk, or not to walk, in Syria. A video I just posted keeps my options open.

# FOLLOW THE IDIOT

## CHAPTER PHOTOS

## CHAPTER MAP

# IDIOT-IC FACTS

Idiot-ic readers frequently mention that they find *The Idiot and the Odyssey* books full of facts and figures.

Here are some facts that you'll find in *The Idiot and the Odyssey: Walking the Mediterranean* and *The Idiot and the Odyssey II: Myth, Madness and Magic on the Mediterranean.*

# PART THREE

## A DIVIDED CYPRUS

*Reaching No Man's Land on Cyprus*

*Meeting Aphrodite in the Republic of Cyprus*

*MedTrekking Through the Turkish Republic of Northern Cyprus*

# Reaching No Man's Land on Cyprus

"With Cyprus, we shall acquire the absolute sovereignty of the sea." – *Alexander the Great*

"And lads, feast tonight, for tomorrow we will dine in Hades." – *Alexander the Great*

I plotted a trip to Syria between my autumn and spring MedTrek outings. Without going into too much detail, I worked out a theoretically failsafe plan to slip across the border from Turkey onto the seaside in northern Syria and to undertake a speedy undercover MedTrek down the 193-kilometer long coast. I figured that my under-the-radar walk would take me less than a week.

That winter plan prompted me to frequently fantasize about surreptitiously entering Syria not far from the section of the border that I first crossed in 1972 when I was driving from Paris to Cape Town. At that time, I was subjected to an intense search because the border patrol figured, solely due to the existence of the *Book of Joel* in the Old Testament, that I was Jewish. They spent a day taking my car, a red Simca with French plates, apart to find proof. They came up empty-handed and, after ten hours, let me through.

I visited Syria again in 1977 and, besides now MedTrekking from north to south on the short coast, I thought I might also try to revisit Palmyra, the ancient Semitic city near Homs that dates back to the Neolithic times. I want to witness and assess the recent devastation wreaked by ISIS, which destroyed many priceless monuments when they trashed the ancient ruins. In any event, I am sure that once I MedTrek through Syria there won't be any problem getting into refugee-filled Lebanon. To get myself in the mood for the walk I frequently order the Kabob Combo plate (think pita, tabouli, hummus, dolmas, gyros and kabobs) at a Syrian-owned restaurant in Redding, California.

Just before I left the United States, I visited a niece in Maine and her oldest son gave me a parting gift.

"Uncle Joel, because I love maps and want to travel, I'd like you to wear this necklace when you go to Syria on your next adventure so I'll feel like I'm with you," said then nine-year-old Seamus Henry, handing me a silver necklace with a heart-shaped pendant. "It'll keep you safe."

In mid-April 2015 I was ready to go, following the last stage of training to get me in shape for the MedTrek. This happened to occur amidst the Mayan ruins in the Tikal National Park in northern Guatemala where, among other things, I tested packing smart and traveling light for my lightning Middle East MedTrek outing.

What will I be carrying?

Here are some of the practical accessories and compact travel gear in my lightweight pack for the speedy stroll through Syria: a headlamp, an Idiot baseball cap, a Swiss army knife, euros and dollars, a pen, my passport, a GPS, a pedometer, a plug for Syrian sockets, an iPhone and iPad, two quick-drying pairs of shorts, three pairs of underwear, three pairs of socks, one light pair of pants, three T-shirts, one short sleeved perma-press shirt, a Speedo swimsuit, goggles, lightweight hiking shoes, a pair of Teva sandals, and toiletries, including a few band aids and bandages. Although I don't subscribe to any particular regime or dietary trend beyond the basic Mediterranean diet, I eat frugally the month before my departure to psych myself up and to feel lean and mean.

Despite the earlier warnings by the Turks I met, and a steady flow of adverse travel advisories and warnings from the US State Department and the UK Foreign Office, I am ready to go. Then Liz points out what an absolute pain in the ass it will be if I am arrested or kidnapped by ISIS or any of the other dysfunctional players in the Syrian conflict.

"Your totally selfishly motivated MedTrek could eventually be a time-consuming and worrying burden for more people than you'd like, from your mother and kids to your government and girlfriend," she says, perhaps still a bit upset that I don't plan to have her come along. "Not to mention that it could become a total embarrassment or, almost worse, lead to your death."

"Well," I reply, smiling. "A bookseller in Tasmania told me that the best way to sell my books would be to be killed on the MedTrek."

A few days before I get on the plane from Boston to Europe, I decide instead to first hike 648-kilometers around Cyprus, the third largest island in the Mediterranean Sea located off the coasts of Syria and Lebanon. In the end that will become 796 kilometers due to various detours and topographical challenges.

Once I made the decision – to go to Cyprus – I felt a bit stupid to have even considered going to Syria, admitting that, though it could have been an uneventful excursion, it might conceivably have led to my arrest, kidnapping, decapitation, murder or suicide. When I arrive in Frankfurt, I am feeling somewhat satisfied that I sagely decided to fly to Larnaca on Cyprus and MedTrek around that historically rich island, where human activity and archaeological remains date to the 10th millennium BC. It is a serendipitous reward for postponing (and I underline the word "postponing") Syria, because I'm not sure I would have gone to Cyprus at all had I been able to MedTrek in Syria.

The past – both the ancient past and the present past – on Cyprus is omnipresent. I've always been impressed that the island has been inhabited since the Neolithic era and colonized by the Mycenaeans, Phoenicians, Assyrians, Egyptians, Persians, Greeks, Romans, Arabs, French, Venetians, Ottomans and British. Ptolemy I, one of Alexander's generals and later the king of Egypt, took over Cyprus in 295 BC and his dynasty on the strategic island lasted until it was annexed by the Romans and made part of the province of Cilicia in 58 BC.

The oldest towns on Cyprus – including Citium or Kition as present-day Larnaca was called; Amathus, as contemporary Limassol was known; and Old Paphos, which is now simply Paphos – were buzzing Phoenician settlements that later were eclipsed by the Greek colonies, like Salamis, Soli, and New Paphos. Here's a bit of information for your next trivia contest that I wasn't aware of until now: Cyprus was called Geth in Hebrew and its inhabitants were known as Oittim.

It isn't just the glorious past that intrigues me about the strategically located island. It is also the fact that it has experienced an array of political, social, cultural and economic developments during the last fifty years that can only be described as surreal, Orwellian, Kafkaesque or, well, outta this world.

It's the current era, since independence from Britain in 1960 to the present, which really differentiates Cyprus from other Mediterranean islands and has intrigued me since I began following its evolution in high school more than fifty years ago.

Cyprus, and excuse me if you already know this, is partitioned into two states – the Greek Cypriot Republic of Cyprus in the south with about 60 percent of the land and the Turkish Republic of Northern Cyprus (TRNC). The result is a schizophrenic divide and hard-to-fathom separation that is policed, patrolled and occasionally maintained by the United Nations.

That perhaps doesn't sound unreasonable until you remember that the UN arrived here in 1964 and, well over five decades later, still maintains a peacekeeping force to monitor a 180-kilometer, or 112-mile, buffer zone that divides the island. There's even one Greek community in the north that is still supplied with food by the UN once a week.

That's not all. Britain still has two Sovereign Base Areas that they've kept since they granted Cyprus independence on August 16, 1960. When the British left they optimistically hoped that the Greek Cypriots and the Turkish Cypriots would live happily and peacefully in their respective areas. Fourteen years later, however, a military junta ruling Greece initiated a *coup d'état* in Cyprus with the aim of annexing the island and ruling it from Athens. Five days later on July 20, 1974, Turkey launched an invasion or, if you prefer their version, an intervention, that enabled them to ultimately create the Turkish Republic of Northern Cyprus in 1983. Today the Greek Cypriot National Guard and other countries and institutions have a military, or a more-than-just-diplomatic presence, and Russia is currently trying to establish a foothold.

The result is two languages (Turkish in the north, Greek in the south), two currencies (the Turkish lira in the north, the euro in the south), two religions (Islam in the north, Greek Orthodox in the south) and two of almost everything else. It's the Noah's Ark of Mediterranean islands. Although almost everyone agrees that the status quo is unacceptable, peace generally reigns and, despite numerous talks between the two sides, there's still no way to predict how Cyprus will evolve.

I repeat: Totally surreal, totally schizoid, totally strange.

As I fly over İzmir and down the Turkish coast in mid-April, I have an in-flight chat with a young Greek Cypriot psychologist who lives in Brussels and studies the impact of reality TV shows on participants' personalities. We agree these insipid shows are perfect for entitled, self-important Americans seeking 15 minutes of fame and some $, but acknowledge that they completely baffle much of the rest of the world, where there are, if you can believe it, more important preoccupations.

Then we discuss the situation in Cyprus – what divided the island, the recent discovery and exploitation of oil (which sparked increased interest by President Putin and the Russians), the general good terms between Turkish and Greek Cypriots on the streets, the fact that Cyprus might be isolated but is a pleasant place to get away from the European grey weather. Although he claims it's no problem going from one side of the island to the other unless you're a Turk from Turkey, he's only been to the north once in his life.

"We're all refugees and those of us who came south in 1974 find it very depressing to see Turks living in our homes," he says, talking about the division that forced Turks to head north and Greeks to move south. "And I'm sure the Turks who wound up in the north feel the same way."

The taxi driver who takes me to my just-booked Airbnb flat on Avenue Archbishop Makarios in Larnaca tells me, more than once, "This place is shit. Cypriots are crazy."

"Who in the world would put the UN, Turks and Greeks on one island that now seems to be mainly populated by the British?" he asks, suggesting that I walk through a British cemetery to see all the fresh graves in Larnaca and then visit a British army barracks in Dhekelia. "We also can show you Russian, Romanian, Albanian and immigrant workers who have come here to work. And did you hear about our financial collapse a few years ago? Things won't get better in Cyprus and I wish I hadn't been born here."

"Why don't you have something smaller than a €50 note?" he asks when I try to pay the fare.

My base camp is a cozy but spacious fifth-floor apartment with balconies looking onto the sea and port. Within an hour of arriving, I send a GPS from the rooftop just above my flat, take a quick shower and walk through the nearby British cemetery. I'm looking forward to my first MedTrek steps early the next morning.

I awaken to the chirping of dozens of different birds and a view of the rising sun over the Larnaca harbor before I have a meditation and stretching session on the roof and cook three sunny-side-up eggs over two pieces of toast for breakfast. I'm energized and prepared to kick off the day and begin six weeks of physical, spiritual, emotional and mental MedTrekking that will take me who knows or cares where while I circumnavigate the Cyprus coast.

Before I take off I send Ibrahim Cabbaroglu, who cooked us dinner on our last night in Turkey last October, a message on Facebook that reads: "Happy Birthday from Larnaca, Cyprus! I didn't realize when you cooked Liz and me that wonderful fish dinner at your home in Samandağ last October that I'd be restarting the MedTrek on your birthday.

"I somewhat reluctantly decided after our chat, and the visit to the Syrian border with your dad, not to walk into Syria but rather to MedTrek around Cyprus," I write him. "I'm starting this morning but wanted to let you know that your hospitality was not only the true definition of *misafir*, but also a highlight of our last outing in Turkey. Very gracious! *Teşekkür ederim*!"

That visit seems like eons ago as I admire the fully rounded orange-pink sun as it continues rising above the cranes and ships in the Larnaca harbor while going-to-work traffic gradually fills the seaside street below. I walk down five flights of stairs, turn right on Avenue Archbishop Makarios and enthusiastically kick off the MedTrek around Cyprus with gusto (I love the word gusto) – once again saying to myself, "Ah, I'm back on the path again."

The sun moves into the clouds above the port and, although there are some bright displays in a few shops, Larnaca still seems hung over and a bit dreary after the island's 2012 financial meltdown. The port is as seemingly quiet as the bike and walking path (they drive on the left here, so I'm facing traffic as I walk on the seaside) and there's only one fisherman at the first sandy beach that I reach just before 8 a.m.

Without thinking about it, I walk at a relaxing five-kilometer-an-hour pace and am delighted to pass the storage and industrial facilities found in every port and then just enjoy being back on the Med. I'm a bit disenchanted when, after about ten kilometers, I hit a very serious, heavy-duty fence that turns out to be barring my entrance to not just any military installation but to the HQ of "The Princess of Wales's Royal Regiment – Second Battalion – Alexander Barracks."

On the street is a café serving traditional British breakfasts, a grocery store with a British shop assistant and, even, a van with UK license plates purporting to sell "real British fish – haddock and salmon." Coals to Newcastle? I wonder. I feel I'm entering a back-to-the-past time-warp when I stroll by street signs for Mandalay Drive, Agincourt Lane and Waterloo Road. In fact, this is actually British soil – known as a Sovereign Base Area (SBA) – which might seem comforting to some but doesn't please everyone. A paint-sprayed bit of graffiti, which covers the original advertising message on a billboard, reads "SBA OUT."

When the British granted Cyprus independence in 1960, a key part of the deal was the establishment of several SBAs that shrewdly, and possibly forever, give Britain a strategic military foothold in the southern Mediterranean.

Enter any of these numerous fenced-off SBAs (at your peril if you don't have a base pass) and you'll find more street names like Suffolk and Worcester, attractive greens and parks, private beach clubs and typical English cinemas. I don't even consider challenging the military fences to enter one base as I walk down Derbyshire Road, pass St. John's School and descend into Happy Valley.

After the SBA, my next hurdle is the well-known electric power plant in Dhekelia, one of only three in the country, run by the Electricity Authority of Cyprus (EAC). Although it prevents me walking next to the sea, I notice that there's also an EAC Refugee Settlement, one of many established after July 1974 when the Turkish invasion created 200,000

Greek Cypriot refugees. I learn that the EAC houses 7,000 refugees mainly from Famagusta but that only ten work at the power station. I silently applaud this seemingly charitable corporate action while, as I walk further east, I see two white cars with an oversized UN written on them in black letters.

I continue between the sea and the autoroute through fields of rich red earth, then on lava-like beaches, unused dirt roads and even a five-kilometer stretch of autoroute, which I think is safe because I'm wearing my fluorescent green vest and walk facing traffic.

I stop briefly at a petrol station to buy water and a decent map of Cyprus (which I'm consulting as I write this), then at a food truck in Xylofagou for a pork, cucumber and tomato sandwich. I continue on rural roads and traipse through the Xylofagou industrial zone and farmers' fields to Pyla, one of the few towns on Cyprus with a Greek-and-Turk population mix.

I arrive in quiet villa-filled Agia Thekla where there's almost no living soul but lots of empty villas. I'm glad, though it may be a sensible investment, that I never bought one of these much-vaunted use-it-for-a-month vacation homes here or anywhere else in the world. They certainly don't look like a good investment now. There are too many "For Sale" and "For Rent" signs, though the situation may change when the summer crowd arrives.

I'm ready to call it a day until, after 39 kilometers, I stumble on a pristine, calming seaside Greek Orthodox chapel that inspires me to keep walking. A bit further is a publicized swimming beach for dogs on the outskirts of Agia Napa, one of the best-known party/hotel/beach resorts on Cyprus, even though Agia means "holy."

After 45 kilometers, I stop at Nissis Beach – and summer or not, there are already babes on the beaches and young hunks in the hotels – and wait an hour for a bus back to Larnaca.

The next morning, for one of the first times in MedTrek history, or at least since my passport was swept away by the Mediterranean Sea in Morocco over a decade ago, I'm carrying my actual passport, rather than a photocopy. That's because I expect, today or tomorrow, to make it to the Green Line that separates the Greek Cypriot Republic of Cyprus from the Turkish Republic of Northern Cyprus.

Getting to the "border" involves a pleasant walk on Agia Napa's beaches through a number of stylish hotels before a refreshing rural stroll around Cape Greco. I kick off the day in sandals, then go barefoot, then sandals on an excellent stone path, then hiking shoes on pathless volcanic rock to the tip of the cape.

Cape Greco, which translates as "Greek Cape," is officially at the southern end of Famagusta Bay and between the resorts of Agia Napa and Protaras. A protected nature park, the cliffy cape is reputed to be the home of the "Agia Napa sea monster" and the cliffs feature intriguing sea caves. Between us, I find it more productive to explore the sea caves than search for the sea monster.

I stop short of Protaras for a Greek salad at a kiosk on Konnos Beach and then continue along the sea to sample some soft ice cream at Fig Tree Bay in Protaras. I begin calling it the Bay of Figs and make up all sorts of Cuba-related rhymes.

I can probably make it to the United Nations buffer zone, or Green Line, separating the two parts of Cyprus before day's end but decide, after I speak to a travel agent who fled Northern Cyprus in 1974, to return fresh to Agia Triada in the morning.

"You have no idea what it was like then – to lose everything," he said. "You can't know unless you lost it. You're wasting your time walking on the sea to the buffer zone. It's dangerous. The people manning it are boys, children. If the Greek army or the UN doesn't get you then the Turks will."

Typically no one I talk to throughout the day knows precisely how far away, or even exactly where, the Green Line is but I don't want to be pressed for time. My new plan is hike up the coast to the buffer zone tomorrow and, ready to flash my passport, see what happens.

Just being this close reminds me how much I enjoy visiting countries on the cusp of change – think Burma, Cuba and Tibet, places I've visited during the past ten years. Although Cyprus has been on the cusp of change for decades, we all know that nothing lasts forever.

I return the next morning and walk north towards Famagusta, the seaside resort where the southern quarter of Varosha has been shut off to former residents and the world since 1974 when the Turks took it over. Varosha is described as a Ghost Town on posters that advertise boating expeditions to the area (the boats stop offshore and the tourists stay on board) and everything, from the dust-covered cars on the street to the breakfast dishes left on tables during the evacuation, is frozen in time.

I wear bright orange shorts, my flashiest red shirt and a blue cap to ensure that the Greeks, the UN and the Turks know that I'm not trying to make a subtle, sneaky seaside entry into Northern Cyprus when I reach the eastern edge of the 180-kilometer (112-miles)-long Green Line. This is the "no man's land" buffer zone that has divided Cyprus since the Turks invaded.

Getting here involves a pleasant morning stroll along the seaside that begins at the Golden Castle Hotel, where I left off yesterday. I'm so relaxed that I'm amused by a watermelon garden surrounded by signs that read "SMILE – You're on camera" and plants under plastic with signs that firmly declare "POISON." Despite those warnings, there are sandy beaches, lovely swimming holes, small marinas with fishing boats, a dredger taking sand out of the sea and earth-moving equipment carving a new beach area.

It all seems so normal.

That's perhaps why I'm surprised when, after six or seven kilometers, I see in the distance the expansive, empty ghost town of Varosha, a jet-set resort in the early 70s with sandy beaches and high-rise hotels, in the distance. As I approach I can make out a white panel that, as I get closer, reads "UN BUFFER ZONE NO ENTRY."

"Is that Famagusta? Is that Varosha?" I ask a Cypriot walking in my direction.

"That's it – and it's a sad sight," he says. "I still have a house in Varosha and left when I was a child."

"Can I get there from here?" I ask. "Maybe get permission to cross the border for a quick day visit?"

"No, you'll have to go to the Vrysoules checkpoint on the British Army Base because no one's dumb enough to try to cross the Green Line here," he said. "Anyway, the only ones allowed in Varosha itself are the Turkish military."

"How has this lasted more than 40 years?" I ask.

"Who knows? What can we do?" he says as he shrugs his shoulders. "We keep hoping things will change but..."

As I get closer, I'm not very impressed with the dilapidated UN watchtower and weathered, tattered blue UN flag at the top of the hill with no physical UN presence. I ask another Cypriot, who's got a Karl Lagerfeld-like accent when he speaks English (he is, or was, obviously a *Gästarbeiter*, or guest worker, in Germany) if I can risk a run into Famagusta and, once there, try to enter Varosha.

"Have you seen the movie *Midnight Express*?" he asks. "Well, you don't want to be arrested by the Turks patrolling the Green Line because they're the same as the ones that you saw in that film. Those are real Turks over there, not actors. They might not shoot you but they'll definitely arrest you. They'll claim you don't have a visa or something and make your life miserable. Your embassy will probably get you out but that'll take time. Why waste a couple days? Go to Vrysoules."

I climb to the top of the hill, make a short video featuring the dilapidated UN watchtower, take some photos and notice that there's a spiffier guard stand with a Turkish flag on the beach below. I walk back to Agia Terada and celebrate my arrival at the Green Line with a swordfish kebab and vegetable lunch.

To avoid seemingly certain arrest by Turkish troops, I decide to return to Larnaca and resume MedTrekking southwest through the Republic of Cyprus. I'll save Famagusta and Varosha until I've walked around the entire island.

Then I post an Earth Day (April 22) story entitled "Why Does a Green Zone Stop The Idiot in his Tracks Just Before Earth Day?"

I can't help but wonder what Alexander the Great would think of the status quo here today. After all, when his troops arrived, "Those who governed in Cyprus put that island into his possession."

Where is he now that they really need him?

# ALL ALONG THE WATCHTOWER

Ah, another sunrise start from the middle of Larnaca! Though this morning I have cereal with a banana rather than eggs. Today is probably not going to be quite as exciting as the walk to the Green Line, though that's perhaps what inspires me to brazenly and defiantly cross another restricted barrier.

It is, as usual, a delight to take off from my Larnaca base camp and simply go left out the door and saunter pleasantly west on Avenue Archbishop Makarios to pick up a warm *bougatsa crema* at Zorbas, my favorite local bakery, before walking on the marina, promenade and longish Mackenzie Beach.

My first blockage is a fence on the city side of the airport that pronounces in CAPITAL LETTERS "DANGER: PLANES TAKING OFF AND LANDING. NO TRESPASSING." There is a somewhat serious topped-with-razor wire fence around the airport itself, but it would be easy for anyone to skip around the end of the fence that extends less than two meters into the water and continue down the beach.

There is, of course, no one walking beyond the fence and I ask around before I take my first steps in possibly forbidden territory.

"Those are the rules," says one woman who's walking the beach. "You might get arrested."

"Don't take it too seriously," says a male walker. "They've had problems with immigrants sneaking into the airport but I doubt that they'll bother you if you stay near the water."

And that's what I, a Green Line vet, do. I'm walking alone on the beach until I pass the airport and, just FYI, there's no fence of any sort on the far side. Must be the Larnaca crowd that really worries the authorities.

I continue uneventfully on the seaside through a few uninhabited resorts and farmers' fields. There's a bit of preparation-for-the-season construction at the end of Cape Kiti, where a new complex is on the rise and they're grading a road around the end of the cape, but no people, markets or cafés. I buy a few oranges a bit further on when I walk through Perivolia, just to have some contact with another human (somehow I get the orange seller to understand that I need napkins), but otherwise, it's me and deserted beaches, often lined by vacant summer homes on a slightly windy slightly cooler-than-usual Monday. I make a video of a plastic tarp draped over some vegetables because from a distance it looks like wavy water.

## EARTHLY WAVES

I stop at a café near the wreck of the *Zenobia*, which sank off Larnaca in 1980 during her maiden voyage and is rated one of the top ten wreck dives in the world. I regret that today the water is too wild for a swim out to the abandoned ship that I presume is named after the 3rd century AD queen of the Syria-based Palmyrene Empire.

I wonder if the island's feeling of desolation is partly due to overbuilding and a lack of buying spurred on by the 2012 financial mess here. Although there are a lot of places for sale, there's no real estate agent around to sell them or any potential customers to buy them. After 18 kilometers, when I stop to stretch, I can count the number of people walking on one hand and the number of people reading a newspaper in their car on one finger.

The last ten kilometers are on the beach or on a road paralleling the beach. Kite surfing is promoted on this stretch of sea, where there are signs advertising future housing developments, and I pass a Camel Park with no camels. I'm hoping there will be something open on the beach in Mazotos, but there's nothing to open up even if it were in season. I'm grateful when, in the early afternoon, a shepherd whistles at me and waves to me. A single human spark in this emptiness. It's absolutely wonderful that he whistles.

In mid-afternoon, I walk three kilometers inland to the center of Mazotos where some schoolgirls tell me there's a bus to Larnaca at 4 p.m. and, pointing, indicate that there are markets and cafés further up the road. I order a pork kebab with tomatoes and cucumbers in pita bread for a late lunch/early dinner and almost miss the bus when it arrives ten minutes early with apparently no intention of waiting until the scheduled stop at four.

When we get back to Larnaca, the bus driver tells me the time of a return bus the next morning (7:30 a.m.) and I'm thrilled that a shop next to my apartment has a battery to replace the dead one in my pedometer.

It's a very cliffy, very windy, very large-pebbly and small-stony day on an often-impassable narrow beach. That results in choice between walking on the road abutting the sea or in thistle-filled fields of grain. There are the usual clusters of vacant houses, but I see only one hotel the entire day. That's the German-frequented Aldiana where two guests are practicing karate on the beach when I walk by at 8:30 a.m. and many more are here for kitesurfing. "Facilities are for guests only," a sign informs me.

When I reach Zygi I must admit that my mind had pictured a "town inhabited by friendly gypsy children" – from the French word *tzigane*, which means gypsy. But instead I find a seaside city full of radio towers, the Vasiliko Cement Plant, an oil storage products depot, a power station and a naval base that blew to smithereens in July 2011. And absolutely no gypsies.

Things are so quiet that I consider it momentous when a Slovakian woman at the Romena Frappe stand on the road speaks English and makes me a cappuccino, though I'm sure that's not her main source of income. I sip at the cappuccino and feel strangely transported back to France, where I lived for so many years. Much of the countryside has mountainous terrain and wind that reminds me of Narbonne in the south of France. The memories, the concordance of landscape and time – it's not an unpleasant sensation. She must have used a special blend.

I wait for an hour outside the Zygi Naval Base to catch another scheduled bus back to Larnaca and when it doesn't show, I hitchhike for the first time on Cyprus. The first car stops and the occupants, Sisie and George, ask me if I've ever been to Lefkara (*lefka* means white in Greek and *ori* means hills), a hilltop town in the Troodos Mountains famous for its lace, silverware and edible Cyprus delights. As I haven't, they take me there. The high point of the day – and I must admit it's nice to get away from the sea for an hour – is touring the village, having a coffee with them and discussing the devastating (and it was devastating) impact the financial collapse had on George and his family.

They're all broke.

Ah, the yin-and-yang of MedTrekking. And I'm not just talking about the changing weather expected to bring rain tomorrow. Yesterday was narrow big-pebbled beaches, road walking, fields with thistles, heavy industry and tea time in the mountains. Today, beginning at Zygi Naval Base, I walk west to Governor's Beach, on a dirt road, and continue along the tempestuous seaside for 12 kilometers into Limassol on a brick walkway that becomes a wood walkway that again becomes a brick walkway. It goes on and on for 15 kilometers until I reach Limassol's old port after a 30-kilometer hiking day with lots of intense Mediterranean sounds and waves.

There are scores of seafront hotels that begin in Amathous, the ancient royal city about six miles east of contemporary Limassol that was the locale of a cult of Aphrodite. Though it's still too early in the season for any of the hotels to look too vibrant, they display lots of brand names – Four Seasons and Crowne Plaza, among them – and there are funky local venues, like the Blue Berry café. Limassol itself has, besides its impressive seaside path, a spiffy enough seafront, but across the main street, many buildings are in poor shape, even those on Avenue Franklin Roosevelt.

I take a day off – and it turns out to be a very cloudy, rainy, haily day off – to move my base camp from Larnaca to a spacious first-floor, two-bedroom seafront Airbnb apartment in Limassol. I sleep in the back bedroom to avoid street noise and lounge around a gigantic kitchen and an even more gigantic living room, and enjoy all the comforts of home. The prices for these seaside flats are above my usual MedTrek average – €50 in Larnaca and €75 in Limassol – but I figure the Cypriot economy needs my help and they both have washing machines (laundry is a big MedTrek challenge when I have only the few clothes I'd allocated for the sprint through Syria).

I walk 171 kilometers – three days on either side of Larnaca – during my first week here and enjoy lots of social encounters that bring me up to speed on the feelings of the Greek Cypriots regarding their divided country, their basket-case economy and, despite all that, their generally relaxed attitude ("Stay Calm and Carry On" is written on the wall above my bed in Limassol).

I also get in touch with an old friend, Cyprus-born Michael de Glanville, who I first met when our kids attended the Pouces Verts Montessori School in the south of France in 1984. Among other things, Michael taught me massage for a couple of years in the 1990s and, though he now lives near Girne (or Kyrenia to the Greeks) in the Turkish-occupied north, we plan to get back together when I attend a "Secrets of the Breath" class that he's leading with his Venezuelan wife Viola in Limassol.

"You will enjoy the west end of the island, especially the Akamas Reserve, and you can cross over into the Turkish zone some 20 kilometers east of Polis," Michael wrote before we meet up a couple days later. "Very lovely scenery, the hills come right down to the shoreline. The North East Peninsula of the island is the real jewel, and it's all in the Turkish zone so no hassles with border crossings.

"I wonder," he continued, "if you can get hold of a copy of *Journey into Cyprus*, a Penguin Book published in 1986, written by Colin Thubron about his 600-mile trek around Cyprus on foot in the last year before the division of the island in 1974 now over forty years ago.

Looking forward to meeting up again, quite a few years and many miles from Mougins (in the south of France)."

I get a copy of Thubron's informative book and look forward to circumnavigating the rest of the island after I learn, from Michael and Viola, the "Secrets of the Breath." Today, though, I've meditated and hamstring-stretched to some Tibetan chants (a hangover from my days at the Lerab Ling lamasery near Montpellier, France) and I'm looking forward to heading out the door at sunrise (6:05 a.m.). I'm always exhilarated about getting in a good day's MedTrek between two days off and relish the early sunrise start.

As I prepare to head out of my spacious seaside squat towards Akrotiri and, beyond that, the iconic ruins at Kourion, there are lights from a dozen waiting-to-dock ships visible from my window.

When I leave at 6 a.m., the sun is just rising and it's still chilly but there's a burst of action and animation on the seaside promenade – fishermen, walkers, exercisers, joggers, cyclists, even swimmers – as I ramble towards the old port, the new port and the fabulously named Lady's Mile Beach on the peninsula west of Limassol that separates Akrotiri and Episkopi bays.

First some good and very noteworthy news: many free public toilets complement Limassol's superb long-distance walking path from one end of town to the other. Trust me, I've walked a lot on the Mediterranean and free toilets are a rarity. Two other tidbits:

1. The first bus, the #30, runs west at 6:40 a.m. and, like all public buses in Cyprus, costs €1.50 whatever the distance.

2. Odds are that the person serving you in a café is Bulgarian, Romanian or Russian.

I continue past the new port and then move a bit back from the sea to walk past the gigantic harbor before stopping for a *bougatsa crema*, always a delish MedTrekking treat. Then I walk on Lady's Mile Beach past some fairly serious bird watchers. I'm the only person walking barefoot which is how I show up – barefoot and eager – for a hot chocolate at the Captain's Cabin bar.

I'd heard about the UK's Sovereign Base Area in Akrotiri, just after the Lady's Mile Beach, but when I arrive, I find a fairly simple fence with a hard-to-read sign and, on the other side, see a beach club with sunbathers and someone giving windsurfing lessons. It looks so casual and loose that I walk around the fence in the sea, say "G'day" to the sunbathers and continue unperturbed for 400 meters – until I encounter gun-toting army guards who call the military police.

As I put it in my blog: "The Idiot mistakenly entered the British Royal Air Force Akrotiri base, which blocks access to the end of a peninsula west of Limassol, because he couldn't read the small print on the sign and didn't let the fence, which extends only a short distance into the sea, bother him.

"When stopped by gun-toting guards after walking 400 meters onto the base, he feigned ignorance, apologized, suggested a larger sign and a more serious fence, and was pleasantly escorted back onto Cypriot soil to resume the MedTrek after the military analyzed his passport, questioned him, asked what he wrote on a piece of paper (I simply put "RAF/US" because there were some US troops among the windsurfers and sunbathers at the Beach Club), and said they would like to follow The Idiot."

After reading this, Idiot fan Kathleen Breslin wrote: "What the hell!!! Thinking of you and hope you stay safe in the insanity of the current state of affairs..."

"Don't worry," I reply. "Everything's peachy and smooth on the current MedTrek outing despite the decades-long dispute between the Cypriots and the Turkish invaders, the ridiculous Green Line and the haunting ghost town of Varosha in Famagusta. I'm 'safe in the insanity of the current state of affairs' and am abiding by the 1,333 step theory (that's the number of steps there are in a kilometer) and taking one step at a time..."

I walk along the inland perimeter of the camp back to the sea, take a right and spend another two hours on pebbly beaches hiking to the Kourion Archeological Site, which gradually comes into view at the top of a hill. Definitely a great place to locate a BC or AD town, I think to myself.

I have lunch (The Cyprus Special, it's called) on the beach before relaxing at ruins that have been described as "the Acropolis of Cyprus" and, from the hilltop vantage point, taking photos of where I walked today and where I will walk in a couple of days. Ahead, I must admit, are cliffs that prevent walking on the beach and make me happy that I'm taking a day off for a breathing class.

The next day I meet Michael for the first time in a decade and am reinvigorated by his breathing class – which basically teaches and practices breathing techniques to broaden my human, physical, emotional, mental and spiritual condition. After dinner, we return to my apartment and discuss the state of our aging and impermanent bodies on the balcony.

At one point Michael asks me about the genesis and the evolution of the MedTrek, which was conceived and launched shortly after he left the French Riviera to live in Cyprus in 1998.

Here's a rough résumé of my verbal report just in case you, too, missed the first decade of my walk:

"When my walk around the Mediterranean Sea kicked off with the first steps near the Picasso Museum in Antibes I wasn't sure if I'd even make it to the Spanish border," I tell Michael. "After all, as you know, I'm generally a sprinter rather than a long-distance kind of guy. And I hadn't made any vainglorious pronouncements about walking around the entire Sea nor bet anyone that I'd do it.

"At the time, I simply wanted to get away from daily journalism, reflect a bit on my sixteen-year marriage and embark on a new adventure when I turned 50. I didn't have an agenda, any expectations, a camera or a GPS. I didn't even plan to write about the walk when I started. I was just going to take off and see what happened. But a first night in the Cistercian monastery off Cannes followed by an amusing stroll through the nudist colony at Cap d'Agde changed my mind. I began writing newspaper and magazine articles for *Time* and a variety of other publications.

"One thing led to another as I pursued a path, or actually the lack of a path most of the time, around the Med," I continue. "I adopted a simple philosophy borrowed from Lao Tsu – 'The goal is the path, the path is the goal' – and an even simpler daily *modus operandi*: 'One step at a time.' I gradually realized that I was not just undertaking a journey but also embarking on a long meditation on my life. The physical journey and the inward path quickly became one."

I stand up, stretch and walk to the kitchen to boil water for some organic Moroccan mint tea that I carry with me. Michael follows me and we both notice a map of the Mediterranean on the wall. I point to the south of France and move my finger from Antibes along the sea to the Spanish border.

"After I crossed France and reached Spain," I continue, as we stand in front of the map, "I decided to emulate Odysseus, Homer's Greek hero in the *Odyssey* who spent twenty years venturing to fight the Trojan War and return to his palace, wife and son on the Greek island of Ithaca. This gave me a new way to view the landscape and immerse myself in the marvelously storied and wild past of the actual and mythical Mediterranean.

"The twenty-year walk – which I began calling a MedTrek because of its medicinal, meditative and Mediterranean nature – wasn't a full-time pursuit because, as you know, I had a wife, two teenage kids and a daily workload. But I've now devoted almost two decades of my life to this poetic quest and matured, or changed anyway, with every step and unexpected sensation. And today I have no wife and the kids, like your three sons, are in their 30s."

Michael, who knew my wife and kids when they were much younger, laughs (guffaws actually) and I resume my tale as we shuffle back to the balcony with our tea, the moon-illuminated Mediterranean across the promenade.

"What started as a seaside stroll gradually became a midlife passion (okay, maybe at times a midlife crisis too). Though some people openly questioned my sanity, this seemed like the right timeline for a theoretically stress-free hiking project around a sea that has, according to a map I have that was published in 1857, a 16,000-kilometer perimeter.

"Although I took notes every day, I certainly didn't know that I'd eventually write three books and post daily updates during the adventurous outing," I explain. "The first book, *The Idiot and the Odyssey: Walking the Mediterranean,* appeared in 2008; a *Follow The Idiot* blog and website (www.followtheidiot.com) was online by 2009; and a second book, *The Idiot and the Odyssey II: Myth, Madness and Magic on the Mediterranean,* appeared in 2013."

"Here," I said, as I tapped on my iPhone, "take a look at this video we made to promote it."

### SHAMELESS PROMOTION

"Pretty high tech," says Michael, when he sees how interactive the book, complete with maps and links, is.

"Anyway, since then, I've been writing *Where Is The Idiot Today?* A photograph, usually an original one that I've taken, always accompanies these daily items that enable readers to keep up with me wherever I am, on or away from the Mediterranean. I don't think I've missed a day in more than five years.

"I definitely didn't know at the outset that I'd be kicking off this third volume in *The Idiot and the Odyssey* trilogy by returning to northern Greece to participate in the Alexander the Great Marathon before following Alexander's footsteps from Greece to find you in Cyprus," I conclude.

"That deserves a toast," says Michael, raising his glass. "I look forward to MedTrekking with you."

# FOLLOW THE IDIOT

## CHAPTER PHOTOS

## CHAPTER MAP

# Meeting Aphrodite in the Republic of Cyprus

"Everyone in this land can be called an Alexander."
– Alexander the Great

I've booked a communal taxi to pick me up in front of TGI Friday's to ferry me from Limassol back to the Kourion Archeological Site. There I spend two hours exploring ruins that have been described as "the Acropolis of Cyprus" before starting the 33-kilometer cliff-and-road MedTrek to Aphrodite's Rock, the purported birthplace of the goddess of love, beauty and sexuality.

I immediately learn on the walking path to the Sanctuary of Apollo Hylates, a site dating mostly from the first century AD, that it would be wise not to stray into the forest. Signs tell me that I'll encounter prickly burnet, buckthorn, thorny shrub, *pinius brutia* (Calabrian pine), thyme, *pistacia lentiseus* (lentisk), olive trees, *rubia tenuifolia* (madder) and other not-always-so-friendly plants. In fact, I'm overly cautious during the day and feel that I stick to the road perhaps more than necessary. However, it's better to err on the side of caution than to get stuck at the bottom of a cliff or have to walk through the aforementioned flora.

Meanwhile at the Apollo sanctuary, after walking through and

219

touching parts of the temple, I come away with a quote from Strabo, the famous Greek geographer, purporting that "those who touched the sacred altar of Apollo were flung into the sea." And speaking of the sea, I see an ad for a diving company that promises "Sea life like never before."

I stupidly wear sandals for the entire hike, violating a personal MedTrek credo to change shoes after every 20 kilometers, and as a result of breaking the rules I get a slight blister, one of the few on the entire MedTrek. I'm swearing to myself as I walk up and down hills through the budding and much-advertised Cyprus Wine Route past the hillside town of Pissouri.

A police officer tells me that the food at "the cafe near the mosque in Parmali" is pretty decent and I take his advice and stop for the €8 "Mix Portion" of meat with salad and fries before continuing a few more hours to make the final downhill stroll to the sea and along the coast towards the Rock of Aphrodite. As I look back at the cliffs, I no longer think it a total mistake to spend so much time on the road.

Perhaps that is partially because I am still under the influence of the energizing "Secrets of the Breath" workshop that transported me to a(n) (n)etherworld of calm and contentment and makes me even more physically, emotionally, spiritually and mentally able to continue the Cyprus MedTrek.

At the end of the day, I get three interesting rides while hitchhiking back to my base camp in Limassol.

The first is with a nerdy, methodical and anally well-planned Austrian – an IT engineer who has seven days to see Cyprus and has diligently planned how to drive through one-seventh of the island each day and still make it back to his hotel in Agia Napa for dinner. Say hello to Helmut, the master of hyper-organization and genuinely bizarre categorization.

Helmut has been collecting rocks (he stores them in his dress shoes in the back seat) for his grandmother; doesn't want to visit Limassol "because I live in Vienna"; doesn't want to use my good-for-the-day ticket stub to get into Apollo's tomb at Kourion because "The people I work with respect me because I'm honest"; and definitely doesn't want any surprises.

"I want to wake up in the same bed and know what kind of food I'm going to get and know where I'm going every day," he explains. "Yesterday I made it from the farthest point on the west to the farthest point on the east and still got back for dinner."

I don't argue with any of this, of course, but let the orderly, nerdy, methodical and eccentric Austrian, whose pack is already weighed down by rocks, get his life off his chest. He talks the whole way and never asks what I'm doing in Cyprus when he drops me off at the Kourion Stadium, where I'd started the day.

It's the second lift that truly amazes me. A Kenyan, one of the few blacks I see on Cyprus, stops a couple hundred yards down the road, so far away that I don't think he's stopped for me. When I reach his car he asks if I am okay.

"Sure, I just didn't realize that you were stopping for me," I tell him. "I thought you were using your phone."

I've been to Kenya numerous times and kick the conversation off with a sampling of my limited Swahili while explaining in English that I'm walking around Cyprus.

"Hey, were you the one they stopped on the base the other day?" he asks. "That was pretty wild, walking into an armed base like that. You're crazy, man."

Remarkably the story of my brief detention at the British military base has already become a minor local legend, and he heard it because he is from Leeds visiting his cousin who works with the RAF at the base.

"I do recall saying hello to one black soldier," I tell him. "That was obviously your cousin but the whole thing really wasn't a big deal."

My third hitch is with a pair of drunks who want to borrow money for a drink. In fact, I'm so worried about their erratic driving that when we reach the outskirts of Limassol I point to a café and tell them I'll be happy to buy them a beer.

When I tell the taxi driver who takes me to my Airbnb squat from the edge of town about the rides, he cracks up as I describe each lift.

He too is exceptional. He had moved back to Cyprus from Toronto, calls me "dude" (one of my ten least favorite words), talks about "all the tan Scandinavian tits side-by-side at Lady's Beach" and describes all the reasons that he prefers Cyprus over Canada.

I spend a fourth night in my gigantic Limassol apartment before moving the base camp down the coast to Paphos, where Liz will be arriving in a couple days.

When I take an early bus from Paphos back to Aphrodite's Rock the next morning to resume the MedTrek, the "Tourist Pavilion," where I was hoping to have another decent Nescafé with milk, is closed.

Still, I have a blissfully flat, seaside-all-the-way walk to Paphos with numerous signs of Aphrodite throughout the day. There's a temple dedicated to her, there's the Aphrodite Hills Resort (where there is also a development called Alexander Heights), there's property sold with her imprimatur near Venus Rock (Venus is Aphrodite's Latinized name), there's a brown "historical" road sign proclaiming Aphrodite's Birthplace and, of course, I'll reach the renowned Baths of Aphrodite in a few days.

The Aphrodite Hills resort and hotel is just a few kilometers from the Rock of Aphrodite, where the goddess of love and sexuality was purportedly born, though many tourists are there to swim and admire the natural rock sculptures in the sea rather than explore their own sexuality.

My seaside saunter includes a fantastic few kilometers of windy nature trails and there are pebbly beaches the entire way (one sign warns "Pebbles Loosely"). There are almost no people, just a tranquil sea, an occasional detour through agriculture fields, some swampy areas, one aquaculture business and another light industrial factory, a short stretch of 15-meter high red cliffs and, as I near the Paphos airport, planes flying lower and lower above me.

It's an easy walk, even on the beach next to the security fence at the airport (a sign in town says it's 17 kilometers to the airport), and I cruise the last few kilometers through a long strip of hotels that, in a salute to the second warm day in a row, are comparatively crowded with guests, though I must admit that the Alexander the Great Beach hotel could use a redo.

The next morning, I leave my three-bedroom apartment base camp in Paphos, head down to the harbor after getting a *bougasta crema* at the local Zorbas Bakery, and immediately begin the day's MedTrek on a wide seaside path around a fenced-in archaeological site, presumably the Tomb of the Kings that I'll return to investigate with Liz when she arrives. Besides watching my fellow walkers, I'm entranced with shade-providing benches (what a concept!) that enable people to sit in sunless comfort and look at the sea. I take half a dozen photographs of the different bus stop-like structures and wonder why the idea hasn't been exported.

The popular flat walk (I'm in for another blissfully flat day) continues to the Lighthouse Beach Bar (there's a lighthouse within the archaeological area) and I MedTrek north along a string of hotels that are much less dense than on the southern side of Paphos. Again, it looks like summer occurred overnight because most of the hotels, like the Elysium, where I squat the toilet, appear to be full.

Besides the hotels, there are lots of "tourist villages" in various states of repair (or disrepair) and a number of poolside yoga classes are underway, with much less loud music than in Turkey. A nice touch of the day is a trumpeter playing not so well at the end of a pier and an advertisement for "foot golf," which is basically, I gather, soccer on a golf course. There are even signs pointing out the danger of rip currents and how to get out of them.

I stop for a village salad at the Sunset Beach bar in Coral Bay and then continue north above some minor-league cliffs to the Cavallia Beach Hotel, which has a 50-meter swimming pool (locked unfortunately, though I'm close enough to read the masters' teams workout posted on a board), and pass signs for the Paphos Zoo (I pass) and lots of banana plantations.

I post a photo of the still-shipwrecked EDRO III, a rusting Albanian-owned, Sierre Leone-flagged ship that's been on the rocks near Coral Bay since December 2011 and isn't getting any more attractive.

I meditatively make my way to Agios Georgios at Pegeia, where I visit the 6th-century basilica that was once a major pilgrimage destination. Three early Christian basilicas and a bath, all 6th century, were excavated in the early 1950s to reveal an extensive unwalled settlement that flourished on the cape in the Roman and early Christian periods.

The advantageous position of the cliffside settlement, which had its heyday during the reign of Byzantine Emperor Justinian I from 527 to 565 AD, suggests that it was probably a port of call for ships transporting grain from Egypt to Constantinople. A small chapel from the late 13th century is also named after Agios Georgios and I contemplate it all at the end of the day when I down a 1.5 liter bottle of water and a Nescafé in the café.

The owner of my large Paphos apartment encourages her father to give me a lift back to the path the next morning at 6:30. That generous gesture gives me an early start on my walk through the Akamas Peninsula National Park on the last day of April.

Demetra, schooled in Southampton, is a businesswoman and single mother who oversees a three-story property in central Paphos with her parents on the bottom and my rental on the top. She and her wild-haired son Leonidas are in the middle.

"The whole problem with Cyprus is corruption and bribery," Demetra said when she picked me up on the bus from Limassol a few days ago.

It's a MedTrekker's delight to have a ride to the beginning of the path and Demetra's dad, though he speaks no English, gets a pat on the back for dropping me off on the way to some tractor work in his home village of Kathikas.

It's obvious that no other walkers had such personal delivery service this morning because the only other people in the Akamas Park (according to locals, Akamas gets its name from Akamantas, an Athenian warrior and the son of Theseus who came here after the Trojan War) this early are half a dozen fishermen and two surfers.

I walk on the dirt track that goes along the coast for 18 kilometers and is occasionally identified as part of the E4 long-distance European hiking path that now totals over 10,000 kilometers. On Cyprus, the E4 takes hikers through Cape Greco, into the Troodos Mountains and through the Akamas region, where I am at the moment.

I stop at the Lara Beach Turtle Shelter and Hatchery, a facility that, since 1976, has saved the lives of, and created a habitat for, many endangered green and loggerhead marine turtles. Although I see no turtles as I walk by, a sheltered photo display gives me a quick course in nest protection (a frame is placed over the under-the-sand nests and cars are encouraged not to drive on the beach), predators (foxes and humans) and turtle breeding and living habits.

Practicing the breathing method I picked up at my course the other day, I continue to stroll through a national park that is rich in flora (the juniper bush is one of the local stars), smells, sea air and nature. This is the longest stretch of semi-pristine hiking I've had on Cyprus and I relish the landscape and five hundred different types of plants as I head toward Cape Arnaouti.

Why semi-pristine?

Although there are signs about respecting the environment and not littering, visitors litter. I pick up lots of trashy things during my walk and meet a cleaning team that, like the last cleaning team I met near Aphrodite's Rock, shake their heads in a frustrated-but-not-too-angry "What are we going to do?" dismay.

In addition, although there are hundreds of signs proclaiming "Wildlife Conservation Area – Hunting Prohibited" I'm not sure if I've ever seen so many spent shotgun shells. They easily outnumber discarded and empty cigarette packs, usually the *numero uno* litter item throughout the world. There are also signs reading "No Camping – No Fires," but at the end of my walk, I run into 20 Russian women who are obviously, from their gear, intending to camp and, presumably, light fires.

There are few cars and it's apparent after 18 kilometers, at a place identified as Tzioni, that the only way to go is forward. But I take a detour to Agios Konon (a nondescript-from-the-outside chapel with some intriguing icons inside) and meet some hunters having lunch who invite me to sit down for a beer and give me directions to Blue Lagoon.

At 2 p.m., after pacing over 30 kilometers, I get a wonderful view of the Blue Lagoon and run into two hikers. Rod is a retired London bobby who speaks Russian and worked as a detective in the United States and Russia. His girlfriend Mary, a Lithuanian who also speaks Russian, works for a Princeton, New Jersey firm, keeping them up to speed on illegal Russian shenanigans on the internet (this was in 2015, well before everyone found out about the wide range of illicit activities by online Russians).

The couple had just hiked over an hour into the Akamas Park from the Baths of Aphrodite and, when we part company, they say they'll give me a lift back to Paphos if they see me on the road. A couple hours later, they do see me at a bus stop and, true to their word, give me a lift to a bus going to Paphos from Coral Bay. On the way, we stop at a pub called The Jail in Pegeia, where Rod and I discuss our lives while Mary speaks to the Lithuanian barmaid.

When I get to Paphos, I visit the Carrefour hypermarket that, like every other shop in the Kings Avenue Mall, will be closed tomorrow because it's May 1 – a day I too plan to take off before fetching Liz at the airport. I issue a short and sweet press release:

"It's two weeks since I took my first MedTrekking steps in Cyprus and I've now hiked 11.5 days for a total of 334 kilometers, or an average of just under 32 kilometers a day."

In Paphos, I again take off two days in a row. When Liz arrives, I let her sleep late in one of the three bedrooms in our two bathroom apartment with a balcony, kitchen, washing machine, marble staircase, some street noise and a view of the distant sea. This, the third large place I've rented on this outing, costs a whopping $46 a night.

We spend Liz's first full day in town exploring the Paphos archaeological sites, including vestiges of the prehistoric era, the Tombs of the Kings, the harbor and downtown, the American-like Kings Avenue Mall, the Church of Agia Kyriaki, an Ottoman bath and a medieval fort, before we have lunch on the seaside.

Our leisurely exploration of this UNESCO (United Nations Educational, Scientific and Cultural Organization) World Heritage Site will end tomorrow morning when we return to the Baths of Aphrodite and MedTrek towards the Turkish-occupied northern part of the country. There breathing specialists Michael and Viola, who together know all the Cypriot ropes, will ferry us across the UN Green Line that separates the two parts of the island.

A sign says the water at the Baths of Aphrodite isn't drinkable and that there's no swimming allowed under the old fig tree hanging over the grotto where the goddess of love, beauty and sexuality purportedly used to bathe and, says one myth, have trysts with her lover Adonis (which is why there are both Adonis and Aphrodite Nature Trails in the vicinity).

I'm not too impressed by the baths, but Liz doesn't agree.

"I love Aphrodite's baths because of the setting, the fauna, the myth," she says. "I can imagine being Aphrodite and seeing Adonis waiting in the wings. Get with the program!"

Instead I head to the Baths of Aphrodite Restaurant to have a tea and appreciate the stunning sea views.

The flat sea walk along the coast into Latchi is pleasantly uneventful on sandy and pebbly beaches and through bountiful orchards and fruitful fields to the Anassa (it means "queen" in ancient Greek) Hotel, which reminds me of the Hotel du Cap near Antibes, France. The most exciting photo of the walk is a picture of the *Mayflower*, a rowboat in a seaside grassy spot overflowing with colorful flowers.

At 1:30 p.m. we stop for a delicious and filling lunch at the Psaropoulous family restaurant where we're served village salad, village bread with village oil, and grilled calamari before we get back on the road for another ten kilometers. There's a pleasant sidewalk promenade on the Polis Beach (Polis itself is a kilometer or two inland) and we walk on rocky beaches until we arrive at an odd-for-the-Mediterranean state-of-the-art pier constructed "for the use of all" by Cyprus Limni Resorts. Two kilometers beyond this and we're in Argaka, where we end the hike at the

Fly Again Irish Pub and meet a German couple – Christian and Christiana – who give us a ride back to Polis. Like Rod, the former London bobby, Christian insisted on paying for coffee. That, I figure, must be part of the social code on the western end of Cyprus.

Liz and I return the next morning to the Fly Again Pub after riding on a minibus with a Jamaican Brit, a server at a bar in Argaka who's been here ten years but has never been to the north and rarely discusses it with his Greek Cypriot friends. He tells us that locals like him are able to squat Turkish Cypriot homes for free if they maintain them.

We take off from Argaka on the continually flat coast, with the high Troodos mountains to the east, moving toward the elephantine sounding village of Pachyammos, then we go through Agia Marina (where we have another village salad for lunch after walking eight kilometers), and we continue on the lava beaches near Nea Dimmata, and on the pebbly beaches into Pomos.

There we meet a woman named Nina who lives in a €400 a month flat and cleans beaches with her rescue dogs while she's here from Denmark. Then we pass a place called The Wave, presumably because of the shape of its roof, with a room at €400 a night. Each town has the same welcome/goodbye sculpture/symbol that enables us to define the city boundaries.

The following day we move the MedTrek base camp from Paphos to Pachyammos at the end of the beach road. Our €40-per-night multi-windowed flat looks onto the sea and the Turkish-controlled, historically rich and symbolic coastal enclave of Kokkina that is patrolled/guarded/defended by UN, Greek Cypriot and Turkish troops. Liz stays at our rural seaside place while I take a late afternoon walk and chat with the Greek Cypriot soldiers who make it clear that I can't enter Kokkina. They tell me that I should sit still and enjoy the sunset, which I do from a local cemetery that also has the tombs of some Turkish soldiers.

Because we're not allowed to enter Kokkina, to get around it requires a long walk inland on a serpentine road that takes us from Pachyammos to Monsoura on the other side. Basically, we walk 20 kilometers to accomplish a mere ten kilometers on the MedTrek today, including a few kilometers along a mostly deserted pebbled beach and road to get as close as possible to Kokkina. Again, I encounter the Greek Cypriot military and am told to walk no further.

"This is the little Green Line and if we don't stop you, the Turks will stop you forever," says one of the five young soldiers I talk to as they point over my shoulders to a Turkish outpost in the hills.

We move the base camp from Pachyammos to Kato Pyrgos, which necessitates waiting an hour for a bus to take us on the windy drive in the hills around the enclave, and check into the Tylos Beach Hotel. Liz takes the day off while I start walking through Pyrgos along the beach in an attempt to reach the Green Line on the seaside.

At the end of the pebbled beach, I climb a cliff and am surprised to learn on my GPS that I'm actually within the boundaries of the big Green Line. Though I can see buoys demarcating the "border" in the water and see a fence a few hundred meters away, I am completely unaware that I have wandered into the actual buffer zone.

The look back at the last beach in western Cyprus from the top of a cliff inside the buffer zone is relaxing and in the other direction, on the Turkish side, I can see the beaches of Morfou Bay leading to Cape Kormakitis. We'll begin hiking there tomorrow when we're joined by Michael de Glanville and cross into the TRNC.

After soaking up the views, I feel unable to safely climb down the cliff that I climbed up (it's crumbly and I fear a fall). Instead I am butchered by thorns, thistles and everything else that bites, pricks, scratches and cuts as I work my way down the hill. It's the worst brambling since Pig's Bay in Turkey and there are so many splinters, scrapes and scratches that I'm embarrassed to take a picture. Obviously, there are no paths in the green zone and I keep telling myself that I prefer the superficial scratches and scrapes to a serious fall.

When I return to the Tylos Beach Hotel, I'm reminded how nice it is to have a base camp with a washing machine and other amenities, including space. "We're still out of season," says the owner. "The tourists won't come until June." Fortunately, Liz stocked up on fruit, water, yoghurt and biscuits while I was out.

There are so many peaceful sights and sites on the MedTrek along the 383-kilometer coast of the Republic of Cyprus that perhaps only an Idiot would want to cross the United Nations-patrolled Green Line, the buffer zone that divides the island country, into Turkish-occupied northern Cyprus.

But it turns out that I'm wrong again.

# FOLLOW THE IDIOT

## CHAPTER PHOTOS

## CHAPTER MAP

# WHAT ARE THE IDIOT'S TEN MOST MEMORABLE SWIMMING HOLES IN CYPRUS?

# MedTrekking Through the Turkish Republic of Northern Cyprus

"It was an empire not of land and gold but of the mind."
– *Ptolemy*

Michael and Viola de Glanville pick us up at the Tylos Hotel and we cross the border into the Turkish Republic of Northern Cyprus (*Kuzey Kibris* in Turkish), a non-country country recognized only by Turkey. We get our visas on a separate piece of paper rather than in our passports (apparently we'll be hassled by the Greek Cypriots coming back to the south if we have a visa from the TRNC in our passports) and Liz, Michael and I begin the MedTrek into and through the Turkish Republic of Northern Cyprus.

It doesn't take long to realize we're no longer in the south. The Turkish Lira is the currency and towns have different names in Turkish than in Greek. The names are obviously not the same on my Greek map as they are on a Turkish Cypriot map and, for me anyway, the dual nomenclature wreaks havoc. I resolve, when I'm done with the MedTrek, to create a map with both Turkish and Greek names. Though they still drive on the left and use British electric plugs, the language, the culture, the time zone and most other things in the two sections of Cyprus are slightly – if not radically – different. Many locals estimate that the north is 5 to15 years behind the south in terms of development.

We immediately take a left off the main road to descend to the beach, blithely passing a sign indicating that this is a military zone. We're met by six Turkish soldiers who exchange niceties and wish us a nice walk. They seem friendly enough but, still, they're soldiers in a conflicted area. There's an undercurrent of war here, even if it's dormant at the moment. And there are all the stories from our Greek friends about how harsh and rough Turkish soldiers can be. So we move ahead with caution, and nothing happens – yet. I consider it a favorable omen that MedTrekking doesn't devolve into MedRunning away from soldiers during our first ramble in a "FORBIDDEN ZONE" in the TRNC.

When we reach the beach after a few kilometers on a path through not-as-cutting-as-yesterday vegetation, we get social at a café where we order a round of lemon squash and chat with the owner who's lived in London. As we sit looking at – and fully appreciating – the dark blue sea, we discuss life in the TRNC while the owner dives into the almonds that Michael has brought and tells us that the place that Michael has booked to stay tonight, the Aphrodite Beachfront Village, is "as posh as it gets." Viola is dropping our gear there while we're hiking.

A debate follows about whether there's a path to the hilltop ruins of Vouni or if we'll have to walk there on the main road. Though we later learn that there is a path, we take the main road that brings us into more social contact, including a conversation with a Sufi from Italy making a spiritual visit to a center in nearby Lefke. He needs our help negotiating the price of strawberries – and tells me that "you're a combination of Ernest Hemingway and Jack Kerouac" when he learns about my walk and my books. We help him buy strawberries, we buy strawberries and we all have strawberry-flavored water while Liz complains about the status of two penned-up dogs who are hunters and, says the owner, allowed out of their cages only a few days a year.

"It might bother you two," Liz says to Michael and me, "but I am always going to stop to help any animal or person in need."

Michael and I climb to the hilltop Vouni (located near a town now called Bademliköy), as Liz rests on a bus stop bench, and are rewarded with one of the best views from a ruin anywhere on the Mediterranean. There are panoramic overviews of Morfou Bay (or Güzelyurt Bay in Turkish), which we'll be walking around for the next few days, as well as a vista of the Troodos Mountains and another mountain range above distant Kyrenia (or Girne in Turkish), the vibrant tourist capital of the TRNC.

At 250 meters above sea level, Vouni dates from the Neolithic period and was later settled by Persians to keep an eye on the Greeks at

Soli/Karavostasi/Gemikonaği (the ancient name/the Greek name/the Turkish name). There's a Temple of Athena over the statuesque Yeşilirmak Rock, where there was once a palace with 137 rooms. I particularly love the fact that the different rooms in the erstwhile palace are identified simply as "Bathroom," "Cistern," "Bedroom," without much noise about the site's glorious past.

Our appreciation heightens as we walk away from Vouni through strawberry fields and olive trees amid the smell of sage and thyme. We take a narrow road back to the beach and saunter into the site of ancient Soli, where we meet a Turkish professor from nearby Lefke (Lefke is fortunately Lefke in both Turkish and Greek) European University in Gemikonaği (aka Soli), which was founded in 1990 with 3,000 students from 30 countries.

Once the three of us endure two kilometers on the road to get out of Soli, which is highlighted by the intriguing and detailed Roman imperial mosaics that are protected by a permanent roof cover, the breezy nine-kilometer walk from Gemikonaği to the Aphrodite Beachfront Club (it's actually Aphrodite Beachfront Village, but I prefer the ABC acronym) is a piece of *baklava*.

At one point, we find ourselves in the CMC (Cypress Mediterranean Coast) Golf Club – not to be confused with the Cyprus Mining Corp. (CMC) which began mining here as an American company in 1914 and created this golf course in Yeşilyurt for its management staff – and traverse its synthetic tees, weedy fairways and hard sand greens that stretch along the seaside for more than a kilometer. Near Gemikonaği we pass the Monument of Cengiz Topel commemorating the heroism of a Turkish Air Force pilot. After that, it's a five-kilometer walk parallel to the pebbly beach on a dirt road to our penthouse apartment at ABC.

Michael, who was born on Cyprus to non-Cypriot English parents, is a wealth of intriguing information about the evolution of the country since his youth, explaining that he was here until 1959, returned sporadically in the 1970s and then came back permanently after 1998.

He recounts the Greek Cypriot genocide (a Greek would not agree with this choice of words) beginning in 1963 that precipitated and led to the intervention (a Greek would call it an invasion) by Turkey in 1974, the subsequent attacks on Turkish enclaves by Greek Cypriot "liberation" groups, the attempts at Greek unity, the long-time presence of the UN, the welcoming the Turks got before they began their four-decade occupation (as the Greeks would call it) or liberation (as the Turks would call it) of the Turkish Republic of Northern Cyprus (TRNC) and the numerous attempts over the decades to resolve the frustrating deadlock.

"No one on either side is willing to own up to any mistakes – the genocide by the Greek Cypriots, the occupation by the Turks – which is necessary for any successful negotiations," Michael explained. "And those in power have no reason to change the status quo."

Michael, who began impressing me with his array of arcane knowledge when we were friends in the south of France in the 1980s and 90s, is a great guide, well informed about everything, and he would rather talk than eat. He gives a list of back exercises to a barman with back problems, explains to a German couple in detail how to get to a beach, lectures a taxi driver named Sully about directions and distances and talks about the waves, the wind, the clouds and everything else under the sun. He's a great MedTrek companion because he sees things and knows things that I don't.

The next morning at the ABC – where prices are quoted in $, €, ₺, £ and ₽ (dollars, euros, Turkish lira, pounds and rubles) – we watch a dolphin diving and swimming offshore and, during a traditional Turkish breakfast, observe six TRNC tanks drive in front of us between the pool and the sea. I'm not thinking about the military implications, or speculating about the future of Cyprus, but instead am delighted that the tanks have prepared a tank-track route for us to more easily walk to Akdeniz on the sea. In fact, when more tanks whiz by the three of us shortly after we leave the ABC, we exchange waves and smiles as they churn up dust on the sandy, earthy trail they create on the very pebbly beach.

After 15 kilometers, the three of us arrive at the Caretta (named after the *Caretta caretta*, or loggerhead turtle) Beach Restaurant about three kilometers from Akdeniz. At some point, without even realizing it, I pass the 11,000th kilometer mark on the MedTrek.

Liz and I get separated from Michael when he takes an inland route (we stick to the tank tracks through the big pebbles and finally on sand for the last few kilometers) but hook up with him at the restaurant and share the windy ride back to our base camp with three different drivers on roads that do anything but parallel the sea.

The first lift takes us to Akdeniz, where we're given a ride to the main road by a friendly I've-been-passionate-about-dance-since-I-was-five grammar school dance instructor, who takes time out from a folk dance class. The next ride is to agriculturally rich (oranges, grapefruits, melons) Güzelyurt (we pass Saint Mamas Church and the Güzelyurt Museum of Nature and Archeology) and we make it to the front door of the ABC with a just-engaged couple.

All these brief encounters further demonstrate Turkish friendliness and *misafir.*

"The Greek Cypriots always want more than their neighbor and want improvements," says Michael. "The Turks are chilled out and enjoy benign neglect."

Based on what little I've seen, it seems Turkish rule in Cyprus is benevolently paternalistic (in contrast to dramatically authoritarian) and I take it in stride during the five-day MedTrek around Güzelyurt Körtezi (aka Morphou Bay) and Cape Koruçam to Girne (aka Kyrenia). Turkish rule certainly hasn't impaired the exquisite views and sometimes rugged, sometimes easy MedTrekking.

We take a day off and visit Lefke's aqueducts, historical mansions, mosques, olive mills, water tanks, palms, trees and the Soli ruins, which remind us that the first inhabitants arrived here around 7000 BC and that the island was colonized by Phoenicians, Achaeans, Assyrians, Egyptians and Persians until it was annexed by Rome in 58 BC. Roman control lasted until 343 AD when Cyprus, which gets its name from the word "copper," was conquered by the Byzantines, who ruled the area until the English king Richard the Lionheart took possession in 1192.

Although Alexander didn't come here (and I might not have come, had I not chosen to postpone the hike down the coast of Syria), he did value the Cypriot navy and the island's strategic location.

Fresh from a day off that also took us to the joyous celebration of the first anniversary of the death of Sufi Sheik Nazir in Lefke, we move our base camp to the Mountain View Hotel outside Girne/Kyrenia. The next morning we return to Caretta Beach and launch the hike around Cape Kormakitis to officially arrive on the northern coast of the TRNC.

To get there, we again hire Sully, the noble and informative and opinionated and everything else taxi driver whom Michael debates about some forgettable subject during each drive, to squire us at 6:30 a.m. across the TRNC to return to Akdeniz and the Caretta Beach. At the beach we set up a table and spend 45 minutes breakfasting on tomatoes, bread, almonds, bananas and other treats just right for a long seaside MedTrek.

Then, for the next six hours, it's a no-other-human-contact delightful MedTrek to the lighthouse at Cape Kormakitis through numerous sandy coves (I spend the day in sandals which are put on and off for barefoot hiking) and along even more numerous pebbleless lava beaches for a seaside day that embody MedTrekking at its finest. We stop to watch a man catch baby barracudas, admire the different colors and textures of rocks and shrubs, and marvel at the transfixing turquoise water.

We go slowly, taking breaks for edible and visual treats and swims, but can't help remarking how much litter is swept in from the sea (it's obvious that it's from the sea because people can't access this place easily enough to leave their own litter). Liz says, despite the plastic and litter on the beaches and a dead cow on the trail, that this is "the prettiest walk during my two years on the path with you."

After an hour-long lunch at the lighthouse, I give a bag of garbage I'd collected to a young German couple with a car and tell them that taking it out to dump in a trash bin would be "a good thing to do for humanity." Then we hike the last four kilometers into Sadrazamköy where we stop at the Colya Cafe and Restaurant, owned by the very dignified and educated

Mazhar (Maz) Ozkol. Maz tells us he worked as a radio engineer and now runs this simple cafe in a tourist village to serve us a well-presented Sprite (in a tall glass with lemon) and Nescafé (frothed with a cappuccino-like foam).

Maz offers us a ride to Camlibel to catch a *dolmuş* back to our base camp and, extending even greater hospitality, also offers to meet us in Camlibel in the morning to give us a ride back to Sadrazamköy to enable us to start the walk to Kayalar. Wherever we wind up, a glorious new attraction is the Kyrenia mountain range that towers above us as we wend our way between the sea and the mountains.

We see a new dam for water pumped across the Med from Turkey; drop into a folk dance festival in Akdeniz; visit Kormakitis, one of four Maronite Christian villages in Cyprus; and investigate houses that were begun, presumably by Greeks, in 1974, and are in the same early stage of construction more than 40 years later.

Liz tells me she's now able to practice walking meditation while MedTrekking.

"I used to have a defined pattern of worrying about things and walked miles with my thoughts and preoccupations hanging over me," she confides. "But suddenly I'm not thinking those thoughts but am thinking more of others and my surroundings. A third person changes the dynamic of MedTrekking, but Michael is good for you because he's got all the knowledge and keeps up with you. He has huge strides and can talk about everything when he walks."

The Maz Connection works. He meets us the next morning at the petrol station in Camlibel, takes us over the winding road to the Colya Café, and we have three Nescafés before we set off along the seaside towards Girne/Kyrenia. We walk on beaches and rocks without any problem for an hour but then are thistled and thorned until we make our way back to the small country road that parallels the sea.

Once we take a long enough break to remove the thistles and thorns, eat some cookies, and change socks we continue along the road and beach, at times sandy, at times rocky, at times easy, at times a pain in the leg/arm/foot/ass. We pass a new Turkish Cypriot graveyard, with death dates beginning during the past decade, and then arrive at a Greek chapel on the sea that's been cleared of all crosses and icons. It's completely barren, has bars on the windows, and is locked to prevent, I presume, further desecration. It's a frightening image, both stark and hostile. The church without its icons seems to me like a face with its eyes gouged out.

During a swim stop I find an odd modern treasure in the Med: dozens of computer hard drives, tossed off the point presumably to be rendered very unreadable. Liz swims for the first time on the Cyprus MedTrek and we're rejuvenated enough to continue the climb on the seaside road with stunning views until we get to Kayalar, a little over halfway to the urban road. The sight of Kayalar replaces five days of rural bucolic scenery with a strip of hotels and shops leading into Girne/ Kyrenia.

First, though, we're treated to the stunning sight of goats perched on the highest rocks of a hilltop. I post that we are "Making a revolutionary discovery about cliffside goats near Kayalar in the Turkish Republic of Northern Cyprus (TRNC): After serious study and evaluation, The Idiot has determined that goats in the TRNC look, act and smell exactly the same as goats in the Republic of Cyprus."

Aren't you excited to know that?

Then taking a "shortcut" on the beach to avoid the upward turns and twists on the road, we run into another herd of goats (the shepherd has a prosthetic leg and isn't too happy that we've forced his flock into an inaccessible, or slightly inaccessible, canyon) as we make our way back up the hillside to the road.

I usually make a point of staying on the side of road, off the tarmac, when I walk, but Michael's attitude is, as a former cyclist, that "they'll see me and they all have steering wheels." So he tends to walk in the middle of the road. We speak a bit about the dynamics, challenges and parameters of hiking as a threesome and agree that I should always be in visible contact with everyone. Michael can go his speed, Liz can go hers and I'll stay in the middle of the herd.

Indeed, every MedTrekker has his or her own interests, ambitions and distractions that can amuse even the most patient Idiot, though I try to acknowledge, accept and applaud individuals' idiosyncrasies.

Liz, for example, not only insists on greeting and getting intimate with every dog on this island country, as she did in Turkey, but also relishes having lengthy conversations with fellow humans. Although her affection for every dog on Cyprus frequently holds up the MedTrek, I support her (and try to keep my mouth shut).

"Caring for and feeding dogs is the theme of my odyssey on the Mediterranean," Liz says as she buys dog food and leashes to carry in her backpack.

And Michael enjoys human social interactions, which I often choose to avoid, and I listen as he provides a detailed account of the island's history to some visitors from the UK.

As we descend the country road to hook up with the urban road to Girne/Kyrenia, we pass the pipeline bringing water to the TRNC from Turkey to fill lakes and bathtubs. It's been delayed a couple of years, but Recep Tayyip Erdoğan, the former Turkish prime minister and current president, opened it in 2015 and it's now reputed to be the world's longest undersea water pipeline, part of a $538 million project to bring fresh water beneath the Mediterranean to northern Cyprus.

The next day's MedTrek through Lapta, Alsancak and Karaoğlanoğlu to Girne, the zippiest town on the Mediterranean in the TRNC, runs between the mountains and the sea, a natural delight despite the fact that romantic-sounding places like Stumble Inn, Real Dream Hotel and Sam's Place don't live up to their seductive names. Trust me, I checked them all out during a day on my own.

The road is a breeze at 6:45 a.m., but by 7:30 the Monday business traffic into Girne is in full swing and I walk on the beach whenever there's enough distance to do so. There are some pleasant spots – the road through Lapta is almost in the sea and Escape Beach, where the Turkish landed when they invaded in 1974 (there's a monstrous memorial), looks particularly upmarket – and parallel roads edge by lavish homes and luxurious hotels.

I return to the Mountain View Hotel at 9:45 a.m. in time to catch breakfast and take off again around noon with Liz for the final push into Girne/Kyrenia.

We shoot directly to the seashore and kick off on the day's best seaside walking until we hit the first of two fenced-and-posted military installations that send us to the main road. It's a cool day, the clouds over the mountains portend rain and when it rains, around 1:30 p.m. after 18-plus kilometers, it rains buckets. We take refuge at Ronnie's, a furniture store/restaurant-to-be run by two Kurdish brothers who came to Cyprus 15 years ago. The nearby university is building a medical school which, coupled with a furniture business slowdown due to the economic slump, prompted the brothers to become restaurateurs. They give us tea and we discuss the situation in Cyprus until the rain stops an hour later.

We continue on the main road until we find Gloria Jean's coffee shop that is Liz's landmark for the Elif & Elif hairdressing salon, where she has an appointment the next day. Once we check out the location of the hairdressers and assess their capabilities, we walk through a depressing, debilitated apartment zone and zigzag back to the seaside.

We gradually wind our way down to the harbor where we have a late lunch of mixed kebab (me) and salad (Liz) and then spend over an hour exploring Girne/Kyrenia's iconic castle. We meet a group of young women from Ankara who are amazed that we've come all the way from the US and one guesses, or misguesses, our ages (maximum 40 for Liz, maximum 50 for me). We love her.

The castle highlights for me, besides the overview of the harbor, are the remains of a ship that sank just after the time of Alexander the Great (it was carrying almonds and other artifacts dating from 280 BC) and vestiges (blades, tools, utensils) of the Neolithic period about 6,000 years ago and the more recent Bronze Age.

We stay until closing time, when all the dogs in the castle follow

Liz out the gate.

Everyone at the castle says *güle güle* (goodbye in Turkish) as we depart, but I forget the Turkish word to signal a stop on the *dolmuş* and thank a Russian working girl for yelling *Inecek var!* on our behalf. We make our stop and I profusely thank her with *spasibo* ("thank you" in Russian).

I'm a little worried about the walk east of Girne because Chris Elliott, the co-founder and chief editor of the "cyprusscene" website, told me, after he interviewed me about all things MedTrek, about the obstacles I'd face on the walk.

"You won't be able to get around the new harbor, there are lots of fenced military installations, the hotels have tight security, there's a mosque and there are cliffs," he said. "You'll have to walk most of the way on the main road."

"Well, if that's the case, we might make a diversion to Bellapais and see the home where Lawrence Durrell lived while accumulating information for his book *Bitter Lemons*," I said, just to show Chris that I knew Durrell had written a book about life in Cyprus.

When Chris arrives at Michael's home, where we have been invited to stay (Thanks again, guys!), the next morning at 7:30 he takes five of us – himself, Liz, Michael, Viola and me – on a drive to check out his aforementioned MedTrekking hazards before accompanying us to the start of the hike near the castle. Indeed, he was right. There is a new harbor, as well as lots of fenced military installations, hotels with tight security, a mosque and cliffs.

"Shouldn't be a problem," I tell a skeptical Chris, who MedTreks a couple kilometers with us. "The path is the goal and we're in absolutely no hurry."

Though he makes one misstep into the water, Chris has an opportunity to witness us walking close to the sea, on rocks, on a narrow board across a stream and over fences before he leaves us, taking Liz and Viola with him. Then Michael and I are able to MedTrek the next 23 kilometers without once diverting from the sea (except for a when we cut up to Michael's home for a fish/vegetable/rice/pure health lunch).

The major pre-lunch dramatic event occurs when we stumble upon a beach blocked by boulders in front of two gargantuan garish monster mansions with a private pier.

"I'd like to put diesel in their swimming pool or use a tank to destroy their rock wall," says Michael, somewhat betraying his image as a generally calm and soft-spoken body therapist. "We've petitioned the mayor to do something about these Russians who overstep their boundaries on one of our favorite beaches but they've paid off someone above the mayor. The rocks illegally blocking public access to the beach irritate me and everyone else."

We then maneuver over boulders, climb over fences, stride on the seaside, hike through fields and manage to walk through two hotels (the Oscar Resort and the Cratos, both with sweet beaches and guns-for-hire security guards), the new harbor and two military installations without being stopped or even questioned.

Fortunately, our next stop is a calming mosque/memorial for Hazreti Ömer Türbesi where, we learn from Chris, six martyrs were told to come to Cyprus.

The most memorable post-lunch dramatic event is the walk through the last military installation of the day. After hiking unimpeded for ten minutes, we are finally stopped by a young military officer who asks what we're doing on the fine-sanded military Peace Beach and where we are going.

When I randomly say "Acapulco," the resort I can see beyond the base, he smiles and lets us proceed.

"Acapulco," I joke to Michael, "is definitely the password of the day."

The last stop, before a power station that forces us to the road for a while, is the site of the largest hotel I've seen on Cyprus that is being constructed above Lara Beach. Who will fill the many rooms is as much a mystery as who spends money to build resorts that never seem to reach completion. However, the Lara Beach Hotel with 2,000 rooms does get built and I expect that hotels like this gargantuan, sprawling behemoth will consume more and more coast in the TRNC.

I take a fall and get a couple new lacerations during a day that is primarily rocks, boulders and beaches and many more kilometers than usual. Michael continues to feed me more information about Cyprus as we discuss our past marriages and attitudes towards aging.

Then he delivers a very favorable compliment about MedTrekking.

"I consider the MedTrek around Cyprus to be as memorable as a transatlantic sea crossing and I want to do it all," he says.

The Alagadi Turtle Beach (turtles usually choose the best beaches) is a delightful, sandy kick off to the next day's walk and it's an easy stroll to Korineum Beach and the nearby Korineum Golf & Country Club, where there's real green grass (watered by the club's own desalination unit), a wooden pier, brand new lawn chairs and a just-constructed seawall.

"None of this will last through a season," predicts Michael after inspecting the dubious construction of the wall and low level of the wooden pier that, he's certain, will soon be covered by the sea and seaweed.

We again tackle boulders, pebbles, thistles, cliffs and up-and-down trails (or a lack of them) through coves and headlands on another satisfying outing. Throughout the day, I photograph Michael for a "How The Idiot Keeps Up With Fellow MedTrekkers" story as he takes photos of flowers and rock formations.

Michael's having a minor tiff with Viola (it happens to the best of relationship counselors) and when we stop so he can send a text, a very white Russian swimmer in his 70s tells me that we've just walked into Turtle Bay Village. We admire large villas occupied mainly by Russians, who are tanning en masse and probably wonder why we're climbing the keep-us-in-and-them-out escarpments on both sides of their resort.

We walk on the Old Coast Road (OCR) in order to meet the *dolmuş* bringing Liz from Girne/Kyrenia and have a very decent cod lunch at Amore just past Esentepe. Heading out of town, we stumble on to a deserted Magic Bus on the side of the OCR, which prompts me to tell the story of author Ken Kesey and his Merry Pranksters and encourages me to suggest that we convert the Magic Bus into a Peace Bus to tour both sides of Cyprus. I forget about that idea a few minutes later when we take a refreshing naked swim just after Stazousa Point.

We pass numerous started-and-stopped tourist village developments and call it a day when we arrive at Residence Morlais, one of many posh seaside resorts run by the Carrington Company.

"You look like Alexander the Great with your sandals, soldier attitude and rapid conquering of headlands, coves and the sea," Liz tells me when we walk up to the OCR near Bahçeli to hitchhike back to Michael's.

"Am I turning into Alexander?" I ask Michael as we try to hitch a ride back to our base camp.

"You do look a little like Alexander the Great," he agrees. "But I don't think anyone will pick us up with your wild hairstyle."

My two accompanying skeptics are surprised when the first passing car picks up three hitchhiking MedTrekkers and I ask the driver, a DHL deliverer, why he stopped.

"Because of your savage hair style," he said. "I thought you probably needed help."

We take a day off to attend the Kuzey Kibris Yoga Festival in Çatalköy, the first of its kind in the TRNC, and take another breathing class with Michael and Viola on the inaugural day before moving our base camp to Kaplica.

Then we return to Bahçeli and begin the day with a downhill walk on the close-to-the-seaside OCR. The road has generally been abandoned and is a fantastic MedTrekking path, through the village of Kuçukerenköy (Turkish names that mix Ks and çs always send a shiver down my spine), complete with typical English bars and English music.

It turns out that 90 percent of the walk today is on the OCR (five percent is on the dangerous, daunting New Coast Road and only five percent is on the beach) which, after days of bouldering with Michael is a welcome change. We never stray very far from the sea, occasionally wander through tourist villages with names like SeaTerra and, on a Sunday, see lots of fishermen, bikers, walkers, barbecuers and roadside attractions. Liz poses for a photo with a woman making dolmas, I pose with two kids selling tomatoes and peppers, and we join a young couple in a nifty modern house who invite us to have a few bits of chicken off their bbq, though we don't take them up on the offer.

Instead we have two salads for lunch at the Café Kösk at a cliffside table looking onto the sea near Tatlisu. It's a long and pleasant lunch. We spend an hour discussing Cyprus with the owner.

Mesut Murter was born in a village near Larnaca, grew up speaking both Turkish and Greek, fought with the Turks, served in the office of a past president of the TRNC and had a stroke 22 years ago. Holding a "clock flower" (it actually looks like the face of a clock), he recounts how women and children in a Turkish village were killed and buried by Greeks, tells us President Erdoğan has gone too far too fast in Turkey, and mentions a UN friend who also saw Cyprus as "two of everything, including nationalities, religions, languages and social mores."

It's not surprising that everyone, local or foreign, has some comment about the composition of Cyprus.

"The Greeks always seem to want more – a bigger house, more money, a nicer car – even if they already have everything, which is one reason they all went overboard during the financial crisis in 2012," Michael had told me. "The Turks are content with what they have, whatever state they're in, and they love the earth."

"Forgive me if I sound racist," said a British resident in the TRNC, "but the Greeks are avaricious and like bling and throwing money around. The Turks seem more content."

"You can't even drink the water in the TRNC," says a Greek in Nicosia. "It has no international recognition, there's a pervasive feeling of being valued less than real Turks and the place has absolutely no flair."

We pass an older Turkish man collecting capers and meet the owner of the Zambak Holiday village, run by the Tatlisu Municipality. Zambak is a gem – wooden bungalows that include a Sultan Villa and a restaurant on stilts over the sea – and we're given a free tea when we stop for half an hour.

Another eight kilometers on the delicious sea enables me to play with a herd of sheep, photograph an old carob warehouse, admire the coastline and meditate to soothing sea sounds. We arrive at our base camp in Kaplica and get installed in a gigantic room with AC, a balcony with sea views and enjoy a Sunday sundowner sunset. The 80₺ "for both of you" price I was promised in an email is 80₺ per person when we get here. I don't argue.

A Welsh cyclist vacationing in Esentepe sees Liz and me walking beyond Kaplica the next morning, pulls over and, after we exchange the usual greetings and gestures of active people on the road, says: "Your accent gives you away. You're the American I read about yesterday." He was referring to an article about The Idiot and the MedTrek in a Cyprus newspaper.

We kick the day off with about five kilometers on the Old Coast Road, which will soon cut inland, and pass the Mavi Hotel accompanied by dogs, a lovely sunrise, fresh morning air, a calm sea and singing birds. But the surprise of the day is the discovery of an extended New Coast Road, a just-paved seaside superhighway that abuts the rocky coast that we have to ourselves, with not one car, for 18 kilometers.

The well-designed road with planted trees and vegetation, sophisticated drainage and lots of high-tech security precautions is a welcomed expenditure by the European Union, whose funds built many of Cyprus' new roads. It cuts through boulders, cliffs and thorny thistly fields and features the first few meters of paved access roads to beaches. Oddly, though, there is no one, except the Welshman and two Americans, on it.

"No one knows about it," said the cyclist. "It's not on my Garmin maps."

"Or on my Google maps," I reply.

When the NCR finally cuts inland, we dip down to the Med and have a naked swim and a meager lunch of oranges and cookies before tackling a green-marked trail along the sea for seven kilometers, moving through golden wheat fields and wide ravines. Due to fatigue and the heat, we finally cut uphill to Yeşilköy on a faint trail through strawberry fields.

Liz, as we huff and puff up the steep hillside, tells me that I should applaud her MedTrek efforts more frequently and that what we did today is commendable "starting at 6 a.m. and going 32 kilometers without a major stop." I clap.

After we consume three ice cream bars and buy two liters of water in Yeşilköy, and after the sedentary, obese storeowner gives us the thumbs up for our walking and our purchases, we hitch back to our base camp and are picked up by a German. I ask him why there's no one on the speedy new road.

"People don't know it's there," he says.

I'm so enchanted with the road, I decide to rent a car for a day when we next move the base camp so I can drive Cyprus' "Big Sur" in both directions.

The following day we return to the same store in Yeşilköy and the owner leaps with joy to see us again and sell us two 1.5-liter bottles of water for the day's hike. We take off towards Yenierenköy and get occasional glimpses of the Med, pass the road to Sipahi and wander through a no-longer-in-use tobacco factory in Yenierenköy called KKK. When we arrive "downtown," there are bands, cheerleaders and athletes parading around for the National Sports Day and we observe a requested moment of silence before continuing to the new Karpaz Gate Marina.

The plush and posh marina was launched in 2005 by David Lewis, an Israeli-British Cyprusphile, and, like the Lara Beach Hotel and the New Coast Road, is another example of the blossoming infrastructure in the TRNC. And like the hotel and the new road, I have no idea it exists until I see it. It's so enticing that Liz abandons the MedTrek and spends the day lounging at the Beach Club and the sleek, spic and span Ernest Hemingway Bar & Resto. The operations manager Oykun Erüreten, who worked with the British Sovereign Base Area (SBA) for 18 years, had also read the article in "Cyprus Today" ("A US MedTrekker Hits Cyprus Coast") and says he'll offer me a good deal on a one-day car rental when I return later that afternoon.

I leave Liz, set off solo on the Old Coast Road and arrive at Agios Thyrsos after five kilometers to visit a half-underground considered-holy Greek chapel filled with icons and with a pool of water inside. I stop for lunch at a Turkish restaurant a few kilometers later and am the only customer. I'm invited to join a group of ten family members and employees (including two Filipinas and one Vietnamese who somehow have wound up working here). We sit around the kitchen table and are served copious portions of beans and rice. When I offer to pay, the owner smiles and says *güle güle*.

A few kilometers later I enter the Karpaz Natural Park (wild donkeys, an assortment of birds and white sand beaches are among its well-known attractions) where I follow another green-marked trail along the seaside. I stop just short of the Oasis, a guesthouse that Michael was involved in for years with his Kurdish partner Mashallah (things went south and Michael had to go to court to recoup his investment). I think it might make a great base camp. But I reject the idea and boycott the place due to my friend's legal squabble.

Instead, I hike inland to Dipkarpaz and take a quick tour of the town before hitching back to the Marina with a female high school history teacher and her 78-year-old mother, who looks over 100.

It's Wednesday, and there seem to be lots of UN vehicles on the road. The teacher tells me that the UN comes each Wednesday, as they have for over four decades, to deliver food to the 500 Greek Cypriots in Dipkarpaz, who are the largest contingent of Greeks in the TRNC.

I find Liz, who's bought me a dashing, long-sleeved Karpaz Marina T-shirt as a gift (I never buy gifts), rent the car for a pittance, pick up some ice cream bars from our favorite store in Yeşilköy and relish the drive on the sexy new road back to the Kaplica Beach Hotel.

We spend the next day moving the base camp from Kaplica to Dipkarpaz and, after lunching on a calamari salad at the Marina en route, find a room at Arch House, which unfortunately is run by the local municipality and tourism office. Cleanliness is obviously not one of their strengths and Liz's habitual cleaning obsession goes into action mode – mopping, toilet cleaning, alcohol spraying and demanding new sheets and toilet paper until the room passes the lower limit of her rigorous inspection standards.

Dipkarpaz is a mix of Greek Cypriot, Turkish Cypriot, Turkish and Kurdish cultures, a wild mélange of languages and cuisine that is a refreshing breath of multiculturalism in this divided island country. An Orthodox church next to a mosque is an appropriate symbol and Greek is frequently spoken by local residents, including by the family running the Dilara Restaurant where we wind up having dinner every night.

The church/mosque proximity reminds me that, in theory, both sides on Cyprus agreed over a decade ago that monuments of cultural significance, mostly deserted centers of worship, were to be restored as part of a "common heritage which should be protected and preserved for future generations." Inshallah.

The next morning I wake Liz after the 4:33 a.m. call to prayer and am eager to kick off the MedTrek around the Karpaz Peninsula. At first light, we walk to Ayfilon (aka Agios Philon), again boycott the Oasis (which, of course, has no clue that it's being boycotted by two hikers) and follow dirt roads and beaches along a seaside featuring white sand, clear water and high cliffs abutting agricultural fields, forests and mountains.

We pass Byzantine chapels and stroll around Cape Apostolos Andreas, but any timetable we have is seriously delayed when it takes almost an hour to walk 300 meters through fallen rocks on the slippery seaside under a high mountain. The only people we see are shepherds with flocks of goats and farmers working in their fields. Not even a fisherman.

But there are lots of constantly braying wild donkeys (a donkey in the TRNC who doesn't bray is, I'm told, known as a no brayner) and Liz says "it's a beautiful, arduous, challenging, steep and invigorating hike."

When we finally reach the Holy Monastery of Apostolos Andreas, it's closed and in the midst of a €5 million renovation as part of the cultural heritage program under United Nations auspices that combines Greek-and-Turkish Cypriot oversight and collaboration.

I fully support the program and thank some workers for doing it when they pick us up hitching back to Dipkarpaz after we've walked another few kilometers to end the day at Big Sand Beach.

The next day kicks off, after we hitch a ride back to Big Sand Beach from Dipkarpaz with three Poles, with a glorious walk on two expansive sandy beaches, including the famous Karpaz Golden Beach. After yesterday's 37-kilometer walk, we're ready to take it easy. We not only get a comparatively late start, but Liz takes an earlier-than-usual morning dip after only 1.4-kilometers. (For the record, The Idiot rarely swims until the middle or end of a MedTrek day because he dislikes the salt-and-sand feeling that will plague him until he finds a shower).

The highlight of the sandy beach walk is an encounter with eight Turkish Cypriots, mostly schoolteachers, and a Brit called Barry, a schoolteacher who met the group when he was teaching here 15 years ago. The gang has erected one of the most complete camps I've seen anywhere for one of their two annual "Karpaz man weekends" in May and October. The full regalia include a large covered tent for communal gatherings, stocked with lots of liquor, and independent tents for each "member" ("We're a closed group," says one, who had attended the physics program at Ankara University with three of the others).

# THE KARPAZ PENINSULA

One teacher is gathering wood, another is actually catching fish and a third is making us cups of Earl Grey tea as they tell us about the importance of regular male bonding getaways and the current peace talks in Cyprus ("The TRNC always gets the short end of the stick," says one). It is a refreshing scene and, they tell me, their getaways are the envy of all their friends.

We continue on the seaside road and beaches until, after 18 kilometers, we have lunch at Nico's semi-Greek restaurant and tavern where the owner's British wife makes us a delicious cabbage-based salad. Another six kilometers take us to the Gold Island Restaurant and Bungalows on the Dipkarpaz Beach about six kilometers from the town center.

Liz reserves two bungalows for early June when Michael Knipe will fly in from London to join us on the 100-plus kilometers to Famagusta and the completion of the Cyprus MedTrek.

The next day, we hear my pre-recorded program on Denise Philips' BRT International show where I was asked to chose songs – *Born in the USA, I Feel The Earth Move, Knockin' on Heaven's Door, Summertime, All You Need Is Love* – to provide a commentary about my life (I trace it from North Dakota to the anticipated conclusion of my Mediterranean walking project in 2018) and discuss the MedTrek (I describe the comparative ease of MedTrekking and hitchhiking in Cyprus but, although I mention sleeping with Helen of Troy, no sex or politics is allowed on the program). Denise says I resemble Michael Douglas, seem very fit and don't look my age.

I've heard worse.

## BTR RADIO

I get more press in the TRNC, largely thanks to Viola, than anywhere else I've walked. A number of items appear in cyprusscene.com; there is a front-page teaser and the aforementioned article piece in *New Cyprus*, and an hour on a television program called *A Cup of Conversation*.

That night I reveal my next movements:

"The Idiot MedTrekked over 700 kilometers around Cyprus in April and May when he abruptly flew to Dubrovnik, Croatia. Why did he abandon the path when he needed only a few more MedTrekking days to complete the circumnavigation of the third largest island in the Mediterranean?

Because Alexander the Great had told him, during their discussion in Antalya, Turkey, to visit Marco Polo on the Croatian island of Korčula to get some advice about how to proceed on the MedTrek's next outing."

Liz and I abandon our Arch House squat in Dipkarpaz and take a *dolmuş* and taxi to Famagusta, where we survey the perimeter of the Varosha section left to rot since Turkey invaded in 1974. We get another taxi across the border to Larnaca and our constantly frowning and solemn driver finally smiles when I encourage him stop at the Kolonaki "Refugees from Famagusta" taxi stand on Athens Avenue to get directions to our Airbnb base camp.

It turns out that our taciturn TRNC taxi driver knows the "Refugees from Famagusta" driver who I fetch to give us directions and belts out, with a rare smile, "Now I feel good."

Early the next morning another "Refugees from Famagusta" taxi takes us to the Larnaca Airport for the flight to Croatia.

In Dubrovnik, we join Gordon and Anne Kling for a week's sail off the Croatian coast on the *Adamus*, a 38-foot Leopard catamaran. We sail to various islands – Lopod, where we dine on fresh calamari after walking two kilometers across the island in the dark; Mljet, where we hike to a saltwater lake that a very few scholars believe is the site of the cave where Odysseus spent seven years with Kalypso; Lastovo, where we moor in Pasadur, get in a swim and have a terrace lunch and use the Wi-Fi at the local hotel; Vela Luke, where I get a $7 haircut and $3 shower before a tasty fish stew dinner; Ston, where a fellow traveler South African June Temple says "The Idiot is an amusing philosopher"; and again in northern Mljet, where we walk up the hill to a 14th-century church and swim in Okuklje Bay. Somewhere in between all that, we stop in the town of Korçula, where I find adventurous Marco Polo.

Although some claim he was born in Venice, the local lore is that Marco Polo was born in Korčula in 1254. I visit his purported first home on a street now called Depolo but don't buy any polo shirts on sale at the front door. Instead, I marvel at the rooftop tower, which would have inspired any adventurer with its circular view. From there, I reflect on Marco's life and travels as I look out on the channel where the battle fought between the Genoans and the Venetians in 1298 led to Marco's capture, imprisonment and jail cell confession and description of his journey to Kubla Khan with his father and uncle.

After visiting numerous Marco Polo shops throughout town, I go to the Marco Polo Museum and see the famed adventurer sitting at a table and talking to, quite oddly I think, a mouse. Marco, who died here in 1324, provides me with new details about his journeys and tells me to forget walking in Syria.

"It's time to let Syria go for good," he tells me. "It won't happen because the fighting won't end before the scheduled end of your MedTrek. Instead, go directly to Lebanon and from there to Israel and Egypt."

When we return to Cyprus, Liz and I meet former London Times correspondent and my longtime friend Michael Knipe for a delightful and informative lunch with former Associated Press correspondent Andy Torchia and his wife Marian. We, apparently all formers, swap war stories and get each other's perspectives and thoughts about Cyprus at Bennigan's near Mackenzie Beach in Larnaca.

The next day Liz, Michael and I travel to Lefkoşa/Nicosia to appear on Bayrak Radio and TV's hour-long *A Cup of Conversation*, where host Can Gazi interviews us about all things MedTrek, including Liz's penchant for stray dogs and Michael's approach to walking. That night, we drive to Dipkarpaz and have dinner at Dilara before returning to the coast to check into the Golden Island Bungalows on the beach. Liz, who will be our designated driver for the next few days, speed cleans the rooms with antiseptic.

# *"A CUP OF CONVERSATION" TV APPEARANCE*

I awaken at 4:30 a.m. and have breakfast in Michael's bungalow before we get an early start under a path-illuminating full moon. Though we've been told that we won't be able to walk more than 250 meters on the seaside, and that it would be smarter to take the road, I confidently lead Michael down the seaside path.

"I've been walking on Primrose Hill or Hampstead Heath every day for twelve miles to prepare for this," Michael says as we start off slowly on a large-boulder beach.

This isn't Primrose Hill, of course, but I'm impressed with Michael's pace and, hoping that I'll be able to walk that well when I'm his age (he's 76), get the impression that he's ready for all types of terrain and a very long day.

We reach the Boyou Cafe after 15 comfortable kilometers and I ask Michael if he feels like stopping to avoid overdoing it on the first day. I tell him that I can contact Liz and have her pick him up and continue alone. However, he wants to go on and I, somewhat stupidly in retrospect, let him.

Michael and I first met in Cape Town, South Africa, in 1973 when I'd arrived after driving from Paris through Africa writing stories for US newspapers. My standard outfit, my only outfit, in those youthful traveling days, consisted of jeans, a T-shirt and sandals.

At the urgent request of fellow journalist Peter Younghusband, who invited me to Cape Town when we met in Kenya a few months earlier, Michael introduced me to his tailor and got me enough store credit to dress it up a bit. Typically compulsive, I bought four suits and a few ties, to fit in with the way people dressed for meals and movies in the restrained, constrained and constipated South Africa of that day when apartheid was in full throttle.

Michael and I both covered Africa for a few years and did lots of social things (think drinking) in Cape Town and wherever we found ourselves. More importantly, we maintained contact over the decades. He came to both the first and the fortieth anniversary of *The Paris Metro* magazine that I was involved with in Paris from 1976-79, and hosted my 64th birthday party at his home in London. I long ago booked his band (he's a drummer) to play at my funeral, did some writing for him at *The Times* of London and was pleased that he edited *The Idiot and the Odyssey II: Myth, Madness and Magic on the Mediterranean.*

But that long-time relationship doesn't prevent his walking abilities from gradually deteriorating during the next two hours and, after we climb up and down a few mountains, he can barely move. I try to cheer him up by telling him that he's just become the oldest MedTrekker to hike over 20 kilometers, but that doesn't seem to do the trick.

"After six solid hours of trekking, I couldn't go on," recalled Michael later. "Clambering over rocks, leaping across crevices, shuffling on and through sand, stumbling across fields of hay, going up and down rocky hills, wading through bramble bushes and staggering across a cliff-top plateau with no obvious un-precipitous decent path was definitely not the Cyprus equivalent of Primrose Hill."

Around noon we joyously meet up with the other Michael (de Glanville), who'd been trying to catch up with us for a couple hours after a much later start, and the three of us walk together on a lovely beachside path (the highlight on the beaches are sets of turtle tracks) and the two Michaels get along famously. After all, they're both English and eagerly discuss a variety of topics, from Cyprus to breathing exercises.

"I only managed to keep going without taking a serious fall thanks to Joel carrying my rucksack, as well as his own, while gripping my arm," Michael wrote later. "But it's also thanks to Joel that I was in this predicament in the first place! I was exhausted and asked to retire from the MedTrek on a beach at 12.30 p.m. while Joel trekked on for another couple of hours. I was told to wait until he and Liz returned to get me."

This sounds like a decent plan when I made it. I initially tell Liz to meet us at a mosque in Teşlica at 10 a.m. and she texts me that she's been there and left a note and a blue towel on the mosque gate. I'm probably still two hours from the mosque, which will make me five hours late if that's correct, and we decide that the two Michaels will wait at Kourkova Beach and I'll continue to the mosque and return with Liz.

"My mission is to help Joel reach his goal but when he didn't turn up at the mosque by 11 o'clock I drove the entire coast looking for signs of the lost MedTrekkers," recalls Liz. "I drove back to the Boyou Cafe and took numerous small roads down to the sea but we never connected, despite lots of texts. I finally decided to wait at the mosque, one of the closest drivable meeting points to the sea, where Joel showed up five hours behind schedule."

Renting cars and appointing someone chauffeur, I've learned over the years, often presents more problems than benefits for MedTrekking, and this was one of those occasions. I walk another two hours to Teşlica, finally meet Liz after a 35-kilometer, day and we return expecting to find the two Michaels. Instead we find some notes.

"Gone Swimming," wrote Michael de Glanville.

"As I've been sitting here for four hours and you haven't found me I'm not sure that you will. So I'm going to walk up the path in the hope that we'll meet up," wrote Michael Knipe.

The delays and lost MedTrekkers illustrate that I should have tweaked the plan a bit, but in the end I find Liz and we find the two Michaels. One (de Glanville) is walking around a village a few kilometers from the sea and the other (Knipe) is hiking inland from the beach. The four of us have a delicious dinner in Kumyali and we drive to our next base camp in Boğaz, where our rooms at the seaside Boğaz Beach Hotel are steps away from the smooth Med and a day's walk from Famagusta.

I awaken at 5 a.m. to start another MedTrekking day without the two Michaels. Michael de Glanville has returned home and Michael Knipe becomes the driver and takes us back to Kumyali, where Liz and I kick off a day's walk that is between Karpaz rusticity and Girne urbanity. A string of garish hotels, like Noah's Ark and the Artemis, have the usual seaside rooms and pools with relaxing guests, over-vigilant security guards (I have the usual battle with one at the Artemis) and nice toilets (I try one at the Artemis).

After strolling on a squeaky clean promenade, we continue around a blunted cape to the Thalassa Apartment complex where I swim, due to the alluring presence of freshwater showers. Drying off, I meet Karl Marshall, a 23-year-old Englishman confined to a wheelchair due to lack of oxygen at birth. He's a karaoke fanatic who eagerly relates detail after detail about his life. He's been to the US five times, he's bored at Thalassa, he sings tunes by The Mamas & The Papas, and he asks if there are lots of single girls on the MedTrek. Each sentence takes a long time to form, speak and understand. And each sentence increases my admiration, and we invite him to join us for a salad at a British-owned cafe.

As we leave Thalassa, I admire Liz's multicultural, multicolored vintage MedTrek look as she scales seemingly insurmountable rocks. But after an hour we're thwarted by dense vegetation and are not even able to climb to a lighthouse due to thick shrubbery. We're forced to cut inland for what becomes an hour's walk until we hit the main road, hitch to the beach north of Boğaz and walk through the marina into town.

Liz takes the next day off and I complete the circling, circumnavigatory MedTrek around Cyprus the next day, which begins with an early 10-kilometer stroll with a revived Michael Knipe who accompanies me on the road and on walking/cycling paths from Boğaz to Long Beach. We have a big buffet breakfast at a seaside hotel and when he decides to stay by the swimming pool, I trot off towards Famagusta on the sandy seaside, barefoot most of the time. I pass a few not-too-upmarket hotels until I am stopped at a military zone just north of town.

After an easy, meditative, thoughtful walk, I continue into town on the main road past the military facility, past the port and into the moat that's part of Famagusta's glorious walled fortification, rich with distinguished still-standing memories from its past. I'm mentally celebrating my circling of Cyprus when the visibly vast number of Africans strikes me – far more than I've seen in Cyprus in five weeks and all of whom, it turns out, are attending the Eastern Mediterranean University.

A secretary at the Tourist Information office says "Bravo" when she learns that I circumnavigated her island and offers me a free brochure about Famagusta, with its main seaside sector cordoned off by Turkish troops. The forbidden stretch of seaside, which separates the Greek and Turkish sides of the divided island, is not open to the public and Varosha, or Maraş as it's called in Turkish, the one-time hub of tourism, has become a haunting ghost town.

After MedTrekking almost 800 kilometers around the island and entering Famagusta's walled city, I head to the Palm Beach Hotel, which is painted with vivid Greek blue and white colors, and celebrate with a bottle of Perrier. Then I send a GPS from the beach near decaying Maraş (Turkish) or Varosha (Greek), the empty and heaving guarded southern quarter of Famagusta high rises and resorts that's been a virtual ghost town since the Turks took it over in 1974.

I watch and listen to a Turkish soldier shrilly whistling at me and many other people in a futile effort to stop us from taking photographs. Naturally, I get a couple shots of myself with the sign saying "No Photographs." Then I swim out into the sea to gaze at the ruins and reflect on the people I met who are still hoping to return to live, or at least visit, their former homes in a city frozen in time.

After I shower, Liz and Michael show up at the beach with congratulatory balloons before the three of us explore the ruins at Salamis, founded in the 11th century BC and once the capital city on the island, and we further celebrate with excellent fresh lemonade at the refreshment stand. It's worth noting that the Romans – who ruled Salamis after the Assyrians, Greeks and Persians – built one public latrine that could handle 44 simultaneous users. That'll show Ephesus who's boss.

Cyprus Stats:
Total kilometers: 796
Walking days/half days: 29
Average daily distance: 27.45 kilometers.
Fact: Alexander the Great's sword was made in Cyprus.

What's next?
The Idiot, following the advice of Marco Polo, plans to MedTrek through Lebanon, Israel and Gaza in September.

# FOLLOW THE IDIOT

## CHAPTER PHOTOS

## CHAPTER MAP

# WHAT WERE THE IDIOT'S MOST MEMORABLE MEDTREK MOMENTS IN CYPRUS?

# WHO DID THE IDIOT ENCOUNTER WHEN HE MEDTREKKED AROUND CYPRUS?

# PART FOUR

## LEBANON AND ISRAEL

*Falling in Love in Lebanon*

*Getting Arrested for Being an Israeli Spy*

*The Closed Border Between Lebanon and Israel*

*Walking in Israel with the World's Oldest
MedTrekker and a Teenage Niece*

*Reaching Gaza and the Sinai Peninsula*

*The Tires Wear Out*

# Falling in Love
# in Lebanon

"How great are the dangers I face to win a good name in
Athens." – Alexander the Great

I spent two weeks on the Pacific Ocean coastline training for my
upcoming MedTrek down the coasts of Lebanon and Israel. Although the
dramatic, wild northern California oceanside contrasts starkly with the
soothing southeastern Mediterranean seaside, the refreshingly cool
weather and mix of rocky and sandy beaches make for an ideal hiking and
training locale.

Another of my favorite MedTrek training hikes in Northern
California between June and September took me through a majestic
redwood forest to some of the world's tallest trees. As I mentioned earlier,
the 16.6-mile round-trip stroll on the Redwood Creek Trail to the
renowned Tall Trees Grove is on a generally clear path with little exposure
to the sun, only minor ups and downs, and not too many deer, bear, elk or
slugs. Combined with numerous walks along the Pacific Ocean, I was
ready for my trek down the coasts of Lebanon and Israel.

During one drive back through the Trinity Alps to my Northern
California base camp in Redding, I watched old school blacksmiths in

Shasta City forge metal to produce tools and cooking utensils. Naturally, I asked if they could create a replica of the sword used by Alexander the Great in 336 BC.

"Why not?" the smithy replied as we planned the project. "We'll have it ready for you in six months."

I spent a week just before my flight to Beirut hiking on the Atlantic Ocean. Once again I noticed a number of striking similarities between the Mediterranean seaside and the Massachusetts oceanside. For example, the view of the Atlantic from the medieval-style Hammond Castle in Gloucester, Massachusetts, is similar to Mediterranean vistas from cliff-top villas in France and Italy. And some coastal rock formations remind me of parts of Spain's Costa Brava and many of the rugged stretches in Turkey.

I even hiked around and through Lebanon, New Hampshire, figuring that a walk in the inland Lebanon in New England, which was established in 1761, is an apt symbolic preparation for the MedTrek in a seaside Lebanon where the earliest civilization dates back more than 7,000 years.

My decision to return to the MedTrek in Lebanon, and walk from the Syrian border in the north to the border of Israel in the south, inspires the *Redding Record Searchlight*, my hometown daily newspaper, to confirm my Idiot status in an article touted on the front page.

"Bound for Lebanon: Hiker Taking Trek to Mideast," read the title for the story that was subtitled "Self-described 'idiot' planning Lebanon trip..."

The Idiot, though, tries to reassure everyone that while Syria is definitely dangerous, Lebanon is merely dicey.

It doesn't take long to experience its diceyness. On my first full day in Beirut, in contrast to my plan to immediately head north to the Syrian border, I have to MedTrek south for 20 kilometers to pick up my lost-in-flight duffle bag at the Beirut–Rafic Hariri International Airport.

As I set off, I'm so excited about walking with such a tangible objective that it doesn't bother me that I'm not wearing my usual MedTrekking attire. I blithely head out of the Lebanese capital without a cap, sunscreen, pack, shorts, hiking shoes or other accoutrements that are in my misdirected luggage. I feel so energetic that I walk past the airport through the seaside cities of Khalde and Doha/Dawha to Naameh before returning on a minibus to get my bag late in the afternoon.

That turns out to be a mistake. Among other things, I am slightly sunburned and exhausted by the 30°C degree heat within the first hour. But at least I enthusiastically kick off my autumn MedTrek outing in style during a day of schizophrenic contrasts. These include a camouflaged tank defending the Saudi Arabian Embassy, which I see during the first minute into my first day's walk from my Airbnb at an aptly named suite complex called Bliss near the American University of Beirut. This is a sharp reminder that in spite of Lebanon's currently peaceful state, the civil war that raged for 15 years until 1990 has left its mark.

The obvious military presence is noticeable throughout my stroll south along a seaside that features many off-limit barbed wire military-controlled beaches abutting luxurious beach resorts, like the Kempinski group's new Summerland complex and the Villa Mar, where entering cars routinely undergo thorough security checks.

The intriguing natural offshore rock formations contrast with unattractive urban sprawl, squalor and lack of sanitation in a refugee-filled urban blight call Ouzai. An American journalist friend in Beirut tells me the next day that "I would have warned you to avoid Ouzai because it's the worst patch between Beirut and Tyre, full of refugees that began with the Palestinians, then the Muslims from the south and now the Syrians. It's more than dicey; it's dangerous."

Indeed, Ouzai is as dilapidated as anything I've seen or smelled on the Mediterranean. I'm reminded of the slogan "You Stink!" that was used as a political rallying call against the government during Beirut's recent citywide garbage strike. "You Stink" is what I silently think when I walk through Ouzai, which is definitely in contrast to the generally glitzy Beirut *Corniche* seaside promenade that I amble along before reaching the outskirts of the town on the Avenue Paris and the Avenue General de Gaulle.

I wonder if some of the begging Syrian refugees in Beirut come in from Ouzai for the day. If so, they deserve a donation, because Ouzai is cramped, ramshackle, crowded and abuts a sea that seems dark brown rather than sparkling blue, as though a mirror image of the on-shore squalid living conditions.

I continue past that blight and then pass the Beirut-Rafic Hariri International Airport to Naameh where I take a break in a café in Ramlet al Bayda. An hour later, after a fifteen-minute lay down on a smelly seaside rock, a 20-something shop owner, after selling me a 1.5 liter bottle of water for an extortionist price, shouts at me.

"I hate America, FUCK AMERICA, but I like some Americans," he screams in my face, making it clear that I am not among the Americans he likes. I leave quickly with the water that costs me double the usual price "because we're on the beach."

My hamstrings are killing me and my stride has slowed to a shuffle after this first adverse encounter.

The state of the seaside – dotted with obstructive military installations and tumbledown homes with unsanitary living conditions that vividly contrast with sophisticated beach clubs, chic marinas and lavish construction projects – tells part of the story. These, and many other eerie and surreal yang-and-yin contradictions, are what make Lebanon so intriguing. Within steps, inches really, of the intimidating tanks and smelly sewage-filled seaside hovels are calm and clean sidewalks, spotless marinas and new buildings on the rise.

Lebanon was known by its Grecian name of Phoenicia in Alexander the Great's day and I like to think the name is derived from the Greek word phoenix, or a type of palm tree, since they're still found throughout the country and are used as logos for some of the towns. The Phoenicians, who spoke Carthaginian and get credit for influencing the form of written Greek letters, were also known as the People of the Purple because they made a dye from a sea snail.

Phoenicia, sometimes called the purple country, was, back in the day, between 12-30 miles wide, which was one factor that led Phoenicians to explore the sea and become renowned as ship builders and traders. The northern coast of Africa was lined with their colonies, including Carthage that rose to become one of the great powers of the world and which you'll visit at the end of the MedTrek. The historian Strabo says there were also 300 colonies on the western coast of Africa, while another ancient academic noted "their flag waved at the same time in Britain and the India Ocean." There is some buzz that they might have circumnavigated Africa.

Things were a bit different when the first historians took a look at Lebanon two thousand years ago. Arrian wrote that, because of its central location, Phoenicia developed as a commercial power, and early exchanges with foreign nations produced an advanced state of civilization and refinement. This was during the aforementioned era when its colonies spread "from Cyprus to Crete and the Cyclades, thence to Euboea, Greece and Thrace. The coasts of Asia Minor and Bithynia were dotted with their settlements, and they carried their commerce into the Black Sea. They also had colonies in Sicily, Sardinia, Italy, and Spain, where they founded Cadiz."

When I arrive, I am not completely prepared for everything in contemporary Lebanon, a nation of 4.4 million people that has, as a percentage of its population, the most refugees in the world. Although the refugee situation is jarring and disturbing, it takes just three days of MedTrekking on the Lebanon coast north and south of Beirut to remind me of the unique historical, cultural, religious, ethnic, military and political diversity found at this historic Mediterranean basin crossroads now sandwiched between Syria and Israel.

After all, except for the "FUCK AMERICA" incident, I don't experience any hassles or bad moments and I'm sure almost everyone from everywhere finds the longstanding dilapidated, unsanitary housing conditions of the Palestinians, descendants of the refugees who arrived after the creation of the modern Israel, and the constant presence of begging, bewildered, bothered and broke more contemporary Syrian refugees very dispiriting.

As I walk, I have enough social interactions with inhabitants who've set up stands selling fruit, vegetables, fresh fish, and junked cars to empathize with their plight. I also understand why most of the people I consult about the sanity of my stroll through Lebanon suggest that I walk the Lebanon Mountain Trail (LMT) rather than the congested coast.

"The good news is I can't see any problem with the general plan to walk through Lebanon," Catherine Philp of *The Times* of London responded when asked about my intended MedTrek. "Lebanon's resilience in the face of all the chaos on its borders is extraordinary. The strain imposed by the refugee burden is of course immense and there is insecurity along the border with Syria and in part of the Bekaa, but otherwise it is incredibly stable.

"From my limited knowledge I would question any attempt to walk the actual coast, from a perspective of practicality rather than security. The coast is very narrow before it becomes the mountains and is dominated by a busy highway and lots of unattractive urban sprawl. Might I suggest instead the Lebanon Mountain Trail which is a recent initiative to open up hiking the length of Lebanon?"

Patricia Nabti, who went to Stanford with me in the late 1960s, agrees:

"I have lived in Lebanon for 23 years and have traveled extensively throughout the country," she emails me. "While it is a small country – roughly 140 miles by 40 – it seems much larger because of the mountains and its amazing diversity in terms of its history, culture, natural beauty, and so much more.

"I think you could hike the coast without any serious problems, though I don't think that doing so is the most interesting way to see Lebanon. If you want to do more than just say you did it, and count the miles, you need to go inland a bit...The most interesting route to hike the length of the country is the Lebanese Mountain Trail (LMT) that has been developed to mostly hike along the ridge of the Lebanon Mountains."

I insist, of course, that it's the sea that I want to walk. I'll be content on this visit to see historical and cultural sites close to the coast in Tripoli, Byblos, Beirut, Sidon, and Tyre and skip the caves of Jeita, the ruins of Baalbek, the inspiring cedars and the sea view from the mountains.

After I pick up my bag, my plan is to head to the Syrian border the next morning to begin the MedTrek south. The buzz, though, is that getting from the border to the town of Tripoli in northern Lebanon might be a challenge and could require a bodyguard because there are gangs and militias in the north looking for easy prey to rob or hold for ransom.

Coming back into Beirut from the airport on a bus, I get these opinions.

"People in Beirut always think the worst about the northern part of the country," says Nada, a Lebanese woman. "It's actually quite safe."

"Don't go alone and be careful whom you get to go with you," says a British woman on the bus who moved to Lebanon from Syria.

In fact, some other comments give me pause about starting the MedTrek at the Syrian border.

"There's nothing political about it, nothing too sophisticated," my American journalist friend tells me. "They're just figuring out who to kidnap or rob for the most profit. Don't take it personally."

My friend Philippe, who was born in Beirut but has been living in Florida, expands on the subject when we have dinner.

"It's not political or religious militia you have to worry about," he says "Just gangs who will rob you for money. They might not even kill you if you pay up. In fact, they returned one captive with a box of candy to thank his family for paying."

The woman who greets me when I return to my Airbnb says "I used to go to Syrian beaches a decade ago but it wouldn't even occur to me to do that anymore. I don't know who all these suspicious people are north of Tripoli. They might even be Lebanese but I wouldn't think of going there."

A government official I interview says "Lebanon is fine between Beirut and Tripoli, though I wouldn't camp out overnight. However, north of Tripoli is dangerous. It's very sensitive."

My new friend Ibrahim Muhanna, chairman of The Muhanna Foundation, says "I wouldn't advise you to go without an Arabic-speaking bodyguard and guide to let you know which people might be a problem." He adds "Gangs are taking advantage of the confusion caused by the abundance of refugees. You simply can't be a foreigner walking north of Tripoli. As Arabs, we can tell whom we meet by their accent and intonation. We can read their intentions. You can't. It's almost a given that you'll be kidnapped for either detention, barter (for political prisoners) or ransom."

The anti-travel advisories from the US Embassy, with whom I'm in contact and have registered my presence, are so dire that I feel like an idiot being here at all and the next day Ibrahim introduces me to the mayor of Tripoli who echoes the popular refrain.

"You might have a problem, you might not," he says, giving me his cell phone number. "Get a local bodyguard who will keep an eye on you."

This advice about safety and security gives me not only an idea but also a new *modus operandi*, or MO.

I email Liz who, for the first time in years, does not accompany me on a MedTrek due to my concerns about her safety.

"Got a great nine-hour sleep after a long, hot, sweaty first 20-kilometer day of MedTrekking in street clothes to pick up my dislocated bag at the airport," I tell her. "Long pants and no cap are not advised in this heat but it's great to have all my gear back and I love my new Delorme GPS, which has more bells and whistles than the Garmin SPOT that I've been using for years, including the ability to send and receive texts.

"And," I continue, "I've just come up with a great idea, a new M.O. Because Lebanon is so small (its Mediterranean coast is only 225 kilometers, or 140 miles, in length) and buzzing Beirut is such a convenient base camp, I'll create a different MedTrekking MO than usual. I'll walk north towards Tripoli and Syria from Beirut and, once that's accomplished, head south from Beirut towards Israel. Even though there might be some logistical headaches, I'll keep my base camp here for the whole trip and rely on public transport to get back and forth."

Another plus about heading north from Beirut is that the predominantly Christian part of the country between here and Tripoli, 90 kilometers away, is considered safe and I'll postpone dealing with the purported gangs and militias near the Syrian border until I reach Tripoli and reassess the situation.

My sixth floor room at Bliss looks beyond the American University of Beirut, which I visited when I was first here in early 1973, to the Mediterranean Sea. Today the AUB, which was founded in 1866, has more than 8,000 students of whom more than 500 hundred are from the United States.

I awaken at the call to prayer just after 4 a.m. and take off after a copious and very hearty buffet breakfast (cereal, eggs, cheese, tomatoes, cucumbers, bread and olives are my takings among the offerings) on the top floor of Bliss. I head down to the sea through the AUB campus, which I refer to as Stanford-on-a-Mediterranean-seaside-hillside due to the similarities in architecture, and am surprised and delighted to see the Nabil Boustany Auditorium.

Boustany, who bought and renovated the Mêtropole Hotel in Monaco when I was living in the south of France during the 1980s, was Lebanese and returned here after his Monte Carlo experience to become a politician. My main memory of him, besides his generous nature and some conferences he organized for me at his hotel, is a dinner we had in Monaco and a prescient comment I made that ingratiated me to him forever as a profound undercover seer.

"They could be bombing Tripoli (the one in Libya, not Lebanon) right now," I told Boustany as we dined at the Hôtel de Paris in Monaco on April 15, 1986. And that night the US did indeed bomb Libya in retaliation for a West Berlin discotheque bombing and one of the forty Libyan casualties was a baby girl, who was reported to be Muammar Gaddafi's daughter Hana.

Boustany, who has since passed away, called me the next morning, sure that I had an inside track on secret info inside the US government. I didn't attempt to dissuade him.

I leave the campus and take a right on the wide Beirut *Corniche* and pass the towering Citadelle skyscraper that's symbolic of ongoing reconstruction in a city still filled with empty, half-built and war-ravaged buildings. I slowly stroll by the Phoenicia Hotel where I had drinks and hung out, but couldn't afford to stay, when I was first here in January 1973.

The hotel, which gets its name from Lebanon's Phoenician past, has been redone and looks lavish when I take a few steps inside. Then I walk through the upmarket Saint Georges Yacht Club and Marina with retail outlets like Paul, PF Chang and Starbucks. If Beirut is still the Paris of the Middle East, as it used to be called, then the marina is the Monaco of the Middle East. A blonde rollerblader in shorts seems to embody the hoped-for image of contemporary Beirut. A nearby army tank is the yang to her yin, or vice versa if you prefer.

Unfortunately, this refreshing start to the day only lasts until I get to the city's working port, which has a worn and bedraggled appearance that isn't helped by the heat, pollution, garbage, incessant morning traffic congestion and constant military presence, from tanks to troops. The actual sea is blocked first by a naval base, then the never-ending port, then frequently by the presence of military troops and fences.

The only thing that breaks the monotony during the next eight kilometers is the City Mall that, though it's probably like any other contemporary urban mall, offers a respite from the noxious traffic fumes. But I really don't get a fresh breath of sea air until I reach Dbayeh, where there's a massive Waterfront City project that involves a marina and eight apartment buildings paralleling the sea.

That breath of fresh air doesn't last long either and I begin to realize that what I've hiked during the past two days, south past the airport and north to here, is sprawling greater Beirut rolling on and on in both directions. I've been trapped in the asphalt jungle and I need a lungful of clean air. Today, however, my walk is not filled with as much low-level poverty as yesterday's walk, though the power plant in Jounieh is another blight on the sea, as are the continual string of military bases, private beaches and the congested highway that runs parallel to the seaside road. I feel some relief when green-covered mountains appear to the east with lots of paragliders enjoying the air currents.

I'm beginning to understand the much-mentioned allure of the Lebanese Mountain Trail. I'm definitely in a Christian part of the country. Numerous churches, statues of Jesus and, most visibly, buses that scream out "GOD BLESS" in large letters are testimony to that. In fact, the town of Bkerké, 600 meters above the bay of Jounieh, is the headquarters of the Maronite Catholic Patriarchate.

## *VITAMINS*

It's a few kilometers from the southern outskirts to the northern outskirts of the city of Jounieh, where private we-charge-you-to-get-wet beaches block the sea. I continue north of the town to the Casino du Liban to get beyond all this and hitch-and-bus back to Beirut in the late afternoon. Alexander the Great was awarded crowns of gold when he entered Byblos and Sidon and took Phoenicia, so maybe I'll get the same greeting from the blackjack tables when I return in the morning.

My goal the next day – due to abnormally tight and painful hamstring and hip muscles which prompt me to tell my daughter Sonia, on her September 15th birthday, that I'm contemplating taking a day off in her honor – is to make it at least 17 kilometers to Byblos, one of the oldest continuously inhabited cities of the world.

The morning starts at the casino where I plan, or at least hope, to have winnings that will finance this entire MedTrek outing. But I am quickly disappointed, when I arrive at 8 a.m., to learn that the slots don't open until 10 a.m. and the table games, which is what I play, don't open until four in the afternoon. So I head down the hill to the exact spot where I stopped MedTrekking yesterday and begin walking north along the seaside through Safra towards Byblos.

The walk kicks off auspiciously when a shopkeeper, after I buy some bottled water, gives me a notebook and a vendor at the vegetable market gives me a free banana (they're a dollar a kilo here versus 50-80 cents a pound in the US). Incidentally, US dollars are the currency of preference in Lebanon and during my visit the exchange rate is fixed throughout the country at 1,500 Lebanese Pounds (LBP) per dollar.

After three walking days north and south of Beirut, I finally see some agriculture on the coast, and I learn that Syrian evacuees have taken over a few apartment buildings in Safra, where a Lebanese woman surprises me with the accent she picked up in Melbourne.

There are numerous mid-level hotels on this part of the coast and this is obviously an affordable playground for the casino and vacationing crowd. There are night clubs with names like Lido, Monaco and Paris that, I learn, employ many Russian, Ukrainian and Maldovian hookers, or so

I'm told by a fellow I meet who sells sexy fashion items to the hookers and, he tells me when I ask him whether Lebanese women buy this type of garb, almost none to the locals. No interest in saucy lingerie from the local ladies, only from out-of-town working girls. Again, I'm irritated by pay-to-swim beaches and get in a minor argument with one guard about walking on a fenced-in beach. I keep up my ongoing fractious relationship with security personnel; that's now become my MO and street cred(ibility).

I'm delighted when I arrive in Byblos (Jbail in Arabic), about forty kilometers north of Beirut, to find exotic brown-and-chestnut Arabesque buildings, narrow labyrinthine alleyways and scores of shops and hole-in-the-wall cafes which, I like to think, date back to its origins between 8800 and 7000 BC.

As part of a quick history lesson, I check out the Bronze Age temples, the Persian fortifications, a Roman road, some Byzantine churches and the Medieval and Ottoman old towns before I visit the ruins (8,000 LBP to enter) and absolutely swoon when I explore the crusader's citadel. After I meditatively enjoy views from the top of the castle, the obelisks and small theater are the highlights of my citadyllic walkabout. I learn that the Phoenicians sold lots of cedar here, particularly to the Egyptians, who influenced much of their culture, including the alphabet. To think that I didn't know any of this when I stayed at the Hotel Byblos in Saint-Tropez.

I'm again reminded that I'm in a predominately Christian part of Lebanon when the bus back to Beirut passes numerous icon-and-statue selling shops on the main road. The only thing that might outnumber the Christian retail outlets are the Dunkin' Donuts shops and the only thing that might have a better reputation than Christianity is the air-conditioned City Mall.

I swear that I can't go by the City Mall, in a bus or minibus or cab, without being told, by another passenger or the driver, how cool and refreshing and clean it is inside, though I never bother to pay it a visit. Another thing that grabs my interest is an advertising campaign for the 18-24 set by the Byblos Bank. It calls them The Makers and tells them how cool they are with ads that say "The Makers Keep In Touch" and "The Makers Always Travel." Smart marketing, I think, that makes even me feel like a Maker.

The call to prayer from a nearby mosque just before 5 a.m. on another sultry, sweltering daybreak in Beirut is a MedTrekker's call to meditation, stretching and social media – followed by the 7 a.m. breakfast, my heartiest meal of the day, on the panoramic rooftop of Bliss.

I still think it's smart (or not too stupid anyway) to continue using Beirut as a base camp despite the increasingly long commute back to the MedTrek. I kick off the walking today at the exact place that I left off north of Byblos after taking two minibuses out of Beirut. The total trip time is 90 minutes and it costs me $2, making travel here a cheap, if time consuming, deal (or ordeal).

I head north along a road between the sea and the "autoroute" (a misnomer that locals apply to the two-lane, often congested road from Beirut to Tripoli) and, due to construction that involves the closure of a lengthy stretch of road, I'm about to walk without traffic for a while, though another military base blocks my access to the sea.

Once again, it's way too hot for MedTrekking, but the high point of the morning occurs when I "run" into thirty Lebanese soldiers who, one of the officers tells me, are on a 120-kilometer "walk." They look considerably more wiped out than I do and I know how two of them must feel when an ambulance picks them up. When I see the troops, I visualize Alexander's trip down the coast and the battles being fought in Sidon and Tyre. The head soldier tells me not to take photographs but, unfortunately, only after I've taken photographs.

I walk past a new development called Amchit Bay Beach Residences that claims to be "close to the capital but luxuriously calm" and offers "a life of absolute serenity." I can only dream about it and walk on. In fact, there's no one working on a Wednesday morning, so maybe the contractor and developer are dreaming too.

It's nice to be away from the clamor, crowds and congestion of Beirut and I enjoy a dozen kilometers on a tranquil seaside oddly decorated with a few isolated upmarket private beach homes that seem completely out of place, though they'd look normal in the south of France. I also love the constant smell of figs, which are not quite in season but seem to be the preferred fruit in the fields around the villages of Monsef and Barbara. The landscape becomes starker and dryer, the beaches rockier, the garbage still omnipresent. In fact, I've decided that Lebanon could be the worst environmental blight on the Mediterranean and again fully understand why people told me not to walk the coast.

Hours later, I prance around a promontory called Nouri and enter the center of the country's cement production when I stop in a place called Chekka, which also has a sugar refinery. I drop into a simple seaside hotel where the owner tells me rooms go for $100 a night as she serves me an Earl Grey tea with milk by the pool.

I take the next day off in Beirut to interview Ibrahim Muhanna who, one of my contacts tells me, is "destined to be Lebanon's future minister of finance." Then the next day I'll head back to Chekka on a slow minibus that trudges along the coastal road, rather than the speedy "autoroute," and walk into Tripoli.

The day off rolls like this: an interview in the morning, half a roasted chicken for lunch in my hood (which is the hood to be in) and a swim/Jacuzzi/sauna/massage when I discover that there's a free-for-me-as-a-guest underground gym beneath the Bliss apartment building. I hadn't realized it existed because I haven't been around here at all except to sleep. Late that afternoon, I meet another American journalist who has written a book about Hezbollah and get his impressions of the country as we walk around Beirut.

But most of the newsy and informative info I get during the day is from Ibrahim, whose foundation established in 1994 promotes actuarial education and civic work. Ibrahim travels constantly and is continuing the outgoing tradition and image of Lebanon as a multinational commercial center.

Describing himself as non-sectarian and secular, Ibrahim gives me numerous insights into Lebanon and the Lebanese when we meet in his spacious third floor office on rue John Kennedy. He shows me his collection of "Do Not Disturb" signs from hotels throughout the world and also gives me a local phone to use while I'm in the country. There's a mannequin decorated as a skier with used ski passes and he tells me about a skiing accident he had that injured his leg (he shows me a long scar) and shoulder.

We're about the same age and have similar lifestyles and that gets us off to a good start and a long freewheeling conversation. Here are some intriguing excerpts from our chats in his office and during a lunch and dinner together a few days later. They're as true today as when he offered them in the spring of 2015.

"We are definitely strained by the influx of 1.2 million Syrian refugees which, for a tiny country of 4 million people, is completely unsustainable. Something's got to give because their presence is a ticking time bomb. The land and water shortages, and the population density were difficult to manage even without the refugees. Now it's untenable.

"A third of the current population is Syrian – and the worst of Syria at that – and they are stressing every part of the system, including health, education and sewage. Their presence has led to human trafficking and they're also a drain on the economy, because the money they make goes back to Syria. They present a danger to Lebanon and must be relocated to a peaceful part of Syria.

"We should also kick out the many foreigners doing housework and other jobs here and open them to Syrians. But we're worried that they, the Syrians, speak our language and will steal from us. There are 200,000 foreign housekeepers from Sri Lanka, Ethiopia and Bangladesh in this country earning $100 to $300 a month, while Egyptians run the gas stations and bakeries. Housewives have become complacent, and this has created a serious social problem that's not being addressed. It will take generations to change our inherited behavior.

"We Lebanese still have a commercial mentality and that means that we survive by making deals and all of us can be bought and sold. We're financially oriented and individualistic with lots of ego issues. We constantly try to beat the system and take the easy way out. I learned to steal electricity from the grid when I was ten. We're more criminal than visionary. All of our billionaires stole the money to reach that level...Lebanon's lovely like that. We're an open community. I'm a Christian working in West Beirut, which is Muslim. You can't tell if my secretary is Muslim or Christian.

"There seems to be a peaceful coexistence between our many factions, political and religious, including the military and Hezbollah. Nobody, not the 'You Stink!' movement or anyone else, can upset the balance of stability created by the Lebanese Army and Hezbollah. Neither side has any interest in taking over, because they would lose everything they have achieved. The Christians have a working relationship with Hezbollah. Their intelligence networks are very strong. The situation works. But people are fed up with corruption. And with Saudis and other Arab countries playing politics here.

"The Lebanese government, plagued with corruption and disfunctionality, will only be changed by a crackdown. We need leadership. I would love a military *coup d'etat* and rule with an iron fist for two years with a timetable back to democracy. All politicians should be put under house arrest and every corrupt politician – that means every politician – should face a civil or military trial. We've got to clean things up."

The next day, I take a minibus back to Chekka, where I left off the other day, to walk into Tripoli and decide whether to proceed to the Syrian border, with or without an Arabic-speaking escort, despite being warned that the area between Tripoli and the Syrian borders to the north is not meant for foreign MedTrekkers.

I email Liz: "I've been making lots of contacts here so something might work out, though I'm not insistent that it does. If it doesn't, I'll start heading south tomorrow (gosh, it'll only be a week since I got here) and the coast is clear until about 30 kilometers north of the Israeli border when I'll have to get permission from the military to walk any further. Or, who knows, maybe I'll figure something out today – though I'll be triply (make that Tripoli) sure that it's safe.

"In any event, I'll keep this place as a base camp because it's too difficult to move north if I'm stopping in Tripoli. And I hear the place is dodgy and a bit of a dump compared to Beirut."

This day, in fact, introduces me to two unique protagonists, a nun and a bodyguard, who outweigh the importance of the walk to Tripoli and the Lebanon-Syria border.

The first is Mother Thekla, the abbess of the Saint John the Baptist convent in Enfeh, between Chekka and Tripoli. I see a few English/Arabic signs as I walk into Enfeh and make a beeline to the convent that is still under construction. I ask a gardener if I can visit, he says yes and I cross over the garden and rocks to the church, which has both indoor and outside pews.

Then I'm approached by Mother Thekla who informs me that she's the lone nun, that she's been in charge of construction since 2010 and that the archbishop from Tripoli is coming to visit next Tuesday. She has a "build it and they will come" attitude towards attracting other nuns and work is underway on the two-story nunnery. She tells me she speaks seven languages ("but please quote that like most Lebanese, I really speak only Arabic, French and English"). She shows me her future burial plot, which has flowers growing from the rich earth. Then we visit the church and a grotto which, she tells me, is 5,000 years old and was the site of a pagan ritual.

"All in God's time," she says when we discuss the timetable for the completion of the convent and my own MedTrek project as she offers me, and her workers, some fresh lemonade and a biscuit.

"You are a true hermit to walk all of Lebanon by yourself," she says after I describe my solo MedTrek in Lebanon, noting that she hopes I am a Christian. To keep things simple I say, "Yes, I am" and she gives me a 'mobile' prayer to recite when I walk.

"Jesus, son of God, pray for me for I am a sinner."

During an hour at her convent, Mother Thekla insists that The Idiot be photographed with one of her workers rather than with her. She encourages me to visit the twelve houses of prayer in Enfeh and we clasp hands as I leave and head through a field to the coast road to Tripoli, taking some shots of both the abbey and the town's attractive port with me.

I would be hard pressed to encourage anyone to walk around the littered *corniche* and promenade into Tripoli, from the football field south of town to the congested port on the north side. Although there's a university, a nice ice cream place with Wi-Fi and some decent urban bits (everyone seems to like the Mina district), the beaches are nondescript, lots of sewage flows into the sea and, though not quite as bad as Ouzai, there's a general disagreeable state of sleaziness.

I also immediately sense aggressiveness in Tripoli, Lebanon's second largest city. Cars slow down and honk to get my attention and if they weren't trying to get money out of me, I'd feel like a celebrity. Instead, they want me to jump in the car or, after all I've heard about the north, might be setting me up for some kind of sting.

There are some nice people and I have a friendly chat with a young policewoman ("Are you a policeman?" I ask. "A policewoman," she smiles) and a young woman going to a hairdresser who says "Welcome to

Lebanon." But there's a tinge of rudeness to the hustle and bustle that makes me glad I kept my base camp in Beirut.

The next day when I return to the port, I meet a burly and surly Lebanese man who tells me that he lives in Aarida near the seaside border entrance into Syria and offers to serve as my bodyguard. Maurice (he winks to indicate this isn't his real name) says he's a Christian and offers to ensure my safety to the border in exchange for conversation in French and English. He shows me that he's carrying a gun and that his fresh-waxed black SUV has an excellent air conditioner, which really impresses me on what will be another sizzling day.

I get in and he tells me that we'll drive to Aarida, check out the border and he'll drive parallel to me on the road while I'm walking on the beach. I admit that I don't ask for references or do any kind of background check, but I am impressed by his professional demeanor (he's wearing a suit and looks like a successful and retired nightclub bouncer); the air conditioner (especially the air conditioner); and the fact that he is from Aarida. Weighing all the bad things I've heard about the north and calculating the low odds of this guy being one of the bad guys, I formally ask him to be my bodyguard and offer him a reasonable amount of compensation to take me to the border and to drive south while I walk on the beach.

"Just your conversation is enough for me," smiles the clean-shaven and stocky bodyguard-to-be who adds that he's 37, married, has two kids and works for an automobile import firm just south of town. He doesn't wink so I presume this is close to the truth.

"No, I insist on paying you if you keep me safe and alive during my walk," I tell him, repeating my offer.

We chat for fifteen minutes as we head north and I confirm that his name isn't really Maurice, though that's what he wants me to call him, that he was brought up near the border and knows the area, and the locals, like the back of his slightly hairy hand.

Then, a few minutes into the ride, he bluntly asks a question that was among the furthest things from my mind at that particular moment.

"Do you like sex?" he asks, winking again.

"Sure," I say, adding, to keep things straight, "but only with women."

He pushes a button on an iPad on the dash and there's a video of two women going down on each other; he pushes another button and a woman is giving a guy a blowjob.

"Do you like this?" he asks, winking and smiling at the same time.

Then – and remember that we've been associated for less than twenty minutes and are driving on a coastal road north of Tripoli, Lebanon – he goes into a long rap about how much he likes me and that it's not all about sex, but intimacy and friendship which he says he lacks in his marriage.

He's had a *coup de foudre*, he explains, but knows that this is true love and how would I like it if he just strokes my leg (I'm wearing shorts, a T-shirt and carrying a backpack) and my thighs and rubs my back. He says he likes older guys and wonders out loud how I'm functioning at 67 (I tell him I was diagnosed a few years ago with AHT, or abnormally high testosterone, and that I'm still functioning); if I can still do it (I tell him I not only can still do but like doing it "with women only," I repeat); how long my, uh, cocksure organ is (very long, I say, jokingly extending my arms as though I caught a gigantic fish); and whether I can do two women at once (three, I say).

"But only with women," I repeat, as I belatedly begin to see what's happening. "Basically I'm just a boring straight guy. I just never seem to be on anyone's gaydar."

It's true. The only gay guy who showed any interest in me, at Elaine's in New York in November 1971, was really drunk and even he said, "Don't get any ideas. I don't just do it with anyone, you know!"

"Don't worry," Maurice says. "We'll just do *que voulez vous*. If you don't want to have sex we won't have sex. I just want to be close to you. I love you. I actually don't like to fuck. We can just be close."

"Well, keep your eyes on the road and your hands on the wheel" I say, repeating the lyrics from a '60s song as I wonder if he's working a bit of reverse psychology on me.

"Do you want to fuck me?" he adds, after many moments of silence. "Can I just put my hand on your knee?"

Now we're far enough away from Tripoli that I don't want to abandon or lose my bodyguard and I figure that I could probably, what with my AHT and all, restrain Maurice, if necessary, despite our age gap. So I let him touch my leg and he begins stroking the sensitive inner thigh area above my left knee.

"Just touching and no sex," I say, as we converse in English and French. "Let's just get to the border and I'll walk on the beach and when we get back to Tripoli, I'd love to buy you dinner. We'll be friends."

"Don't you like me?" he pouts as he strokes me again, displaying a forlorn expression that he's obviously been perfecting since he was a baby.

OMG, I think to myself, is this what I used to look, sound and act like when I attempted to seduce girls in my teens with similarly lame lines? ("I love you, just let me do this, we won't do more, just let me touch you there, I won't do that, I just want to be a friend.") Everything Maurice says sounds like me as a broken record from decades ago.

"Is it really dangerous up here?" I ask to change the subject as we approach the no man's land before the border. "I've heard a lot of stories."

"Very dangerous," he says. "You're lucky to have me as a bodyguard."

There is no one on the beach and no cars going to or coming from the border. It certainly doesn't look like the place for a gang or militia to hang out in hopes of snagging MedTrekkers.

"Everything will be fine if you stay with me," Maurice says. "Most of them just want money. Just don't make eye contact with anyone or talk to anybody or go into anyone's house wearing those short shorts and you'll be fine. Don't let anyone see you're wearing shorts. And don't talk to anyone, especially anyone who looks like a soldier, because they don't speak English or French, just Arabic. People in the south think people in Aarida and the Akhar district are poor and ignorant, but we think people in Beirut are rich and ignorant."

This is the longest stretch of virginal and clean beach I've seen in Lebanon, and there are rich fields on my right. No hotels, no nothing, not even anyone swimming, though Maurice tells me that the beaches will be packed in the late afternoon and most women swim wearing full-body suits. There aren't even any refugees coming through the border today. Quite refreshing. And it certainly looks like I'll get to the border without getting robbed or raped, though Maurice has managed to move his hand up my leg. Much to my surprise, his thigh stroking actually seems to relax my painful hamstrings and does, I admit, cause pleasurable mini-tremors in my hardening organ.

Hmmm, I think to myself. I actually don't mind this, though I have no intention of letting him do anything else to me. But do I have the patience and tolerance, and maybe even the right amount of restraint, to avoid getting angry with Maurice or maybe jump out of his SUV with the great AC or maybe succumb just for the experience? Just what the hell am I doing here?

Maurice pulls off the road after we visit the boring, busyless border so I can walk on the seaside and I ask him to take some photos of me before he drives on the road while I walk on the sea. He wants, he says, just one photo of me naked but I say "No." He wants just five minutes of embracing on the sand but I say "No." He wants me to call him Sunday so he can come to Beirut to massage me with cream and I say, "Yes" (to placate him and shut him up, I thought).

"I like you, I like you, I like you, I love you, I love you, I love you, *je t'aime, je t'aime, je t'aime*," he says in a mix of French and English.

It occurs to me that this is as far as I've ever gone, as a full-blown hetero with no homosexual experience, with another guy and I'm quite surprised that not only am I not completely turned off by it, neither by his emotions nor by his touch, but also that I quite enjoy it.

I walk for a few hours and Maurice drives on the carless road and there's absolutely no problem with gangs or militia or, because I'm not in the car, Maurice's wandering right hand. When we get to Tripoli, with me walking and him driving, I tell Maurice that I've got to get back to Beirut and he buys me a bottle of water, refuses my wad of Lebanese Pounds and puts me into a minibus into Tripoli. We hug and kiss on both cheeks.

"I'll love you forever, do you love me?" he asks.

I tell Maurice that I do like him and that I'll call on Sunday and let him know about dinner in Beirut. Though Liz, after I explain what happened, doesn't think getting together with him is a very good idea, I, being a man of my word, do call him on Sunday. I tell him that my wife wants me to come back to the US immediately because she senses that something serious might happen between us, and she could tell that I actually have feelings for Maurice.

"I think she's right; I don't think I could control myself if you come to Beirut," I admit. "I might have sex with you and then I wouldn't let you go and I'd wreck your marriage and then where will we be?"

"That will be fine," he says. "I'm excited."

I end the conversation with "I'll love you forever, do you love me?"

I recount the story to Philippe, my Lebanese friend living in Florida, and he says, "Oh, I forgot to tell you that they like men in Tripoli."

"Now you know how women feel when we say 'NO'," says Cristina, another American journalist in Beirut when I tell her about Maurice. "Welcome to my life!"

# FOLLOW THE IDIOT

## CHAPTER PHOTOS

## CHAPTER MAP

# Getting Arrested for Being an Israeli Spy

"Of course you have fears, we all have fears. Because no one has ever come this far before." – *Alexander the Great*

I keep Beirut as my base camp and continue to take always-running but usually pretty decrepit minibuses to and from my exact MedTrek location at the start and end of each day. These trips cost between $1 to $2 depending on the distance while a deluxe bus, which I sprang for once from Beirut to Tripoli, cost me a whopping $3. The difference: it's a 70-minute trip on the deluxe bus versus a couple hours on the minibus. All this, despite the logistics, beats hauling my gear to a new base camp. Also I've grown to love my Beirut hood and being entertained by man-about-town Ibrahim Muhanna and some American journalists.

I make the mistake of launching the next day's MedTrek outing south of Naameh, where I wound up while walking to the airport on my first day here. It's a very hot day and I'm suffering from a minor bout of food poisoning (perhaps a chocolate croissant at the Tripoli bus station is what kept me up during the night) and I wonder if Maurice, my erstwhile bodyguard, might have something to do with it. That, coupled with my sore hamstrings, is so debilitating that I wind up sleeping every twenty minutes: under a banana leaf, on the broiling seaside rocks, during a visit to the Soap Museum in the Sidon souk and everywhere else, including, even, an hour nap in the minibus on my return to Beirut.

The MedTrek takes me to Sidon, a bit sick and still shuffling, through Damour, Mechref and the two J cities of Jihey and Jadra, all with a few decent beaches like Sunset Beach, Chateaux de Mer, Havana Beach and Sands Rock Beach. I notice a fully clothed female swimmer when I awaken from one siesta on a fine bit of public beach (similar to the stretch of sand in Beirut) going into Sidon, where I see the iconic Sea Castle jutting into the water and I like the looks of minarets popping up throughout the town.

Sidon (aka Saida, the name means fortress), the third largest city in Lebanon, was the first city founded by the Phoenicians, was governed by its own kings and is mentioned in the Bible 71 times. Homer wrote that it was famous for its embroidered robes, metal utensils, glass and linen, but the Sidonians are also renowned for building exceptional ships. After exploring the Sea Castle, built by the Crusaders, I spend two hours wandering through the town's souk and maze of labyrinthine alleys, taking catnaps wherever I can.

When I get back to Bliss, I go to bed at eight and wake up with the call to prayer at 4:47 a.m. Completely wiped due to hiking in the heat to Sidon and whatever I ate at the bus station in Tripoli, I don't plan to eat for a while. I definitely need, and will take, a day off. I make myself a Nescafé (I couldn't even drink coffee yesterday) but am not ready for a big breakfast. I need to fully recover before returning to Sidon tomorrow to continue walking on what is easily one of the dirtiest parts of the Mediterranean coast that I've encountered, with all kinds of pollution, from litter and sewage to polluted air and water.

In fact, despite being sick and shuffling, everything is going well and, although there are some problems obtaining army permission to walk on the coast as I approach Israel, I only have three or four days of MedTrekking left in Lebanon. Military permission, which I may or may not obtain, is required to keep walking about 15 kilometers north of the Israel border, but I'll keep going until they stop me and hope to reach the border which is closed and impassable.

I have a day-off lunch with Ibrahim near the AUB followed by a visit to the luscious Phoenicia Hotel, where I came for drinks in luxury in January 1973, and then ginger tea at AltCity cafe, an incubator for start-ups run by Patricia Nabti's son.

A delightful rain cools things down the next morning as I MedTrek out of Sidon towards Tyre. After I get out of town, past the urban sprawl and beach-blocking power station, I walk alongside refreshing banana, orange, grape, avocado, lime, pomegranate and flower plantations, and fields complemented by a number of greenhouses. There is little traffic and few people, except families working in the fields which, compared to the noise/congestion/pollution elsewhere, makes this area seem almost bucolic. And I love the way that the growers artistically arrange their vegetables and fruits in the fields with the pride of farmers who have watched their crops develop from seed to sale.

Another rainstorm hits at 10:30 a.m. and I take refuge in a bar near Safar. By noon, after more walking on or near the beach, I have to admit that I am again sick and tired of the smell of running and standing sewage, the incessant piles of garbage, the half-completed buildings and empty structures, the shabby high rises on virginal hillsides, the dirty mechanics shops, the general pollution and congestion, and the honking devils-on-wheels attitude of Lebanese drivers ("Why don't they take his license away?" I asked one friend in Beirut whose brother had totaled two cars. "Get real," she replied. "This is Lebanon.").

Naturally there are some things I like, such as the modestly dressed women and the fact that no one really bothers, or attacks, me. As I try to think of a few more items to add to the list of my disgruntled dislikes, a fellow, who appears to be a handyman at a ramshackle house, sees me taking pictures of the various messes and pollution and yells something at me in Arabic. I ignore him and walk on. I didn't have my antennae out and missed the vibe. But I would catch it soon enough.

Fifteen minutes later, the thin and haggard handyman and a friend, who looks like a burly car mechanic, or so I deduce from the grease stains on his clothes and hands, yell at me to "STOP" as I approach a seaside banana plantation just after Adloun.

The mechanic, who speaks French, tells me the police have been called and are coming to talk to me because "you're a suspicious foreigner who can't speak Arabic and is taking pictures."

Rather than rant, rave or create a problem by continuing to walk, I decide to wait for the police. By the time two undercover cops in their mid-20s arrive fifteen minutes later in a nondescript, aging and tiny private car I'm joking with a table of six 20-somethings picnicking on the beach. I sit down with them, refuse their offer of a drink and am slightly relieved when one member of the group says the guy who made the call, the handyman, is the "village idiot" (they have no clue, I gather, that I am The Idiot).

The apparently undercover policemen, both with shaved heads and wearing jeans, look like any two young Lebanese men in their mid-20s and I think this is possibly a scam, maybe a robbery. But when I ask them for some ID, in response to their request that I show them my passport and answer some questions, they flash their plastic ID cards with Internal Security Forces emblazoned on them. They're apparently the real thing, though I wonder how smart they are when one lets me take a photograph of him and his ID.

I calmly allow them to check my papers, which consist of

photocopies of my passport and my California driver's license, and they joke with the people around the table that I'm a VIP American. The atmosphere and discussion are very casual and they tell me that I'll be able to continue my walk after they call their boss, whom they call "The Colonel," at the Saida office. Unfortunately, he tells them to bring me in.

"Don't worry, but we've got to take you to the office in Saida," says the one who let me photograph his ID. "It's just a formality and won't take long (I'm always pretty sure that it will always take long when someone says that to me). You'll be back here in an hour."

It turns out that the man who called the police, the village idiot, is some kind of low-level informer. He and the mechanic leave and I get in the car with the two undercover ISF officers and we drive half an hour to the police station in Saida.

While sitting in a nondescript room and waiting for whatever happens next, I wonder what trouble Alexander might have gotten into when he approached Tyre, the scene of one of his most difficult and prolonged battles. I also want you to know that was not the only time Alexander would voyage down the Mediterranean Coast through Sidon to Tyre.

He returned here after his death in Babylon and his lavish bier, decorated with solid gold, glittering gems, chiming bells, and drawn by sixty-four mules, contained a sarcophagus and in it a simple cedar coffin where Alexander lay amid spices and herbs. According to someone who was there, the sarcophagus was eighteen feet long and adorned with wreaths and crowns and a frieze illustrating the greater exploits of Alexander.

Someone joked at the time that if Alexander's attendants were as careful of him when he was alive as they were when he was dead, he wouldn't have died. His fame prompted constant attention and sacrifices, including the sacrifice of a bull in Issos followed by a feast, where Ptolemy said that Alexander's wish was to be returned to lie in rest in Siwa, a desert oasis near the Libyan border that I'll tell you about when I get there. The cortege continued past the towns – Sidon, Tyre and Gaza – that Alexander had passed through alive with his troops eleven years earlier.

When the procession reached Egypt, it headed south to avoid the marshes and the coffin was placed in Memphis-Saqqara until the official tomb was finished in Alexandria. His remains were moved there by Ptolemy I or Philadelpheus between 282-305 BC and then, during the reign of Ptolemy IV, he was transferred to Siwa.

During my fifteen-minute wait, I'm given water and allowed to use the rest room before two different almost-lookalike police officers very politely take me, after repeating that "This won't take long," to see "The Colonel" in a small office where a very overweight, very greasy 40-

something colonel-for-life pumps his plump self up behind a very small, paper-littered desk.

It's obvious the second I enter the room that "The Colonel" doesn't like me and wants to prove to the young officers that he is vigilant and in control. He asks me not to cross my legs and instructs the ten plain-clothed cops in the room to go through the photos on my phone, investigate my GPS, check my phone calls and take my backpack apart.

It occurs to me just then that "this won't take long" is not going to prove to be an appropriate phrase and I feel lucky that I am walking solo in Lebanon rather than with Liz. I am still polite, humble and quiet but I immediately realize it will take a bit of time, and probably even test my patience, before I get out of here.

"The Colonel," using French-and-English-speaking policemen to translate his questions from Arabic, is fixated on my high-tech GPS. This, he makes quite clear to his junior officers, indicates that I am a high-level spy capturing and recording state secrets involving people, places and things on Lebanon's coast. He tells them, citing his years of experience, that I am probably an Israeli spy and gloats, with a smug expression that indicates, "We've caught a big one here."

It takes the local Sherlock Holmes/Inspector Clouseau just thirty minutes to interrogate, insult, mug-shoot, fingerprint, book, arrest and put me in handcuffs. Then another fifteen minutes for him to write a detailed description of me and my crimes in Arabic on a police report.

No one speaks adequate English or French and doesn't, in accordance with the sign on the wall about a prisoner's rights, call the US Embassy or bring me a translator after they take my mug shots and photograph me. Not that I'm bothered enough to point that out.

"The Colonel" definitely loses it when I refuse to sign the document that he has painstakingly written in Arabic, though he is very conscientious about checking that I agree with the list of items that his officers have confiscated. These include my high-tech GPS, my iPhone, the local phone that Ibrahim lent me, and my Swiss Army knife. They consider removing the gold bracelet on my right wrist, but I refuse to let them touch it and I refuse to sign whatever the sleazy colonel wrote in Arabic. After all these refusals, I can see that "The Colonel" adds something negative to his report about my attitude (this is later translated for me as "rude, disagreeable and uncooperative").

Everyone except the colonel is still joking during my processing and they frequently tell me that I'll be released as soon as they take me to Beirut and check my passport, which is in a safe at Bliss, my Airbnb rental. There are even a few funny moments as they go through the photos on my iPhone. One of the cops sees Liz's photo in a swimming suit and asks if she is my daughter.

"No, she's my mother," I joke. "Actually, she's my partner."

"She much too young for you," he says.
"Not true; she's 59," I reply.
"Well, she looks 29."
I know Liz will like that.

The greasy colonel calls his superiors in Beirut and presumably tells them that he's captured Mata Hari, only a male one. They tell him to send me immediately to the ISF HQ in Beirut and I'm taken, handcuffed, to a civilian car with three policemen.

As we drive north, I silently review the situation and feel that I should have simply been questioned and released on the beach and that this obnoxious colonel wants to prove to his underlings and superiors that he's capable of capturing a spy. However, once the ball gets rolling, it keeps rolling.

Within three hours, I have been transported from the beach, detained as a "suspicious foreigner," placed under arrest in Saida and transported to the top floor of the main ISF headquarters in Beirut, which I now consider a combination of the police, FBI and CIA in the US.

For the next six hours I'm interrogated by various officers using everything from a good cop/bad cop method, which lasts four hours, to forcing me to repeat my story, from start to finish, to various officials who each laboriously write everything down in Arabic while looking for inconsistencies.

Throughout the process everyone wants to get a look at the Lebanese visa in my real passport to ensure I have entered the country legally. At one point they are going to bring the safe in my room at Bliss to HQ; at another they are going to go to the room, open the safe and presumably search the room. I'm told that everything they're doing is being approved or not approved by a judge, who apparently does not allow them to search my room (or so they tell me). I'm not mistreated and I am not forced to sign a statement, but things do go on longer than I wish.

I begin to frequently point to a sign in the interrogation room (the same sign I saw in Saida) that states I am entitled to a translator, a phone call and assistance. When I ask for a translator, the bad cop says "I'm the translator" and I tell him that won't do. At this point, they are trying to pin everything bad going on in Lebanon on me. They've been through all of the photos on my phone, scoured and copied my Facebook account and my list of friends, and looked at my phones and analyzed my GPS, which they treated like a nuclear device. They call the Airbnb to check me out, which will later make me a celebrity of sorts at Bliss.

They ask detailed questions about a couple of photos (it's illegal to take photographs of military buildings in Lebanon, which I knew and, luckily, hadn't taken), especially one indicating the location of the Khiam prison. I am surprised that they aren't fazed by my shot of sweaty and tired Lebanese troops on that long hike or numerous photographs of military outposts behind barbed wire on the beaches.

The questioning becomes more intense as the night goes on and involves spying, gun running, mysterious phone calls to Belgium (on Ibrahim's local Lebanese phone by whoever used it before I did), drug use, my family, my profession, my books, my walking, the MedTrek, Buddhism, my life. They want the password to my Facebook account and email, which I refuse to give them, and I occasionally demand that they contact the US Embassy, though I learn from the Embassy the next morning that they legally have 24 hours to make that call and that they did make it at 10 a.m. the next day – about 19 hours after my official arrest – which means they complied with international law.

I only exhibit a minor loss of temper at one point when I stare down the bad cop and shout, "What the fuck do you expect to find? What can you conceivably expect to find? You're wasting my time and yours." I think he actually believed that I was innocent from that point on.

Although I expect to spend the night in a nondescript room or cell, around 11 p.m. an ISF agent named Khalid drives me back to Bliss in a black town car. I'm told that I'm restricted to my Airbnb until 9 a.m. the next morning when someone will come to fetch my passport and me.

When I'm taken back to the ISF HQ in the morning and give them my passport, it takes four more hours to have a new statement taken, written and translated for me with the aid of a bilingual interpreter. They ask, for the first time, whether I've ever been in Israel and I tell them about a number of trips to the Holy Land (they don't call it the Holy Land, of course) in the 1980s and 90s when I was producing stories for *Time* and the *International Herald Tribune*.

"Why didn't you tell us that before?" the officer, who I haven't seen until this morning, inquires.

"Because no one asked," I reply.

I have to detail everything I did in Israel well over two decades earlier and they diligently include it in my statement. When my "confession" is complete, I have the translator, a woman in her thirties, read it back to me, make one or two minor changes and sign it. I'm told I'll be released in fifteen minutes.

After an hour, this is the only time that I really begin to worry. I wonder if my trips to Israel might be causing a problem. However, I'm finally taken into the office of a top officer who apologizes for the inconvenience, tells me I can go and suggests that I leave the country within the next few days.

He tells me the reason that they were so insistent during the interrogation last night is that they felt I might have been signaling the location of military installations on the coast with this new high-tech GPS given to me by my mother as a Fathers Day present. The charge wasn't that ludicrous from their point of view and "you would have been in serious trouble if we found it to be true."

"I understand and apologize for any confusion I might have caused," I say. "I know things are a bit tense here but I still want to walk into and beyond Tyre."

"Be careful," he replies more sternly than necessary. "And don't get too close to the border. We're not the only ones watching you. And don't stay too much longer."

I promise the interrogators in Beirut that I will not reveal the undercover agent's identity and I keep that promise until I leave the country. I still have not shown the arresting officer's face to anyone.

When I'm released I call the US Embassy and speak to Lydia Avakian in Consular Services.

"I strongly suggest that you be happy you made it this far without being permanently arrested, attacked or killed," she says. "You can't believe how many death certificates I sign, and how many body bags I ship back to the US, simply because Americans were in the wrong place at the wrong time. It's not worth it. Enjoy Beirut for a few days and then leave."

Though I was considered a suspicious foreigner, I was treated like a VIP once I was in custody in Beirut because I'm an American (they definitely don't treat Syrians like this). It took a while but the ISF finally determined that I wasn't a spy, wasn't guilty of anything, wasn't hiding anything and was completely upfront about what I'm doing here. They checked out the photos on my iPhone, Facebook and Twitter pages, blog, website and everything else to establish my credibility. I'm glad I put everything on social media. It supported everything I said.

I have dinner with an American journalist that night who agrees that I'm lucky.

"If you're going to be arrested and detained, the ISF is the most responsible organization in the country," he tells me. "It would be worse to be taken by the military or Hezbollah. And you shouldn't be too surprised this happened. The actual spies can look just like we do."

A week later, I'm having lunch in Tel Aviv with a group of Israelis that includes an official working in the prime minister's office. I vividly describe the Lebanon arrest and the prime minister's aide says, "I mean absolutely no disrespect to you or The Idiot's importance but if the Lebanese think that's how we get our information they're in pretty sad shape."

# FOLLOW THE IDIOT

## CHAPTER PHOTOS

## CHAPTER MAP

# The Closed Border Between Lebanon and Israel

"I send you a kaffis of mustard seed, that you may taste and acknowledge the bitterness of my victory."
– *Alexander the Great*

The next morning I return to the beach in Adloun where I was taken into custody with the intention of restarting my MedTrek to Tyre and the Lebanon-Israel border.

Before departing, I briefly relive the scene when the handyman and the mechanic told me to quit walking and how I patiently (and perhaps stupidly) waited, seated with six people under an umbrella, for what I thought would be a five-minute conversation with the cops. In retrospect, I should have known I was in trouble when one of the ISF agents said "VIP" after he looked at the photocopy of my passport and saw I was American. He couldn't lose face in front of his informant. And "The Colonel" couldn't lose face in front of his men.

I let that go and start walking near the water.

288

Almost the entire distance into Tyre is between the sea and a seemingly never-ending banana plantations. The bunches of bananas are each individually wrapped in blue plastic for, I presume, protection from insects, or perhaps excessive sunlight. The morning wind gives me the feeling that I'm between two wavy seas of blue as I wend my way down the sandy coast with no one noticing me – or accusing me of looking like a "suspicious foreigner taking photographs."

I am, for the first time since I hiked south of Beirut to pick up my missing luggage, wearing long pants and carrying my passport to avoid offending anyone. My slightly insecure behavior reminds me of the time I was robbed by three drunken 20-something Gypsies in Italy. For months after that encounter, I was overly cautious, paranoid perhaps, about nearing groups of guys, no matter how innocent they looked. Today, I am definitely on the lookout for informers, ISF agents and handymen.

It's an uneventful and surprisingly short hike into Tyre and I almost totally ignore the port, fishing marina, souk and narrow streets of the old town in order to make a beeline to ruins that vividly evoke layers of civilizations and centuries of life here on a very hot autumn (it's autumn now) morning.

The Hebrew name for Tyre is Tsor, or rock, and this ancient Phoenician city, which was originally an island, was best-known for producing the royal purple dye from the murex snail and spawning colonies from Carthage, Cádiz and Corsica to Egypt and Sicily. I recall that Alexander's grueling siege of this city – thought to be impregnable due to its fortified harbor and towering walls – lasted seven months.

Tyre displayed admirable resistance and Alexander's army had to construct a half-mile-long causeway and 150-feet-high towers capped with catapults to finally take the town. It's estimated that 8,000 Persians and 400 Macedonians were killed during a siege that lasted from January to August in 332 BC. Curtius claims that Alexander crucified 2,000 men of military age when he took Tyre and sold an additional 30,000 into slavery.

Alexander considered Tyre – which was later occupied by the Romans, Byzantines, Muslims, Crusaders and Ottomans – an essential strategic goal.

"If Tyre were captured, the whole of Phoenicia would be in our possession, and the fleet of the Phoenicians, which is the most numerous and the best in the Persian navy, would in all probability come over to us," Alexander told his Companions, according to Arrian. "The Phoenician sailors and marines will not put to sea to incur danger when their own cities are occupied by us."

Alexander conveyed a dream to his troops that indicated Tyre would only be captured through Herculean efforts (he claims to have seen Hercules on the Tyrian walls in his dream) after "seven of the most exasperating months of his life," wrote John Maxwell O'Brien in

*Alexander the Great: The Invisible Enemy.*

My favorite story from Tyre is when, at one point during the siege, ambassadors came to Alexander from Darius III, the Persian king, with peace terms that included offers of lots of money, lots of land and a marriage between Alexander and Darius's daughter Statira to create an alliance.

When these proposals were announced in a conference of the Companions, a general named Parmenion said that "If I were Alexander I would be delighted to put an end to the war on these terms."

Alexander's priceless reply was, "I would do so also if I were you, Parmenion, but I'm not."

Alexander refused the money, the territory and the daughter, who, under his own terms, he later married for political purposes.

I have a joyous time exploring the ruins of Tyre, founded in 2750 BC and often called Sour in contemporary Lebanon, and relish my walk around the seaside Triumphal Arch, the ancient columns, the hippodrome and the excavated theater in a flat Tyre that is no longer an island and lacks its tall wall.

As I leave, I recall that Alexander's victory over the Carthaginians in Tyre, who were the only real competitors to the Greeks to potentially control the Mediterranean basin, led to a flow of immigrants to Carthage on the Mediterranean seaside in what is now Tunisia.

How was Alexander able to take Tyre and never suffer a very serious defeat at the hands of the Persians?

Students of Alexander's tactics and his strategic approach to warfare cite a number of reasons for his string of victories. The attributes of the great military commander included close ties with his troops, his uncanny ability to correctly digest reports from the battlefield and his skill in making correct assessments and issuing swift orders that often baffled the enemy. At the same time, he could be patient when visualizing a long-term strategy that involved both strategic warfare and tactful diplomacy.

Alexander's leadership is variously described as decisive, shrewd, strategic, intelligent, educated, lucky and, even, invincible. It's always mentioned by historians that he made promotions based on merit, treated women with respect and often returned land and prisoners to defeated kings to create alliances. In fact, he frequently kept the kings in power if they swore obedience to him.

"When the wife of Darius died, Alexander ordered a sumptuous funeral becoming the queen of a great empire," wrote Plutarch. "He was as gentle after victory as he is terrible in the field."

Even the defeated king was impressed.

"Alexander's kindness to my mother, my wife, and my children I hope the gods will recompense," said Darius.

Alexander frequently thanked the gods for his victories with magnificent sacrifices, rewarded his friends and followers with large sums of money, and put many of his men in charge of defeated territory. His pep talks included both flattery and reproach, a combination that worked. It once led some of his men to ask him "to lead them wherever he wished."

"Most of you have gold crowns as memorials of your own courage but also of the honor that I have accorded you," Alexander told his men, according to Arrian. "This will perhaps win you a fine reputation with men and will doubtless be holy in the sight of heaven."

He was not, however, complacent. Anyone suspected of insubordination or graft faced flogging, stoning or drowning and, in one case in Asia, trampling by elephants. He had a terrible temper and could sometimes murder close advisors, friends and anyone else who got in his way.

"My logisticians are a humorless lot," he said once. "They know if my campaign fails, they are the first ones I will slay."

If he was ever bored or had a "restless brain," his cure was a return to the battlefield with a new arsenal of clever theatrical and dramatic military tactics. He often created camps that would make the enemy think he had three times the number of men he actually had. Or built oversized beds and couches to make the enemy think they were facing giants, not men.

One time he made Darius prepare for an imminent attack that kept the Persian troops on edge for so long that they faltered when the attack finally occurred. Another time Alexander rejected advice that he attack at night because he refused to "steal my victory" under the cover of darkness.

He never considered victory a given or certainty.

"I think that the Persians will regain courage, as being a match in war for Macedonians, since up to the present time they have suffered no defeat from me to warrant the fear they entertain," he said.

Incidentally, this was not the last time Alexander would be in Tyre. He would return in the spring of 331 after he conquered Egypt to make sacrifices to Hercules and to hold athletic and dramatic contests before heading to Babylon. And it was on that campaign, after his battle with the Indian king Porus, that he introduced elephants to western warfare.

I sneak out of the Tyre ruins over a back wall and climb down a ladder to reach the clean and comfortable promenade along the long, sandy beach in the modern south section of town where there's even a Starbucks. A sign says I'm now in the Tyre Coast Nature Reserve. Then I reach the end of a beach that heralds the beginning of a high security zone and off-limit walking terrain between here and the border with Israel. The next stretch is controlled by Hezbollah in conjunction with the army and I'm told that I won't make it far without special permission.

The last person I spoke to at the Internal Security Forces strongly suggested that I not MedTrek any further and bluntly told me that either the ISF, Hezbollah, the army or the UN would nab me within five kilometers of Tyre – and that it might not be a friendly reception.

I am even more influenced by a conversation with a US journalist who's written a book about Hezbollah and tells me about numerous credentialed journalists who had been held incommunicado by Hezbollah or the army for days "though it's unlikely they'll kill you."

I've MedTrekked almost 200 kilometers with very painful hamstrings during the past two weeks and am delighted that my last day in Beirut coincides with the Eid Al-Adha holiday, which means the city is blissfully free of traffic, honking horns and car pollution. There's an ongoing call to prayer and everyone attends services at the mosques on this day of the feast held in honor of both Abraham, who was willing to sacrifice his son Isaac to God, and the end of the haj pilgrimage to Mecca.

I'm glad to have a few days off to rest my worn-out hamstrings and take it very slowly. My laundry's been turned in and it will be returned pressed and clean by the Bangladeshi women who also keep my room clean at Bliss. I have a long swim, sauna and Jacuzzi session when the gym opens and then a late lunch with my former Stanford classmate Patricia Nabti, who is married to a Lebanese and is involved in establishing various volunteer social programs.

She went to the American Universtiy of Beirut during her sophomore year at Stanford and we discuss the state of the seaside, politics and her effort to increase work by volunteers during lunch at Oliver's. Then I drop by Ibrahim's office to return his phone and present him with a "Don't Disturb" sign from Bliss to add to his collection.

Tyre is not too far north of the Lebanon/Israel border. But the border is closed – Lebanese troops on one side, Israeli troops on the other, UN peacekeepers in the middle – and it takes two days to travel just a few kilometers and kick off the MedTrek on the Israeli side. There, if all goes well, I'll start the hike to Gaza on the sandy and bustling beach at the same time of year that Sukkot and other Jewish holidays bring thousands of serious campers to the seaside.

I decide to enter Israel by way of Jordan (I could have returned to Cyprus and gotten a flight to Tel Aviv). To get there requires a taxi ride to the Beirut airport, a flight to Amman and another taxi to the Marriott Hotel, where I hit the pool shortly after my 4:30 p.m. arrival. I witness a swearing, posturing and shoving "fight" between two Jordanians that security for some reason allows to go on for an hour. I walk away in frustration and complain to the manager about how poorly it was handled by his security staff. He sends me to the Jacuzzi to warm up and cool down.

After the Jacuzzi and sauna I walk downtown and have a lamb

kebab and rice at a hole-in-the-wall that I feature in my "Where Is The Idiot Today?" item: "Amman, Jordan's capital, has become the chic and cosmopolitan crossroads of the Middle East but the food looks the same as when I first visited in 1973."

The next day, I go through the laborious customs procedure at the King Hussein/Allenby Bridge border at the Jordan River. I leave Amman at 7 a.m. to cross into Israel because I figure it will be crowded at the end of Eid Al-Adha and the haj holidays. Although it's only a five hour door-to-door trip, the numerous check points at the crowded border post require more than three hours of lining up, standing, going through security and getting a stamp on a piece of paper rather than my passport.

Then I bus to Jerusalem for another night before proceeding by taxi and bus to Tel Aviv, Haifa and Nahariya to reach the seaside Israel/Lebanon border at Rosh HaNikra.

During the journey, as I adapt to the unhurried pace of public transport and government agencies, I write emails to numerous friends, most notably Liz, who can't come to Israel because she's helping her father move into assisted living accommodation. Here's a snippet of one email to my pal Lex Hames, who traveled and hiked with me to Machu Picchu and Tibet:

"Yeah, Lebanon was a trip and I was fortunate to have been nabbed by the Internal Security Forces instead of Hezbollah or the military in order to obtain some great fodder for the next book. I remember the Lima prison entry (NB: I had talked my way into a woman's prison in Lima to interview Lori Berenson, a New Yorker serving a 20-year sentence for collaboration with terrorists) and this time I actually kept my mouth shut, except to answer questions, when I was in custody. I told the whole truth as they investigated my iPhotos, Facebook pages and anything else I had with me. Sometimes calm, patience and humility do the trick. I consider myself very fortunate.

"And wait until I tell you the details about my gay/bisexual bodyguard from Tripoli to the Syrian border who groped, propositioned and cooed to me during the entire trip. Naturally I had to grin and bear it rather than risk losing my 'protector.' Felt like I must have made women feel when I got involved with them in high school and maybe even at Stanford – 'I really love you for your mind, I love you way too much to make love with you, I won't touch anything but your knee'.... Pretty feeble bullshit when you're on the other end."

During the wait at the border, I read an article about existing Israel coastline development restrictions and efforts by a local legal eagle named Rachelle Alterman, an urban land-use and policy expert at the Technion-Israel Institute of Technology, to see that they are enforced.

"Over the millennia, the Mediterranean Sea has become much more than a transport hub for empires that control the region: It links nations, feeds countries, and its shores hold some of the world's most expensive real estate and natural beauty," the article reads.

Keeping human development in check along the Mediterranean isn't only a goal for environmentalists. Already back in 2004 the United Nations created directives and policies on how coastal development in the Med region should look. And most of the countries in the region signed on.

Professor Alterman initiated Mare Nostrum, a new project that will unite 11 Mediterranean countries and stakeholders in finding ways to better enforce shoreline development regulations..."

Israel is one of the most densely populated countries in the region and has only 2.5 centimeters of coastline per citizen. That's why it was an early adopter and enforcer of coastline development laws, before the UN created its regional protocol in 2004. Alterman says that Israel's coastal control laws are pretty well developed and, except for France, quite possibly the most developed in the Mediterranean region.

The legally binding treaty that most of the Mediterranean countries signed is called the Integrated Coastal Zone Management Protocol of the Barcelona Convention. Among its directives is that development should be set back 100 meters from shore.

"The distance between lofty declarations and what's on the ground gets messy," says Alterman. "There are major disparities between countries in the Med."

She should visit Lebanon.

# FOLLOW THE IDIOT

## CHAPTER PHOTOS

## CHAPTER MAP

# Walking in Israel with the World's Oldest MedTrekker and a Teenage Niece

"A king isn't born, Alexander, he is made. By steel and by suffering. A king must know how to hurt those he loves. It's lonely." – *King Philip, Alexander's father*

"I am not my father! I've taken you farther than my father ever dreamed!" – *Alexander the Great*

The bus drops me at the Golden Walls Hotel across from the Damascus Gate and when I see the scores of people at breakfast the next morning I realize I was lucky to get a room. Sukkot, the season of the Jewish Tabernacle, began this morning and hotels in Jerusalem are packed.

I visit the Old City, which I've been to numerous times since the

1970s, in the afternoon and have dinner with my longtime Israeli-living-in-London friend Michal Shor-Knipe at the YMCA across from the iconic King David Hotel, a lavish lodging where I stayed decades ago when I had an expense account. Michal, the wife of my MedTrekking companion Michael Knipe, frequently visits her family near Tel Aviv and brings me up to speed on current political and security discussions in Israel, where there are always discussions about politics and security.

The next morning, early, I meander along Jerusalem's empty ramparts, alleys, nooks and crannies and wander by Old City landmarks like the Tower of David and the Western Wall, though the Temple Mount is currently off-limits to non-Muslims, which a sullen machine gun-carrying guard at the gate makes very clear to me.

The day after that I share a taxi from Jerusalem to Tel Aviv with a 23-year-old woman from Indiana who spins an interesting tale about how she got a job teaching in a Bethlehem elementary school but, because she's a Palestinian American, is getting much less salary than her American Jewish counterpart.

Fluent in English, Hebrew and Arabic, she quit in protest and is now broke, bewildered and dejected, an upmarket version of the Syrian refugees in Beirut. I suggest she go back to the school and try to negotiate "using your ability to speak three languages and being an asset to the school as your argument. If that doesn't work, contact the media and scream DISCRIMINATION."

Unfortunately this is not an infrequent situation in Israel, which has a population of 8.6 million people, of whom 74 percent are Jewish and 20.8 percent are Arabs. Of the Jews, just over half are religious. Nine percent of them are ultra-religious and 44 percent are secular while 80 percent of the Arabs are Muslims. Each of the two groups tends to live in their own communities and, not surprisingly, inequality frequently exists.

Immediately upon arrival in Tel Aviv, I take a bus north to Haifa and check into my clean and tidy $37-a-night Airbnb apartment in an Arab hillside neighborhood. The apartment looks over the sprawling port out into the Mediterranean Sea and I walk into town to explore the German colony, first settled in 1868 by German Protestant Christians committed to revitalizing the Holy Land. One iconic site in Haifa is the nifty Baha'i Gardens created by the Baha'i faith community that originated in Persia in the 16th century on Mount Carmel – 1,700 steps and 19 terraces up to the Shrine of the Bab, where the remains of the founder of the faith are apparently buried.

The downtown college campus and other areas of Haifa are completely quiet due to the Tabernacles holidays. I send a GPS from the seaside and tweet that "The Idiot is on Israel's Mediterranean seaside and resumes the MedTrek at the Lebanon border tomorrow."

I determine that Haifa, a bustling but beautiful port city, has been polluted by tankers at sea and industry on its shores and is a deserving case study for the implementation of Rachelle Alterman's Mare Nostrum project.

I kick off the MedTrek heading down the coast of Israel to Gaza not far from where I left off south of Tyre in Lebanon – as the proverbial crow flies. But to get here, as I explained to my Airbnb host, took a three-day intentionally relaxed journey to Amman by air, then to the multi-queued customs and border crossing at the King Hussein Bridge by taxi and then to Jerusalem by bus, on to Tel Aviv in a shared taxi, and to Haifa in a communal bus. Early the next morning I plan to take a shared bus and a "special" taxi from Haifa up to Nahariya and Rosh HaNikra at the border with Lebanon.

My host is impressed and peppers me with questions about the situation in Lebanon and what the people I met think about Israel.

"Most people in Lebanon hate Israel with the same passion I witnessed when I was there in the early 1970s," I say. "One Lebanese told me that 'I love all people on earth except the Israelis.'"

It's still very hot here which is why I'm out the door at the first hint of light to make it to the Lebanon border (there's no public transport because of the holidays) early in the day. My plan is to walk back to my apartment by MedTrekking about thirty-five kilometers.

The border, which features a gigantic mural indicating the distances to Beirut (120 kilometers) and Jerusalem (205 kilometers), is atop the picturesque and iconic Rosh HaNikra chalk-white cliff and above grottoes that many tourists visit by boat. Not far away, but not on the sea, is the Rosh HaNikra kibbutz, whose former kibbutzniks include comedian/actor Sasha Baron Cohen whom I met in Hollywood when he was promoting his movie *Borat*.

I pose in front of the sign with some friendly cyclists who have just arrived from Haifa and send a GPS that fails to convey how excited I am to be here after the circuitous journey. After all, four days ago I was less than 20 kilometers away on a beach south of Tyre.

I squint through the wire gate into Lebanon and am told by an Israeli soldier, who lives in the US but is undergoing a three-year military stint in Israel, that all is quiet on the northern front.

"You can see the Lebanese lookout posts from just over there," he says as he points, "but there are UN peacekeepers between our troops and theirs."

"And if I try to walk on the water's edge and or swim across the border marked by buoys in the water?"

"Our water patrol will be happy to meet you," he said. "Trust me, trespassers are prosecuted without many questions being asked."

I marvel about where I am and how I got here before taking some photographs of the "Border Closed," "Border Ahead No Entrance," "No Photos" and "No Trespassing" signs, and the beach that lies ahead before scampering down a path, which is part of the Rosh HaNikra Coast Reserve and parallels the Achziv National Park.

It doesn't take long for me to realize that the beaches, whether sandy or rocky, are much cleaner than their counterparts in Lebanon. There are not only lots of garbage cans, including some see-through recycling containers that, though probably introduced for security, provide a look at what people drink on the beach (lots of water, in fact), and I'm delighted to see workers throughout the day, despite the fact that it's a holiday, actually picking up garbage.

It will be refreshing, after MedTrekking on garbage-filled and mostly empty beaches in Lebanon, to walk on Israel's comparatively clean seaside filled with holiday campers and bathers.

Loads of Israelis have hit the beaches to enjoy the holidays and the method of room and board here is small or sprawling tents close to the sea on public beaches that tend to have hiker-intimidating fences at both ends. I go around, through or over the fences, of course, and think it odd that public beaches, which charge sunbathing customers and campers, have fences to keep out the public. I'm not sure if Sukkot has anything to do with the fishing, but I see more fishermen today, using poles and nets (which actually seem to snag lots of fish), than anywhere on the MedTrek.

The first real city I hit, the northernmost seaside city in Israel, is Nahariya (the name means "rest and recreation"), which was started as an agricultural station in 1935 and is about ten kilometers south of the border. I have a couple cups of coffee and use the Wi-Fi before continuing on the sandy/rocky coast towards Akko or Acre, the historic city at the north end of the horseshoe-shaped Bay of Haifa where, even from this distance, I can see more than twenty ships waiting to dock.

I spend an hour walking around the sea walls in Acre, which is jam packed with holiday makers, and get a delicious photo through a wall of the bluer-than-blue Mediterranean and another of a soccer field that has been built in the city's out-of-commission moat. I investigate Knights Templar caves, an underground prisoners museum and the historic citadel before watching daredevil kids jumping off the walls – while totally ignoring signs that say "Don't Climb The Walls" – into the refreshing sea.

Acre is one of the "oldest continuously inhabited cities in the Middle East" (lots of places make this claim) but there's no question that a number of changes have occurred since the Crusades.

In fact, a nicely timed email from Lex Hames brings me up to speed as I walk: "One of the great battles of the Crusades was in Acre, in 1191, between the Christian Knights led by Richard the Lionheart, and the Muslim forces (or Saracens) led by Saladin. There was a fort on the edge of the sea that was besieged for two years. The Crusaders attacked with siege engines and catapults – the Saracens fought back with bows and arrows. Awesome battle – the Crusaders finally won. I wonder if the old fort is still there...?"

"The old fort is here and if you're looking for something to make the outmoded moat around your citadel a little more utilitarian? Acre has the answer," I write Lex, attaching a photo of the soccer field.

I also share a joke with Lex.

"What do you call The Idiot in Acre?"

"Right – a wiseacre."

It's a straight shot along the sandy seaside into Haifa, Israel's third largest city and a booming center of shipping, heavy industry, high-tech (the Google offices are on the beach just south of town) and education. At the end of the afternoon I am alone on the stretch of virginal seaside between Acre and Haifa and feel comforted by a sign that reads "Go In Peace" written in Hebrew, English and Arabic.

I'm amazed that I have the ten-kilometer long coast to Haifa to myself, but that's perhaps because I ignore a sign that says "Firing Range – No Photos – No Passage." Somehow I am not worried. My reasoning is thus: (1) I figure I can't run into trouble this quickly after my bodyguard and security issues in Lebanon and (2) I doubt that anyone would shoot me on a Jewish holiday. That said, I walk intently and quickly on a seaside stretch that brings me unscathed to Haifa's northernmost coastal urban sprawl.

At one point I hear a whistle and think I'm cooked (I prepare to send an SOS signal with my GPS if things get serious) but then – and for some reason this takes me five minutes to figure out as I continually look over my left shoulder toward the military installation – I realize it's a bird. Whew. I make it through.

The last five urban kilometers into Haifa pass the port, a university, lots of industry and a big Cinemall. Fortunately, my apartment, in a tranquil neighborhood I was told is "risky" by my Jewish taxi driver, is on the first hill at the north end of town and I end the twelve-hour day before sunset.

The next day, I leave my clean apartment and walk a few kilometers into town to Ben Gurion Avenue where I'm scheduled to meet Michael Knipe and his wife Michal for my first round of social MedTrekking on this outing. As you may recall Michael, who was based in Jerusalem as a correspondent for *The Times* of London from 1977 to 79, walked with me in Cyprus and is joining me for the 172-kilometer trek from Haifa to Gaza. He'll be 77 in two weeks and will increase his record distance as the oldest MedTrekker to accompany me. Michal is coming along for the first time.

I fear that we'll begin with a long walk along the busy but dreary Haifa port, but it turns out that most of the port's industrial action is in the north, where I walked into town the day before, and after a couple kilometers – after we pass numerous hospitals for children and cancer research – we're down at the water and heading around the Haifa promontory.

Michal, a former (think over 30 years ago former) Israeli Army soldier attached to a paratroop regiment, moves into MedTrek command mode and gets instructions from people we meet that take us along the sea until we're thwarted by a military base. A bit later, she chastises a compatriot for illegally removing stones from the beach and, very argumentatively, he tells her "your house will burn down." Ah, the humble and polite Israelis take charge.

Forget any Jewish or Israeli preconceptions you might have, particularly regarding money. Michal, who hosted my 64th birthday party in London a few years ago, is always tipping, even when the tip is included because "the waiter never gets the money." She does have an Israeli attitude about Arabs and is concerned about my walk to certain troublesome places in Jerusalem and is also amazed that my Airbnb in Haifa is owned by Arabs. She may not be happy about comments by Palestinians and others that Jews have no right to be in the Promised Land but she's very conscious about paying for street parking and walking legally in street crosswalks.

We're soon on a paved path that takes us along a seaside with numerous restaurants, sophisticated bathing facilities and lifeguards. There are Orthodox Jews bathing fully clothed next to nicely bikini'd unOrthodox whatevertheyares. It's an animated walk, though my hamstrings are killing me and forcing me to constantly bend over or stop for short breaks. I trudge on.

Michal is of Yemeni heritage and both Michael and I are somewhat amused and baffled that she's bothered by the heat, and, after leading the way for the first eight kilometers at a faster pace than mine, drops out for the day. Michael and I continue for another 2.5 hours along the wide sandy beach that takes us by Google, Microsoft and Intel offices; past a large dead turtle with mollusks on its not-yet-decayed shell; and onto the first male-frequented nudist beach I've seen in Lebanon or Israel. When we finally reach Atlit, Michal (who has offered to be our chauffeur) is waiting and I have an easy return to my base camp after drinks in downtown Haifa.

It turns out that Atlit is where Michal's parents were processed when they came from Yemen to Israel in 1949 and we all notice a sign in English that says "Detention Camp."

Michael and I agree to take the next day off to ease muscle pain, especially in my hamstrings, because there's no need to hurry down the coast. I've got two weeks to MedTrek only 190 kilometers and that distance might be shortened if the situation in Gaza stops me in my tracks.

I email Liz that she would appreciate the dog situation in both Israel and Lebanon because there are very few stray dogs – and the ones in Israel all seem to accompany attentive owners. I only saw a few homeless dogs in Lebanon and far fewer than in Turkey or Cyprus. There are, however, lots of cats in both countries, including outside my bedroom window in Haifa.

The plan is that Michal and Michael will arrive at my Haifa apartment and that Michal will move my gear down the coast to a new base camp in Netanya while Michael and I resume the MedTrek where we left off in Atlit near what was once a Crusaders outpost, which I look forward to exploring before we start walking.

I was intrigued to read these massive signs (and I repeat what's written) when we arrived in Atlit the other day:

"Crusader Cemetery – Atlit beach in Israel is completely preserved with more than 1,700 graves. Were buried knights, pilgrims, resident and professionals working in the fort. Some gravestones are decorated with stylized patterns of crosses and icons indicating the status and profession of the deceased. The site is part of the history and cultural heritage of the land of Israel. Respect the place and help us to preserve it."

Another read: "Atlit fortress was built between 1217-1218 by the Knights Templar with the assistance of pilgrims, hence the name Fort Pilgrims (Chateau Pèlerin). The fortress was one of the largest and most modern in the Kingdom of Jerusalem and was the last stronghold in the Crusaders before their withdrawal from the Holy Land in 1291..."

Unfortunately, the cemetery and fortress are now located on soil occupied by the Israeli Navy, and pilgrims, including us, are no longer allowed in. The guards tell us politely, very politely, that we have to walk around the saltpans and factory to get back to the sea. Fortunately, the attendant at the salt marshes lets us walk on the corporate-controlled paths and we arrive at the seaside after passing through urban Atlit.

It's still hot (30°C) and I don't expect to MedTrek the 50 kilometers to Netanya in one day, which means that I'm disappointed when the large and crowded public beach doesn't have a café for a relaxing mid-morning coffee. By 9 a.m., we're walking barefoot on still-not-too-hot sand and in warm-but-still-not-too-hot seawater. Michael and I discuss Mediterranean beaches and agree these are among the best: fine sand, clear water, little litter, few people (when there aren't holidays), ideal October climate. I mention that Israel is where I'll start telling people to come at this time of year.

Again, I marvel at the complex tent communities that secular Israeli Sukkot vacationers have created on the sand, often with dozens of people in each compound. Religious Jews traditionally erect hut-like structures in their gardens or outside their homes to mark the memory of the 40 years of travel through the wilderness that their ancestors experienced after their exodus from slavery in Egypt. Secular Israelis on the beach usually pitch their version of sukkots – pup tents – under a billowing communal circus tent (a *zula* to Israelis).

We ask at one tent where we might get a coffee and we're invited in not only for coffee ("It's very good," says Yoav who makes it for us, "because I let the water boil seven times") but also for *shakshuka* (a Middle Eastern dish of eggs, poached in a sauce of tomatoes, chili peppers and onions that is expertly spiced with cumin) and an hour-long chat about the Israeli penchant for communal tent life on the beach at this time of year.

We discuss the organization of the community and learn that, in this particular spot, there are eight main organizers who each have their specialty.

"He can dig," Yoav says pointing to one burly man, "but I wouldn't let him near the kitchen. Everyone has a specialty and gravitates towards it. Individuals put money in a jar – there's no set amount – to finance things."

There seem to be enough pots and pans to prepare food for, and feed, an army camp. In fact, this communal Israeli camping spirit is sometimes attributed to the 32-month military conscription that all young Israeli men, except the ultra-religious, undertake. For women, it's 28 months, although religious Jews are not obliged to sign up.

Everyone's interested in my tales and photographs from Lebanon and I discuss my adventures with Edden Friedman Killa, a New Yorker who's been living in Israel for ten years and is teaching English in Jaffa.

Reluctantly we leave our new pals and continue hiking through the Dor HaBonim National Park until, just as we enter HaBonim Beach, where there are showers and coffee and picnic tables, Michael falls on sharp pointed rocks and that results in numerous facial lacerations and some chipped teeth. I take him to the emergency room at the beach, where the park officials are very friendly, and, as he lies prone on a hospital bed in the air-conditioned cubicle, I end the day's hike at noon with a swim and freshwater shower after only ten kilometers.

I'm not sure why the Lebanese don't swim much (the garbage on the beaches and the sewage going into the water could have something to do with it) but the women, when they do swim, all wear a full-body swimming suit, as do the Orthodox Jewish women here. I'm the sexiest one on the beach in both places. I, unrestrained by any religious or other constraints, am a master of liberation and ease, an example of freedom to the repressed masses.

While we're waiting Liz sends Michael a get well email: "Oh no! Dearest precious Michael! All the places that are hurt, bruised and need mending have earned you the Homeric Idiot Badge of honor, courage and bravery! You have zoomed up to a whole new category of bravery!"

Michael sends me an email: "Thanks for your patience and efficiency after my fall."

I send my mother an email: "It'll be a week or so before I get to Gaza and I don't think there's a chance that the Israelis, the Egyptians or the Gazettes will let me in. And I don't think I want to go without bodyguards representing each of these groups. So I'll probably just keep getting good stuff in Israel until I leave."

There are lots of tourists with American accents enjoying the holiday, and I chat with a few of them until Michal comes to fetch Michael a couple hours later and drops me at the Park Hotel in Netanya.

The next morning I return alone to HaBonim Beach with the intention of making the 38-kilometer walk back to Netanya, which I sometimes call Netanyahu in reference to Israel's current prime minister Bibi Netanyahu. I kick things off on more beaches with fine sand, water without pollutants, and communal tents crammed with cozy Israelis. When I reach a small beach with no tents – it's an Arab beach and seems like such a downgrade from a "regular" beach that I recall apartheid during my days in South Africa in the 1970s – I decide to walk inland a couple kilometers to see if the Arab village is as "clean" as Jewish Israel.

It doesn't take me long to find out that it's not. In fact, there's enough garbage to make me feel like I haven't left Lebanon, and the shops on the street look like those in the country to the north as well (one has GROCERYS handwritten on a sign outside). Now either I'm a politically incorrect profiler of Arabs, or there's some serious inequality going on here.

The "regular" beaches and campsites continue on Israel's coast until the next surprise of the day, which is the stunning ruins and stone columns at Caesarea, located midway between Haifa and Tel Aviv. These are an amusing contrast to the tall columns rising from the Rabin Light Power Station a few kilometers further south.

I spend an hour walking through the town built by Herod the Great between 25-13 BC on the ruins of Straton's Tower. It was later controlled by the Muslims, the Crusaders, the Mamluks and in 1884 by Bosniak immigrants. It's a refreshing break to explore the mosaics, hippodrome and other remains of Caesarea and I wind up running into Alexander the Great (where have you been, Alexandros? It's great to see you) to discuss the wisdom of walking into Gaza and the problems he had there.

His take?

"If I could do it, you can do it," he says. And then he fades into the sun-glazed air, and is gone once more. But he will be back. I haven't taken in enough of his wisdom and experience yet. And for that matter, neither has he taken in enough of mine.

## PSYCHIATRIC EVALUATION

Then, in a typical MedTrek yin-and-yang example, the beach stops at a fence encircling the Robin Light Power Station, with its four tall and distinctive cooling towers, and I'm forced to walk, if not on water, inland around it after a yoghurt and fruit salad lunch. I learn that I'm now walking on a part of the 1,012-kilometer long Israel National Trail that was inaugurated in 1995, that goes from Dan in the north to Eilat in the south and is identified by its white, blue and orange vertical stripes.

This is where, like the LMT in Lebanon, I might be hiking if I weren't glued to the coast. The section of the INT that I walk takes me through, on the south side of the plant, patches of greenery and picnic tables in the Hadera River Park and across the river on a footbridge. Very attractive in view of the park's yin-and-yang relationship with the power plant.

Beyond that a new Ramada Hotel is in the making. I leave that rising edifice and move on to some fenced-in marinas and ports near Mikhmoret that are part of the Gador Sea Nature Reserve which, I learn, has calcareous sandstone rock formations near the shore that are loved by loggerhead turtles.

Have I mentioned that Israel is expensive? Water is five or six times the price it was in Lebanon. Hotels, for what you get, are hardly a good deal. I think about this as I give my hamstrings a rest in a random chair found incongruously close to the sea.

All along the way are Israeli men (or mostly men) in the water and in the air – kitesurfing, paddle boarding, waterskiing, fishing – and many of them have been up, like me, since sunrise. Lots of others though can be found still slumbering on mats, in tents and preparing food or doing chores in their campsites.

I run into cliffs about five kilometers north of Netanya, whose tall thin buildings look like they're competing with the columns at both Caesarea and the electricity plant, and am surprised and pleased by all the sunbathers. I cruise into town and send a GPS on the Park Hotel beach where, due to the Sabbath, I'll make do with a dinner of crackers, white chocolate and water.

I have time on my hands and Google "Alexander the Great Israel"

306

and learn about a mosaic depicting him in Huqoq, north of Tiberias, and coins found with his image near Caesarea.

"Mosaic of Alexander the Great meeting a Jewish priest is the first ever non-biblical scene to be discovered inside a synagogue," reads the lengthy title in the London *Daily Mail*.

"Stunning mosaics that may depict Alexander the Great meeting a Jewish priest have been unearthed in Israel," reads the article. "The artwork was uncovered in the east aisle of a fifth-century synagogue in the ancient Jewish village of Huqoq and is the first non-biblical story to be found in an ancient synagogue."

Another article notes that there are still remnants being found from bygone days around the Mediterranean. One shiny object found in eastern Galilee in 2016 was a 2,000-year-old gold coin with the face of the Roman Emperor Augustus, the founder of the Roman Empire, who ruled from 27 BC to AD 14. Emperor Trajan minted the coin in AD 107 as a tribute to the reign of "Divus Augustus," or Augustus the Divine. I mention this because it's said that Alexander was the first person to put his face on a coin.

Shabbat during a holiday season is particularly quiet, and Netanya is like a ghost town. I've never seen a place go from buzzy at 60 miles per hour to a dead stop as rapidly as in Israel. And it happens every Friday afternoon.

Its tangible impact on me? Here are two examples:

(1) Because Orthodox Jews can't operate electricity on Shabbat for religious reasons, one of the two elevators at the Park Hotel stops automatically at each floor going up and down which takes a while if, like me, you're on the ninth floor with a seductive view of the Mediterranean.

(2) Because they can't operate electricity, there's no coffee machine in the morning but just hot water and instant coffee.

This hotel, The Park, became an important symbol to many Israelis after a suicide bombing was carried out by Hamas during a Passover Seder in March 2002. Thirty civilians were killed and 140 were injured. Besides holding memorial services at the hotel, guests have stayed there for years as a sign of both defiance and support. It's a bit late, but I add myself to the list.

In addition, there's a buzz that the mafia used to run bakeries in Netanya and it was once the murder capital of Israel. Mayor Miriam Feirberg Ikar, the first elected female in the city, who took office in 1998, gets much of the credit for cleaning it up and turning it around.

I've just come back from a Yemenite Shabbat brunch at the house in a Tel Aviv suburb where Michal was born. It is a lovely, lively, well-stocked Saturday affair overseen by her 90ish mother and attended by a score of family members.

I have a chat with Michal's pregnant lawyer niece Sari Amrusi-Yishai about the apartheidness of the Arab town I walked through ("It's a cultural thing, it's the way they live," she says) and why she's having lots of kids ("It's a genetic and cultural thing rather than something pushed by the government, and though they did help me with IVF they don't pay or help us raise a large family," she says).

Then I chat with a nephew who served in Gaza in 2009.

"We just kept far away from them, and kept them away from us, because you can't tell who's a threat and who isn't," he says.

Michal tells me that at times she visits every two weeks from London, and, once during a sister's fatal illness, found driving by the Mediterranean each morning a "ray of hope despite death." We talk about her father's arrival from Yemen and the pleasure he got out of serving Ben Gurion; the changes in the family neighborhood from agriculture and small houses then to very tall apartment buildings now, the joy of weekly Shabbat gatherings and an invitation to another dinner tomorrow night. Then there are kisses and hugs from everyone as Shabbat hopefully starts to wind down and Netanya begins to wake up.

Will we make it all the way into Tel Aviv as Michael rebounds after his fall? Not that I'm worried. I've got ample time to get to and, if possible, through Gaza during the next ten days. It appears I may even have a family companion on the MedTrek to Gaza. My 21-year-old niece Sara will be visiting from Egypt, where her archaeological dig with UCLA has been delayed. She has some time off; she can roam the landscape with Uncle Joel, well known for his wit, sagacity, and adventuresome spirit.

Shortly after 7 a.m. we kick off at The Park Hotel – Michael, his niece Sari (not to be confused with Sara) and me – immediately get into sandy beach walk mode after we descend the staircase to the seashore. We find, most happily, a continuation of Israel's sandy beaches that began, with only very few interruptions, at the Lebanon/Israel border only six days ago. The glorious sand rolls on. We shift our hips into beach drive and move out.

Sari and I continue our discussion from yesterday's Shabbat lunch and she becomes the day's "Where Is The Idiot Today?" subject:

"MedTrekking from Netanya towards Tel Aviv with a 30ish liberal Orthodox Israeli lawyer and mother of three...Walking on Mediterranean sand and discussing the fate of Israel ("We're stuck where we are, with periods of war and peace, unless something happens from the outside," said Sari); the Gaza spinoff, Orthodox and not-so-Orthodox Judaism; the coexistence of Arab and Jewish cultures, and the attraction of the seaside."

Sari lives in Netanya and walks the first eight kilometers with us along cliffs and below cliffs, past the towering and too-close-to-the-seaside Season Hotel, and through the end of the newly developed southern Netanya suburbs. Sari explains that all the growth in the city involves towering apartment buildings that are becoming shaky and in need of repair. One incentive the city offers to encourage renovation of these older buildings is to give a contractor or owner who renovates the entire structure the right to add two floors in compensation. And those can be sold at a profit. Sounds sensible to me. Although it does mean that all the apartment buildings on the shoreline in Netanya may soon be two stories higher.

We make a pit stop for coffee and water at a restaurant in the sand. I keep complaining about the ludicrously high price of water and Sari tells me that all water in Israel is fit to drink, so I start filling my water bottle from faucets to boycott the ludicrously high prices.

The cliffs continue, as do we, while we skirt by two kibbutzim that are above and behind the cliffs, and by 11 a.m., there are far fewer big tents and a narrower beach. Sari, though she admits she's never done the walk all the way into Tel Aviv, tells me to expect some nudist beaches. I'm happy to report to her later that I saw about a dozen naked male organs and one set of breasts as I approached Tel Aviv.

Once Sari leaves, I do try to be more social and have three conversations with hikers coming from the other direction.

Here's what I say to a man my age wearing a New York Yankee baseball cap a few days after the team gained a post-season wild card berth.

"Are you a Yankee fan from the US?" I inquire.

"I was, I was."

Another man asks where I'm going.

"Gaza," I say.

"Don't go there! They're all crazy," he responds, sounding ominously like the Turks who told me not to go to Syria with the same tone of voice. "There are no Israelis left in Gaza."

Then I meet a couple whose grandparents left Poland and Austria in the 30s to settle in Israel. The husband explains that the sandstone cliffs stopped getting any higher after the Aswan dam was built, because the dam restricted the movement of sand. Then he begins talking about the refugee problem in Europe.

"We're all refugees here and our grandparents came with nothing and established a new identity, a new life," says the wife. "We know how they feel."

Michael and I get separated when he prefers taking a path up the cliffs to negotiating the giant boulders of the seaside breakwater. We somehow fail to meet on the other side, though I hike up the hill and look for him near the Appolonia ruins (the couple told me these ruins of the Phoenician village of Arsuf from the fifth or sixth century BC aren't worth visiting if I'd seen Caesarea) and the Sidna Ali Mosque. As planned,

Michael and I both continue in the same direction to the marina in Herzliya where, somehow, we still don't reunite.

There are lots of boats in the water as I approach the Herzliya marina, which includes an upscale mall, a Ritz Carlton Hotel, a Carrefour supermarket (I buy cheese, a roll, two bananas and a 1.5 liter bottle of water for lunch), numerous other shops and lots of tanned Jewish holiday bodies playing racquetball, football and Frisbee.

I return by bus and a communal taxi to Netanya where I post my weekly *Follow The Idiot* item entitled "How Does an Idiot-ic MedTrekker in Israel Observe Sukkot, or the Jewish Feast of the Tabernacles?"

"The Idiot didn't have a clue what would impress him most as he MedTrekked down the coastline of Israel in early October when everyone in the country was observing Sukkot, or the Feast of the Tabernacles," the article reads.

"Would it be the state of the wide, clean, sandy beaches that stretch the length of the country crowded with Jewish holiday sunbathers and vacationers?

Was it the hippodrome at the Caesarea ruins...a shipwreck south of Haifa...multi Israel flags flying...a deceased turtle near Atlit...the realization how much easier the MedTrek would be on horseback when he saw these relaxed riders near Mikhmoret...the stroll beneath the cliffs into Netanya...a rare nudist near Herzilya?

Actually, none of the above.

The Idiot was continually intrigued by communal Sukkot tent life that, during the extended Jewish holidays, transformed the Mediterranean coast into the world's longest kibbutz.

Sociologists claim that one reason Israelis like to group together under tents like this is because of fond memories of their shared national service in the military. Tents on Israeli beaches provide a new definition of camping out – or taking absolutely everything you own to the beach."

A day later I return to my last GPS location just south of the Herzliya marina and continue on the sandy beach to Tel Aviv – at least I think I'm on the way to Tel Aviv. Since Michal isn't walking with me to translate signs from Hebrew to English, I can't be absolutely certain.

There are lots of surfers in the water and I meet an Israeli who lived in Newport Beach for eleven years and is about to move back because he thinks "Mediterranean waves are a joke."

"What are they waiting for?" he laughs as looks at the surfers and describes the superior attributes of California and the Pacific Ocean.

Just a few hundred meters into Tel Aviv, the sandy beach is abutted by an elevated concrete path, half dedicated to cyclists, half to walkers and joggers. Michael says, "wouldn't it be great if there were a walkway like this around the entire Mediterranean?" I tell him I'm glad there isn't one.

"Diversity and the unexpected are what make the MedTrek exciting," I say. Truer words were never spoken; surprise is my name, the unlikely is my game!

We find a concrete path that takes us into Tel Aviv as we approach the Sde Dov Airport, which looks like a proverbial landing strip in the desert, although it's close by the ocean. Mirages, miscalculations and mist – it's the Middle East. Michael landed here once coming from Amman, he tells me – back in his old foreign correspondent high life and high danger days. After we pass the Reading Power Station, a fine array of footbridges, sidewalks and decorative promenades lead us through the old Tel Aviv Port and along the beginning lineup of the city's sixteen beaches (we start with the Metzitzim and Nordau Beaches and end the day at the Gordon, Frishman and Bugrashov Beaches). We stroll past hotels that were standing when I was here on reporting assignments in the '80s and '90s. Visually, not much has changed.

It's a pleasant urban walk on beaches that are blissfully close to empty. Yesterday was the last of the long string of Jewish holidays and people are getting back to work. It means fewer folks on the sand, a development I welcome. We end our walk not far from the Opera Tower, at a restaurant on Jerusalem Beach with coffees and cakes, a good way to celebrate the closing of a long day.

From there I repair to my base camp at a two-bedroom Airbnb on Ness Tziona Street, where I will await the arrival of my niece Sara (not to be confused with Sari), whose flight from Egypt has been delayed a day or two. Will she get here in time to walk to and through Gaza with me? Time will tell; it's in the hands of the gods, and there's rather a large smattering of them here in the Middle East, constantly throwing thunderbolts and stirring up the winds and destroying things in general, ending human hopes, wishes and dreams. Inshallah. As God wills it.

An hour later, while I eat a helping of hummus while watching the sun come down behind a rare grove of palm trees on a beach in Tel Aviv, I decide that I'll try to watch the sun set at a different beach, from Hof Hatzuk to the north and Jaffa to the south, each night that I'm in Tel Aviv. A different chair, a different view for each evening's shower of gold over the salty water. A good plan.

The next morning, Michael and I kick off on the Medside boardwalk past Jerusalem Beach, Banana Beach and Charles Clore Beach into Jaffa where we pass the Museum of Jaffa's Liberation, St. Peter's Church, an Armenian church and numerous other remnants of old Jaffa.

It was "only" twenty-five years ago, when I was on a reporting assignment for the *International Herald Tribune*, that I made my first walk from Tel Aviv to Jaffa. Then, it was like an adventure on a wild beach, because there was, comparatively, no development on the coast at that time. I can remember the sense of the "wild" I had when I walked from the

Hilton or the Sheraton south. No longer. The paved promenade makes walking easy and there are hotels and business high rises throughout the route.

On arrival, though, it's easy to find the old Jaffa as we walk through the port and up the narrow alleyways past churches and intriguing doors to the lighthouse. Jaffa's still a mixed city with Jewish and Arab residents and there are a series of posters done by kids that show the different religions and races coexisting.

We head out of Jaffa towards Bat Yam, another high-rise community (I was expecting a low-rise country, but Israel is moving up in the world), featuring the Leonardo Hotel (like in Haifa, there's a guard in front) and an expansive sandy beach. We continue until there's a much-more-serious-than-usual fence across the sand that extends a good distance into the sea.

I'm surprised that this is only the second time I'm stopped in my tracks by an Israeli Defense Force installation (the other was in Atlit) and I'm informed by a soldier that this one blocks the coast for seven kilometers. Unlike the firing range south of Acre, which I walked through to enter Haifa, I'm not taking any chances here.

In fact, as I take pictures of signs telling me not to take pictures, a shell goes off and we quickly begin the inland detour. After walking a few kilometers, and talking to a few more soldiers, it's apparent that we need to take a taxi around the installation to return to the sea at the Palmahim Beach National Park, where we visit the remains of the Yavne-Yam port from the Middle Bronze Age.

The definite highlight of the day is a photograph I take of a young female army soldier who's undergoing national service in the Israel Defense Forces, a rite of passage for almost every young Israeli. A few words with this 20-year-old soldier convey the confidence that Israel's youth have in their country's future. The second highlight is talking to a couple of the National Park rangers who tell me that there's another nature park in Ashkelon.

Why is this a highlight? Because it's here that I get the idea that Gaza could become a National Park or Nature Reserve, though the complicated situation in the Palestinian enclave seemingly precludes that from ever happening.

The military base continues on our left once we restart the MedTrek on the beach. We have the rocky, wild, wavy and deserted beach to ourselves for the next 2.5 hours as we approach and hike toward another sprawling electric power station at the northern edge of Ashdod. Beyond it, I'm surprised to see two gigantic cruise ships in a port that must rival Haifa. We head inland to get around the power plant and have a surprisingly healthy sandwich at a place called Lyon.

Despite healthy sandwiches at Lyon and our calm beach walk,

tensions are again rising between Palestinians and Israelis throughout the country, from the Old City in Jerusalem to the West Bank and suburbs of Tel Aviv. Absolutely no one thinks it will be possible to get into Gaza from the Israeli side, and the usual response is still "You may get in but you won't get out."

Indeed, the generally paranoid US Embassy in Tel Aviv, which will soon be moved to Jerusalem, has nothing good to say about Gaza. They point out that that they won't help stranded Americans, and I learn that many smugglers' tunnels have been destroyed at the other end of Gaza on the Egypt border. There goes my emergency Plan B and exit strategy.

I constantly get advice during my 400-kilometer MedTrek from Syria to Gaza, although most people – of various cultural, national, political, racial and religious persuasions – question my general sanity and are adamant that I abandon my quest if I want to live another day. The suggestion that I quit MedTrekking now intensifies due to increasing unrest and violence throughout Israel, although I've personally witnessed none of it.

Indeed, I not only continue toward Israel's border with Gaza but also feel confident and comfortable enough to invite Sara to accompany us. Liz was also invited along but is unable to make the trip from the US.

I take two days off. One in Tel Aviv to do nothing until my niece Sara finally arrives, 48 hours late from Cairo; another to move my gear to Ashkelon on Israel's southern Mediterranean coast for three nights. That will give Michael, Sara and me a base camp to complete the MedTrek to the Gaza border.

I'm glad to have Sara along, because she frequently accuses me of tormenting her when she was younger. That's not completely false. Whenever I returned to Redding, I would always ask her to choose a number between zero and ten and then tell her that she was really, really close but it was 4, not 3; or 8, not 7; or 10, not 1. It took her years to understand that she was being tricked, and she claims that being misled by a trusted uncle resulted in years of therapy.

More recently we climbed Mount Lassen near Redding together and I'm not worried about her ability to hike, though I know from an earlier experience that I won't let her be the guide on this outing. That's because the only time I tested Sara as a guide was during a 60th birthday party I hosted for myself when Sara was 12 or 13. I hired her to lead guests on a walk across the Sundial Bridge and north on the Sacramento River Trail in Redding. We'd gone over the route, she'd perfected her spiel and I was looking forward to the adventure when we gathered at the bridge at 9 a.m. However, after just a few dozen yards on the trail, Sara stopped in front of a large tree and said, with great confidence: "This is a tree... Time for lunch."

Now that she's older I'm sure all those youthful flippant traits are in the past. Although she dyed her blonde hair brown when she was in Egypt a year earlier, in an effort to be inconspicuous, Sara's got a totally American blonde intelligent surfer girl look when Michal, Michael and I fetch her at the airport. She'll definitely add some zip to our Zenny walk and also be able to give us some details about some of the archaeological sites we pass.

What does she know after studying archaeology in college?

At one point I discovered an array of colored tiles taken from the classical Roman city of Pompeii, Italy, at the Behrens-Eaton House Museum in Redding. I urged the Behrens-Eaton House Museum to return the painted tiles and other stones, taken from Pompeii by Judge Richard B. Eaton while serving in the US Army in World War II.

It was Sara who verified that they were the real thing, which prompted the museum to offer to return the mosaics, tiles and stones to Italy. They are, however, still in the museum today.

Fortunately, Sara has a gigantic duffle suitcase that requires a medium-size rental car to transport it efficiently. This turns out to be a blessing in disguise. It enables the two of us, as we drive the next day from Tel Aviv towards Gaza, to follow the path Michael and I ambled down after Jaffa and check out the coast to Gaza before we walk it.

After Sara and I lunch on another healthy sandwich at Lyon in Ashdod we're reassured about the ease of the 24-kilometer beach walk from there to Ashkelon. It seems like a straight shot, though there may be some military and geographical inconveniences.

The drive south to Gaza reveals that there are not only some beach inconveniences – including the entry fee to the Ashkelon National Park (they want 29 shekels, the robbers), a sprawling power station and several military installations – but it also gives us an insight into the status and significance of Gaza, which has changed as tensions mounted between Israelis and Palestinians over the past ten days.

We drive inland to the Israeli village of Hetiv HaAsara that abuts Gaza. It's well-guarded by Israeli soldiers. One is an American trainee, a paratrooper-to-be, who tells us, "If you touch a fence we'll know you're there," and describes the tall mosaic wall at the border with Gaza.

"This is a normal community and we're just here to ensure that things stay chill," says the American from New York. His voice has a touch of that harsh New York nasal tone. He's accompanied by a few friendly yellow Labradors and suggests we drive down to see the tall walls that separate Gaza from Israel. "There's been some commotion on certain Gaza borders but nothing noisy here. We also think they've dug tunnels into Israel from Gaza."

We go a few kilometers further east and arrive at the closed Erez Crossing, the only land crossing between Israel and Gaza where we hear shouting and gunfire. I imagine that it's Palestinians taunting the Israeli troops, but we can only guess. We listen for five minutes and return to our rented base camp apartment on the marina in Ashkelon and hear on television "Around 500 Palestinian protesters tried to breach the Erez Crossing in northern Gaza Strip and were stopped by the IDF." The next day I learn that four Palestinians were killed.

"This is how we live," says Iris, the owner of our sea view apartment rental who's originally from New Jersey. "Cycles of war and peace, peace and war."

The next morning Sara and I return to Ashdod, meet Michael and kick things off at the West All Suite Hotel. We hike past the expanding towering high-rise housing complexes south of town along a fine-sanded beach populated with all kinds of drones and miniaturized flying machines that zoom down towards us like kamikaze pilots. Everyone from drone pilots to sun worshipers seems blissfully ignorant of yesterday's confrontation at the nearby Gaza border.

The only diversion during the entire hike, that is done barefoot, is the ruins of the ancient Ashdod Harbor but throughout the day, until we arrive in Ashkelon, I admire Michael's ability to walk so well at 77, Sara's fluid pace at 21, and my persistence at 67.

Ashkelon gets its name from an ancient city whose remains are at the Ashkelon National Park. Mentioned in the Bible many times, the first people here were the Canaanites though the main stories are about Samson, who wound up here "because he had a thing for Philistine women," says one gossipy report on the strong man.

It's refreshing to visit the Ashkelon National Park and see the results of a dig that began in 1997. The park is a half hour walk along the seaside from our apartment in the marina, where I found a note on my rental car that said "Park here again and you won't have any wheels the next time you see your car!"

Michael speeds far ahead of us and is out of our sight before we reach the national park. Sara and I continue along the sandstone cliffs as she gives me archaeological descriptions of pottery shards and other findings. Everything goes well – I'd thought we'd have to cut inland because of a gas works and power plant – until we ignore a large sign in Hebrew that apparently says "STOP! PRIVATE! WE'LL SHOOT!" and are approached by two security guys with automatic rifles.

"Just agree with everything I say," I tell Sara, "and back me up if I make any radical outbursts."

My hamstring pain encourages me to refuse to backtrack and we discuss things for half an hour with the security personnel. The plant's manager finally agrees with my recommendation that signs should also be in English and Arabic and ends the standoff when he takes us on a 100-meter drive in his pick-up to get to the other side of the facility.

Then we walk inland for 45 minutes and another 45 minutes through the sand dunes to Zikim Beach where there's a warning sign that says in English, "Restricted area, Entry is Forbidden, Trespassers will be prosecuted according to the low (sic)." We swim, ride the waves, take a sweet water shower and hitch a ride, then bus, then taxi back to our rental in record time.

On the funky beach in Zikim, a former soldier recounts a story about an Israeli who walked to Gaza, threw his pack over the border fence, got inside and is still there. Again, I hear the phrase, "You might be able to get in but you won't be able to get out."

After the break, I'm ready to walk past the military lookout to the border fence and enter dangerous Gaza and the ISIS-frequented Sinai Peninsula to reach Egypt. I'll find out if the dire warnings are accurate or not.

# FOLLOW THE IDIOT

## CHAPTER PHOTOS

## CHAPTER MAP

# Reaching Gaza and the Sinai Peninsula

"O king, thou wilt indeed capture the city, but thou must take
care of thyself on this day."
— *Aristander the soothsayer* in Gaza

I've got to admit that not one person in Israel endorsed the idea
that I go into Gaza. In fact, no one anywhere outside Gaza endorsed the
idea that I venture into Gaza – and, no, I didn't talk to anyone inside.
Gaza's reputation is worse than Syria's. Heck, even Alexander the Great
had more trouble in Gaza (Gaza is the Greek form of the Hebrew name
Azzah or fortress) than he did in Syria.

According to Arrian's account in *The Anabasis of Alexander*, a
commander named Batis (some historians say he was a eunuch) ruled
Gaza with the assistance of Arabian mercenaries when Alexander arrived
on the outskirts of the town built on a tall mound at the edge of the desert.
As in Tyre, the strong wall theoretically made this last city between
Phoenicia and Egypt difficult to attack and conquer. In addition, Batis had
an adequate supply of food and water and was confident that he could
outlast anyone trying to take Gaza.

The siege lasted two months, and the keys to Alexander's success
were the tunnels he dug to collapse the city walls, coupled with a tall

mound he created at the southern end of the city that again enabled him, as it did in Tyre, to launch an attack with catapults. Any Gazans not killed in the battle were slaughtered or sold into slavery. After Batis was executed, his naked body was tied to the back of a chariot driven by Alexander and dragged around the city. That, of course, as the story of the *Iliad* goes, is precisely what Achilles did to Hector after he defeated him at Troy.

The soothsayer Aristander's prediction also proved to be true. When a large bird dropped a clod of earth on Alexander's shoulder that then bounced onto a catapult, it was interpreted by Aristander to mean that Alexander would be wounded before he took the city. Indeed, he was hit and injured by a ball from a catapult, which kept him out of action for a while.

The image of Israeli drones dropping clods of dirt on me has become a regular nightmare. In dreamland I seem to be mixing up Alexander's travails with my own.

With the MedTrek from Syria to Gaza completed, Sara and I catch up on both sleep and news of growing unrest in Israel, including a survey in *The Jerusalem Post* that presents a panorama of viewpoints concerning increased violence throughout the country.

While enjoying a celebratory dinner at Scubar on the port in Ashkelon I ask Sara to give me her opinions about MedTrekking with The Idiot. Over coffee (well, Nescafés) the next morning, I type as she dictates her appreciation of the MedTrek before we go down to the gym in our marina apartment complex for a sauna, steam bath and Jacuzzi. She notes:

"I've been hearing about The Idiot and the MedTrek since I was four years old, and I'm pleased that there's no disparity between my image and the reality," says Sara, who wanted to be a journalist until a year ago. "When I was a kid, I felt it was super glamorous because you were traveling around this mythical place called Europe. Now, wow, I'm doing the thing that I always thought was so neat to do. And it's especially rewarding because I imagined doing it as a youngster.

"There were no dramatic problems, though I'm not sure it's smart of you to be rude to guards with machine guns. Everything that came up required a flexible response and you came up with one. I learned that even walking on beaches can be hard if you have an obsessive intent to get somewhere. It's better to just let the sand slow you down and walk more slowly. Landmarks in the distance get closer, but you can't go faster or you wreck your calves.

"Israeli security men with machine guns are very cute, and all the Israel Defense Forces seemed to be between ages of 20-24, which is just right for me. IDF men and women look normal, not intimidating. I realize they have sisters, brothers, mothers, and grandmothers and are all real people. The women soldiers accessorize and have perfect hair and the boys all have their Ray-Bans and other hot stuff. Describing the MedTrek and what you're doing gives them a bit of a challenge because it seems so weird to them. Lebanon and Gaza are different worlds and their enemies.

"The distance was easy, and it's fun having Michael along because he's a good walking partner. All this makes for a good story. Interesting people that you know can hold their own. I wish I knew what's public land and, though it's not life changing, I have a bad cold."

We pick up Michael at the nearby globe-shaped Holiday Inn and head back to Tel Aviv, where I've booked an Airbnb apartment with a sea view for two nights. Sara can explore the big, zippy city and we'll celebrate Michael's 77th birthday with a lunch on the beach, or somewhere. He flies back to London Tuesday night; Sara leaves Wednesday morning; and my flight is at 11 p.m. on Wednesday. Thus concludes a very successful and somewhat exciting MedTrek through two relatively peaceful countries between two territories, Syria and the self-governing Palestinian territory of Gaza, which are in a state of violent conflict and rarely put on anyone's vacation bucket list.

On the way to Tel Aviv, The Idiot energy factory is beginning to hum. I'm mentally beginning to shift into California action mode, in anticipation of the Stanford/UCLA football game on Thursday night. Plus I'm excited about getting my car serviced, having a haircut, enjoying a facial and participating in an annual "Walk to End Alzheimer's" in Redding. I also have to drive to San Francisco in a week for my annual Alzheimer evaluation as part of a longitudinal research project at UCSF (I'm a healthy research subject) and then go on to a full agenda of 45th reunion events at Stanford.

But I'm immediately brought back to reality in Israel during the drive when Michael shares his MedTrekking memories and reads us a draft of an article he's writing about it:

"Awarded the title 'The World's Oldest MedTrekker' (I'm 77) after my maiden spell accompanying The Idiot around parts of the coast of Cyprus in June, I could hardly refuse his invitation to join him for a similar jaunt down the beaches of Israel this month.

My preparations for the Israeli MedTrek had again been occasional, leisurely hikes on London's Hampstead Heath. One hour to the top of the Heath, a half-hour coffee break, another hour home.

When I'm not rushing for a bus or to the shops, and when I don't have earphones clamped to my ears, I find that walking gives my mind time to ruminate, to wander and to wonder. My body sets its own pace. I can think, analyze issues and recall memories. I can also take in the scenes around me.

That type of walking meditation made me feel that I was ready for the MedTrek.

Things start off fine. The Idiot, having MedTrekked the length of Lebanon and northern Israel from the Syrian border, greets me on the beach at Haifa and we stroll past Microsoft's R&D Center, one of the high-tech industries that sets the pulse of Israel's economy, and pass a beached and deceased sea turtle.

Throughout the sea-turtle egg-laying season, from May to September, inspectors of the Israel Nature and Parks Authority comb the beaches along the entire Israel coast every morning, rescuing female turtles and transferring them to one of five protected breeding farms. When the eggs hatch the baby turtles are shepherded from their nests towards the sea. And some, apparently, return here to die.

We are MedTrekking during the annual Sukkot holiday, when Jews create temporary hut-like structures in memory of their ancestors who trekked through the wilderness after their exodus from Egypt. Fortunately for us, many of the more secular Israelis establish their Sukka in Bedouin-style communal tents on the beach and invite MedTrekkers in for coffee, cakes and even *shakshuka* during the Feast of the Tabernacles.

On the MedTrek, our early start gives me a chance to see the sun rising. Striding or ambling along the Israeli coast, I hear the rhythm of the waves and feel the sea breeze. I see municipal workers collecting and taking away the litter of the day before. And, a little later, Jews and Arabs – of every age and every body shape and size – in uninhibited beachwear, at play: many lone fishermen, swimmers and paddlers, surfers, sunbathers and sun-worshippers, children and their parents building sandcastles. And then you hear and see the men, mostly men, playing *matrot*, a bat and ball game, similar to table tennis, but played more fiercely and ferociously.

MedTrekking, even on Israeli beaches, is no walk in the park. We hiked across a variety of beaches: soft sand (tough going), hard wet sand (the best), shells (painful), shingle (more painful), pebbles (worse), stones and rocks. It was on the sharp rocks that I stumbled, falling flat on my face. Fortunately, we had just left an almost entirely deserted beach and entered a nature reserve where The Idiot, after giving me first aid, took me to a beachside emergency room where a medic laid me out on a stretcher and patched up my cuts.

MedTrekking is not an asocial activity. We passed numerous men fishing and even one grooming his dog in the sea. And while accompanied on the MedTrek by my niece-in-law Sari, we even took a rare coffee break. Although The Idiot doesn't like admitting it, he takes occasional coffee breaks when he's hiking with other people.

Yikes, another encounter with a dead animal. Persian fallow deer, native to Israel from Biblical times, were hunted to extinction in the early 1900s. But in 1978, the Iranian government agreed to give Israel four fallow deer and, as a result, today there are a number of wild herds throughout the country. And we stumble on a dead deer.

322

On two occasions when the beach route was blocked by power stations, I had to trek around them and once when I judged the rocks to be too formidable I left the Mountain Goat Idiot to venture into the interior.

Our generally pleasant seaside MedTrek on sandy beaches continued for over 100 kilometers (The least appealing sight and sound? Mostly men in motorized hang-gliders whizzing along the beach just above my head) until the first barbed wire barrier signaled, and blocked, the border into Gaza. My MedTrek in Israel ended when I neared the border with Gaza, but I hope The Idiot will invite me to join him in Egypt."

"What glints of wisdom did you gain on the McdTrek?" I asked Sara when Michael finished reading. A day later, she read me her response:

"Travel can be a soul-breaking and strength-forging activity: the chronicles of my uncle's own wanderings on his walk around the Mediterranean Sea are the most recent amongst the accumulations of such accounts.

But what would I find?

Maybe personal epiphanies or some bigger truths from exposure to The Idiot's always electrified environment (preferably, with some anecdotes to write home about).

After a week of walking, talking, and watching The Idiot talk himself out of sticky situations, my findings were more practical than esoteric. Beyond the sensation that is *shakshuka* (if you have not had it, eat it immediately), here are my discoveries:

1. Find an essential cafe. If the coffee is good and the food is local, be loyal to it. My favorite cafe in Tel Aviv is just steps away from our Airbnb sea view apartment.

2. I'll give The Idiot credit where credit is due: he can make a damn good cup of Nescafé. Known abroad as "American coffee," despite the many times that I protest that it is not, Nescafé is essential for early MedTrekking starts and suitable for pre-caffeination purposes before walking to my favorite cafe.

3. Appreciate what little lessons the locals can teach you, even without the use of words.

From Jaffa to Zikim Beach, beach bums looked content, if not pleasantly bored, just standing at the water's edge with a fishing rod.

Were the fish biting? Apparently not.

Does it matter? Apparently not.

Pretense to just zone out by the water. Noted.

4. Don't be content to simply take the road less traveled: toe the line and, if you think you can, stumble across it. Go equally to the odd and the idyllic places. Indulge your curiosity. How would one cross into Gaza? What do the nearby communities look like?

5. Take time to watch the sun set."

One of the remarkable things about the Middle East, or almost any place that constantly fluctuates between war and peace, is how daily life continues despite increased social tension or outbreaks of violence. With the exception of Syria – where hopelessness reigns, half the population has fled and the outcome is unpredictable – there's often an eerie sense of surreal complacency.

"When they were bombing a building or there was a street fight in my neighborhood," Philippe tells me in Beirut, Lebanon. "I just moved down the block to a quieter spot."

"We don't know where all the stabbings this month will lead," says Iris, the owner of my Airbnb in Ashkelon, Israel. "But we've learned to live with uncertainty rather than despair."

People are still baking bread, attending school and serving coffee in Lebanon. Students casually attend class at the American University of Beirut (AUB) and young cooks in a bakery south of Beirut invite The Idiot in to sample their tasty, fresh flatbreads. In Israel some are sunbathing nude (a very few, in fact), cycling, often furiously, and celebrating Jewish holidays.

Naturally, almost everyone almost everywhere in the Middle East is a bit on edge. But in Lebanon, where I was arrested by the Internal Security Forces on charges of spying, and in Israel, where Sara and I heard shouts and gunfire in Gaza that resulted in the death of four Palestinians, life resolutely goes on.

Here are just a few "normal" people who took the time to give The Idiot some insight into their lives, communities and countries during his recent MedTrek between Syria and Gaza on the coasts of Lebanon and Israel.

Israel: The heroine of The Idiot's steps in Israel was Michal Shor-Knipe, who not only provided a history of her Yemenite family's arrival and life in the country over the past 65 years, but also smilingly chauffeured The Idiot and other MedTrekkers, including her husband Michael Knipe, from one leg of the MedTrek to another. תודה רבה.

Lebanon: The hero of The Idiot's time in Lebanon was Ibrahim Muhanna, chairman of The Muhanna Foundation, who provided an intriguing assessment of Lebanon, life and love during many pleasant encounters and meals in Beirut. شكراً

Israel: Sari Amrusi Ishai, who MedTrekked and dined with The Idiot, provided the intriguing viewpoint of a liberal Jewish Orthodox woman/mother/lawyer.

Lebanon: Patricia Mihaly Nabti, who graduated from Stanford University with The Idiot in 1970, described her enthusiasm and concerns about Lebanon, where she's lived since 1992.

I get an urgent text from Sara informing me that she was inquisitioned by Israeli security at the airport and that she gave them the scoop on me and my walk and everything I've been doing, including my arrest in Lebanon. That gets me worried that I'll be pulled aside and interrogated, though I've done nothing wrong and have nothing to hide.

Despite my projection (I'm still capable of blowing snails into dinosaurs or gorillas), I breeze through passport control without any problem.

I get another view of the Middle East after I return to my California base camp just a week after reaching the edge of Gaza on the MedTrek.

I compliment exchange student Nataly Jomaa, 15, following her "Palestine Is My Identity" presentation at Shasta College in Redding, California. Palestinian Jomaa – who is spending a year studying at Shasta High School, which I attended fifty years ago – discussed the challenges and delights of growing up in the State of Palestine and her impressions of Israel, Israeli institutions and Jewish Israelis.

"We are definitely not equal in Israel, but I am very proud to be a Palestinian," she said. "It's nice to be in Redding where there are no walls and military checkpoints."

Nataly, who's staying in the home of a female minister with a Muslim "sister" from the Philippines, is a zippy teen from Ramallah who speaks of the discrimination, separation and second-class status she's faced throughout her life with a this-is-the-way-it-is not-very-hostile tone. She did refuse, however, the idea of going to a camp with Jewish Israeli teens in Maine where "they all play like they're equal when they obviously aren't – I wouldn't play that game." Her chat is complemented by a PowerPoint presentation that she obviously got from the Palestinian Authority, or someone with a distinctly Palestinian point of view, before she left the West Bank.

Her comments on the normalcy of Redding – no checkpoints or visible military – and candid responses to basic questions bring things home to the people in the audience, some whom have visited the Middle East for work or play (her hostess was in Cairo during the Arab Spring and was evacuated by the US Embassy). I go to the talk with my high school English teacher and his wife and am delighted to get a photo of them with Nataly for "Where Is The Idiot Today?"

Although everyone from the entire population of Israel to the US Embassy to my mother thinks it an Idiot-ic pursuit, I begin giving some thought to MedTrekking in Gaza – again. The idea does not seem to want to die. For some reason, it doesn't bother me to hear repeatedly that "you'll be able to get in but you might never get out."

The Israelis may have made it impossible to enter Gaza through the Erez Crossing border point which Sara and I visited – and the current deterioration of relations between the Palestinians and Israel (stabbings in Jerusalem, killings at the border in Gaza, rockets intercepted in Ashkelon) doesn't make this an ideal time for a visit, although there's probably never an ideal time to visit Gaza. The shouting and battle we heard are a reminder that this is serious stuff – as are the stories about many people who've gone in but haven't gotten out.

Consequently, I decide to petition the Egyptian government the following spring when things may have cooled off. Perhaps, they could allow me to enter Gaza at the Rafah border crossing and to MedTrek the 40-kilometer long Mediterranean coast. It could be done in a long day.

If Gaza, and perhaps even the dangerous Sinai, are not meant to be MedTrekked by The Idiot, I'm pleased that Sara provides me with some alternatives and tips concerning Egypt.

"It's not that I mean to dissuade The Idiot from his usual Homeric meanderings," Sara begins, "but security when traveling in Egypt is a weighty determinant of where one may travel. Foreign tourists who venture outside of common cities like Cairo, Luxor, Aswan, or Alexandria typically require their own police detail. The out-of-the-way areas are simply not equipped with the same level of police patrols as the more metropolitan areas.

"It's more often than not that you feel completely safe. You may wonder if it's the extraordinary work of the ten policemen who follow you, or if the headache of coordinating your daily movements with the police is well beyond overkill," she continues. "My recommendation to The Idiot is not to *not go,* but to realize the logistical limitations to his quest in such a place as post-revolutionary Egypt. There are so many beautiful, awe-inspiring things to see – that one has to see. The Greeks obviously took that to heart, as they are documented traveling there well before Alexander's takeover.

"I'd like to suggest that you perhaps restrain your walking in Egypt to the places visited by Alexander the Great and the many historical sites where he hung out back in the day," she says, referring to Alexander's campaign in Egypt in 332-331 BC which, after he had made it through Gaza and the Sinai, took him to the pyramids in Giza, Heliopolis (known to the Greeks as the City of the Sun), Memphis and numerous other well-known destinations, including Alexandria (which wasn't there until he founded it) and the Siwa Oasis, where he met, and had an intriguing Q&A session with the Oracle of Ammon.

"Anyway, there are so many beautiful, awe-inspiring and historically interesting things to see and they will look the same to you as they did to Alexander," Sara adds. "Chill out at the Pyramids, decipher the reverential graffiti that litters the Valley of the Kings, explore Karnak and the Temple of Luxor, pay homage to Alexander wherever you go."

And she's right. Alexander's image is replicated all over Egypt, in both monumental statuary and delicate relief, and his Greek name is still seen translated into hieroglyphs. Sometimes he even appears in the company of the Egyptian gods. wearing traditional Egyptian regalia, including the rams' horns of Ammon as worn by his pharaonic predecessors. And reverential graffiti in Ancient Greek and Latin litter the Valley of the Kings and the Temple of Luxor. Septimius Severus and Hadrian, both Roman emperors, have their own etchings at the Colossi of Memnon. Their goal was much like that of The Idiot: to pay homage to the likes of Alexander and other greats in the hope of being identified with godliness.

I thank Sara for her suggestions and tell her I'll think about her way-too-sensible approach.

Although there are many options, The Idiot's return to Gaza, the Sinai Peninsula, Egypt or anywhere else is delayed. It turns out that I won't make a decision about whether, or how, to approach Gaza, the Sinai or anywhere else until I spend almost a year resolving a troubling health issue that has severely impacted my ability to walk.

I never think of not returning to the MedTrek, of course, and here is an omen that encourages me not to give up: I am high-fived by the pope to commemorate completion of the MedTrek from Syria to Gaza. And that inspires me to continue walking in Egypt amidst, and with, different nationalities, races and religions.

# MedTrek Milestone #12

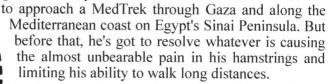

Another milestone, another decision about whether to walk in a dangerous country. This time The Idiot has to decide how to approach a MedTrek through Gaza and along the Mediterranean coast on Egypt's Sinai Peninsula. But before that, he's got to resolve whatever is causing the almost unbearable pain in his hamstrings and limiting his ability to walk long distances.

# WHAT PHOTOGRAPHS DID THE IDIOT TAKE IN LEBANON AND ISRAEL THAT WERE TOO SENSITIVE TO POST?

# WHAT ARE THE DIFFERENCES BETWEEN THE MEDITERRANEAN SEASIDE IN LEBANON AND ISRAEL?

# WHAT SIMILARITIES DID THE IDIOT OBSERVE WHILE MEDTREKKING IN LEBANON AND ISRAEL?

# FOLLOW THE IDIOT

## CHAPTER PHOTOS

# The Tires Wear Out

"My son, thou art invincible."
*– The Oracle at Delphi* to *Alexander the Great*

"The tires wear out."
*– Dr. Matthew Paul*, Orthopedic Surgeon

"Take kindly the counsel of the years, gracefully
surrendering the things of youth." *– Desiderata*

I always contend that I will almost certainly be able to complete my twenty-year walk around the Mediterranean Sea unless I have a debilitating injury or insurmountable health problem. Except for a bad fall in Morocco, an inguinal hernia necessitating surgery in Sicily, an occasional bout of food poisoning, two blisters and too many scrapes and scratches to count, things have generally progressed without a major calamity.

I walk, I stay healthy, I'm in decent shape.

But progressively, beginning in early 2009, my hamstring muscles start aching. My chiropractor, my primary care physician and even, apparently, I myself, are all content to attribute this, for a number of years, to "constant overuse syndrome" due to long-distance walking. At one point I think the muscle pain might be due to a cholesterol-reducing statin. I stop taking it, it isn't the culprit. I accept the pain as part of the walking and aging process, treating it with massages, acupuncture, stretching, yoga and an occasional Advil.

# DR. TRUDI PRATT

By the time I am MedTrekking in Lebanon and Israel in 2015, I am in constant pain, have to stop walking every fifteen minutes, bow over frequently to ease the pain and attempt to conceal my condition whenever anyone asks how I feel. In fact, the pain in both legs not only restricts my ability to walk long distances but also, in some cases, to walk at all. It becomes intolerably uncomfortable.

I'm providing details about my progressively worsening ailment (and I realize that in the global scope of injury or illness this is a comparatively minor affliction) in case any readers or fellow hikers, or even just one reader or one fellow hiker, might have the same problem and, like me, dismiss it, only to later lament that it could have been diagnosed and resolved a bit earlier.

I determine in Lebanon, when I collapse for twenty minutes on a rock on a sandy beach two days south of Beirut, to definitively investigate and determine the source and cause of the pain when I return to California. I certainly don't plan to give up MedTrekking but I resolve not to return to Gaza, Egypt or anywhere else until I do whatever's necessary to properly walk like an Egyptian, or any nationality for that matter.

The diagnosis, surgery and recovery process take over a year. It starts with X-rays, a CT scan and an MRI as well as treatments that involve daily massages, weekly acupuncture treatments, stretching, yoga and, at one point, abstention from any walking for a month. It ultimately leads to cortisone shots at a pain clinic, the decision to have surgery, the search for the right physician, an operation and a recovery.

For decades, I usually spend the last half of October in Redding, California, to fete my mother's birthday. This is the town where I grew up and have a two-story townhouse base camp I rented in 2009 to care for ("amuse" might be a more appropriate word) my nonagenarian mother before she changes her address for the last time. When I moved to town, I thought I'd be in Redding for six months or a year but it's now 2018, my mother's almost 99 and I'm still in the town where I went to high school. Six months have become almost a decade, though, despite the intense summer heat and devastating wildfires, I'm delighted and grateful to be here.

October is also usually the month that my Shasta High School (1966) and Stanford University (1970) reunions are held every five years. I enjoy attending these get togethers to check in with my classmates and even wrote a short essay entitled *How to Prepare for Your 50th High School Reunion.*

Read it?

In the essay I insist that adequate preparation for a reunion definitely includes a pre-reunion physical fitness regime, a medical check-up, a facial, a manicure that promotes school colors (purple and white for Shasta High, cardinal now for Stanford), a T-shirt portraying the school name and mascot (Shasta Wolves in Redding, The Cardinal in Palo Alto) and full-throttle participation in reunion events, from cocktails at Lulu's (a Redding favorite of the late Merle Haggard, who lived just out of town) to the dance floor at the Redding Elks Lodge.

At Stanford, besides catching up with classmates, I thrive on participating in intriguing reunion activities, like Classes Without Quizzes, including one taught by classics professor Richard Martin entitled *Odysseus in Silicon Valley* during my 45th reunion.

"Stanford is an island like Ithaca and you have all, like Odysseus, made a journey home," Martin tells an eager audience of alumni.

"If the voyager Odysseus time-traveled to Silicon Valley, he'd have chosen to be reincarnated as the wandering entrepreneurial warrior/hero Steve Jobs, and seduced by the siren Joan Baez in the early 1980s," I tell Professor Martin before selling and signing copies of my books during a profitable "Authors Meet and Greet" session.

The latter half of October also gives me a chance to catch up with my barber Mike Hernandez, who I always ask to reproduce the Renaissance look of Michelangelo's David, and visit older friends, like my high school English and Critical Thinking teacher Paul Hughes before he died. When I'm in town, I happily and go-luckily concentrate on spinning classes and swimming workouts at the YMCA, walk the local river trail to keep in shape and promote my books whenever and wherever anyone asks me to – and often when they don't.

But that's not how it goes when I return from Lebanon and Israel during the autumn of 2015 and attend my 45th Stanford reunion, where I make the mistake of dancing like I am still 18.

Here's a chronological look at how things evolved and were ultimately resolved during the next year:

November 2015

An X-ray and C-scan reveal a slight fracture of my left femoral head due to a fall I'd taken the previous summer.

"You're a lucky bastard," says Dr. Trudi Pratt, my friend and chiropractor since 2009, after seeing X-rays of my pelvis, spine and hip. "The subchondral fracture of the left femoral head is painful but should heal in a couple months and you've got great spinal disc space. These are the X-rays of a 30-year-old. Take a month without walking or strenuous exercise and we'll get a CT scan if things don't improve."

Comforted by the fact that I've got "great spinal disc space," I spend the non-walking month of November in Massachusetts, where I have a second base camp near Boston in Scituate on the South Shore, and abstain from walking while continuing with regular massages and care for other parts of my body. Think facials, mani-pedis, reflexology and everything else available except a lobotomy.

December 2015

Things don't improve, and Trudi sends me for a CT scan and MRI that indicates I'm afflicted with severe central spinal stenosis (from the Greek word *stenōsis*, which means narrowing), a degenerative nerve disorder caused by pressure on the spinal cord that gradually impacted my ability to walk or swim (I can no longer do flip turns or kick with any strength) for more than five minutes without incurring intolerable pain.

At this point, it is difficult to imagine that six months ago – in Cyprus – I was almost blithely tolerating what I thought was just hamstring pain, MedTrekking over thirty kilometers a day and having no problem with a one-mile open water swim.

Trudi is out of town and I see another chiropractor, Dr. Michael Hanley, who looks at the MRI, explains the problem to me and says, "This is classic. You can try anything you'd like and explore all the options available but in the end the only way to resolve this is with surgery. You've got to remove the bone, ligament and anything else putting pressure on your spinal cord. This won't go away."

Naturally I "explore all the options available" during the next five months, from extending my morning meditation to checking out remedies online to having a hands-on séance and prayer sessions with students getting a degree at Redding's Bethel School of Supernatural Ministry.

I begin discussing the medical situation on a regular basis with an expanding team of doctors, therapists and acquaintances afflicted with stenosis. I have a series of epidural (from the Greek word *epi*, which means "on," and *dura*, or "matter") steroid injections to temper/mask/reduce/resolve the ongoing pain by reducing inflammation.

I still hope, of course, to avoid surgery to remove the malicious growth causing nerve compression. While the surgery itself is fairly simple and usually provides tangible relief, I know that any back operation changes the structure of the spine and might open a Pandora's Box of potential complications.

The first two epidurals temper the pain and encourage me to take a long-planned trip.

January 2016

The pain is reduced enough, following two epidural injections, that my hamstrings no longer feel like taut steel cables and I am able to walk a half mile with a half smile, though I am definitely not in the shape required for a serious six-week round of daily 30-kilometer MedTrekking. I feel, as I embark on a trip to Fiji, New Zealand and Vanuatu, that I am only at 46.57 percent of my usual physical prowess.

After enjoying my last massage of 2015 in Fiji with Liz, who had to return to the United States, my daughter Sonia and I embark on a three-week jaunt around New Zealand and tramp from the Bay of Islands in the north to the Fiordland National Park in the south.

Tramping, of course, is a popular activity in the Down Under nation, though it's known elsewhere as hiking, backpacking, rambling, hill walking, bushwalking or any other kind of walking that lasts more than 47 minutes. The pain-relieving shots enable me to enjoy a number of short hikes, called trampettes, throughout the sheep-filled country, and I rarely meet enough people on the trails to be overwhelmed or, as they say locally, trampled. I dedicate my walks to Donald Tramp and Charlotte Trampling, and learn the pronunciation of key Māori words from Rena at the Waitangi Treaty Grounds.

Sonia and I tramp through protected rain forests, listening to the songs of the kokako, tui and other birds, while learning how possums became one of New Zealand's most despised pests (there are now 40 million possums compared to 30 million sheep). We take an art walk in the Connells Bay Sculpture Park on Waiheke island near Auckland and tiptoe through budding grape vines at a touted vineyard and winery near Blenheim on the South Island. We have a reflective stroll in the Fiordland National Park in the enticing Southern Alps, where crampons are required for the steeper snow-covered mountains, and around the property at a high country retreat called Grasmere Lodge.

Even The Idiot can figure out why Kiwi director Peter Jackson filmed "*The Hobbit*" and "*LotR*" trilogies in his native New Zealand, where specialist tours take visitors to every location where the movies were shot. The entire country is a Tolkienesque stage set, and the trees, rivers, mountains, waterfalls, plains, shires and inhabitants are usually eager to play a role.

As you would expect, bad sheep jokes are very common in New

Zealand.

Here's one of the worst: "Buy a sheep. Name it Relation. You now have a relationsheep."

When I get to Vanuatu during the last week of January, the epidural effect has worn off and I feel the hamstring pain return.

Not that I don't enjoy a beachfront bungalow near Port Vila, discovered by John Keeney, whose company Fast Thinking published *The Idiot and the Odyssey: Walking the Mediterranean* in 2008. Days on the 83-island archipelago in the South Pacific kick off with a breakfast of papaya, lime and pineapple on the terrace, where we each have four-handed, hour-long massages after SCUBA diving amid colorful fish, coral of all shapes, and a few intriguing shipwrecks.

We even feast on the legendary Vanuatu Flying Fox at Le Jardin des Saveurs restaurant in Port Vila, Vanuatu. Chef Francis Mouroux at Restaurant Le Jardin des Saveurs wants his presentation of the Vanuatu Flying Fox dish to "resemble a live flying fox" with visible head, teeth and ears. He succeeds.

It's hard to imagine that The Idiot can be just as stressed in mellow Vanuatu as he was in laid-back New Zealand.

But it's true.

The Idiot's stressometer registers a big goose egg, a gigantic zero, in both countries but the hamstring pain has returned.

February 2016

Thanks to the International Date Line, I live a 43-hour day on February 1 that begins in Vanuatu and ends in Los Angeles. The productive day includes a mid-morning kayak outing on the South Pacific Ocean; lunch in Port Vila, Vanuatu; a 2.5-hour flight from Vanuatu to Fiji; a 10-hour flight from Fiji to Los Angeles; lunch near Venice Beach with my son Luke; an afternoon walk along the Pacific Ocean; and an evening out in Hollywood.

I tell Luke that I have many more social encounters traveling throughout the South Pacific Ocean than I do walking around the Mediterranean Sea.

"That could be because I don't feel obligated in Fiji, New Zealand and Vanuatu to MedTrek between 25-50 kilometers a day," I say. "In fact, right now I'm not sure that I'll ever be able to walk 25 kilometers a day."

Though I frequently run, or walk, into people on the Mediterranean, the get-togethers tend to be brief to avoid breaking the walking pace and getting out of the MedTrek zone. In the South Pacific – when I never walked, or could walk, more than a few kilometers at a stretch and travelled in planes, boats, buses, SUVs and trains – I tend to spend hours each day interacting with other sentient beings.

This much more meditative approach to travel often leads to

extreme behavior, like the time I patiently sat and watched Liz get her hair braided in Fiji. That's something The Idiot has never done on the MedTrek.

Many of my encounters were educational and informative. In New Zealand, I tended to spend a great deal of time getting acquainted with Māori history, culture, traditions and people.

I return to Redding and a third epidural injection has almost no effect. It's now clear that this won't be a long-term solution, and I issue the following press release just after Valentine's Day:

"The Idiot, who planned to fly to Cairo on April Fool's Day to resume the MedTrek, will postpone his walk from Gaza across the Sinai Peninsula to Alexandria, Egypt, due to a medical/MRI diagnosis of 'severe central spinal stenosis.' The nerve-compressing affliction painfully impacts his hamstrings and is what led to an oft-excruciating walk from Syria down the coasts of Lebanon and Israel last autumn.

The discomfort forced The Idiot to take frequent seated breaks and to constantly bend over to alleviate pain caused by compressed spinal nerves, or 'severe crowding of the caudal equine fibers and narrowing of the neural foramina.'

The result: MedTrekking was much less fun, daily distances were much shorter and I constantly leaned forward or bent over (traditional signs exhibited by someone with spinal stenosis) to alleviate constant pain in my hamstrings and legs.

The process to determine that my ailment was more serious than the usual "classic overuse syndrome" included a month of complete physical inactivity complemented by a regimen of massages, chiropractic adjustments, acupuncture and various mystical treatments. It also called for more frequent meditation sessions, including Middle Way meditation with Phra Piya Piyawajako, a Buddhist monk from Chiang Rai, Thailand, that always conclude with a healthy Thai buffet prepared by the sisters at Racha Noodle.

Nothing worked.

Although surgery is likely, The Idiot is still attempting to avoid it."

March 2016

I continue to take short walks – some of them with a spiritual touch like the Peace Labyrinth on the Sacramento River Trail in Redding, CA, and the labyrinth at Glastonbury Abbey in Hingham, Massachusetts, where I love a sign that reads *Solvitur Ambulando*, or "It is solved by walking" – but I am now a limping shadow of my former self.

I still attempt a few hikes – an urban stroll in San Francisco, a walkabout in the hills above San Luis Obispo, a walk with an old friend on the sidewalks in West Hollywood – but they are more pain than pleasure.

After postponing the MedTrek, I decide to have surgery in May and begin meeting and interviewing prospective surgeons in Redding, San

Francisco, Los Angeles and Stanford, while continuing to seek out and consult people who had a similar surgery.

I also throw myself into an alternative project to keep busy, which I mention in an article entitled "What Will The Idiot do After Postponing his Return to Egypt to Continue The MedTrek?"

"The Idiot has been advised to put his return to the MedTrek in Egypt on hold due to a diagnosis of 'severe spinal canal stenosis' that hampers his ability to enjoyably hike over 30 kilometers a day. Although he requires surgery and will be sidelined for a few months, he's got a new project to keep him busy.

In the spring of 1976, The Idiot was part of a small group of American journalists in Paris that launched a tabloid-sized fortnightly magazine called *The Paris Metro*. In the autumn of 2016, the survivors and friends of that memorable meteoric venture will gather in Paris for a 40th reunion.

The Idiot was publisher of the fortnightly magazine (he also wrote numerous articles and a regular column called *On The Money*) that took the French capital by storm from 1976 to 1979. Now he's the co-editor of a commemorative eBook/book of Paris Metro-related anecdotes, memoirs, poems, reflections, stories, vignettes, illustrations and photographs that will be published to coincide with the 40th Anniversary party from September 23-25, 2016.

The book will be written, edited, illustrated and produced by former staff members, freelancers, readers and friends of *The Paris Metro*. The submissions concern the magazine's meaning and mystique, the allure and downsides of the city of Paris and/or a reminiscence of personal (mis)adventures between 1976 and 1980. Submissions are due on April 15, exactly 40 years since the printing of the dummy issue of *The Paris Metro*."

April 2016

The affliction that forces me to postpone the resumption of the MedTrek enables me to attend the 45th class reunion at the Columbia School of Journalism in New York on April 15-16. Not only do I get up close and personal with former classmates, but I also got the scoop on trends in social media, discuss the issue of race in journalism, attend a workshop on virtual reality and talk about *The Idiot and the Odyssey* books.

I invite almost everyone I run into, from social media guru Sree Sreenivasan to classmate and Pulitzer Prize winner Margo Jefferson, to join me on the MedTrek from Gaza to Alexandria, Egypt, next November. This is my way of telling myself that all will be righted after the stenosis surgery.

That isn't the only book promotion I do during my respite. I answer Idiot-ic questions at the Henry Miller Memorial Library ("where nothing ever happens," says a sign) when I drive through Big Sur along the Pacific Ocean from San Francisco to Los Angeles. And a weeklong book promotion tour on the east coast includes stops at Dartmouth College in New Hampshire and the University of Vermont.

After discussing the situation with friends – including Howard Pierce, a long-time stenosis sufferer familiar with the latest medical advances, on Vermont's Lake Champlain, Beth Bradley in Massachusetts and Tom Isaak in California – and interviewing four physicians, I decided to have the surgery at Stanford, performed by the reputable Lawrence M. Shuer, MD.

May 2016

How do I prepare for my May 19 surgery at the Stanford Medical Center?

Although it is perhaps a little dramatic and hopefully premature – and although most people in ancient Greece and Egypt didn't have this done until they were verifiably dead – I have a life/death mask cast. If necessary, the wax cast can be used to create my death mask (think Tutankhamen and Agamemnon) should things go south at the Stanford Medical Center.

To avoid putting the death mask to use, I exceed the doctor's orders to get exercise and stay in a semblance of good shape until the surgery.

I somewhat lamely continue my 5 a.m. spinning class at the Redding YMCA, conducted by Silas Lyons, the editor of the daily *Record Searchlight* newspaper, and grimace during a speedy half-hour weight-lifting session to exercise my upper body.

I take steps (though not many) to look and feel as well and healthy as possible to give myself a pre-op psychological boost. Would anyone think of having surgery without getting a mani-pedi or haircut? Not me. And I eat wisely. Three days before surgery, I prepare fillets of Dover sole on a bed of boiled spinach with virgin olive oil, pepper and organic hulled sunflower seeds.

On May 19, I confidently undergo the stenosis-eradicating surgery.

What sophisticated word does one of America's top neurosurgeons use the day after surgery to describe the bone, cyst and ligament compressing my spinal nerves and restricting my ability to walk around the Mediterranean Sea – and even stand up straight?

"GUNK!"

That's right, GUNK. That's what surgeons remove when they perform a bilateral laminal foraminotomy at the Stanford Medical Center. But getting rid of it works at least one miracle.

Improvement in my posture is noticeable just a few hours after surgery. Patients afflicted with central spinal stenosis tend to slouch (it's said that doctors find prospective clients by seeing who's slouching over their shopping carts in supermarkets) and I am able to stand up straight within hours of surgery. The minor incision used for the procedure doesn't affect the aesthetics of my yin-yang tattoo/tramp stamp decorated with Mediterranean waves.

On May 21, I discuss my bilateral laminal foraminotomy surgical procedure with Thomas Jefferson, well a statue of Thomas Jefferson, in the courtyard of the Stanford Park Hotel, where I spend a few days recovering.

"George, Ben, James, me...we all had severe lumbar spinal stenosis with neurogenic claudification at L4-5. But we sure didn't scream about it as much as you do," says Jefferson.

I am told that a slow recovery period is required to ensure a complete success. No bending, no lifting, no twisting, no sitting for more than 30 minutes. Start taking three five-minute walks a day on flat terrain. Then work up gradually each day.

When I return to Redding, Trudi agrees that limiting postoperative physical activity to walking will help prevent the formation of scar tissue that is a potential cause of post-op pain frequently referred to as *failed back surgery syndrome*.

I wear sturdy low-cut hiking shoes or strapped walking sandals when MedTrekking. But to recover from spinal surgery by taking three 10-minute walks a day on flat terrain, slide sandals solve the problem of being unable to bend over to tie shoes or attach straps. Thanks to my daughter Sonia for the bright idea.

As I patiently recover from the surgery that reduced compression on nerves causing incessant leg pain, I constantly hear one phrase during weeks of post-op rehab: "Don't overdo it!"

My exercise regime – which usually involves spinning, swimming, hiking and pumping iron – is limited to three short daily walks in my neighborhood. After ten days, I increase the trio of strolls to ten minutes each.

June 2016

Are you wondering why The Idiot takes his first 15-minute post-op rehab walk in June before sunrise – and his second one before most people get to work? Early morning is the only cool time of day at this time of year in Redding.

I meet neurosurgeon Dr. Lawrence Shuer on June 19 for a post-op evaluation at Stanford Medical Center and he specifically mentions how happy he is that my lower back tat is intact. I wonder, belatedly, if my tattoo contributed to the development of severe spinal stenosis.

"No and you can swim, spin and hike long distances but wait

another four months until you do something stupid," Dr. Shuer says when I ask if I can ride horses, ski or jump off bridges.

"How about a road trip to Durango, Colorado," I ask, noting that I plan to hunker down with the designers of *The Paris Metro 40ᵗʰAnniversary Issue: The Book About Paris Yesterday* to produce a book that requires excerpts from issues that are decades old.

Ten days later, I survive a 1,059-mile summer road trip from Redding, California, to Durango, Colorado, by adhering to one key rule: Stop every ninety minutes and walk for one mile while lifting five pound weights.

When I arrive after making the road trip through Nevada and Utah, I immediately promote my *Idiot and Odyssey* books at the aptly named Joel's Bar in Durango.

The Idiot's mountainside aerie, near the nesting area of Peregrine falcons, is an ideal place to work with Durango designers Aaron and Jenni Patterson on the upcoming book. He hires his 96-year-old mother to review a proof copy of the book and she reads one of her son's three anecdotes in *The Paris Metro 40ᵗʰ Anniversary Issue: The Book About Paris Yesterday*. The vignette that has her smiling is entitled *How I Lost my Day Job, my Virginity and my First Fortune at The Paris Metro*.

## July 2016

I continue rehab in Durango, where I hike at least two hours a day on the fanciful Animas River Trail, the walkway that stretches seven miles through Durango along the 126-mile-long river.

On July 9, I climb my first decent hill since back surgery seven weeks ago – a section of the scenic 6.3-mile Overend Mountain Trail above Durango.

On July 11, my niece Sara – who MedTrekked with me in Israel and is currently involved in historic preservation projects in Texas, Colorado and Wyoming – interprets petroglyphs during a history-rich walk through the world of ancestral Pueblo people in Mesa Verde National Park.

On July 23, for the first time since my surgery two months ago, I'm back in Redding and walk the six-mile loop on the Sacramento River Trail. A week after that I am hiking the rim of the majestic Pacific Ocean south of Trinidad, California.

## August 2016

I begin broadcasting news about the 40ᵗʰ reunion of *The Paris Metro* from September 23-25 and signing people up for the kick-off cocktail party at Le Tour d'Argent. I also declare that I'll be ready for a return to the MedTrek in November to march from Gaza across Egypt's Sinai Peninsula to Alexandria.

Recovery reaches a new plateau when I painlessly hike 16.4 miles in the California redwoods. The six-hour walk, which I mentioned was one of my favorite training hikes before I went to Lebanon, takes me on a loop from the Redwood Creek trailhead north of Orick to the Tall Trees Grove, the site of some of the world's tallest trees. This is the home of Roosevelt elk that graze in misty roadside meadows and on grassy hillsides throughout the year.

The Redwood Creek Trail is not only an easy walk under shady tall trees but is, with the exception of one missing bridge, also in excellent shape this summer.

During the return hike, The Idiot changes shoes and prepares for the next challenge of his post-op rehab: a hike up and down Mount Lassen not far from Redding.

Liz and I climb to the 10,463-foot peak of Mount Lassen during the full moon on August 18 to celebrate the three-month anniversary of spinal surgery at Stanford University. We start the hike in the late afternoon, enjoy sunset at the summit and descend with headlamps under the full moon. I first climbed Mount Lassen in the 1950s when I was nine years old and have it on the calendar for my 90th birthday in 2038.

September 2016

We go to Paris for a bash celebrating the Paris Metro 40th Anniversary and the just-published book, *The Paris Metro 40th Anniversary Issue: The Book About Paris Yesterday,* which is generating controversy in French media. A story entitled *Naked Tales From The Paris Metro* by Christina de Liagre includes a photo of me skinny-dipping at a Paris Hotel in 1977 and the description, "Just think of it: full frontal nudity featuring our very own, very well-hung publisher, for God's sake."

I celebrate the book and my anticipated return to the MedTrek by feasting on the 1,152,731st French duck at the iconic Tour d'Argent restaurant in Paris with CNN's Jim Bittermann and our lovely American partners. The Idiot first encountered the Tour d'Argent's numbered ducks in 1971 and was at a party celebrating the 1,000,000th duck in 2003. His next goal is to eat the 1,500,000th duck.

October 2016

I find myself still in Redding a year after my return from Israel, but I am now easily able to participate in the three-mile "Walk to End Alzheimer's" across the Sundial Bridge on Oct. 17 when *The Idiot and the Odyssey* team raises over $6,000 for the Alzheimer's Association. The team made a donation of over $12,000 in 2017 and the only person who joins me each year is Trudi Pratt, my faithful chiropractor.

*The Idiot and the Odyssey* team also spearheads **The Helen Stratte Entrance** at One Safe Place, a residential center that provides safety and support for victims of domestic violence and sexual assault in

Redding, CA. The shelter dedicated the entrance to the guests' residence in honor of The Idiot's mother, Helen Stratte, for her 97<sup>th</sup> birthday.

After a thorough physical examination at Stanford University prior to a month-long visit to Egypt, I spent Halloween with my favorite witch in Salem, Massachusetts, to get her opinion about how I should approach my MedTrek in Egypt later that week.

Claiming that she's channeling a message from Alexander the Great, here are her seven key suggestions:

1. "Spend the time before you fly to Cairo on November 3 walking and meditating at Egypt Beach near your oceanside base camp in Scituate to get in the right frame of mind."

2. "Don't walk, as you're planning, from Gaza across the ISIS-frequented Sinai Peninsula to Port Said or you might wind up walking no further."

3. "Get rid of your oceanside base camp near Egypt Beach and put your stuff in storage just in case you're detained and don't make it back in December."

4. "Meet with Eric Almquist, the author of "The (30) Elements of Value," at the Charles Hotel in Cambridge to determine whether your readers really care that you're walking in the footsteps of Alexander the Great in Egypt."

5. "Don't walk the wrong way when you reach the lighthouse in Alexandria, or you'll never make it to Libya."

6. "Plan for all possible outcomes by buying a spot for a memorial bench in Scituate Harbor as a gift to the town."

7. "Don't believe everything you hear from a witch you met twenty years ago on the street in Salem when your daughter was going to school here. Yes, the same one who told you to walk around the Mediterranean."

# FOLLOW THE IDIOT

## CHAPTER PHOTOS

## CHAPTER MAP

# PART FIVE

## EGYPT AND TUNISIA

*A Nilistic Exploration of Egypt*

*From the New Suez Canal to Alexandria*

*Strolling through Chic Alexandria to El-Alamein Battlefields*

*An Armed Escort and the Woman in the Headscarf*

*Consulting The Oracle of Siwa and Reaching Libya*

*Crowned The Idiot Emperor of Carthage*

# A Nilistic Exploration of Egypt

"It takes strong men to rule. Alexander was more: he was Prometheus, a friend to man. He changed the world."
– Ptolemy

I plan to resume the 42-kilometer MedTrek along Gaza's coast and then casually stroll on the 185-kilometer Mediterranean coast of the Sinai Peninsula to Port Said, Egypt. After that, if all goes according to my plan to stay as close to the sea as possible without getting detained or arrested or killed, I'll walk along the Egyptian seaside through Alexandria to Libya.

Piece of cake, right?

Unfortunately not.

Crossing the border into Gaza where, besides the on-and-off battling with the Israelis, there is an ongoing standoff between Hamas and the Palestinian Authority, may be a suicide mission. Israelis, officials at the US Embassy in Tel Aviv (it moved to Jerusalem in 2018) and everyone else familiar with, or even unfamiliar with, the explosive enclave make it clear that they can be of little help to anyone, including me, if they get into trouble in Gaza.

"If you're stupid enough to go there, you're on your own," an

Israeli government official tells The Idiot. "People go in and frequently don't come back. We won't come get you."

The Sinai peninsula on the other side of Gaza has been the scene of the bombing of a Russian passenger jet and numerous attacks on Egyptian security forces, and even crowded mosques, by ISIS jihadist groups, known in much of the Middle East as Daesh, the Arabic acronym that stands for *al-Dawla al-Islamiya fi al-Iraq wa al-Sham*. The Egyptian military's scorched-earth approach to militants in the Daesh-frequented Sinai – including summary executions and the occasional destruction of whole villages – has failed to end the insurgency. The Egyptian military doesn't like interlopers and, in addition, Bedouins have also been kidnapping foreigners. No one is suggesting that I go to the Sinai either.

Alexander might have conquered Gaza, crossed the Sinai Peninsula and been welcomed as a liberator in Egypt, but that stretch of the contemporary Mediterranean coast is definitely dangerous, or problematic at best.

Although an American attaché at the US Embassy in Cairo tells me off the record that "the walk is doable with a guide, bodyguard and military approval," I reluctantly abandoned the Sinai stroll when the Egyptian government refused to give me permission to travel there and many Egyptians cautioned me to be just as wary of the trigger-happy Egyptian military as the kidnapping Bedouins and jet-bombing Daesh militias.

"The northern Sinai Peninsula is a war zone and tensions are very high," a colonel in the Egyptian Army asserts when we discuss the possibility of resuming the MedTrek at Rafah on the Egyptian side of Gaza. "Don't risk it – not that we'd give you the necessary permission to be there – while we're fighting Daesh and have numerous other security concerns in Sinai."

An experienced Egyptian mountain hiker I meet pointed out that "the real problem is the military, which will constantly detain you and never believe you're just there to hike." He said that the Mediterranean coast between Port Said and Libya should be, comparatively, no problem.

"Inshallah," he added.

After a thorough investigation and evaluation, I concede that I'll have to come up with alternative plans. After all, the third book in *The Idiot and the Odyssey* trilogy is not subtitled *Confronting ISIS and Cheating Death in Gaza and on the Sinai Peninsula*.

I decide to pursue Sara's suggestion and, to kick things off, visit the historical sites in the footsteps of Alexander the Great.

Alexander, of course, considered Persian-dominated Egypt an imperative conquest and thought that Greece and Macedonia would no longer be vulnerable to foreigners once he controlled Egypt and the Nile. After conquering Persia's naval bases all along the coastline of Asia Minor and Syria-Palestine, controlling Egypt would also create more coastal bases for his strategic and commercial purposes.

With naval reinforcements following his progress along the coast after his victory in Gaza, Alexander's Macedonian army covered the hazardous 200-plus kilometer distance in a mere seven-day march and reached the heavily fortified coastal town of Pelusium, the most easterly city of Egypt at the time, in late October 332 BC.

Alexander then marched south into Egypt where he remained for a total of six months before resuming his ongoing campaign against the mighty Persian Empire of Darius III.

Egypt, which was conquered by King Cambyses in 525 BC and was controlled mostly by the Persians from then on, welcomed Alexander as a liberator. The local Persian viceroy had no intention of challenging someone who already controlled Phoenicia.

After installing troops to defend Pelusium, Alexander's army marched up the Nile (its Greek name *Neilos* means a valley with a stream) to Memphis with its towering temples and, nearby, the pyramids and sphinx at Giza. When he arrived, the Persian viceroy literally gave him the keys to the country and Alexander was crowned as pharaoh on November 14, 332 BC. He spent two months in the royal palace in Memphis (the capital was first known as Ineb-hedj, or White Walls, and later called Menoph in Egyptian) studying Egyptian laws and customs.

The young king of Macedon made some smart maneuvers to seduce the Egyptians. Among other things, he honored the Egyptian gods, ordered temples in Luxor and elsewhere to be restored, and put Egyptians in positions of authority to rule according to ancient customs. Even the Persian viceroy, knowing he was increasingly isolated and ultimately doomed, went to work for Alexander, who made regular sacrifices to the gods and hosted a number of feasts and athletic contests in Memphis.

Alexander soon became known not only as the king of both Upper and Lower Egypt but also, in accordance with ancient Egyptian tradition, as a "son of the gods" and "the strong ruler, who seizes the lands of the foreigners, *meryamun setepenra* (beloved by Ammon, chosen by Ra) Aleksandros."

Once established, Alexander went further south and was impressed by the temples, obelisks and pyramids in Saqqara, Heliopolis and Giza that were seemingly built for giants. He was continually awed that these structures had occupied the desert for more than 2,000 years before his own lifetime. Devoted to science, Alexander is said to have dispatched an expedition up the Nile to investigate the sources of the river and determine the reason for its frequent flooding.

Again I don't feel comfortable bringing Liz along to Egypt, but try to get a once-daring photographer friend, a former lunatic member of the paparazzi for the British tabloids, to accompany me.

But David Koppel writes, "Thanks for taking the time to write such a detailed description of your plans, which has helped confirm my initial doubts about the sensibility of joining you in Egypt. The Foreign Office is very cautious about any travel to Egypt and my instinct tells me to stay away from such a dangerous part of the world. Your email certainly confirms that.

"Can you guarantee my safety? I doubt it. Much as I'd love to join you and see you, it sounds like an unnecessary risk, when I can just wait to have you buy me dinner in London."

I write back that "I'm obviously concerned about your safety (as well as my own) and would be downright distraught if anything happened to either of us. But I can't guarantee a thing."

Sara, you might recall, encouraged me to first join tourists of all nationalities and walk, in the footsteps of Alexander the Great, through Cairo to the Giza Pyramids. In accordance with her proposed plan and growing concern by everyone from Liz to David Koppel about my safety, I decide, prior to launching the MedTrek on the coast from Port Said to Alexandria and Libya, to first travel to various spots that Alexander visited, or may have visited, when he went up the Nile.

I send Koppel another email: "Heading to Cairo with the intention of exploring Memphis, Giza, Luxor, Aswan and other places for a couple weeks to see how things look. This is safe tourism. Now want to come along?"

"See you in London," he replies.

I know my mother and Liz will be pleased with my sensible itinerary. In fact, one reason I'm taking this route and at the last minute join a tour with a London-based company called Explore, with whom I'd taken a trip to Tibet in 2010, was to placate my mother. She's still amazed that I haven't encountered and endured anything worse than being robbed, sexually harassed, arrested and moderately injured on the MedTrek and, although she doesn't tell me this, I feel she has a vision that something more worrisome might befall me in Gaza, Sinai or Egypt.

I send her an email to illustrate how rational The Idiot has become: "Planning to take a train to Aswan and then cruise down the Nile back to Luxor. This will give me a sense of the mood in the country and the boat will have comparatively extravagant accommodations (in contrast to my usual basic MedTrek digs), good food, a swimming pool and a belly dancer. Can't be much safer than that!"

I arrive in Cairo via Washington, D.C., and Zurich in early November. I begin walking through the city to bring myself up to speed on changes that have occurred since I was last here in 1997 to write a report for the *International Herald Tribune*. More importantly, this is the first time I've been here since the January 2011 Arab Spring revolution that turned Egypt, and much of the Middle East, upside down.

Contemporary Egypt, of course, is still stunned by all of the ramifications of the 2011 revolution, but, although there are comparatively few tourists (this is the first tour Explore has done in six years), things seem to be settling down. Everything's inexpensive (a cappuccino in a chic cafe with a view of the Nile and stunning sunset is $1) and touts are virtually giving away touristic trinkets – scarves, rugs, jewelry, figurines, statuary and everything else – that, despite the price, I still continue to boycott. To ensure that everyone takes me seriously, I use the common greeting "*As-salāmu ʿalaykum,*" or "peace be upon you," to everyone I see, and they respond "*Alaykumu as-salām,*" which means "and upon you, peace."

I spend my first day walking through Tahrir Square and explore Cairo with the continual recollection of how jubilant many Egyptians were in early 2011 when the revolution began in this square – and how devastatingly tragic things became in 2013 when more than 1,000 people were massacred here. I recall how rosy things initially looked when people were demanding their rights and the ousting of President Mubarak in 2011 and how the establishment of the next authoritative and dictatorial military government dashed many of those hopes and accomplishments. In the end, after a failed experiment with an elected radical Islamic regime, one dictator replaced another in a nauseous example of *plus ça change, plus c'est la même chose.* Many former revolutionaries who disagree with the current government are in jail, in exile or dead.

To reach Tahrir Square, I cross the Qasr al Nil Bridge, where a column of 1,000 riot police tried to block the enthusiastic crowd heading to protest from January 28 to February 11, 2011, with water cannon and tear gas. It doesn't take me long to realize that many things, like the now-animated promenade and gardens on the Nile, aren't the same as they were in 332 BC or 1997 or 2011.

I wonder what Alexander would have thought had the banks of the Nile been this lively when he visited Egypt. Gardens and promenades on the river in central Cairo didn't exist to this extent when I was last here, much less during Alexander's triumphant arrival. Each walk on the Nile or in a public park now costs five pounds, or 40 cents, and, applying my "walking should be free" principle, I sometimes boycott paying the fee. I should have just accepted something I later heard from a guide in Luxor: "Everything you do in Egypt costs something."

Tahrir Square is calm and peaceful today, but there's a roadblock created by gigantic cement blocks at the entrance to the US Embassy, where I'm inquisitioned by the head of security. I wonder how long the road has been obstructed and ask "Where are the Marines?" That's because wherever I go all I see are Egyptian security guards (a big employment boom here, like the TSA in the US after 9/11) and military who constantly assure me that "everything is normal."

Recalling food riots in Cairo during the past decades, I visit a few markets to determine whether there is a visible shortage of bread, sugar or other staples. I even ask about the price of a bus ticket (15 US cents) to see whether increased inflation and price hikes might lead to another revolution or social uprising as they have in the past.

I zip down to the river, enter the Muhammed Ali Palace and head towards Helwan, doing some kind things for humanity as I walk. I pick up and return a young man's dropped ticket to a medical convention and am polite to everyone who assails or assaults me with a "Welcome to Egypt" greeting.

It doesn't take me long to be grateful that I don't live in Cairo.

Despite the Nileside attractions, Cairo has continued to grow – and trash, traffic and trouble seem to have grown with it. Indeed, the dreary decay disturbs me and a mere four hours strolling on the Nile makes me happy, and appreciative, that I'm walking around the sea and not up the river.

The most telling sign throughout the day is garbage – everywhere. Remember my complaints about garbage in Italy, Morocco and Lebanon? Well, Cairo, though not on the Mediterranean, is perhaps the dirtiest, and most stultifying, large city in the world.

I dodge back toward town and end the day hanging out with Alexander and Hercules at the Egyptian Museum, after getting the scoop on Egyptian dynasties, mummification and King Tut. The boys are a breath of fresh air, so to speak, after the fetid air and appalling clutter of Cairo. In the room dedicated to the Greco-Roman period (332 BC-AD 395), I discover an alabaster head of a young Alexander and recall that he was a mere 24-years-old when he arrived in Egypt.

I'm assured that Alexander's era will be given more prominence at the Japanese-financed $1 billion Grand Egyptian Museum. The recently constructed 700,000 square foot museum, said to be the world's largest, relocates Egyptian artifacts to the outskirts of Cairo, near the Giza pyramids, removing them from the much smaller building in Tahrir Square.

Then I recall a rumor that Alexander had actually been born in Egypt. The legend, which is part of the narrative known as the *Alexander Romance*, an ancient text about Alexander which began circulating shortly after his death, purports that Alexander was not the son of King Philip of Macedon, but instead the offspring of Pharaoh Nectanebo II of Egypt. This claim was perpetuated by Egyptian elites to justify Alexander's legitimacy and authenticity following his coronation. But maybe that's what made him so keen about worshipping the Egyptian deities. Maybe Alexander was Egyptian.

What advice does Alexander give me about how to proceed in

Egypt on the MedTrek when I see him at the museum?

"Continue up the Nile to visit monuments in Egypt associated with me and you won't be wasting your time," says Alexander, whose place in history happens to fall equidistant between the first dynasty in Egypt and the election of President Donald Trump in the United States.

That night, I watch weekend warriors in Cairo very casually enjoying water pipes, strawberry smoothies, backgammon and a soccer game on TV. Then I return to my seedy $32 room and watch *My Big Fat Greek Wedding 2*, which contends that Alexander is an important historical figure because he spread his seeds, and the seeds of Greece, throughout the world.

"Everyone is Greek," says one character in the film who purports to be a direct descendant of Alexander the Great. That reminds me to have my DNA tested when I'm back in the US to determine whether I too might be a close relation, or perhaps just a distant cousin.

The next day in Giza, I marvel that I am standing in front of the same Sphinx, and the same pyramids, and maybe even on the same sand, as did Alexander. I wonder if he also posed for a "Japanese photo," as locals now call a trick shot that shows me "holding" one of the nine Giza Pyramids in the palm of my hand. If so, I haven't found a copy.

Despite increased pollution, slight crowds (Egyptian tourism is still down 90 percent on 2010 figures) and local hustlers (who seem to be selling three of everything, whatever everything might be, for $1), it seems eerie, and simultaneously satisfying, that the pyramids look about the same today as when Alexander saw them for the first time in 331 BC. As I wander amidst these monumental and enduring burial complexes, which Herodotus, the Greek historian, acknowledged as "ancient" when he visited and wrote about them in his *Histories* in the fifth century BC, I'm pleased that, here anyway, things haven't changed since the era of Alexander the Great.

I start humming or singing, and keep humming or singing for a few weeks, the first few verses of *Walk Like an Egyptian* by The Bangles.

Remember the pertinent lyrics?

"All the old paintings on the tombs
They do the sand dance don't you know
If they move too quick (oh whey oh)
They're falling down like a domino
All the bazaar men by the Nile
They got the money on a bet
Gold crocodiles (oh whey oh)
They snap their teeth on your cigarette
Foreign types with the hookah pipes say

Ay oh whey oh, ay oh whey oh
Walk like an Egyptian."

To think that Alexander never had the good fortune to hear that song.

I patiently delay the resumption of my walk around the Mediterranean Sea when Alexander the Great sends me on a ten-day quest to "explore my legacy along the Nile on a boat before you walk along the sea to the capital city I created at Alexandria, which became the center of Hellenistic culture and commerce."

As a member of the Explore group, I take an overnight train (an experience that makes MedTrekking look like an incredibly sane and productive form of movement) from Cairo south to Aswan, where I spend my first hour investigating "the incomplete obelisk" at a quarry in the city where many of Egypt's obelisks originate.

I'm struck that a colorful wall of pictographs at the quarry has almost completely faded ("No money to repaint it," says my guide Medhat) and that many Aswan hotels are running on empty. Sellers of everything, from camel rides to touristic trash, are virtually giving away their services or wares. "Give me money to care for my horse!" and "Buy from me, no hassling!" are typical ploys.

"There's just no money for anything anymore," says Medhat, as he switches the subject to ancient history while we take a boat to the delightful Philae temple on a nearby island. He tells me, though he admits it's "probable propaganda," that Alexander was told by the Oracle of Ammon at Siwa to "kiss the arms of Egyptians, and you will not be forced to fight them."

Perhaps that advice, and not his fictionalized birth as an Egyptian, is what inspired Alexander to build temples on Egyptian holy sites. Philae, for example, is dedicated to Isis, the goddess of love, and is an attractive, dramatic and gripping mélange of Egyptian/Greek/Roman architectural styles. Medhat walks and talks us through the Greek myths, hieroglyphics and Egyptian history associated with Philae before and after it was transferred to its current site from another island during the construction of the Aswan High Dam in the 1970s.

He also tells me about a more recent temple of love, and explains the romantic ritual of the rose at the pinkish limestone Mausoleum of Aga Khan on the west bank of the Nile overlooking the city. It's news, and new, to me.

The contemporary memorial – constructed long after the country's well-known Egyptian, Greek and Roman monuments – is not only the burial site of the Aga Khan but a poignant symbol of love, because a fresh red rose has been laid on his tomb every day since he died in 1957. The Aga Khan's fourth and last wife initiated the ritual of the rose and there's a story that when not a single rose could be found in Egypt, the flower was sent from Paris by a private plane for six consecutive days. Love it.

Before we part, I ask Medhat if he might be able to arrange me safe passage through the Sinai. Here's his emailed response a few days later:

"Good day from Aswan. Concerning Sinai walking. I checked with a high rank friend and he told me it is no way because it is a war land now and said even to never talk about it to anyone else we do not know otherwise they will consider us a spy. So no going now. Maybe when it gets quiet. All regards, Medhat."

Here are some of the monumental sites I see in southern Egypt at the behest of Alexander and the Explore itinerary:

Alexander insists that I travel up the Nile beyond Aswan to the Sun Temple of Abu Simbel to "pay your regards to 'the great builder' Ramses II and applaud him for his monumental impact on Egyptian civilization."

Abu Simbel, my favorite monumental site in Egypt, is indeed an apt reflection of the megalomania and power of a man who had 66 wives, 150 children, and ruled for 67 years. Ramses' serious statuesque stare on his gigantic creations impresses me as much as it did the Nubians and other visitors. They took one look at the stern visage and dropped any notion of invading or entering Egypt from Africa.

To get to Abu Simbel, I leave Aswan at 3 a.m. on a three-hour bus ride farther south towards the Sudan border to arrive before sunrise. Remarkably, the self-aggrandizing Temple of the Sun constructed by Ramses II in 1200 BC was moved here while Lake Nasser began to fill in the early 1960s. I'm absolutely mesmerized by the site as well as the films and posters providing details of the remarkable transfer as the water rose. I spend a lot of time studying graffiti from the 1800s on some of the interior walls, where pictographs tell the fascinating story of Ramses' position as a god and his prowess in defeating his Nubian and Hittite enemies.

I happen to be in Abu Simbel on the day that President Trump is elected, and an Egyptian journalist interviews me about the results. I suggest that the Egyptians could gain favor with the new administration if they replace the face of megalomaniac Ramses II on gigantic statues at Egypt's Abu Simbel temple with that of the new US president. I mention to the interviewer that "even Alexander the Great didn't have the ego or need to create a similar colossal symbol as Ramses did, but President Trump might like the idea."

"Will face of #President #Trump replace #Ramses on #statues at Abu Simbel #temple in #Egypt?" I ask in a tweet.

Alexander also instructs that I "visit some of the temples on the Nile representing the blend of Ancient Egyptian and Hellenistic architecture that I promoted – and that my successors in the Ptolemaic

Dynasty pursued. This will also give you an idea of the objects of Egyptian idolatry."

That directive leads to my surprisingly lavish quarters on a new Nile cruise liner called the *Blue Shadow* (there's also a yacht named *Alexander the Great* on the Nile but I'm not on it), which is a pleasant contrast to the MedTrek's generally lackluster accommodations.

I've got to admit that I enjoy this luxury excursion and diversion (think excellent food, gigantic sleeping and bathing quarters with Nile views, a big bed made for me every day, an intriguing masseuse and other unexpected delights). I obviously look the part of a typical American tourist because a hulking guy on the boat named Steve, who's now living in Florida, calls me "Sir" and claims that he too is a (a lovely word this) "vagabond."

The 215-kilometer boat trip from Aswan to Luxor kicks off at 5 a.m. and the first stop at 7:30 is the riverside 2$^{nd}$-century BC Kom Ombo Temple, a rare double temple dedicated to two Egyptian deities, Sobek (crocodile god) and Horus (falcon god). Alexander asked me to "get a photograph of a headless Greek" and "take home two mummified crocodiles as an offering to your 97-year-old mother." I do.

I have always admired Horus, the falcon-headed sun god, but also get a lot of information about why crocodiles, particularly the crocodile god Sobek, who is depicted as a crocodile-headed man, were elevated to godly status. Apparently crocs were, and maybe still are, (1) both revered and feared because they had benevolent and frightening characteristics, (2) so powerful that ancient Egyptians prayed to them for protection, strength and fertility and (3) the male was extremely virile and the female was extremely fertile. I send photographs of a couple of mummified crocs to inspire my mother.

The *Blue Shadow* docks in Luxor and, again at Alexander's behest, I visit the no-photos-allowed colorful royal tombs in the Valley of the Kings, and venture deep in the earth to see sarcophagi of Ramses II, King Tut and others before paying a visit to the Temple of Deir el-Bahari, created by my muse Hatshepsut, the longest reigning female pharaoh in Egypt.

Born in 1508 BC, Hatshepsut ruled for 20 years and is considered one of Egypt's most successful pharaohs. As an unusually powerful female leader in ancient Egypt, she's also The Idiot's latest inspiration, which I tell anyone who cares to listen in the café at the Temple of Deir el-Bahari where I wind up discussing the MedTrek and promoting my books.

Alexander also strongly suggests that I visit Luxor Temple, where he claims to have been crowned by the Egyptians and directed the reconstruction of the sanctuary. While Luxor is the site where many of the kings of Egypt were crowned, Alexander's comment to me is the first proof that he actually traveled this far south, though most historians still contend he was never here.

As Alexander requests, I visit Karnak and learn that Alexander inspired construction on the main gate to the sprawling three-kilometer square temple. I find a guide who leads me to a hieroglyphic depiction of a pharaonic Alexander, created by Egyptian workers in the Great Hypostyle Hall with 164 columns. Apparently, the workers were expressing their appreciation for the manner in which the great Macedonian king embraced Egyptian deities.

I write an item about swimming secretively in Karnak's Sacred Lake (I mention that the lake is "spiritually cleansing, physically filthy and The Idiot, according to long-time security officials, is the first one to ever swim laps in the rectangular pool") and return that night for a sound and light show that describes the Karnak columns as "organ pipes" and an obelisk anywhere in the world as "a finger indicating silence."

On my last day on the Nile, after flamboyantly dancing with an Egyptian belly dancer on the boat while wearing my traditional Egyptian ankle-length caftan made of cotton called a *galabeya*, I await a massage while tanning and napping around the ship's pool.

This seems to be the perfect time to decide that the Sun (Ra) is an apt god for me, as it was for the ancient Egyptians. One reason I appreciate Ra is that, whatever happens, the Sun appears daily, bright and cheery or dim and downcast or hidden and hard-to-see, and every twenty-four hours, we experience the cycle of light and darkness. I not only grasp Ra's allure and power but also fully understand, and more importantly feel, that without this god, we are all extinct. Ra, who predates Zeus and most other gods, will do for me.

Speaking of beliefs, I've always considered mummification a very sensible way to prepare for a second (or third or fourth), longer life, especially if I'm transitioning in a tomb decorated with some of my belongings which is an indication that, in fact, "you *can* take it with you."

But if all this seems so clear to me, I have to wonder why 85 percent of the Egyptian population has chosen Allah as their god while, I'm told, there are only 1,500 Ra worshippers in the country today.

On my last Sunday in the Upper Kingdom of the Nile, I awake to the call to prayer just before 5 a.m. with a soothing warm breeze wafting into my top floor room at the Eatabe Hotel in Luxor. I pay a last visit to the marvelous Luxor Temple and the intriguing Luxor Museum where I again find a representation of Alexander that indicates it's time for me to return to the Mediterranean and the MedTrek after "you visit an archaeological dig at Saqqara near Cairo to tell them to quit trying to repair the pyramids."

I also get a reminder about ethics in the hotel lobby when I mistakenly leave a twenty-pound note, instead of a ten-pound note, for tea. The waiter brings the bill back to me in a great example of honesty. Heck,

I might have pocketed it and do, of course, give him the ten as a tip. Then I attend a dinner at the Jamboree restaurant in Luxor's downtown bazaar with some of the people from the Explore group who sailed down the Nile with me. All of them are seasoned travelers and agree this is a sensible way for The Idiot to kick off the MedTrek in Egypt.

I return to Cairo and sprint out to the Saqqara pyramids, where a number of tombs are decorated with story-telling hieroglyphs and pictographs. I shout to two baffled workers at the top of scaffolding on the Step Pyramid: "Alexander the Great told me to tell you to quit trying to repair this pyramid!" Mission accomplished.

Then I visit the crypt in Memphis where Alexander was initially entombed when his body was returned from Babylon. He was, historians agree, buried here for twenty years and there's a simple pedestal indicating his resting place.

Before coming back to Memphis for burial, Alexander sailed out of Memphis in January 331 BC down the western branch of the Nile to inspect the upriver Greek trading colony at Naucratis. When its land-bound position offered no scope for further development, he pressed on toward the coast to reach the ideally located Egyptian fort of Rhakotis that's referred to by both Herodotus and Thucydides.

I leave Memphis in November 2016 and take an inexpensive taxi to Port Said on the Suez Canal, where I will finally launch my walk west towards Alexandria and the Libyan border. Ah, how deliciously fun it is to get back on the MedTrek after, as Sara suggested, exposure to Alexander's footsteps elsewhere in Egypt.

# FOLLOW THE IDIOT

## CHAPTER PHOTOS

## CHAPTER MAP

# From the New Suez Canal to Alexandria

"I had rather excel others in the knowledge of what is excellent, than in the extent of my power and dominion."
— *Alexander the Great*

I arrive in Port Said at mid-morning and initially have difficulty finding a hotel because I'm upset and insulted that the first two charge twice as much for a foreigner as they do for an Egyptian, a not unusual discriminatory policy in many developing countries that today I feel compelled to boycott. Fortunately, I find a ninth floor room at the less-demanding, centrally located, adequately functional and perfectly priced Panorama Hotel above the Al Salam Mosque. It's occasionally a mixed blessing due to the blaring calls to prayer five times a day but I've preserved my principles and my spacious corner room looks onto the mosque, the sea and the Suez Canal.

Forced by now to almost completely abandon my plan to walk across the Sinai Peninsula, I decide to MedTrek from Port Fouad, on the eastern side of the Suez Canal, through Port Said and west toward Alexandria which, founded by Alexander the Great in 331 BC, became Egypt's capital for more than 1,000 years.

I start my first MedTrek stint on this outing by traipsing, on the afternoon of my arrival, to the nearby ferry across the canal. I spend four hours walking through Port Fouad and Port Said, both bustling seaside ports with none of the street hassling and hustling of Luxor and Upper Egypt.

There's only one westerner here, and it's me.

Free auto and pedestrian ferries run constantly across the Suez Canal between Port Fouad in Asia and Port Said in Africa. The canal, which is Egypt's largest earner of foreign exchange since the radical decline in tourism during the past eight years, seems more natural than manmade at this stage of its existence.

As I continue my walkabout east, I espy a ship in the distance in a place where, to the best of my knowledge, there shouldn't be a ship. After all, I know that I just left the Suez Canal behind me, which means, and correct me if you think I'm wrong, that it can't be ahead of me. The canal is straight. It doesn't meander.

I figure I'm just having an acid flash and continue approaching the mysterious ghost ship on a phantom canal until a soldier stops me in my tracks.

"Where am I?" I ask innocently. "What's the deal with the ship? It shouldn't be there."

Apparently I'm out of touch. I'm looking at the New Suez Canal, an $8.2 multi-billion dollar project that's been discussed for decades but was actually launched, without anyone telling me about it, in August 2014 and speedily completed under the orders of Egypt's President Abdel Fattah el-Sisi.

Also known as "The Great Egyptian Dream," the showcase 75-kilometer New Suez Canal begins paralleling the existing canal a few kilometers south of here. It doubles canal capacity – and is projected to double annual income to $12.5 billion dollars – by allowing ships to simultaneously sail in both directions, instead of alternately as they have on the frequently congested old canal since it opened in 1869.

Besides coping with an anticipated increase in traffic (critics contend that the figures are inflated and the projected increase in traffic and revenue won't occur), the New Suez Canal is already spurring the development of numerous canalside cities and connects with an industrial zone, a technology valley and five existing ports. The Egyptian Armed Forces not only helped design and dig the canal but also, as I just learned when I ran into the soldier, protect the area from terrorists from Sinai and MedTrekkers from California.

I'm titillated by this surprising and informative discovery about the Egyptian seaside and continue walking through neighborhoods and on the seaside in Port Fouad before taking the free ferry back to Port Said.

That night, I enjoy the full-moon view of the mosque, the Mediterranean, the Suez Canal and local beaches from my multi-windowed $44 corner room. The price includes a breakfast rumored to start at 6 a.m. the next morning in the tenth floor restaurant, which I can access by a staircase across the hall. It turns out breakfast actually does start at six sharp because the kitchen is preparing takeaway meals for a dozen departing workmen who catch 6:30 a.m. shuttles to their industrial jobs. During the flurry of activity, I quietly enjoy surprisingly good coffee and a fresh buffet with the 360° view that, obviously, gives the Panorama its name.

The full moon, which kissed me goodnight when I got in bed, is still up above the Mediterranean to the west as I excitedly prepare to head out for the first full day of MedTrekking in over a year. After crossing from Asia into Africa yesterday, I'm exhilarated to be back on the path. And, yes, I tell myself, I'll be careful, though everyone is very polite and seems to regard me more as a novelty than an obstruction.

There are so few tourists here, I reason, that they prize the one they've got, and I constantly receive "Welcome to Egypt" greetings.

Port Said, with buildings that eerily resemble a crumbling New Orleans, has seen better days and, like much of Egypt, is abhorrently trashy. I find it odd that it's not in better shape, more clean and spiffy, due to the massive amount of money brought in by the canal. But things begin looking up when I discover a tiny, *faux* Target rip-off store that looks almost as inviting as the real thing.

I head west on the *corniche* for a seventy-five minute walk along Port Said's not-too-animated-at-this-time-of-year-and-day beaches, including one that features a run-aground ship. The beaches presumably cater to a local crowd, with simple amenities and many dilapidated facilities.

My beach reverie ends when I'm screamed at by two guards at a shuttered beach hotel who warn me ("warn" is the wrong word: they scream loudly, make wild hand gestures and wave me back as though I'm approaching certain death like a lemming at the edge of a cliff) that I'm about to enter a military zone, which I learn are a constant on a coast rigorously controlled by the Egyptian military. They get the point across by putting fingers on one shoulder (like stripes on a uniform) and point at me using the same fingers as pistols to indicate that I'll be shot. One of them makes a guillotine movement to his neck with the side of his hand.

I get the point, see a military sentry lookout just ahead, and the security guards kindly let me cut through their closed hotel to the main road where I immediately encounter an automobile checkpoint. Police and troops are checking the cars, but no one is concerned when I walk through and continue on the busy road until I arrive at the inaptly named Port Said International Airport where I plan to stop for a coffee.

No such luck. I'm not allowed past the loudly beeping X-ray body and baggage scanners at the main door without a ticket (every hotel, shop and airport in Egypt has walk-through body and baggage scanning equipment that all beep loudly and incessantly, though the noise never seems to prompt the security staff to check anybody) and then I'm unceremoniously shown out when I ask where I can "get a coffee, a sauna and a massage?"

"No airplane ticket, no entry," says an unamused security officer who is definitely not impressed that I want a coffee, a sauna and a massage.

There are constant traffic checkpoints in Egypt (which, from my vantage point, are about as effective as the X-Ray scanning machines) and I stumble up to another one on the west side of the airport. This time, although I'm not in a car, I'm asked what I'm up to. I explain that I'm out for a walk. The guard asks to see my passport and I tell him it's at the Panorama Hotel in Port Said. That seems satisfactory, and he waves me through.

After a few kilometers, I return to the beach, where teams of fishermen are pulling in gigantic nets that actually contain fish, but within an hour, I'm forced back up to the main road. This time it's not only the military that stops me in my steps, but access to the sea is blocked by industrial works that include the Egyptian Propylene and Polypropylene Co., Petrobel, Petrojet, the Zohar Development Project and (my favorite) Pharaonic Petroleum, all blocking access to the sea. This, I deduce, is where the workmen from the Panorama are employed and bring their takeaway lunches early each morning.

I continue on the main road, known as the International Coastal Road, through a nameless urban development (make that blight) that's another top contender for the worst squalor (indeed it's a superlative definition of "squalor") on the Med. Unlike the many merely unattractive or simply poor developments on the coast, which are out of action for the season or permanently in the dumps due to the economy, this town with no name has dozens of dilapidated but inhabited six-story apartment buildings that feature horrendous odors of sewage, revolting piles of garbage (including a few dead dogs), broken-down electric boxes and crumbling walls. If it weren't for hanging laundry and competing bits of blaring hip-hop music, I would have thought everyone had died from malaria or cholera or the neutron bomb (remember the neutron bomb?). There's no commerce except a single barbershop, and, though I don't sense danger, I'm glad to leave it in the desert dust.

I cross back to the beach and begin seeing or imagining, on this empty, sandy desert without a soupçon of vegetation, mirages of luxury hotels, shopping centers and cafes. I wind up on a new highway under construction right by the water that takes me into El Diba, exactly thirty walking kilometers from the Panorama doorstep. My faith in the MedTrek is restored and, done for the day, I grab a communal minibus back to Port

Said (it costs five Egyptian Pounds, known as EGP or E£, which is equivalent to about thirty US cents).

The next morning, hesitant to move my base camp to a place I call Blightville, I get a minibus back to El Diba from the Panorama after a lively discussion with other early-rising hotel guests, including one workman who offers me a ride when he leaves on the 6:30 a.m. company shuttle for his job at Petrobel. Another guest starts his day by saying to me, in English, "Americans think all we do is ride and fuck camels," and a third asks my age.

"68? You're old way too old to walk like this!" he replies when I tell him. "Go back to bed."

My communal minibus driver speaks a little English and is intently listening to a lyrical version of the Koran sung to music. When we pass the roadside housing blight, aka Blightville, he says, "that little place is disgusting, dirty and dangerous...there's nothing good about it; don't set foot there or you'll be risking your life." I don't bother telling him that I causally sauntered through Blightville the day before.

The minibus drops me in El Diba (spelled Ad Dibar on my GPS), and I'm ready to MedTrek to the eastern branch of the Nile River and the verdant slice of fertile land known as the Nile Delta, until, after only a kilometer, I run into a small army base where an officer asks a soldier to check my backpack.

Soldiers and security officials who empty my backpack in Egypt seem primarily stumped by, and interested in, two things: my functional, multipurpose Swiss Army knife, and my sophisticated looking GPS. They studiously examine a photocopy of my passport and let me know that I am not allowed to walk on beaches in Egypt outside urban areas. They tell me, in an almost friendly and helpful tone that indicates they also feel very sorry for me, to take the heavily trafficked main road to Damietta and beyond if I want to avoid problems.

Fortunately, there's a dirt path in the desert paralleling the main road and I embark on an uneventful and long walk to the bustling city of Damietta. I stop at a rare filling station on the desert road for biscuits and coffee for lunch and meet an army officer with the name Mohamed Samy written on his uniform. He speaks excellent English because he spent time, like many members of the Egyptian armed forces, training in San Diego, California.

"Shouldn't you be in Luxor or Cairo?" he asks me. "We never see foreigners here!"

Then a handsome, well-dressed, obviously-a-jogger fellow in the coffee shop, who it turns out works for the Maersk Line container shipping company, and I discuss the two-tier hotel prices and the fact that many consider the New Suez Canal a white elephant.

"Don't walk outside at night in Port Said," he says as he returns to his car to drive to Alexandria. "Even we don't do that."

What am I missing by walking on the main road or a path through the desert instead of on the beach a couple kilometers away?

My *Rough Guide* to Egypt says, "there's nothing to see in the Nile Delta" but informs me that Damietta got rid of the Crusaders in 1247 by supplying them with fish fed on rotten corpses. Besides fishing, which is still very popular (I've seen as many fishermen on the Med, the lake and the lagoons during the last two days as I've seen anywhere), the town's main product today is wood furniture.

I end the 32-kilometer day, after taking a bridge across the eastern tributary of the Nile and walking alongside the river to Ras El-Bar, the "head of land" at the mouth of the Nile, which is sometimes referred to as the Damietta River. I'm now officially in the Nile Delta and enjoy the contrast between the brown and barren desert that I just traversed and the delta with its palm trees, rich greenery, gardens and abundance of water. It's easy to see why most of the country's population lives within the delta, which is a big splash of green on every map of Egypt.

Ras El-Bar, a not-too-shabby resort with an inviting riverside and seaside promenade, and a variety of hotels and restaurants must be among the more vibrant spots on Egypt's Mediterranean coast during the summer. Even in November and out of season, it's comparatively vibrant and buzzy, with outdoor food markets, cafés and other commerce flowing away from the main mosque and along the river. I have a shave, buy some freshly baked cookies and take pictures of fish being sold and grilled before eating one for dinner.

*SUNSCREEN*

I'm woken in Ras El-Bar by the simultaneous crow of roosters and the call to prayer and I gleefully walk to the market to buy fresh fruit as I embark on the day's walk on sandy Mediterranean beaches. I expect that the gigantic Damietta port, which is 8.5 kilometers away, will be my first barrier to the sea until I mistakenly walk into an unmarked, unfenced and unexpected military base less than five kilometers from town.

Being a practical and sensible guy, I realize my mistake when I see soldiers and barracks and immediately stop in my proverbial tracks. But instead of turning around to scurry off the base (in which case I might have gotten out undetected – or been shot in the back), I choose to nonchalantly walk up to two unobservant soldiers with their backs turned towards me, say good morning, apologize for my mistake and indicate my intent to walk back to the beach and return to the road abutting the sea. That friendly gesture leads to my first detention by the Egyptian Army.

A soldier who introduces himself as Alla takes me to the main encampment where everyone is just waking up. He finds Mohammed, an English-speaking first lieutenant who obviously hasn't had his morning tea, and Mohammed requests that Alla search my backpack. He shows Mohammed my Swiss Army knife and GPS while I explain that I ignorantly and accidentally walked onto the base, that the sentry and soldier hadn't even seen me, and that I turned myself in.

Mohammed chastises the soldiers for not being alert and, like everyone else, is well aware that I hadn't intentionally walked onto the base. He claims that a recent storm had destroyed the sea wall separating the base from the public beach and that a "Keep Out" sign in Egyptian had floated out to sea. He says there never was a sign in English because "there's no one here who can read English." He appreciates that I "turned myself in," says he knows I'm no threat, but claims I can't leave right away.

"We can't just let you go," he smiles. "We have to follow protocol and get in touch with our superiors in Port Said when they get to work. You'll probably be released in a couple hours. Don't worry; be patient."

As I've mentioned, I always suspect problems when I hear the expression "Don't worry" and I'm not completely surprised when "a couple hours" becomes fourteen hours.

I spend the daylight hours with Mohammed and the boys admiring the sea view, watching CNN, drinking tea and coffee, taking short walks on the beach accompanied by two soldiers, discussing Donald Trump, becoming Facebook friends with some of the soldiers and getting Mohammed's views on topics ranging from Egyptian politics to American politics.

Here's Mohammed's take on one topical American subject: "Clinton financed Al-Qaeda, Bush financed Hamas, Obama financed Daesh, Carter gave them all money and we hope Trump, even if he doesn't like Muslims, will cut off the funds to everyone except the Egyptian government. Anyway, don't worry, you'll be out of here in a few hours."

Mohammed and I have lots of coffee and tea while he checks out my blog, admires my photos of Upper Egypt, tries to understand why I only carry a copy of my passport, walks back and forth on the beach with me once or twice (accompanied by two soldiers) and speaks to HQ. He then lets me speak to HQ, in Port Said, where an English-speaking colonel tells me, "You have no problem, but we need to take security precautions and we'll probably let you go early this afternoon." Then we watch Egyptian singing and travelogues on TV, discuss Buddhism, have a fresh shrimp lunch at an outside table, and wait.

I somehow manage to be fairly pleasant to my hosts even when, at the end of the afternoon, I am informed that we have to drive an hour to Port Said to meet with the colonel. After our polite conversation, I am looking forward to seeing the colonel to, among other things, ask him if he might arrange to get me permission to walk on the Sinai Peninsula.

At 4:30 p.m. I send a text alert from my GPS: "I've been detained since 8 a.m. by military outside Ras El-Bar and am now being transferred to Port Said for an 'interview' with an Army colonel."

Unfortunately, the colonel is no longer in the office when we arrive after dark, and I have a bit of a tussle with another officer, also named Mohammed, when I refuse to unlock my iPhone to allow him to look at my photos. We finally agree, after two telephone conversations with the English-speaking colonel, that I will hold my iPhone and let Mohammed II look only at photos that I've taken in Egypt during the past two weeks.

It takes four minutes to review the photos, and another fifteen for Mohammed II to convey my innocence to the colonel. I am deemed "No threat" and released for the drive back to Ras El-Bar. The colonel says, "Sorry to spoil your day and welcome to Egypt." Mohammed II says "Don't walk onto any more military bases, be careful and welcome to Egypt." And Mohammed I says, "Write good stuff about us and welcome to Egypt" when he finally drops me at the Teba Hotel at 11 p.m.

Would it have been smarter if I had simply turned around and walked back to friendly sand on the public beach when I realized I was in a military zone fourteen hours earlier?

The Egyptian army has a reputation of shooting first and not bothering to ask questions later. I figured they might think I'd done something wrong if I turned tail – or perhaps even thought I'd snuck through the entire base from the other side and was about to…who knows what? I feel that I made the right move when Mohammed tells me just before he drops me off that "our instructions are to ask people to stop, shoot once in the air if they don't stop immediately, and if they still don't stop, shoot to kill. You were smart."

The most amusing aspect of the entire day is that, once the colonel agrees I can be released, I'm immediately relieved and relaxed and decide to enjoy traveling with four military guys – one in a special forces uniform, one dressed in summer camouflage gear, Mohammed I wearing a military sweater with a few bars on the shoulders, the driver in plain clothes. I insist that we drop by the Panorama Hotel, which is on our way out of town, where I can use the Wi-Fi and send an "I'm safe" alert. I walk into the lobby, where the hotel manager and lots of guests are watching a soccer game, with my four-man military entourage and everyone, who remembers that I'd stayed there for a couple nights, looks at me in disbelief, thinking I'm a spy, or a senator, or something.

I send a text from the Panorama that reads, "Just finished 'interview' in Port Said and will be heading back to Ras El-Bar. Urged to avoid military areas, though this detention (CNN and shrimp lunch, included) was no one's fault and uneventful. Inshallah."

Then, when we're stuck in traffic at the same checkpoint I encountered when I initially walked out of Port Said on my first day of MedTrekking, I tell the four of them to act like real soldiers and get out and direct traffic to hasten our passage. Three of them get out of the car and immediately start bossing around the other drivers like they know what they're doing (they have no clue) before we bypass the line of cars and continue our ride on the dark, long and lonely road along the Mediterranean Sea.

This experience teaches me to check very carefully to determine if the sandy beaches and coastline are public (which is the case in urban areas like Port Said, Ras El-Bar, Gamasa, Baltim and Al Bourros) or off limits (which is the case when fishermen make a sign of being handcuffed by putting their wrists together).

It's also becoming clear that the cordon the Egyptians have created to protect and defend their Mediterranean coast is as visibly and physically secure as anywhere else on the Mediterranean, which is why there are so few tales of unwanted migrants or refugees entering or leaving Egypt by sea.

For me, this ubiquitous military presence means that I'll have to cherry pick where I walk and come up with a good story when I'm stopped.

I also come to the conclusion that the "Welcome to Egypt" greeting that I get from everyone is an over-used phrase which takes on a much more profound meaning the more I hear it. That is, it means nothing at all.

I try to be pleasant and social during breakfast at the Teba Hotel when I run into a Russian sailor and three British scientists.

"Hey, I understand we're supposed to be best friends now," I say, smiling, to the Russian in the wake of Donald Trump's recent election. He smiles back and says, "Nice to meet you, BFF!" Yes, we're Best Friends Forever.

The three British scientists, two men and a woman in their early thirties, are on assignment for an insurance company investigating a shipment of grain that's gone bad in the nearby Damietta port. They shuttle between the hotel and port each morning and evening and have very little contact with anything or anyone in between. I'm intrigued by their work, and my ambitious MedTrek surprises them.

After yesterday's detention, I'm over-cautious about any military encounters when I kick off the walk after breakfast. I spend the morning gingerly strolling to and around the sprawling port and into the appropriately named town of New Damietta where I wander through neighborhoods and across roads to make my way back to the sea.

Once at the water, I take a left along the new promenade (almost everything, from apartment buildings to the main bus stop in New Damietta, is still comparatively new, especially if you put them up against the pyramids or the Suez Canal) and at one point I follow a seawall that's been built to either stop the sand or stop the sea or both, though it doesn't look to be doing too well at either task. Within an hour, I see a military sentry as I approach an under-construction power plant. I immediately scurry back to the ICR, or International Coastal Road.

The highlight of the day is a selfie I take with an Egyptian who also claims to be walking, if I correctly translate his Arabic, around the Mediterranean Sea. The caption reads, "Two Idiots walking around the Mediterranean Sea are able to pose for one selfie near the Egyptian town of Gamasa."

Once past an electric plant-to-be, I enter Gamasa, where tuk-tuks, or motorized three-wheel rickshaws, are the favored mode of transport and, though there's sparkling greenery everywhere, the town is filthy. The garbage, sanitation (or lack of it) and general malaise are another sign of under-development in Egypt.

It takes me until late in the afternoon to walk the length of the promenade in Gamasa, one of the longest urban seasonal resort promenades in the Nile Delta. It's certainly one of my longest walks without seeing a hotel on or off the beach. The villas, all empty, look so unattractive that it's difficult to imagine that they will attract any residents during the summer. I'm so mellow that I even take a five-minute catnap on a bench.

Almost every Egyptian woman I see today is wearing a headscarf, while others, appareled in full black, wear a *niqab*, which covers their entire face except for the eyes. And many Egyptian men have a prayer bump on their foreheads, a testimony to their faith after constant prayer with their forehead on the ground 35 times a week. I also notice a long nail on the pinky finger of many men, which I thought was because they all played guitar for The Sphinx, the well-known Egyptian band. In fact, it's a traditional symbol indicating that they do no manual labor.

Once I finally make it to the end of the promenade, I walk along the beach barefoot and some fishermen indicate that the military lies in wait just ahead. They again convey this point by touching their shoulders with two fingers to signify military stripes and cross their wrists as though they're in handcuffs.

I see the sentry towers in the near distance and again cut back to walk on the highway when I stumble upon the modernistic Delta

University for Science and Technology. I drop in for a gander and a coffee and, after passing through security, am immediately welcomed by a group of students and invited (as I mentioned, I'm the only American around) to visit the president's office in half an hour. I'd like to stay, but write him a note indicating my name, education (BA Stanford, MS Columbia), my profession (journalist/author), and the fact that I feel compelled to keep walking and will see him next time I come through town.

Half the staff and students in the place friend me on Facebook, and one student writes on my timeline that my visit (I was there fifteen minutes) had a "profound" effect on him. Within minutes, there are over a hundred "likes" on his post and a comment that suggests I be made US Secretary of State.

When I leave the school I ask a scarfless student, who turns out to be from Kuwait, what to expect on the road ahead and she replies "There's just the desert after this. Be careful."

I walk into the desert and inspirationally sing a few more verses of the Bangles hit that I now call *Walk Like An Idiot.*

> "Blonde waitresses take their trays
> They spin around and they cross the floor
> They've got the moves (oh whey oh)
> You drop your drink and they give you more
> All the school kids so sick of books
> They like the punk and the metal band
> When the buzzer rings (oh whey oh)
> They're walking like an Egyptian
> All the kids in the marketplace say
> Ay oh whey oh, ay oh whey oh
> Walk like an Idiot."

When I arrive in hotelless and rural Baltim about a hundred kilometers west of Ras El-Bar, I'm hoping to find something that will serve as my next base camp and serendipitously stumble on the Baltim Resort, an expansive, military-controlled "hotel" for officers. In theory, it's run by the military and is for the military – and not for anyone else.

I meet the resort's English-speaking accountant at the main gate as he leaves for the day, explain my project to him ("I've walked here from Port Fouad and Port Said through Ras El-Bar and Damietta and plan to keep walking to Rasheed, Alexandria, El Alamein, Mersa Matruh and Libya....") and somehow we wind up chatting about his years working in Saudi Arabia, where I've been a few times. Much to my surprise, he invites me to stay for two nights at the hotel because, I think, he's thrilled to have someone with whom to speak English and is, like many Egyptians, being courteous to a stranger.

"I'm sorry, but you'll have to pay 120 pounds a night (that's $7.54 and may be a MedTrek low) and there's a sea view but no Wi-Fi," Wahleed says apologetically. "And we'll bring breakfast to your apartment. Please don't let anyone, especially journalists, know that I let you stay because it really isn't allowed."

"Of course not," I reply. "Mum's the word."

How fortuitous. I'll be staying in a hotel that's not only run by the military but is, to the best of my knowledge, the only thing resembling a "hotel" on this stretch of coast. Though it's theoretically closed to the public, from the outside it looks like a fairly luxurious resort in a place that, says Wikipedia, "lies really isolated on the northernmost point of Egypt in the Kafr-El-Sheikh *gouvernant*."

It's the off-season, of course, which means that there are only two other rooms taken. But I'm delighted that I can hear the waves, feel the sea breeze and see the lights of ships just offshore that I presume are waiting to go through the Suez Canal. Like the yin-and-yang impact of desert and greenery, I'm now experiencing the yin-and-yang impact of being detained by the military one day and being lodged by them the next. In a country where the military controls the coast, this is a perfectly Idiot-ic situation.

No place is perfect, of course, and, though I'm thrilled that the rate for foreign MedTrekkers is the same as the rate for Egyptian soldiers, there are two minor issues with my $7.54 room. There's (1) no Wi-Fi, and (2) my vast three-bedroom lodging is co-inhabited by more buzzing mosquitoes and flies than any place I've ever stayed in Egypt, Saudi Arabia or anywhere else.

I solve the absence of Wi-Fi by taking a tuk-tuk four kilometers inland to "downtown" Baltim and installing myself at the Costa Cafe on Port Said Street where a cappuccino, just to give you an idea of local prices, costs fifty US cents. Bustling Baltim, like Gamasa, has hundreds of tuk-tuks that make traffic in central Baltim, which is on a lake, resemble the bumper cars at Disneyland. I get a tuk-tuk back to the military resort and wear a headlamp during the twenty-minute drive, which is especially perilous on the dark International Coastal Road.

No one told me about, and I hadn't thought about, the presence of mosquitoes and flies that plague me throughout the night as I move from one bedroom to another, looking for sanctuary, searching for an insect-free space, in a sprawling suite with an equipped kitchen and a living room with, I just counted, more than 20 chairs of various types. By morning, I have bites and red spots all over my body and can only hope that there's no West Nile virus, Zika or other plague that will strike me. The first thing I do when I get Wi-Fi is consult various sites to determine which will kill me the quickest, West Nile virus or Zika.

I don't get much sleep, of course, and am eagerly awaiting whatever they bring me for breakfast. I was told there's no coffee, but I'm hoping for tea. In fact, there's no tea either, but I do get a functional tray with two eggs, Egyptian bread, cheeses, yoghurt and honey. That's enough as I embark on the beach – and then the edge of the ICR when I'm forced inland by the military – towards Rasheed, or Rosetta, as the location of the famous Rosetta Stone is called in English.

I pass an empty army fort on Baltim Beach and reach the fishing port of Al Barrlos, which resembles New Damietta and Gamasa. The resort homes and apartment complexes, including one called Paradise Dreams, are once again seemingly uninhabited. I'll have to come back in mid-summer to ensure that there are actually people here.

Al Barrlos is a working fishing port, and the sea wall has been reinforced with dolosse (reinforced concrete blocks) to prevent further erosion. I'm fed up enough with garbage to take pictures of one ugly seaside pile of debris with goats and another filthy pile with birds. I give some water to a tiny crying kitten and some bread to a crazy Arab being calmed down by a sanitation worker. Then I watch a refurbished boat being returned to the water and walk by a lagoon-side school where twenty kids want to follow the Pied Piper Idiot to get out of class.

When I finally stop, an hour later, for a coffee at a roadside stand I have a conversation in English with a guy who says, "America cannot live without war. Why do you always go to war?"

The mosquito bites, the obvious case of West Nile Virus or Zika that I've got, the lack of a morning coffee, the whole thing has made me a little despondent, so all I can say in response to his question is "To keep the economy humming and make people rich. I'm sorry."

Then I start telling him about how Egypt, which is obviously in the throes of an inflationary economic cycle that probably won't be helped by an IMF-approved $12 billion loan this month, is one of the least expensive and filthiest places to visit on the Mediterranean. That doesn't impress him much so I switch subjects.

"Actually, I've seen signs that the government is moving in the right direction and that things are getting better here," I say, while asking him for another Nescafé that costs me ten US cents. "The Suez Canal has been expanded to take more traffic, and I passed two new power stations, visited Delta University and met three young British scientists inspecting cargo at the Damietta port. The traffic is still crazy everywhere. It's all happening here. This is the place to be! You've got a great country."

I'm now on a strip of the ICR highway that has the sea on one side and the expansive Barrlos Lake (the water enters the lake under a big bridge in Al Barrlos) on the other and make it about half way to Rasheed/Rosetta when, after a 37-kilometer day, I get a communal shuttle back to Baltim.

Although I probably erred on the side of caution and avoided some sections of the seaside to walk on the treacherous International

Coastal Road, I'm delighted that I haven't been detained again and that my encounters with the authorities (there are frequent checkpoints and run-ins with the military, border patrol and police throughout the day) and other Egyptians have been uneventful, even friendly.

I take a day off to move my base camp from Baltim to Rasheed and much to my delight wind up in a $7.30, ninth floor corner room at the Rasheed International Hotel with a view down the Nile towards the Mediterranean Sea, eight kilometers downstream. I can't resist spending a couple days in the town that gave us the Rosetta Stone, which I've seen in the British Museum and, in duplicate, in the Egyptian Museum in Cairo and, most recently, in the lobby of my hotel. As I look onto the river from my standing room only balcony, I wonder what Alexander the Great would think of the proliferation of fish farms on the Nile and the small motorboats that scurry back and forth between the east and west banks of the river.

Mention this hotel, the only one in town, to fellow travelers, and the first thing they say doesn't concern the ridiculously low price, the extraordinary view, the ornate dining room (where I was always the only diner), the central location near markets and businesses or even the faux Rosetta Stone in the lobby. They all mention the singing elevator. We're all used to Muzak in elevators, of course, but the elevator here is constantly singing an eclectic selection of Arabic and English classics. Loudly. It drives everyone bonkers.

Just after my arrival, I take a water taxi across the river and begin walking toward the Mediterranean on the eastern side of the western branch (get that?) of the Nile. After a few kilometers, I discover that the small creek running parallel to the main river is the most polluted waterway I've seen anywhere on the Mediterranean. Straight out of the worst parts of the Ganges in India or the Chao Phraya in Thailand, it's filled with trash, smells like a permanently disabled toilet, and features women and girls, mainly of school age, washing dishes, clothes and babies in it. I imagine bringing President Sisi down to show him just how filthy the real Egypt is. I not only want to give him a perspective on garbage but also provide him with a health and sanitation reality check.

Then, for some reason, I recall how Alexander smelled, because his delicious body aroma was the exact opposite of the odor emanating from this slowly flowing cesspool.

Plutarch, the Greek biographer and essayist, tells us in his *Memoirs* that "a most agreeable odor exhaled from (Alexander's) skin, and that his breath and body all over was so fragrant as to perfume the clothes which he wore next him; the cause of which might probably be the hot and adjust temperament of his body."

Yup, that's Alexander for you.

Besides the polluted waterway and disgusting smell, I made the mistake of wearing shorts and a V-neck camouflage-patterned T-shirt on this walk that make me stand out more than usual. I can feel the stares and sense my foreignness. I'll definitely wear long pants tomorrow for the stroll toward Alexandria, or Al-Iskandariya.

I've never heard a call to prayer as long (I swear it continues for an hour) and cacophonous as that in Rosetta/Rasheed when I awaken the next morning. After a simple breakfast in the lobby, I meander through the labyrinthine streets of town – dirty, dusty and disheveled but lively, likeable and inviting – as the place slowly wakes up. It's clear that one of the major preoccupations here, besides the Rosetta Stone and lots of brick-making factories on the banks of the Nile, is producing rope from twine, a manufacturing process that involves long lengths of thread being entwined manually near the western edge of town by men stretching the twine the length of a football pitch.

Dense groves and plantations of fenced-in palm trees prevent me from heading directly to the coast (which is just as well, because the military tightly controls and patrols the shore near the mouth of the Nile). Instead, I take a tuk-tuk (E£3) to the microbus station to get a communal taxi (E£2) to Idku and reach the coast there.

There are many industrial plants (Shell and Bechtel are two names associated with the place) that also make it impractical to walk on the seaside. I take a train (E£2) towards Alexandria and get off when the coast is, literally and figuratively, clear. I spend a few hours walking through Abu Qir with its bay containing legendary shipwrecks along a seafront that's now obstructed by more sea-blocking industrial plants, the Air Defense Academy, the Naval Academy and police stations.

Alexander might be enthralled by all the activity if he time-travelled here, but I could have done with a bit more coastal access.

Abu Qir is also the site of Heracleion, or Thonis, a city founded in the 12th century BC on islands in the Nile. Long before Alexandria and its lighthouse were considered to be the gateway to Egypt, this archipelago at the mouth of the Nile formed Egypt's biggest trading port and was its largest source of revenue. Visitors were greeted by a five-meter high statue of Hapi, the god of the Nile flood, and today, the island city, which gradually sank with the assistance of a tsunami and earthquake, is a subterranean wonderland of historical treasures under just ten meters of water about three kilometers off the coast.

I cut through one green zone and am shown the cuffed wrist sign by a farmer if I continue toward the coast. When I finally reach Maamoura Beach, I'm delighted to see some random western women wearing bikinis on a beach equipped with umbrellas and *chaises longues*. I have a coffee with milk at the Harrods Inn (E£23 pounds versus E£5 in the places I've been going to) and the expensive (but antique) milk they use in the coffee gives me an embarrassingly effusive case of Hapi's revenge a few hours later.

When the beach ends, I enter (E£15) the wondrous, Disneyland-like Montazah Gardens featuring the Haramlik Palace and drop into the Helnan Palestine Hotel, which already has garish Christmas scenes in its lobby on Thanksgiving Day. Seriously? Christmas displays in the lobby of the Helnan Palestine Hotel on Thanksgiving? On the Mediterranean Sea in Egypt, which is 85 percent Muslim? There's even a big Santa next to the security scanner at the hotel entrance.

Seriously?

The McDonald's, the lavish Mykonos restaurant and the restored villa that King Farouk built and President Sadat converted into a guesthouse give the Montazah Gardens an upmarket flavor and feeling. It's about as far from Rasheed's dusty streets, sprawling river, singing elevator and polluted canal as I can get.

As I walk through the gardens, the Harrods Inn milk poisoning hits me and I have to squat, in both senses of the word, the gardeners' toilet, which doesn't make them too happy until they realize the seriousness of my plight, and my embarrassment as I make apologetic signs to them and Allah. I tell them that it's for moments like these that there's always toilet paper in my backpack. Inshallah.

I spend fifteen minutes recuperating at McDonald's and lay down on the grass for half an hour before I feel well enough to return to Rasheed, where I pick up my laundry (E£30, or $2, for everything I've got with me) and have a dinner of vegetable soup and spaghetti. Before leaving, I ask the manager to take a photo of me in the Rasheed International Hotel lobby with the faux Rosetta Stone and tell no one in particular that the British Museum should return the original stone, found here by Jean-Francois Champollion in 1799, to Egypt.

Then, after paying the $17 bill for two nights and lotsa coffees, I take my gear on a microbus to an Airbnb base camp in bustling and busy Alexandria, where I'm looking forward to hitting, probably exactly at the Alexandria Library, the 12,000-kilometer mark on the MedTrek.

Incidentally, you probably wonder why Egypt is so cheap?

Fortuitously, if you're The Idiot, the dollar has doubled in value since I arrived a month ago. It was E£8.85 to the dollar on October 16 and it's E£17.59 today. This was due to a massive devaluation that unpegged the E£ from the US$ in an effort to stabilize the economy and earn foreign exchange. There's a surging black market that I haven't explored and I'm amazed that, at this rate, I bother haggling. The rate is not, of course, such good news for Egyptians, who have seen the price of gas, transport and other staples rise dramatically during my stay.

Nice time for an Idiot-ic visit though.

---

# FOLLOW THE IDIOT

---

 CHAPTER PHOTOS

 CHAPTER MAP

# WALK LIKE AN EGYPTIAN

# LISTEN TO THE BANGLES

# Strolling through Chic Alexandria to El-Alamein Battlefields

"There is an island washed by the open sea lying off Nile mouth – seamen call it Pharos." – Homer, *The Odyssey*

"But, O Macedonians and Grecian allies, stand firm! Glorious are the deeds of those who undergo labor and run the risk of danger; and it is delightful to live a life of valor and to die leaving behind immortal glory."
– *Alexander the Great*

Alexandria's iconic *corniche* begins just west of the Montazah Gardens and I'm excited to arrive from weathered Rasheed and move into my new urban base camp, an Airbnb with a sea view, Wi-Fi and all the trimmings located in the chichi Sheraton Apartments abutting the seaside Sheraton Hotel.
Or so I thought.

The photo of the apartment is completely bogus, and it's nowhere near the Sheraton Hotel, or the sea. I go on booking.com, find a ridiculously inexpensive room at the Sheraton, pay for it in advance and walk through the alarm-sounding security scanning machines into the lobby. The price of the room, however, is also completely bogus, due to the fine print that reads: "Please note that the room type includes 'Egyptians and residents only' and is exclusive for Egyptians and residents only. Additional charges are applicable if a valid Egyptian ID, Egyptian passport or Egyptian evidence is not presented upon check in."

I do better with $7.50 rooms at military bases or hotels with singing elevators.

Despite my scruffy and bedraggled MedTrek appearance, I become a hero at the Sheraton when I reveal both scams – which I consider detrimental to MedTrekkers, detrimental to the hotel, detrimental to humanity – on both apps to the appalled and grateful manager of the Sheraton.

"Booking.com advertises prices in English that are available only to Egyptians but allows me to pay in advance," I explain to him. "Airbnb and someone named Oman use a photo of your hotel to advertise a room in the Sheraton Apartment's Plaza, which doesn't exist."

The manager thanks me for bringing these global online shockers to his attention and instructs an aide to contact both sites and rectify the egregious errors. Then he introduces me to the young VIP Coordinator with instructions to honor my "Egyptian only" price.

My discussion with Iythar Khedr, the delightful 20-something VIP Coordinator fresh out of a Cairo hospitality college, reminds me how rural and out of touch I've been while MedTrekking here from Port Said. She's never heard of, much less been to, Baltim, Gamasa or Rasheed and the idea of a $7.50 room or a walk across northern Egypt's desert and the Nile Delta is an absolutely bizarre concept to her. It occurs to me that, except for the British scientists in Ras El-Bar, I haven't spoken fluent English to anyone, or seen many women without a headscarf, or been in a place where I could completely let down my guard, for ten days.

Not that it's been unpleasant, but I was definitely on another planet far, far away.

Iythar honors my "Egyptian only" room rate, which is less than $50, and, though the Sheraton's comparative luxury is in complete contrast to my usual basic MedTrek base camps, I check in and do what anyone who's been "away" from civilization for a while would do. I take a bubble bath, get a massage, have a Big Mamma pizza for Thanksgiving dinner, watch the BBC news and fall asleep in front an old American movie on a TV with a clear screen (everything was fuzzy on every TV I looked at during the MedTrek). The next morning during breakfast, I have a normal discussion with a visiting Ukrainian businesswoman selling timber to

Egypt and I make or break Iythar Khedr's future when I mention how efficient she's been on the Sheraton website and their Facebook page.

This type of over-the-top appreciation for hotel "luxury," or normalcy by anyone else's standards, hasn't happened to me in years, maybe since I took a month-long trek in the Himalayas in the 1980s, because the contrast between rural and urban hasn't been quite as distinct until now. Perhaps it was the pollution on the Nile or maybe the mosquitoes in my military resort room, but I really enjoy checking into the sixth floor Sheraton room with a view of the sea and the Montazah Gardens. It takes me exactly six seconds to make the mental, physical and spiritual transition.

Although the Sheraton is on the wrong (east) side of Alexandria for a sensible long-term base camp, it's so comfy, friendly and reasonable, with such an exceptional view and price (The Four Seasons down the *corniche* is $350 a night) that, despite the travel time I'll face to return to my MedTrek starting points after the first day, I decide to stay for a while as I march towards El-Alamein, Mersa Matruh and Libya in the footsteps of Alexander the Great.

Alexander presumably first learned about this ideal spot when Homer mentioned it in the *Odyssey* ("There is an island washed by the open sea lying off the Nile mouth – seamen call it Pharos") and he was obviously attracted by the deep waters of its well-sheltered, natural harbor.

Although he never saw the city bearing his name being constructed or completed when he was alive (he was here for a while after he died), Alexander gets credit for choosing the location of Alexandria in 331 BC. He outlined its physical layout with the assistance and advice of Deinocrates of Rhodes, who was an experienced architect, the stonemason Numenios, and a technical adviser named Hyponomos who planned the royal palace and worked out a complex system of underground drains and sewers.

"He was immediately struck by the excellence of the site, and convinced that if a city were built upon it, it would certainly prosper," Arrian wrote, noting that Alexander's general layout included a marketplace and temples.

One of the most frequent stories associated with Alexandria is that Alexander sprinkled barley flour on the ground to mark the future city's roads, temples and other features. The story goes that while he was expressing satisfaction with the design, birds swooped down and ate all the flour. In any event, Alexander didn't give the final go ahead for construction until he consulted the Oracle of Ammon in Siwa, where I'll soon be taking you.

Alexandria became, of course, the intellectual capital of the Hellenistic world a couple centuries before Christ, with a celebrated library (it burned down three centuries after it was constructed) and a renowned lighthouse (it collapsed in 1300) on the aforementioned island of Pharos.

Alexander didn't stop playing the name-the-city-after-myself game here. Over the next decade, he founded more than 20 cities, most of them in Persia, with the name of Alexandria. Many were on trade routes and include, besides Iskender where we were in Turkey, Iskandariya in Iraq and Kandahar (shortened from Iskandahar) in Afghanistan. For the record, Alexandria, Virginia, is not named after Alexander the Great but in honor of a landowner named John Alexander.

The *corniche* in Alexandria (everyone calls it Alex and greets me with a hearty "Welcome to Alex" salutation) is more than 20 kilometers long but it's only 13 kilometers, or eight miles, from the Sheraton to the Library – all of it flat and along the sea with beaches on my right and a mélange of faded and crumbling buildings with occasional chic new complexes on my left. The sprawling San Stefano development, which includes The Four Seasons Hotel, a Starbucks and a chic mall with an organic-only supermarket, is the pacesetter. But I estimate that eighty percent of the buildings on the horn-honking, congested-with-morning traffic promenade still need a makeover.

I stop at Starbucks, which is exactly halfway between the Sheraton and the library, for a venti cappuccino ($1.50) and shot of Wi-Fi before visiting the mall long enough for me to be impressed with a natural food store and disappointed that there's no ice cream available anywhere until 11:30 a.m. I continue walking past the Malibu Beach, the Dream Tower building and lots of other seaside restaurants preparing to open.

Alexandria beaches – with names like Cleopatra, San Stefano, Camp Cesar and Stanley – are all pleasantly inviting, and the promenade, though being dug up at many places with road work projects that will be going on for a while, is full of baby strollers "driven" by all types of adults (couples, young parents and young kids, old parents and old kids) and, on the beach, lots of fishermen, who actually are catching fish.

I fall in love with Stanley Beach the second I MedTrek across Stanley Bridge. The horseshoe-shaped beach, located on a little bay on the inland urban side of the bridge, features tiers of 1920s British-built bathing cabins and nicely manicured sand. I can't resist a quick dip and make it my selection as the "Most Alluring Urban Beach In Egypt" after having an early lunch and enjoying the view at the restaurant in the San Giovanni Hotel.

When I get to the Library, my calculations are correct. I celebrate the 12,000-kilometerstone of my ongoing walk around the Mediterranean Sea by taking a selfie with Alexander the Great in the empty courtyard. It's Friday and the museum is closed, but when I'm talking to the security guard about checking out the concert hall on the sly, I meet 20-something Ronnie Vance, an oboist from Seattle who plays with the town's symphony orchestra.

Ronnie is the first one I tell about my 12,000-kilometer achievement and he's so impressed that he and his equally American wife Bethany, who plays the French Horn, offer me a free ticket to Beethoven's 9th in the Library's "Great Hall" the next night. Bethany also teaches at an international school, and we discuss how the recently strong dollar has, because they're paid in local currency, cut their income in half.

I thank the young couple and tell them I look forward to hearing them roll over Beethoven the next night after I've visited the library, the Cavafy Museum, the catacombs and other Alexandria sites. Within minutes, Ronnie mentions on Facebook that he met a guy who had just walked 12,000 kilometers and an Egyptian journalist friend of his, a music and culture critic, contacts me to do a story.

After I meet Ronnie, I walk away from the sea to the Greco-Roman Museum that, it turns out, has been closed for renovation for as long as anyone can remember. That afternoon, I enjoy an urban walk to the town's high spots, including Kom El-Dekka (it means "mound of rubble") that is billed as the "ancient city of Alexandria." I take a photo of a bathtub that, proclaims the local buzz, Alexander used during the short period he was here. I also get some shots of the mainly Roman ruins, including a Roman theater with marble seating for 700. There are also some decent mosaics and digging is underway by Polish archaeologists searching for Alexander's tomb.

I walk from Kom El-Dekka to the Alexandria National Museum, which is in an Italianesque mansion and features hoards of Hellenistic artifacts. I sneak a shot of a bust of Alexander looking like a god and photograph a panel explaining why he chose Alexandria as a site for the new capital (its strategic naval location, commercial potential and abundance of water are three reasons). I hear a museum guide telling an American couple that Alexander is definitely buried at the main "street" in Kom El-Dekka.

I get lost heading to the Cavafy Museum that was the former home of Alexandria-born Greek poet Constantine Cavafy (1863-1933), whose poem *Ithaka* contributed to my desire to walk around the Mediterranean Sea. It begins, you might recall, "As you set out for Ithaka hope that the voyage is a long one, full of adventure, full of discovery" and, after getting a photo of myself with Cavafy's bust, I'm impressed to see that the epitaph on his grave in the city's Greek Cemetery reads simply. "Poet."

At mid-afternoon, I find myself at the Kom El-Shuqafa Monuments, or catacombs, where I meet a well-informed guide named Saber Elhadry whose business card proclaims that he's celebrating his silver jublee (sic) as a guide (1991-2016). Saber not only talks about the transitional nature of the catacombs, specifically between the pharaohs and Greco-Roman era, but also about where Alexander the Great might be

# "KILOMETERSTONES" ON THE MEDTREK

When I revealed in April 2016 that I'd reached the 12,000[th] kilometer on my walk around the Mediterranean Sea in Alexandria, Egypt, a *Follow The Idiot* fan asked, "Where did you celebrate other 000 'kilometerstones,' which I presume is how a milestone is expressed in kilometers?"

Here are the places I reached the 1,000[th] to 12,000[th] "kilometerstones" on the MedTrek:

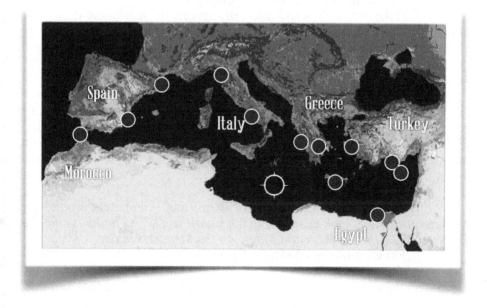

### 1,000 kilometers – Santa Margarita, Spain

"At the 1,000-kilometer MedTrek mark, a potentially momentous milestone, I find myself in a German bakery near a fake Mississippi riverboat parked on a canal in Santa Margarita, Spain.
'And we walked 1,000-kilometers for this?" my toes ask in unison'." – *The Idiot and The Odyssey: Walking The Mediterranean.*

### 2,000 kilometers – Calapiteres, Spain

"When we arrive at the beach in Calapiteres, I hit the 2,000-kilometer mark and anoint my lips, Cassie's lips and Leonardo's lips with seawater. A few days later Cassie gives me a tiny, varnished rock taken from the beach that says, in red nail polish: **K 2000**" – *The Idiot and The Odyssey: Walking The Mediterranean.*

### 3,000 kilometers – Mirador de Perdicaris, Morocco

"When I hear the loud blare of a cruise ship's horn heralding its entry into the Strait of Gibraltar, I realize that it's time for a serious commemoration. I've just reached the 3,000-kilometer (or K) mark of the MedTrek. Cassie, who was with me at the 2,000-K kilometerstone, refers to this as KKK." – *The Idiot and The Odyssey: Walking The Mediterranean.*

### 4,000 kilometers – Viareggio, Italy

"The town's landmark gigantic clock is the 4,000-kilometer mark on my MedTrek. To celebrate, I have a seafood salad at the Gran Caffé Margherita dominated by a Baroque cupola." – *The Idiot and The Odyssey: Walking The Mediterranean.*

### 5,000 kilometers – Point Licosa, Italy

"I hike through a number of agreeable seaside and hillside villages; make a steep climb up a nearly vertical cliff; and almost forget to observe the 5,000-kilometer mark because I'm counting olives, figs, and grapes." – *The Idiot and The Odyssey II: Myth, Madness and Magic on the Mediterranean.*

### 6,000 kilometers – Ithaca, Greece

"I walk along a long, sandy beach and find myself in a pristine cove where I celebrate the 6,000-kilometer mark on my MedTrek with a leisurely skinny dip in the clear and cleansing water before laying down on the warm pebbles to dry." – *The Idiot and The Odyssey II: Myth, Madness and Magic on the Mediterranean.*

### 7,000 kilometers – Delphi, Greece

"My feet, after walking more than 7,000 kilometers around the Mediterranean Sea, look exactly like the Charioteer's." – *The Idiot and The Odyssey II: Myth, Madness and Magic on the Mediterranean.*

### 8,000 kilometers – Mátala, Crete

"After walking 8,000 kilometers I find that the Mátala caves and the town's beaches (the "Red Beach," just FYI, is for nudists only), a hippie allure forty years ago, are now major tourist draws with the usual pros and cons associated with such development." – *The Idiot and The Odyssey II: Myth, Madness and Magic on the Mediterranean.*

### 9,000 kilometers – Ürkmez, Turkey

"I blog that The Idiot is 'dancing in the surf' after reaching 9,000 kilometers (5,592 miles) on the MedTrek." – *The Idiot and The Odyssey III: Twenty Years Walking The Mediterranean.*

### 10,000 kilometers – Gazipaşa, Turkey

On June 5$^{th}$ (2014) The Idiot reaches the 10,000-kilometer (6,214 miles) mark on Nanu Beach near the village of Gazipaşa in southern Turkey." – *The Idiot and The Odyssey III: Twenty Years Walking The Mediterranean.*

### 11,000 kilometers – Caretta Beach, Northern Cyprus

"The three of us hike four hours to arrive, after 15 kilometers, at the Caretta (named after the *Caretta caretta* or loggerhead turtle) Beach Restaurant about three kilometers from Akdeniz. At some point, without even realizing it, I pass the 11,000-kilometer mark on the MedTrek." – *The Idiot and The Odyssey III: Twenty Years Walking The Mediterranean.*

### 12,000 kilometers – Alexandria, Egypt

"Looking forward on my first day's walk to hitting the 12,000-kilometer mark on the MedTrek when I reach the 'new' Alexandria Library, which was under construction when I was last here in 1997." – *The Idiot and The Odyssey III: Twenty Years Walking The Mediterranean.*

When my twenty-year walk around the Mediterranean Sea was unceremoniously launched in France on January 1, 1998, I did not foresee many of the adventures I would have on the path during the next two decades. Or imagine that I would MedTrek over 12,000 kilometers.

I obviously had no way of knowing that I would stumble through the world's largest nudist colony in France, meet a peripatetic sorceress in Spain, take a serious fall off a goat path in Morocco or despairingly watch as my passport and credit cards disappeared in the Mediterranean Sea near the Algeria border.

I couldn't predict that I would be robbed by drunken Gypsies in southern Italy, chat with Zeus after climbing to the summit of Mount Olympus in Greece, swim across the Hellespont in Turkey, get arrested on charges of spying in Lebanon or reach the Alexandria Library in Egypt while walking in the footsteps of Alexander the Great.

What's next, I wonder?

interred. Alexandria? Siwa? Kom El-Dekka? He admits he doesn't know (a rare admission for a guide) but lists the possibilities with enthusiasm.

I end the day on a high note at Amud El-Sawari, or Pompey's Pillar, an ancient Acropolis on the highest point in town.

The next day, I dip into the Bibliotheca Alexandrina, or the Library of Alexandria, to research Alexander the Great in the world's largest reading area with 330 wired computers, free Wi-Fi and chairs for 2,000 readers at a time, There are two million books (500,000 were a gift from France and 1,700 are in Braille) when I visit, and room for three million more.

A guided tour gives me an informative historical and architectural perspective. The library's museum has artifacts from different eras, including a smooth marble bust of Alexander, and sections devoted to mummification and items found during the construction of the library.

Brigitte Grob, an avid *Idiot and the Odyssey* reader in Monaco, suggests in an email that I look for a papyrus fragment with three lines from Book 20 in Homer's *Odyssey* that are no longer in the standard text today. That text apparently dates from the early Hellenistic period between 285 – 250 BC and is an indication that various "editions" were floating around at that time. Homer's works, of course, are a key part of the library's collections, and there are copies of Homeric poems "published" in different Greek regions.

When I later learned that Brigitte had died, I recall the time that we stopped for a tea in a café on Le Rocher, or The Rock, in Monaco. The multilingual Brigitte told me one of her "favorite Idiot stories."

"I continue to laugh out loud whenever I recall your anecdote about an encounter with a waiter in Naples," Brigitte said. "The Idiot had refused to pay for a stale pastry that he ordered and told the waiter in Italian 'No, no, I'm not going to pay for something that's inedible.'

"Then the waiter, who obviously hadn't encountered anyone who wouldn't pay for something they had ordered, screamed '*NO?!? Come no, come no?*' as you casually walked away with your son through the Galleria Umberto I," Brigitte continued. "I laugh out loud whenever I think of that incident because its idiocy really cracks me up."

When my son Luke, who MedTrekked with me into Naples and didn't even bother ordering a stale-looking pastry, or I use the word "No" in a conversation one of us will invariably and instinctively scream, "*NO?!? Come no, come no?*"

I wonder if, back in the day, Alexander's thirst for reading Homer and other authors might have somehow inspired the creation of the first comprehensive public library founded here after his death by the Ptolemaic kings. When he was in Egypt he had to ask Harpalus to send him books from Macedon that included Philistus's History; plays by Euripides, Sophocles, and Aeschylus; some dithyrambic odes, composed by Telestes and Philoxenus; and "anything by Xenophon."

"One can't know too much of Xenophon," Alexander told me, mentioning that next to Homer his favorite book was X's *The Upbringing of Kyros* and one of his favorite lines was "A ruler should not only be truly a better man than those he rules, he should cast a kind of spell on them."

This slow delivery method for books, in pre-Amazon days, could have been avoided had Alexander been able to check them out of the local library rather than rely on snail mail.

The visit to the library and Alexandria prompts me, as I sit in one of the reading areas, to recall my favorite lines from Lawrence Durrell's *The Alexandria Quartet* about this "exotic city of constant interactions between cultures and religions."

I've randomly strung together, with apologies in advance to the author, some selected phrases and words from Durrell's four books – *Justine, Balthazar, Mountolive, Clea* – that, among other things, refer to Cavafy as the "old poet of the city." Durrell's depictions of Alexandria portray a yin-and-yang city if there ever was one (think Arabs and Europeans, wealth and poverty, Muslims and Jews and Christians, jealousy and love, palms and minarets, and, in his words, "princesses and whores") in the 1930s and 1940s:

"In the great quietness of these winter evenings there is one clock: the sea...The Mediterranean is an absurdly small sea; the length and greatness of its history makes us dream it larger than it is...There is no spring in the Delta, no sense of refreshment and renewal of things. One is plunged out of winter into a wax effigy of a summer too hot to breathe... Everything – trees, minarets, monuments and people – have been caught in the final eddy of some great whirlpool...The country is still here – everything that is heteroclyte, devious, polymorph, infractuous, equivocal, opaque, ambiguous, many-branched or just plain dotty...Even the place-names on the old tram routes echo the unforgotten names of the founders...Dusk was the best hour of the day in Alexandria – the streets turning slowly to the metallic blue of carbon paper but still giving off the heat of the sun...the one city which for me always hovered between illusion and reality, between the substance and poetic images which its very name aroused in me.

"This great sprawling jellyfish which is Alexandria today...the communities still live and communicate – Turks with Jews, Arabs and Copts and Syrians with Armenians and Italians and Greeks...Alexandria, outwardly so peaceful, was not really a safe place for Christians... Standing on the balcony I watch the sky darkening over the harbour and hear the sullen hooting of ship's sirens, emphasizing our loneliness here, our isolation from the warm Gulf Stream of European feelings and ideas...

Alexander the Great had asses' ears though only one person knew his secret. That was his barber who was a Greek...Nessim says that in the museum at Alexandria there is a portrait of Alexander wearing the horns of Ammon....Then he walked quietly along the arcades and through the street of the cafes, past a mauve mosque (sky-floating), a library, a temple (grilled: 'Here once lay the body of the great Alexander'); and so down the long curving inclines of the street which took one to the seashore... Walking these streets again in my imagination I knew once more that they spanned, not merely human history, but the whole biological scale of the heart's affections from the painted ecstasies of Cleopatra...Walking down the remembered grooves of streets which extended on every side, radiating out like the arms of a starfish from the axis of its founder's tomb."

And, finally, a selection from *Mountolive*: "The Alexandrians themselves were strangers and exiles to the Egypt which existed below the glittering surface of their dreams, ringed by the hot deserts and fanned by the bleakness of a faith which renounced worldly pleasure: the Egypt of rags and sores, of beauty and desperation. Alexandria was still Europe – the capital of Asiatic Europe, if such a thing could exist. It could never be like Cairo where his whole life had an Egyptian cast, where he spoke ample Arabic; here French, Italian and Greek dominated the scene. The ambiance, the social manner, everything was different, was cast in a European mould where somehow the camels and palm-trees and cloaked natives existed only as a brilliantly colored frieze, a backcloth to a life divided in its origins."

The Library visit and reminiscences of *The Alexandria Quartet* contribute to my growing knowledge of Alexander the Great and will, I'm sure, help me resolve the historical and archaeological conundrum concerning his final burial spot after his death in Babylon, transit in Memphis and entombment in Alexandria.

But all this peripatetic activity apparently makes me very sleepy and, with Ronnie on the oboe and Bethany on the French horn, I admit to nodding off, going in and out of consciousness actually, throughout Beethoven's 9th. But it was fun to get out, and as I leave the concert hall and walk along the seaside back towards my obscenely luxurious base camp at the Sheraton, I'm reminded of Durrell's nearly Homeric phrase in *Justine* about the "sea-gleaming milk-white Alexandrian midnight."

The next morning I take a minibus to the Library for twenty cents after the call to prayer at 5 a.m. and the Sheraton buffet breakfast at six o'clock. In what Durrell called "the pale lavender light of dawn," I continue my MedTrek from the Library along Alexandria's long *corniche* to the tip of Ras el-Tin (Cape of Figs) and then past the grimy port to the western edge of town.

The day gets off to the right start when I begin walking from the

Tomb of the Unknown Soldier past the now German-run Hotel Cecil (this is the spot in the city where Durrell, E.M. Forster, Noel Coward, Josephine Baker and everyone else hung out) and along the Eastern Harbor to Fort Qaitbey. I'm in the Anfushi quarter, with mosques and ramshackle buildings, and I'm as enchanted by a sign with ICE CRAEM misspelled as I am with the majesty of the 1480 Ottoman-built fort, though I'm disturbed that I am not allowed to approach the location of the old Pharos, or lighthouse, that was once one of the Seven Wonders of the World.

A contemporary fish-filled mosaic points the way to the famous Ras el-Tin fish market and, though the bustle is over by the time I arrive at 9 a.m., I do see representative samples of fish for sale, including a skinned Egyptian diving sea cobra.

The day continues in the right vein when I drop into the third century BC Anfushi Tombs that blend Greek and Egyptian burial rites. Despite instructions banning photos, I visit and get a shot of what I believe might have been Alexander's Alexandria grave, especially since I know that Greek Alexandrians adopted Ancient Egyptian burial rites. Maybe Alexander was the first to go this way.

After that, things go sideways as I walk for miles along the sea-interrupting Port of Alexander (as it's identified on a gigantic sign at one of its many entrances) and through the El Max industrial area. Totally boring and an example of the yin/yang theory of MedTrekking, which is that ugly makes beauty more appreciated. I continue around the port until FINALLY there is a beach with sand that I'm able to walk barefoot on for almost ten kilometers. I pass lots of fishermen, a few snorkeling teenagers, two manned military outposts and lots of sleepy resorts on a placid sea to arrive at dusk at Hanoville/El-Agami Pigosh near the Mersa Matruh Road.

The next day, I spend a morning chillin' at the Sheraton and visit the Fitness Room and pool before I return to the Hotel Cecil for a rooftop Chinese lunch/dinner.

"I walked slowly along the *corniche* towards the Cecil," Durrell writes in *Clea*, "where I proposed to take a room, have a bath and shave, and prepare myself for the visit to the country house. I stood for a while staring down at the still sea."

Then an early night and an early (6:30 a.m.) start get me back to the MedTrek about 20 miles from here. My last reflections at the Sheraton: "Definitely fulfilling, mission-accomplished and amusing days in Alexandria that included four different museums, lots of ruins, the world's largest library and lunch at one of the city's most celebrated and celebrity-frequented hotels. My break for noodles and beef at the Hotel Cecil's rooftop terrace China House restaurant let me experience how much the German-owned hotel retains some of its past glory."

It is perhaps not a brilliant decision to keep using the Sheraton as a base camp, despite its comfy feel and discounted price. It takes me two hours to get to Hanoville and more than that to return to Alexandria from Sidi Kyrair, after an almost all-barefoot day on sandy beaches dotted with temporary shacks, buildings under construction and winter-dead resorts. When I run into a military barrier, a man living alone in a mammoth resort helps me get back to the main road without being seen.

It's definitely time to move on.

"Having selected the optimum location for Alexandria, Alexander set out west along the coastal road to Paraetonium (Mersa Matruh) in late January 331 BC," writes one historian. "His military escort included his friends and Companions together with local guides, and as they advanced 200 miles along the coast toward Libya they received envoys from the Greek colony of Cyrene offering their allegiance, together with lavish gifts including 300 horses and a golden crown."

Was Alexander ever interred in the Anfushi Tombs, or anywhere else, in Alexandria? Did his corpse spend any time in the catacombs of Kom es-Shoqafa? Is there truth to the buzz that his remains were once at Kom el-Dikka? Is his elusive tomb in the Soma Mausoleum? Can the Sphinx at Pompey's Pillar contribute to the heated and controversial discussion concerning Alexander's final burial site?

I leave Alexandria, not overly preoccupied by these questions or feeling a need to make any pronouncements concerning the location of Alexander the Great's final resting place, and follow in Alexander's footsteps towards the famous World War II battlefield at El-Alamein, which, of course, had not yet occurred when Alexander marched through. Like Alexander, I'll pay a visit to the Oracle of Siwa in the Western Sahara desert and not draw any conclusions until I find the definitive spot where he was buried after being interred in Alexandria.

There's nothing better than MedTrekking on empty winter-dormant beaches after a busy week on the trail of Alexander the Great in the library, museums, monuments, memorials and alleyways of frenetic Alexandria. I often relish walking alone and barefoot on sand where a beached boat, long shadows and a few fishermen are excitement enough. Indeed, there are lots of fishermen, even a few snorkeling fishermen, but not much of anyone else west of Alexandria and I constantly ask them if there are any soldiers I should worry about. They constantly say no. And they are constantly correct.

This stretch of the Mediterranean coast is theoretically packed with vacationing Egyptians during the summer but, except for security guards at various empty resorts and a few signs of the allegedly omnipresent military, it's virtually dead during the waning days of November. Beaches are untended, resorts are completely empty, everything is for rent for almost nothing, and a new Carrefour supermarket has an insignificant number of customers.

On the next day shoes are only required twice – once to get around a military outpost (there were two that day, each manned by only one visible soldier) and another time to get around a tall wall barricading a seaside electric power plant and the adjoining Air Force Resort Club.

Still wearing my shoes, I transform this obstacle into an opportunity when I walk to the Carrefour supermarket on the road to the Borg al-Arab Airport, which crosses the once lovely but now brackish Lake Mariout, for a sandwich and fruit salad (a 38 cent fruit salad, as I again benefit from the strength of the US dollar and the devaluation of the Egyptian pound) lunch. I take the opportunity to stock up on dates, rice pudding, more fruit salad and other essentials for the next few days.

It is at a beach near here, incidentally, that the Irish narrator in *The Alexandria Quartet* describes his conversation with Justine, a beautiful, rich, mysterious Jewish woman married to a wealthy Egyptian Copt called Nessim. They exchange their first kisses on a beach with "carpets of fresh sand the color of oxidized mercury" and "walked ankle deep in the splurge of shallow dimpled pools." Later that evening. he can still see "the imprint of Justine's foot in the wet sand."

Security guards at virtually all of the empty winter-dead seaside resorts (with names like Granada, Valencia, Riviera, Nice, Marbella Marina, Virginia Beach, Costa del Sol and Long Beach) try to prevent me from gaining access to the sea. But I usually succeed by slipping down between two different resorts and stay on the beach until I hit a military zone and am forced back up to the International Coast Road (ICR). I find some of these areas are worse than the most overbuilt parts of Spain because so many of them are not completed and all of them are garbage-filled.

I'm continually irked that walls, fences and resorts with security guards constantly block the view of, and access to, the sea. At one point, I'm walking on the beach and cut up through one resort called Costa del Sol to avoid approaching a military beach. It takes me fifteen minutes of explanations and phone calls to get OUT of the resort and back on the highway-to-be, a nice relief from the tight lanes and speedy traffic on the International Coastal Road.

Nothing's open, no one's around and I'm slightly upset that Pizza Hut, KFC, McDonalds and other fast-food junky outlets are closed. It's hard to imagine that, as everyone tries to tell me, this is the place to be and party in the summer (June, July and August) when it would almost certainly be too hellishly hot for the Idiot.

On the first day of December, I start the MedTrek in El Hamam at 8:45 a.m. It's the first day of rain I've encountered, which makes the sky dark and the sea explosive, with lots of waves and a terrific, threateningly dark turquoise palate. I'm wearing a black fleece and black gloves but still singing in the rain as I spend most of the day on an evolving bed of a new highway-to-be which isn't as bad as it sounds because 1) it provides a hard surface in the rain and 2) I'm tired of walking on sand next to dead (or, being polite, dormant) seaside resorts.

In addition to the rain, there's paradoxically a lot of dust from a sandstorm and lots of noise from some earth-moving equipment, which is better than speedy cars on the International Coast Road. No one seems to mind me walking in a construction zone but that could be because of my lime-colored fluorescent vest.

The only way to get on and off the beach in this part of Egypt is as quickly as possible. No resort will actually allow me, much less invite me, in. I have to scamper down to the beach between housing developments or at the edge of towns, villages or military-restricted beaches. Naturally, the security guards at each gated residence are bored out of their minds and take full responsibility and move into action when they have a rare opportunity to do so. I also have to continue to be very vigilant about not walking on a military or police beach, which are difficult to identify if I'm not being forewarned by either a lack of fishermen/people, or guard towers, flags or men in uniform.

It doesn't take me long to be equally bothered by all the new construction as I was by the empty aged, dirty and outmoded facilities that seem to exist just to employ security guards to keep MedTrekkers from getting to and from the beach. And while I'm venting, another thing that irritates me are the *faux* palm trees that serve as very unattractive cell phone towers on Egypt's Mediterranean coast. They make the plethora of winter-deserted coastal resorts between Alexandria and El Alamein appear even less attractive than they already are.

But maybe I have the wrong optic. Maybe I'm intolerant.

Mahmoud Elsory Elmasry, a taxi driver I begin using in Alexandria, (30-something, married with two kids, switching from a cab to buying his own new car to start Ubering) tells me: "You've got to come and see how active it is in the summer and realize that revamping these developments, and even building new ones, will be big business in the future. Plus, it makes people happy to have a place on the sea. Chill out."

In any event, it is truly a thrill, and probably a good omen, to see a splendid double rainbow on a rare unbuilt, albeit military controlled, beach after I stop for a rain break "lunch" of salty potato chips and a Nescafé in a hole-in-the wall café. Then I end my feast with an El Bawadi Halawa bar made from pure sesame seeds in nearby Borg Al-Arab City. These bars became my favorite treat when two were given to me each day at breakfast at the army resort in Baltim. All the shisha smokers, who like me are happy to be out of the rain, look at me like I'm a drug addict.

The new highway, of course, might be finished by the time this book is published and getting from A(lexandria) to A(Alamein) will be much easier, but at the moment it's a slog to drive but a breeze to

MedTrek.

At the end of the afternoon, I see a big new Mobil gas station and far beyond, an array of colorful high-rises that look like Oz. In fact, I've just stumbled on my next base camp at the Porto Marina Resorts and Spa in El Alamein, more than 100-plus kilometers from Alexandria.

The seven-complex development includes Porto Marina Three, with brightly colored tall towers and an adjacent hotel that can be seen from miles away. The Porto Marina Resort and Spa hotel has over 330 rooms, but only four are occupied on the night I check in. There are also twelve apartment towers with over 200 empty apartments in each one.

Located on the interior of a bay/lagoon just east of El Alamein, this faux Venetian resort is the first place I've seen that actually looks like it has the potential to be a successful summer party place with a Venetian theme (think gondolas and canals, though not quite as glitzy as the one in Las Vegas) and vibrant, earthy colors (think ochre and sienna). There's a working spa, 12 restaurants (only Chili's is open in the winter) and lots of boutiques. My decent $30 sea view room with an expansive balcony goes for over $150 in the summer and I've got the whole place to myself.

An ideal base camp for the last three days of this MedTrek outing.

There's no Wi-Fi in my lagoon-facing room, but at 2 a.m. (with a headlamp), and again at 7 a.m. (without one), I walk through the labyrinthine halls to the lobby to get online.

It's windy with an eerie stormy feeling (winter is definitely in the air, so my seasonal timing for the MedTrek was perfect) as I wake up on my second-to-last morning on the Med in Egypt, intending to hike a few kilometers west into El Alamein and visit the memorials and cemeteries. I breakfast, again, on the fruit and other goodies from Carrefour and use the little sachets of Nescafé and creamer taken from the Sheraton as a poor excuse for coffee. I'm also pleased that, for the first time in a year due to the back surgery and non-exercising recovery, I'm down to exactly 80 kilos, or 176 pounds. MedTrekking has always had a weight-loss aspect to it.

I take off along the seven Porto Marina complexes (the Porto group, one of the largest hotel owners in Egypt with branches throughout the country, includes investors from Egypt, Dubai and Saudi Arabia) and figure that it will take two hours to walk along the exterior wall from one end of the property to the other. The different complexes have taken over the entire seaside, often on both sides of the highway, I'm reminded when I see the Porto Marina Golf Course. The massive stretch of private resorts ends just west of El Alamein, though construction makes it apparent that more will be coming. This is one of the longest non-military, non-industrial, well-guarded blockages on the entire Egyptian Mediterranean that, with security everywhere, is perhaps as effective as military outposts.

The blustery, cloudy and grey morning seems an appropriate time to pay a visit to El Alamein, known for the key role it played during back-and-forth battles between Axis and Allied troops during World War II. This is North Africa's most memorable site of World War II carnage and many remnants and memories, cemeteries and memorials, still exist, as do rumors about a few mines on many of the battlefields.

After a nine-kilometer walk along the continuing roadside wall of the seemingly never-ending Porto Marina development, I spend an hour at the El Alamein War Museum before paying my respects at the numerous cemeteries and memorials for more than 50,000 soldiers who lost their lives during the 1941-43 engagements.

I visit the memorial for "the Greeks fallen in the battle of El Alamein," the El Alamein War Cemetery with over 7,200 Commonwealth graves (including 800 which are unidentified); the sober and Spartan German war graves and memorial on the seaside a few kilometers further west and the Italian memorial a bit further west than that. The visits, which bring the vivid reality of not-so-distant history alive, make this a memorable MedTrekking day.

While the British cemetery is impressive, I find the setting of the German citadel-like memorial hauntingly stoic and serene. One of the attendants at the German museum makes it clear that the military told him not to let any guests walk on the beach but adds that "it's not because of mines because they don't seem to worry about those anymore, it's just general security."

After dropping into the aesthetic Italian memorial, I continue MedTrekking into the village of Sidi Abd El-Rahman, where I'm 240 kilometers west of Alexandria and 222 kilometers from the Libyan border.

When I arrive in Sidi Abd El-Rahman, there seems to be another extensive development signaled by a seductive billboard: "Marassi: Sahel's most exclusive square kilometer."

The series of billboards have clever illustrations or amusing photos that accompany text that reads:

Get ready for Marassi.
Get silly for Marassi.
Get nature for Marassi.
Get cool for Marassi (with a photo of a dog with shades).
Get wild for Marassi.

I ask a policeman at a traffic control stop how to get to the beach and whether there's a simple hotel anywhere in town. The only housing option, and the best way to try to get to the beach, he tells me, is the Al Alamein Hotel in the Marassi complex, though that will require getting through security.

I walk back a kilometer to the entrance to this complex and have a long discussion with the security boss, who speaks excellent English and was in San Diego for military training (he even asks me if I know someone in San Diego and I'm forced to tell him that California is a more populated state now than when he was there a couple decades ago), and he has a member of his staff drive me to the Alamein Hotel. There I meet the PR officer, visit a few rooms and consider it an ideal spot for my next base camp. It occurs to me that with the dearth of regular hotels, the next part of the MedTrek may involve resort hopping, which is one way to avoid the problem with security officials: stay in a resort with sea access that goes on for miles.

It turns out Mirna Ghorab, the 20-something customer relations officer at the Al Alamein Hotel, went to school with Iythar Khedr, the 20-something customer relations officer at the Alexandria Sheraton. Well-trained like her counterpart in the big city, Mirna shows me around the hotel, and I choose a first-floor room with a view of the sea and reserve it. Winter rate for a room with a sea view, Wi-Fi and breakfast? $32.35.

"I'll see you in March," I say, remarking that this is an ideal location. I'm 131 kilometers from Alexandria and 159 from Mersa Matruh.

"Inshallah," she replies.

I take a communal minibus back to Porto Marina for my last night on the Egyptian Mediterranean and learn that the Tourism Police (the official name is Tourism and Antiquities Police), whom I've heard about but never encountered on the MedTrek because of the under-the-radar places I tend to stay, have been looking for me. When they learn I've returned they visit my hotel and ask for a minute-by-minute account of my actions during the day. Fortunately, photos and my GPS come in handy to back up my verbal account.

"We just want you to be safe," says one of the policemen, indicating that they'll send a vehicle to accompany me to the highway leading to Cairo Airport. "And we'll see you when you return in March."

I calculate that for 19 nights, the rooms on this outing averaged under $40 a night and ranged from $7.10 in Rasheed to $50-something at the Sheraton in Alexandria – all with breakfast included except the last stay at Porto Marina 3 where I made it three days on dates, fruit, bread, rice pudding and cookies that I picked up at Carrefour for E£115 ($6.50). Nescafé and tea were compliments of the hotel.

I decide to use Mahmoud Elsory Elmasry, my Alexandria taxi driver who's just got a new car and has begun driving for Uber, to get to the Cairo Airport without going through Alexandria. He tells me that "you're my friend, not a customer" and when he comes to pick me up is ecstatic when I give him my worn Merrell hiking shoes, done-for-this-lifetime Teva sandals and random hotel toiletries for his wife. He also wants my *The Idiot and Odyssey II* cap (which I tell him he can have after my walk in March) and Speedo swimming suit (which I tell him he can have after my walk in March), after I complete the MedTrek through Egypt.

The police question Mahmoud when he returns to pick me up and, after he's cleared, they provide an escort for thirty kilometers or so on the comparatively new highway that cuts up to Cairo through the desert.

"I'll see you in March and you can take me back to the hotel in Sidi Abd El-Rahman," I announce when Mahmoud drops me at the airport.

"Inshallah," he replies, kissing me eight times on both cheeks.

# FOLLOW THE IDIOT

## CHAPTER PHOTOS

## CHAPTER MAP

# An Armed Escort and the Woman in the Headscarf

"There's only one thing better than winning a battle, son, and that's the taste of a new woman! You'll find it far sweeter than self-pity." – King Philip II to his son Alexander

"All your life, beware of women. They are far more dangerous than men." – King Philip II to his son Alexander

"The US Department of State warns US citizens of threats from terrorist and violent political opposition groups in Egypt and to consider the risks of travel to the country." – December 23, 2016

The Idiot, who has a momentous appointment scheduled with the renowned Oracle of Siwa in Egypt on the Ides of March, is particularly attentive to auspicious and ominous signs as he prepares for a meeting that is expected, among other things, to lead him to the final burial site of

Alexander the Great.

That's why he doesn't hike with family members on the Big Island in Hawaii in December just to get a taste of abundant waterfalls, verdant forests, lush botanical gardens and wild Pacific Ocean coasts. He also has a discussion with the Hawaiian volcano goddess Pele near the increasingly active Kīlauea volcano to discuss his rendezvous with the Oracle and receive advice from Pele pertaining to his upcoming sacred conversations.

He doesn't participate in a nationwide Women's March in January solely to demand dignity and equality for all sentient beings, but also to talk to a sorceress who claims she can channel the Oracle. That'll give him an idea of what might transpire in Siwa.

And he doesn't schuss on fresh snow at Mount Shasta, where he learned to ski in the 1960s, just to have a day on the slopes. He also holds a consultation with Bigfoot, the well-known Northern California version of a Himalayan yeti, in a hidden crevice.

But the most memorable message, a much more ominous message, is delivered the very moment The Idiot's trip to Egypt commences at the airport in Redding, California, when an Idiot-ic tweet at 5 a.m. evolves into a national news story.

The Idiot is among the first passengers to encounter the Transport Security Administration's (TSA's) new, more intimate and totally inane pat-down regulations that were introduced without fanfare on the morning he flew east on March 2, 2017.

"You're not going to like the new pat-down regulations that came into effect this morning," says the TSA agent who regularly pats him down at the small airport where there are only a few departing flights each day. "They've discovered that bad people conceal weapons in their pants, and we've got to do more extensive vertical and horizontal pat-downs if you set off the alarm."

The Idiot, who is regularly separated from the travel herd and patted down because he has been wearing a permanent gold bracelet on his right wrist since 1969 that sets off every alarm he encounters at airports in the United States (but few in Europe), takes the announcement in stride.

"Well, what do you think about this increased intimacy being introduced so long after 9/11?" asks The Idiot, who has learned to practice patience and tolerance during his frequent individual security checks in US airports, even when they're performed with much more profound feeling.

"We don't like it either," the inspector tells The Idiot as he's about to embark on the first leg of a multi-flight return to the MedTrek in Egypt via Boston, Washington, D.C., and Zurich.

I quickly tweet the intimate details: New #TSA agent pat downs increase #groin scrutiny for #travelers in #USA #airports. #travel #security #pat-downs

The story made national headlines. It is initially picked up by *USA*

*Today*, whose parent company owns the newspaper in Redding, and then spreads throughout the world like a thunderbolt from Mount Olympus. In Boston, ABC and NBC interview The Idiot and the story appears in numerous other media outlets, ranging from CBS, UPI, AOL and *The New American* to *Raw Story* and *TravelMole*. The Idiot tells NBC News his day kicked off with "the most intriguing, intense and invasive pat down I've had by the TSA since they came into existence in response to the September 11, 2001, attacks."

Is this a warning from the Oracle to come unarmed to the temple in Siwa? Is it an effort to tell him that if he wasn't arrested in Redding he will be safe? Is it simply a sign to be careful? Does it mean he should start wearing a groin protector? Or is there some other mystical message?

Fortunately, The Idiot is able to opt for a full-body scan to avoid the more intimate and invasive TSA pat-down at Boston's Logan Airport three days later. And following a lunch in Washington, D.C., The Idiot opts to have another scan at Dulles Airport to evade what a TSA agent called "a groin anomaly pat down."

Postscript: "You'll be arrested the next time you fly out of Redding," suggests Marc Beauchamp, a Redding journalist The Idiot has known since high school.

Not quite. When The Idiot flies out of Redding on his next trip, wearing a martial arts groin protector, the groping TSA agent only has one question for him: "Why didn't you use my name in your article?"

The Idiot, who has now walked 12,162 kilometers around the Mediterranean Sea, had forgotten all about the TSA and pat-downs when he arrives in Cairo looking forward to MedTrekking towards the Libyan border.

Michael Knipe, the former Middle East correspondent for *The Times* of London, whom you met in Cyprus and Israel, joins me at the Cairo Airport and together we make the four-hour drive to the Al Alamein Hotel Marassi in Sidi Abdel Rahman with Mahmoud Elsory Elmasry, now a prosperous Uber driver and still the proud possessor of my shoes, shirts and other passed-on items from last year's MedTrek.

Awakening precisely at sunrise the next morning, Michael and I kick off the next stage of the MedTrek on a fine-sanded beach just steps from our sea view rooms about 15 kilometers west of the famed World War II El Alamein battlefields.

Saber, the hotel receptionist, tries to tell us that the police will refuse to let us walk on the beach, that there are bad people (especially bad Libyans) who will do bad things to us on the bad beach, that the Egyptian military tightly controls the beaches and will stop us after just a kilometer's walk, and that that that... We invite Saber to come along but he claims he has to work. It doesn't take me long to realize that once again,

I've been fed alternative facts.

We pass a closed, obviously seasonal Starbucks (the first I've ever seen in the sand on the Mediterranean), and walk barefoot for six kilometers until we reach a small military outpost.

"It's illegal to walk on the beach for the next 500 meters and in five kilometers you'll meet more military personnel like us," says a friendly young soldier, who tells us to cut inland for a kilometer before returning to the beach, where we'll be able to continue walking past lots of deserted developments and an abnormal amount of new construction until we run into his colleagues.

Again, it's as difficult to imagine in March as it was in December that these gigantic housing developments will be full and lively in a few months – and that there are enough buyers in Egypt for all of the new homes being constructed on the seaside.

I'm again impressed that Michael is walking so well at 78, and, though I'm feeling spry, we're both somewhat fatigued after only sixteen kilometers, because of the constant wind, though we agree it's a delight to be simultaneously serenaded by the chorus of waves and wind as we joyfully recommence a new leg of the MedTrek.

The next morning, I wake up to a BBC report about extensive suppression under the current military regime in Egypt. It recounts increased imprisonment, a more determined dictatorship and greater polarization of Egyptian society during an interview with director Mohamed Diab whose recent film *Clash* is about co-existence and tries to humanize the Muslim Brotherhood, the state and the military.

"The effect of the Arab Spring and Tahrir Square does not look good today, but it may later," says Diab. "Unfortunately, the only thing that matters in Egypt today is money and the economy, which are both in bad shape. They've become more important than human rights. Everyone expects a revolution."

Everyone, from the hotel receptionist to omnipresent security guards attempting to exert their power by traumatizing MedTrekkers, certainly seems a bit uneasy and, even, paranoid. But there is nothing for The Idiot to be paranoid about when he hikes alone for the next thirty kilometers from Rixos to the Vista Bay complex. Michael, to ease himself into the rigors of MedTrekking, spends the day visiting El Alamein war memorials.

The Idiot isn't paranoid walking astride a 16-kilometer concrete wall that protects and/or hides the El Dabaa seaside nuclear plant being constructed by the Russian State Nuclear Energy Corporation, although it, and a number of other resorts and industrial developments, keep him further away than he would wish from the sea for much of the day.

He isn't paranoid when he has what becomes a pleasant discussion with selfie-snapping Major Mohammad near the army barracks at El

Dabaa, after the Major sternly asks him "What the hell are you doing walking here by yourself?"

He isn't paranoid when he senses a large volume of stares because he is wearing shorts into a café in El Dabaa for lunch, or when he argues with the security guards at Vista Bay after they refuse to let him enter the property and approach the sea, or even take a photo.

And he isn't paranoid when he is picked up hitchhiking back to the hotel, after walking well over thirty kilometers, by a pickup truck carrying workmen that fortuitously drops him off at the front gate of the Marassi complex.

The Major does warn him that "the army is everywhere on the coast and will stop you frequently, but have fun and don't be paranoid." He, and everyone else he meets during the day, insist on taking selfies with an American that they immediately post on Instagram or Facebook.

The next day, Michael and I return over 40 kilometers to Vista Bay and, because we can't get down to the beach due to the resorts' security and/or the military, walk eleven kilometers on the highway divider on the International Coastal Road in a very strong wind that prevents us from wearing baseball caps despite the blinding sunshine.

We arrive at the much-touted Emirates Heights Resort (it's been advertised as the "Capital of the North Coast" on billboards as far away as Alexandria) where, to my astonishment, the guards not only let us in but have a security vehicle pick us up and take us to the head office. Bassem Fares, the customer service manager, who must think that we're potential clients, serves us tea and takes us on a tour of the not-yet-completed-or-even-much-built fledgling gigantic resort that will include two new hotels and many other amenities.

Although Bassem assures us that everything is on schedule, it doesn't look like Phase One will be finished in two months, despite the presence of 320 workers, as he claims. Whether it is or not, he tells us the entire resort won't be completed until well into the 2020s.

I tell him that I lack the vision and patience required to appreciate the growing pains of a resort like this because Emirates Heights, like every other compound on the coast, is a real mess at this time of year.

Bassem kindly drops us at the seashore and we walk west, knowing that we're risking, if not death, at least an encounter with the military. We manage to uneventfully walk five kilometers on the stunning seaside before we enter an unsignposted, unfenced resort called, we learn later, The Shores, and see a prominent military outpost on the top of the hill on the other side.

Playing it safe, I lead the way through this fledgling development (they all seem to be fledgling) toward the road and I'm very polite when we're asked to go to the head office and are detained by the pretentious head of security who, with lots of time on his hands, calls the military for backup. Although a number of civil engineers in the office clearly think we should be released, and say so, we waste another half hour (on top of the hour at Emirates) waiting for the army to arrive, until I finally tell the security boss that I'm leaving and walk out the door.

"The security guy has too much time on his hands," says one engineer apologetically. "It's hard for us to meet Arab girls," says the other.

An army officer drives up in a military vehicle as soon we start walking on the highway and, after looking at copies of our passports and, pretending not to be impressed with my selfie with Major Mohammad, tells us "everything five kilometers from the sea is under military control and you can't walk there." We agree that we won't and continue another seven kilometers on the road to a new school where, after 21 kilometers, we call it a day. Little do we know that when we return here the next morning we won't be alone.

Egypt's Tourism Police are waiting for us when we return to the Al Alamein Hotel and inform me that they'll be accompanying us on the remainder of our MedTrek to Mersa Matruh and beyond.

"We protect tourists; that's our job," says one. "It doesn't cost you a cent, and it's for your own protection."

Actually I'm slightly surprised that, except for the interview with the Tourism Police at Porto Marina and the police escort on the desert road to Cairo, I have stayed under the radar and had avoided the Tourism Police for so long – since Port Said. It must be because I base camped and slept in offbeat places. And the Tourism Police simply didn't bother with me after I made it through security at the front door of the Sheraton in Alexandria. Though they saw me leaving everyday with a backpack, they weren't aware why I was in the country.

Although I'm regularly stopped by military officers who check my documents and inform me that it's forbidden to walk on the seaside, the Army obviously doesn't communicate with the Tourism Police and, of course, there haven't (yet) been any seriously troublesome incidents on the MedTrek.

But now, apparently having no choice in the matter, Michael and I patiently welcome an armed detail to insure our safety and, when they arrive, we profusely thank them for their service and protection. The MedTrekkers are marching with their own armed guard!

It takes two hours for the Tourism Police to get organized before we return to the exact spot where we ended the hike yesterday. The delay is partly my fault.

To assert my independence, I refuse to be driven back to our MedTrek starting spot by the policemen and insist on making a point by illustrating how "fiscally astute" I am before I accept the right ride at the right price from the right minibus. I refuse a number of overpriced offers that, I think, impresses the policemen and lets them know I'm not going to pay any *baksheesh*, or bribes, for their services (which, with one minor exception, I never do).

Our protection unit consists of four men, one or two who will occasionally walk with us, and a pickup with the other two officers that will keep up with our MedTrekking group on a nearby highway. I feel that calling this much attention to our presence and the MedTrek might be counterproductive but keep my mouth shut.

At the outset, two young policemen, one armed with an automatic rifle, walk with Michael and me for two hours, but then both gradually retreat to the back of their pickup and join their colleagues while Michael and I confront a very serious sandstorm that blinds us throughout another blustery day. I finally begin to appreciate and agree with the civil engineer who, when I made light of the sandstorm the day before, said: "This is what we call bad weather."

In fact, it is wicked bad weather and sand gets into our every (yes, every) orifice, including mouth and ears and eyes and all those other orifices, as we walk into it throughout the day. In addition to impressing the cops with my independence and financial skills, I now have to demonstrate my physical stamina. We walk for six straight hours, with no stops, except to munch on some rolls and buy some chocolate bars and biscuits, until we get to Fuka (yes, Fuka, as in Fuka Off).

Just FYI, MedTrekking in a serious sandstorm is tedious and somewhat difficult, but our stoic and steadfast approach shows the Egyptian police what we're made of.

Because these are cops, and they are obviously aware that it's generally illegal to walk on the coast, we are forced to hike on the highway, or on the dividing strip between the two directions of the highway, throughout the day. The sea is only a kilometer or so away but, although in our sight, we never get close to it. Instead we pass occasional resorts – Sea View, Mountain View, Coral Hills Resort, Fuka Bay – and Michael is amazed when I inform him that not only do people buy apartments here for two months maximum use per year, but they also buy the apartments before they're built – a dubious proposition if you ask the physically fit and fiscally shrewd Idiot.

There is one serious advantage of having the Tourism Police along: we get a fast ride back to the hotel in a comfortable van commandeered by our private police chief with a driver who is impressed that we have the clout to get the cops to order him to take us. As we get in the van, the police announce they'll be following us and will see us at the hotel.

We're only about 70 kilometers from Mersa Matruh, the only large town on the coast between here and the Libyan border, but as we drive back to the Al Alamein Hotel, it's difficult to recognize anything specific in the it-all-looks-the-same coastal desert terrain. The only things that stand out, beside the empty resorts, are the hundreds of big blue billboards that have no ads. Another entrepreneur's idea gone bad.

I tweet a photo of one of our armed guards:

The Idiot is accompanied by a 4-man #armed #Egypt #Tourism #Police #escort as he #walks to #Fuka on the #Mediterranean #Sea.

I also run an item in "Where Is The Idiot Today?" with a caption:

"Egypt's Tourism Police insisted on accompanying The Idiot on today's MedTrek between Al Alamein and Mersa Matruh, Egypt. The protection unit consisted of four men, two of whom occasionally walked with The Idiot and his MedTrekking partner Michael Knipe, and a pickup with the other two police officers that kept up with the MedTrekkers on a nearby highway. There have not been any incidents during The Idiot's MedTrek across northern Egypt..."

I realize again the next morning that the primary positive aspect about having the Tourism Police on my case is that they can commandeer private cars to transport us to and from the MedTrek, saving a lot of time, negotiation and money. Last night, after they requisitioned that plush van, we made it back to the hotel in record time, and this morning, having already proven that I'm financially astute, I allow the agent to commandeer a college bus going to the nursing school in Fuka. When we return at the end of the day, I loosen up a bit and let the three agents accompanying Michael and me drive us 90 minutes from the tip of the Ras El Hekma peninsula back to the hotel, though we are crammed in the back of their covered pickup. We not only have security (which I don't particularly want) but also a seemingly endless supply of chauffeurs (which, I don't mind admitting, is a treat).

There is a different team of men the next day, but, following my directions, we kick off the walk exactly where we left off – at a developing shopping center in Fuka that is called Jumeirah, which is already adorned with a classy neon sign but not much else – and after five kilometers take a right to walk 17 kilometers to the end, or near the end, of Ras El Hekma peninsula (aka Jumeirah Bay). The Bay – 212 kilometers from Alexandria and 66 from Mersa Matruh – is one of the largest on the Egyptian coast, stretching 18 kilometers into the sea and creating a natural block for waves and currents.

The "bad weather" is over, and we gleefully switch back to shorts to enjoy ideal walking conditions – no wind, blue sky, wonderful desert terrain, sun and sea. The oldest policeman in our contingent teaches us Egyptian military marching techniques, think goose-stepping, when he joins us on the road for a few kilometers.

At the end of the cape we encounter a member of the President's elite Republican Guard who informs us that the presidential palace at the tip of the bay has been used by every Egyptian president since it was

410

constructed during the reign of King Farouk, who ruled from 1926 until 1952. He allows us to continue to walk, though warns us not to take pictures or talk to local women, and we meet a young shepherd named Faisal who invites the five of us to his home for tea, which he serves on a sprawling carpet that he unrolls on the ground outside.

That night, we celebrate Michael's successful completion of another MedTrekking stint on the Mediterranean Sea in Egypt before his return to London. Mirna Ghorab, the hotel's manager of customer relations, presents a *Follow The Idiot* cap to the aged MedTrekker.

Though still feeling especially spry, I take a rare two days off and spend the first day ensuring that Michael gets into a cab to Cairo before lounging around the Al Alamein Hotel, even tanning on the beach for an hour. I write about MedTrekking with an armed escort and, after eight nights at this peaceful and pleasurable base camp, plan to move down the coast without informing the Tourism Police.

The next morning, I quietly leave my moonlit, sea-lapped base camp in Sidi Abdel Rahman to set up a new MedTrekking HQ further west on Egypt's Mediterranean coast. The new base camp, in Almaza Bay, 122 kilometers west of the Al Alamein, is a garish and blingy hotel (and the only one open on the coast between here and Mersa Matruh) designed, if the six RAI channels on TV are any indicator, for Italians who are genetically programmed to adore ornate chandeliers, gold bathroom fixtures, marble floors and multiple swimming pools. Trip Advisor calls it "Mediterranean style."

I'm not only one of the very few guests in the seaside Jaz Almaza Beach Resort (they tell me the Italians will arrive at Easter) but am also not sure whether or not I permanently lost the armed Tourism Police escort. Fathy, the driver who brings me here, is a Bedouin who takes me by his home in El Dabaa for tea on the way and points out some two-story homes that were built to provide housing for Bedouins by the government. During tea and our drive, he describes the Bedouins' negative feelings toward Egyptians and explains that Bedouins account for most of the population in northwestern Egypt. He's vocally anti-Sisi, anti-military, anti-nuclear plant and proud to be a member of a nomadic Arab people, who have historically inhabited the desert regions in North Africa.

Even the employees at the Jaz acknowledge that its extreme emptiness is a bit eerie, but claim there will be 5,000 people (primarily Italians, Ukrainians and Egyptians) residing here in two months. All the other guests (I think we're seven in total) have dinner in their rooms, but I eat in the empty restaurant after ordering in advance from four different menu choices. I get a Greek salad, potato soup, lamb chops and *crème caramel*, which is ready and waiting when I'm shown to my table.

Otherwise, there are no bad tidings on the Ides of March, and I have a few extra days to get to Mersa Matruh because the Oracle of

Ammon changed our meeting date in Siwa from the Ides to the equinox on the more auspicious first day of spring.

At dawn after my first night at the beachy Jaz Almaza there is no sign of the Tourism Police. I walk, very jazzed, out of the Jaz the next morning and meet a civil engineer and an accountant working on a new resort project next door (as an aside, civil engineers and accountants working on construction projects, that seem never ending on the Egyptian coast, are the friendliest and most proficient English-speaking people I meet during my walk across northern Egypt and, you'll recall, it was an accountant who offered me a room at the military resort in Baltim). I decide to try the beach option.

This turns out to be the best decision of the day, because I'm on the beach for 30 kilometers walking back toward the western tip of the country's longest peninsula where we ended the MedTrek a couple days ago.

During the first three hours of my walk I only see, besides men working on numerous construction projects, the Mediterranean Sea, three shepherds, 67 goats, 42 sheep, and a few intriguing rock formations. Now on Rommel Beach (that's what it's called on my GPS map, though no one seems to know it as such) I'm amidst some very nice seaside villas (among the most attractive private villas I've seen in Egypt, in fact) with a solitary dog barking at me. I continue barefoot for another hour and finally meet the day's first pair of military men in Bagosh after I've walked about 15 kilometers, alternatively shod and barefoot, on the sand.

The soldiers tell me beaches are not safe, that it's all dangerous desert and that there are robbers but paradoxically let me pass after a young English-speaking military conscript calls his superiors to get permission. This concession is so rare that I silently treasure my good fortune even when I'm told "There are dangerous people there who might rob you and it's unprotected, but you can go ahead." This changes my attitude toward the military, and, though it would presumably irritate the Tourism Police, I assume they're letting me through simply because there are not many people here.

The first soldiers spread the word to their colleagues, and soldiers at the next two military posts (there are five young men at each) greet me amicably and let me continue along the coast to the place where we met the Republican Guard and had tea with the shepherd. One soldier at the first outpost checks the copy of my passport and at the second outpost, a camel – yes a camel – demands a selfie – and won't let me leave until he approves the photo. A few soldiers, also very much in selfie mode, ask The Idiot to pose with them and I gladly comply. But this camel on the Mediterranean is so insistent that, as the photo reveals, I don't even have time to do something with my hair.

"You don't have to worry about anything walking around here," said one soldier who's a friend of the camel. "There are just Arabs, shepherds, a few camels and desert."

The military camps suddenly remind me of the many outposts in Morocco on hillocks a few kilometers apart. I tell all the soldiers I meet today that they're blessed (*Mashallah*) that Allah has given them the sun, the sea and the air, and for that they should be thankful.

When I conclude the walk, it takes me another hour to walk to the main road and get a lift back to Jaz. I notice the fig trees are starting to bloom, and everyone I run into seems startled but happy to see an Idiot on the march. When I return on a minibus to my almost private resort, I again see the accountant. He says he wants my job and urges me to "let me know if you need anything in Mersa Matruh."

The Tourism Police approach me during dinner (I am again the only one in the dining room for exceptional lamb chops and grilled vegetables) and inform me that they'll accompany me tomorrow on the 36-kilometer MedTrek to Mersa Matruh.

"Please don't try to leave without us," they tell me.

It's a chilly, blustery, cloudy day, and the sea is, for the first time on this outing, seriously tempestuous and wild. Although I was a free spirit during my seaside solo walk into Almaza Bay yesterday, today I'm accompanied by Tourism Police officers from the moment I leave the Jaz until we arrive on the outskirts of Mersa Matruh and they escort me back to the resort.

Not only are my protectors pleasant companions, but they have enough cachet or clout to get us invited into three different military outposts during the day, for chai and a brief respite. Maybe it's because I'm a bit further west, but these policemen are more playful than the Al Dabaa security crowd – echoing my "*Mashallah*" when I say we're all lucky to be enjoying the open air, sun, sea and sky; echoing my "Godawala" when I repeatedly shout the name of a nearby village and "pray" that we'll find a good Nescafé ahead. They cheerfully repeat the seven phrases I know in Arabic (they speak no English) and echo the names of towns that I've walked through since I left Port Said, which I continue to utter or mutter in sequence to show locals that I've been walking for a while and know my way around.

I'm impressed that a 32-year-old officer and his younger colleague, both toting German-made machine guns, make the entire MedTrek with me without complaint and encourage me to take photos of the wild sea and rock formations. This turns out to be a glorious seaside desert hike with stupendous sea views and only a very few of the uninhabited resorts or apartment compounds that blemish so much of the Mediterranean shore in Egypt. We pass one empty place called Santa Monica and a few other developments that have either been abandoned during construction or are simply derelict. In fact, my memories of those atrocious vestiges of human zeal will rival the exceptional feel of the fine-grained sand (some which was exported to Cleopatra's Island in Turkey that I saw and felt when I sailed there with Gordon Kling while MedTrekking in Turkey a few years ago) on this part of the Egyptian beach.

The cops love posing for selfies and taking photos, and, most importantly, they let me choose the path, which means we spend the entire day as close as possible to the churning and chortling sea. They also give me a lift back to my Almaza Bay base camp and are absolutely amazed that they too are capable of walking more than thirty kilometers.

The next day, the Tourism Police are on me the second I head out of my new base camp at the Beau Site Hotel, where my third floor room looks east across the expansive Mersa Matruh bay and beyond the seaside *corniche* where we ended the MedTrek yesterday. Four cops in a red car begin following me as soon I head down the *corniche* to hike twelve kilometers to the exact point where I ended yesterday's walk.

I have a peaceful stroll along the *corniche* past the beaches, naval yard and downtown until I arrive at a large inland "lake" and walk across a bridge to take the outer seaside road around it. I greet and acknowledge the policemen with a thumbs up from time to time, but we don't speak until I reach the point where their pickup can't follow me. Two of my Tourism Police security staff, Ahmed and Walid, walk with me for the last three kilometers of the day, after Colonel Sayyid approves the plan to drive their official vehicle down the coast and meet us in an hour. At the end of the day, we're all good buddies and they return me to the Beau Site where I buy them a coffee and they look at my photos and gleefully identify their colleagues who were with me during the hike into Mersa Matruh.

By the end of my seven-day, 190-kilometer MedTrek from Sidi Abdel Rahman to Mersa Matruh, I've actually become accustomed to having a private bodyguard of at least two armed soldiers who follow me whenever I leave the Beau Site hotel to walk around Mersa Matruh. If I'm able to sneak out without their knowledge, which I try to do on occasion, within half an hour they find me getting a shave, having a coffee or going shopping downtown.

I presume these guys think I'm close to crazy, though once they get into the walk they seem to love the idea and execution of the MedTrek. At first the officers Sayyid ordered to walk with me act like they got the shortest straw, but then they begin to feel "superior" because they are being somewhat physical, getting exercise and being exposed to a foreigner. They call Sayyid "old school" and love the idea of being blessed by the sun, sea and sky and hearing about my plans to go to Siwa. I tell them I'll see them on the return from the desert oasis for the walk further west to Cleopatra Beaches and Sidi Barrani.

After completing the MedTrek to Mersa Matruh, I was definitely looking forward to an important date with the Oracle of Ammon at the Siwa Oasis in the Sahara Desert on the Spring Equinox.

I didn't get there the same way Alexander did in 332 BC.

Alexander also traveled along the coast as far as Mersa Matruh, which was then called Paraetonium, but he then marched south "through deserted, though not waterless, country, for a distance of 1,600 stades (280 kilometers)," according to Aristobulus, whose version of events is reported by Arrian.

He followed an ancient caravan route through the desert and, it's said, two speaking snakes, or two ravens, depending on who you believe, led the way like a contemporary GPS to the oasis at Siwa. Ptolemy, another of Arrian's sources, insists that Alexander's guides took the form of two snakes. Whilst unsure whether they were snakes or ravens, Arrian confesses that "I have no doubt whatever that he had divine assistance of some kind."

It was not an easy trip back in the day. The Persian forces led by Cambyses had been obliterated in exactly the same circumstances in their attempts to reach Siwa two centuries earlier. But Alexander was seized by an ardent desire to visit Ammon in Libya, partly in order to consult the god about his own origins, because the Oracle was reputed to be exact in its information, and both Perseus and Heracles were said to have consulted it.

Alexander's journey, which involved sandstorms and rainstorms and dehydration, took six weeks but he absolutely felt it necessary to get an oracular reality check before he returned to fight the Persians in Asia. After all, the Oracle was right up there with the oracles at Delphi and Dodona in Greece, and besides trying to determine whether he was indeed of divine birth, he needed some practical travel advice about whether he should head toward Babylon and confirmation that he should give the go-ahead for a new capital in what would become Alexandria.

More than 2,340 years later, I also leave the Mediterranean Sea to travel a bit less than 300 kilometers south to the Siwa Oasis through the vacant Sahara Desert (Egyptians call it the Western Desert) to keep my vernal equinox appointment on the first day of Spring with the Oracle of Ammon. I expect to get guidance from the Oracle regarding the conclusion of my 20-year MedTrek and answers to some very key questions, including the long-time mystery concerning where Alexander the Great is now buried.

I take a late afternoon four-hour bus ride ($2.50) and am amused that the armed Tourism Police stay with me until my bus leaves the station and follows the paved, two-lane road through the sand in the vast, deserted desert. I make the trip on March 19th to scope out the mythical oasis before the equinox and consider it a good omen when another momentous MedTrek moment occurs after we stop for a midway break at a nondescript hole-in-the-wall gas-stationless truck stop that obviously wasn't here when Alexander made his excruciating journey.

After holding my nose to use the urinal at the excuse for a restroom behind the hole-in-the-wall café, I sit at a table with a few men (like most cafés in rural Egypt, it is filled only with men) drinking a tea, eating some dates and chatting with a young British guy named Walt, who says he's on "an existential quest with no money," and two middle-aged (well, younger than me anyway) Egyptians, one from Cairo and the other from Alexandria.

Then, without any warning, a slender woman wearing a leopard-patterned tan headscarf and oversized Ferragamo sunglasses does the best don't-dare-approach-me entry and strut through the café that I've ever seen at a rest stop in the Egyptian desert or anywhere else. Well-dressed with black slacks and a pearl necklace, she is of indeterminate age because her face is completely hidden by the scarf and sunglasses.

Thinking she is an extraordinary American blonde actress or maybe, due to her erect posture, poised carriage and proud manner, a typical French woman, I immediately conjure an image of Grace Kelly or Catherine Deneuve. I am both surprised and admiring as she stops conversation and attracts every eyeball in the place while purposefully and silently approaching the cashier and buying a small package of outdated potato chips.

When she strides out with the same determined don't-fuck-with-me stride, I notice a wedding band on the fourth finger of her left hand (the Romans believe that the vein in that finger runs directly to the heart, which is why it is referred to as *vena amoris* or vein of love). Most western women in Egypt, married or not, usually wear a "wedding ring" to deter the incessant advances of Egyptian men, who paradoxically have a great respect for another man's wife. In fact, I imagine that "The Woman in the Scarf," as I nickname her, has simply, like most women, turned a ruby ring around on her finger as a pretense. That's because she doesn't look like a woman any man could handle.

The scene (and remember that we are, really, in Bumfuck, Egypt) is so surreal that I briefly think I should approach her, though I consider her close to unapproachable, to make sure she's all right in the male-dominated truck stop in the middle of the desert. But she obviously doesn't need any help from me, and I simply wonder if she's going or coming to Siwa and what she'll think of the excuse for a toilet behind the café which, I must admit, isn't something that I'd ever picture Grace Kelly or Catherine Deneuve using.

I wonder if she could be the American coffee heiress who, I've heard through the grapevine, has a secluded place in the desert in Siwa. Or maybe the author of the next *Eat, Pray, Love* on a mystical spiritual Equinox quest in the desert. Or perhaps, though I doubt this, the wife of a rich Egyptian in Cairo. I have no clue.

I imagine, though, that she's the type of person who arrives in a private limo with a number of courtiers and am surprised when I see her get into the front seat of a minibus that's carrying a dozen other passengers. Like many with some spare change, she probably bought the two front seats to avoid sitting next to anyone. I forget to notice if her minibus heads towards Siwa or Mersa Matruh and just chalk her appearance up to another intriguing, mysterious and ominous MedTrek moment.

But I keep wondering and ask out loud to Walt and the two Egyptians, "Who is that woman in the scarf?"

"Not anyone who would have anything to do with us," says the class-conscious Brit.

For some reason, his comment gets me thinking about women, and I launch into a description of Alexander the Great's trudge across the desert and the women in his life.

"Did you know that," I begin....

Alexander's mother Olympias frequently insisted that he find a woman of class but her son said he had no time to "hold marriage feasts and await the birth of children" before he led the campaign to Persia. His mother also noted that Alexander seemed to prefer boys, which was not unusual during that era.

Olympias, who never gave Alexander too much guff about his bisexuality or his life-long friendship with Hephaestion, was extremely bothered that he didn't have a male heir before he left for Asia.

"You will be nineteen this summer and the girls already say you don't like them, you like Hephaestion more," Olympias lamented. "I understand it is natural for a young man."

But Alexander resisted his mother's admonitions.

"If I'd married in Macedon, as my mother wanted, before I crossed to Asia, the boy would have been twelve by now. But there was never time. There is never time enough," retorted Alexander.

Alexander faithfully wrote letters to his mother that were carried by courier back to Macedon and he constantly sent Olympias gifts, admitting to me that "she charged pretty high rent for the nine months lodging she provided for me and she played me against my father for years."

"My mother also used me to get back at my father," Alexander told me. "When I was in her stomach my nurse told me that my mother said 'In my womb I carry my avenger'!"

"Look at you! Look at you! You are everything he (Philip) was not," Olympias once told Alexander. "He was coarse, you are refined. He was a general, you are a king. He could not rule himself...and you shall rule the world."

That's how it turned out, of course, but sometimes Alexander wasn't sure about himself.

"When I was a child my mother thought me divine and my father weak... which one am I? Weak or divine?" he asked me.

Alexander did have a documented affair with a woman in his early 20s and fathered a son named Hercules with Barsine, the widowed daughter of a Persian father and Greek mother. And he married three times once he left the Oracle at Siwa, who might have suggested to him that it was time to get serious.

His first marriage in the early spring of 327 BC was to Roxana, whose name means "little star," a 16-year-old who was reputed to be one of the most beautiful young women in Asia. Plutarch describes their meeting as "love at first sight and they were united in the Macedonian and Iranian tradition by jointly slicing a loaf of bread." Roxana once caught Alexander getting it on with Hephaestion, and he told her "There are many ways to love."

The two Egyptian men at the table smile at that.

Although they spoke different languages, Roxana accompanied Alexander on his campaign to India. But their son, Alexander III, wasn't born until just after his father's death. Roxana and her son, Alexander IV, returned to Macedonia, where they were later murdered in Amphipolis and put out of the political picture.

While married to Roxana, Alexander took two more wives, relatives of former Persian kings, whom he married on the same day in 324 BC. He was betrothed to Stateira II, the eldest daughter of Darius III, and Parysatis, the youngest daughter of Artaxeres III, at a wedding in Susa with nine thousand guests, each of whom received a golden cup in a goody bag. It was a grand wedding.

Those marriages, obviously for political purposes, fused two branches of the royal family of the Achaemenid Empire and enabled Alexander to forge closer relationships with his empire's subjects. When Alexander died, the pregnant Roxana summoned Stateira and Parysatis to Babylon and had them killed.

Alexander encouraged his troops to intermarry with the Persians and gave all of his Companions – including Craterus, Ptolemy, Bumenes, Nearchus and Seleucus – Persian wives. Hephaestion married Drypetis, another daughter of Darius III, because Alexander wanted Hephaestion's children to be first cousins to his own.

"I wonder what he would have thought of 'The Woman in the Scarf'?" I ask Walt and the two Egyptians.

# FOLLOW THE IDIOT

## CHAPTER PHOTOS

## CHAPTER MAP

# Consulting The Oracle of Siwa and Reaching Libya

"Toil and risk are the price of glory, but it is a lovely thing to live with courage, and die leaving an everlasting fame." – Alexander the Great

"A tomb now suffices him for whom the whole world was not sufficient." – The epitaph on Alexander the Great's tombstone

I feel, even though I'm on an air-conditioned, comfortable bus speeding through Egypt's Western Desert to the Siwa Oasis, that I am now truly and purposefully following in the footsteps of Alexander the Great. A look at the austere terrain he traversed encourages me to respect the effort he made. It gives me a better understanding of his fervent desire to visit the Oracle of Siwa, who was reputed to be infallible with an ability to resolve Alexander's queries about his divinity and provide him with guidance on numerous more practical matters. Of course he had to go.

Alexander's primary objective was to determine if he was a god, and, though it would have been vainglorious for The Idiot to imagine that I might also be of divine heritage, I initially set up my consultation with the Oracle to obtain information key to the future of the MedTrek and determine where Alexander is currently entombed.

Simple stuff. Or so I thought.

I learn when I arrive in the Siwa Oasis that the Spring Equinox is a much more auspicious date for a séance than my originally scheduled, then postponed meeting on the Ides of March. Julius Caesar and William Shakespeare, of course, hadn't been born when Alexander was alive, so at that time, The Ides of March had no meaning at all. But, ah, the equinox, when daytime and nighttime are the same length and the seasons change from winter to spring, has been revered almost forever. The word, in case you're wondering, is derived from the Latin *aequinoctium*, from *aequus* (equal) and *nox* (night).

Siwa, a green fertile oasis in the middle of a vast desert, is full of cultivated trees, olives and palms with a stream and lakes that have always given it a paradisiacal image. Alexander, like every other visitor, including me, was immediately struck with wonder after his trudge through the sand (talk about yin and yang!) to the Oracle of the God Ammon, who was considered synonymous with Zeus.

Besides the surprisingly verdant natural beauty and a feeling of befuddled wonder about the existence of such a haven, there is something immediately special, satisfying and spiritual about the Berber-inhabited, below-sea-level oasis that today attracts many foreign visitors – often to experience equinox solar alignments while seeking solitude under the desert stars. People come for a return to nature at electricity-free ecolodges, meditation sessions at the Temple of the Oracle, or even yoga, massages or full-throttle Quantum Healing Hypnosis Therapy. The seductive spot is sometimes referred to as "Bali in the Desert."

I've heard about Siwa's allure, of course, but don't feel or appreciate its energy until the moment I arrive. I wish my traveling companion Walt good luck, and check into the hippieish, and heritage, Albabenshal Hotel in the center of town abutting Shali, the old mud-brick section of Siwa. Khaled, the Siwan who welcomes me and shows me to my $13 a night room, which Walt said would be too expensive for him, tells me he's taking two Americans to a temple west of town early in the morning to see the sunrise on the day before the equinox.

"Would you like to come?" asks Khaled, who seems too polite and soft-spoken to also be a local fixer. "And I can take you anywhere else you want to go, whether it's to a garden full of olive and palm trees, our salt seas, Cleopatra's freshwater bath or the Mountain of the Dead."

"Can you bring me a kettle to boil water?" I ask.
He does.

I awaken at the rooster-crowing, call-to-prayer break of dawn just before 5 a.m. and, because it's well before the hotel's official breakfast time, make a cup of Nescafé and feast on dates and biscuits that I brought from Mersa Matruh. Then at 6 a.m. sharp, Khaled picks me up in front of the hotel and drives three Americans in the cool dark dawn about 12 kilometers west of town to watch the last sunrise of winter from the remains of the Timasirayn Temple. According to my calendar, the equinox is officially later today but the first sunrise of spring will be tomorrow.

While we pass Lake Siwa and arrive at the ruins of the temple ten minutes before sunrise, I chat with Dustin T. Donaldson and his wife Robynn Iwata who claim to have discovered that the Timasirayn Temple is perfectly aligned with the Temple of the Oracle. On the equinox sunrise tomorrow morning, the sun passes directly and perfectly over the sanctuary of the Oracle of Siwa, they explain.

Although not the official equinox, everything is aligned well enough for me this morning, and I get a wonderfully tranquil photograph of Robynn taking a mouth-watering picture of the last-day-of-winter sunrise over the Temple of the Oracle from the ancient viewing window at Timasirayn Temple.

Dustin and Robynn tell me they discovered this intriguing solar fact and posit that a former viewing window at the temple is what I'm "looking through" today. They claim to have made "a new and important discovery of ancient solar calendar science and archaeo-astronomical engineering" and consider it possible that this temple was constructed primarily to watch the sunrise and view the equinox.

I don't know about that, but this is definitely an exciting place to be for the equinox – and apparently many people come here season after season for their spring renewal. Even a day early, before it's perfect (actually it is perfect), there's an obvious alignment of the sun at sunrise with the Oracle's temple.

The slight quiver I experience when I hear about, and witness, the alignment gets me very jazzed about my session with the Oracle of Siwa at noon tomorrow after I return here early in the morning for the first-day-of-spring sunrise.

And I'm equally titillated when Dustin points out a villa not far away owned, he says, by an American coffee heiress.

"Does she wear a headscarf?" I ask.

After the sunrise, Khaled drops Dustin and Robynn at the home they've been renting for five years and takes me to a nearby villa, a Dutch-owned house he takes care of near Darkur Mountain, for my last winter breakfast. We walk through the date palm garden into the kitchen, where he prepares a breakfast that includes fig jam, *halawa*, dates (dates are a big deal here, and Khaled gives me some delicious ones that have almonds replacing the pits), pita bread, Domiati cheese, fruit off the trees and mint tea.

I slowly stroll through the verdant garden while Khaled is preparing breakfast and recall that some Berbers, or Barbari, still speak Hamitic, an ancient language preserved in the inscriptions and papyri of ancient Egypt. It's one of some 50 languages and over 70 dialects identified in Africa north of the Equator, and I'm happy to spend the last morning of winter with an authentic Berber in Siwa.

During breakfast – I hesitate before I write that it is a heavenly breakfast, which might seem over the top, but, what the hell, it is a heavenly breakfast – I learn that Khaled, a handsome man whose white *galabeya* never seems to get dusty or dirty, is in his late twenties and is courting a woman for a possible arranged marriage. I tell him about the MedTrek, my marriages, Liz and my outlook on life as I experience my 69th Spring Equinox.

"Look, I know it's not your custom and might sound like a very foreign concept to you, but I strongly suggest that you live with your proposed wife and make love with your proposed wife, before you marry your proposed wife," I say sagely. "That'll give you some insight about what you're getting into and whether you want to get into it."

"What are you talking about?" he responds.

After we do the dishes, I thank Khaled for the tranquil but revealing morning outing and tell him that I'll spend the rest of the day walking and exploring by myself.

The first thing I do is climb nearby Darkur Mountain to get an overview of Siwa and the Temple of the Oracle. From the top, I can see Timasirayn Temple, where we watched the sunrise, and, much closer, the Aghurmi Temple, where I'll meet the Oracle the next day. Beyond the greenery and lakes that are Siwa is, on every side, the enticingly empty and seemingly never-ending desert.

After an hour at the top of the mountain, I descend and continue toward the Oracle's temple. I stop for a swim at Cleopatra's Spring (aka Cleopatra's Pool or the Spring of Juba), where I have my fourth mint tea of the day. Then I walk past the Temple of Umm Ubayd. It has a broken column that might have been shipped here from Aswan, where, as I learned during my exploration up the Nile, columns were carved and transported north down the river.

I make my first visit to the Temple of the Oracle of Ammon at 11 a.m. to check things out 25 hours before my private consultation with the Oracle in a sanctuary the next day. Dustin tells me that an aide frequently receives questions and delivers responses to the Oracle on papyrus, but I tell him that I believe that I'll have a personal audience with real-time questions.

"I think it would be smart to write the questions on papyrus anyway," he suggests.

As I enter the temple and walk up the red-dirt hill toward the Oracle's chambers, I feel the comforting sense of calm and contentment that often pleasantly overwhelms me when I visit holy and sacred places. An invisible security blanket shields and protects me from any doubts, expectations or projections. I am where I am.

Alexander's journey to Siwa was an arduous and dangerous one, complicated by no water, too much wind and the unfamiliar and dangerous desert terrain. As he and his exhausted men entered Siwa, which was located in what was then Libya, their eyes relished the rejuvenating beauty of this dewy, lush and fertile hidden-in-the-desert treasure. Shady groves of palms and fruit trees bordering waters that gushed forth in abundance from a subterranean spring in a near-mystical paradise were in complete contrast to the arid sand they traversed to get here.

Anxious to visit the Oracle as soon as possible, Alexander went immediately to the Temple of Ammon on the high rock outcrop of Aghurmi, where the Oracle, when asked if the king would be granted divine honors, replied, "This would please Ammon." As both the King of Macedon and the Pharaoh of Egypt, Alexander was granted the privilege of communing with the Oracle directly within the heavily scented and completely dark sacred inner sanctuary and allowed to put his questions personally to the Oracle, though he couldn't actually see whom he was addressing.

Nobody knows for certain what Alexander asked, or precisely what the Oracle replied, but it is surmised that Megas Alexandros was told that he was both a son of Zeus, the supreme Greek god, and the Libyan god Ammon (dual paternity was acceptable back then), which made him a divine being. In any event, following his audience, Alexander started to think of himself as the son of Zeus/Ammon, which certainly made his journey through the desert worthwhile.

Alexander also asked the Oracle if his father's murderers had been fully avenged. "Yes," was the gist of the response; whether he should create a new capital in Alexandria ("Yes"); whether he should take his military campaign to Babylon ("Yes"); and if he could ultimately be buried in Siwa ("Yes").

The Oracle also instructed Megas Alexandros about how to peacefully and successfully seduce and rule the Egyptians.

"Kiss the arms of Egyptians and you will not be forced to fight them," the Oracle advised. "Work with them, give them power and you will all prosper."

That directive involved, as I mentioned earlier, physically and spiritually blending Greek and Egyptian religious practices and Alexander, who was already ruling with a soft touch, subsequently ordered the construction of numerous temples on Egyptian holy sites, such as Philae near contemporary Aswan.

The Oracle – besides affirming that Alexander should proceed with the construction of Alexandria on the Mediterranean Sea and expand his empire-expanding military campaign to Babylon and India – encouraged Alexander to marry and produce a male heir to prevent disputes and internecine warfare among his potential successors. The Oracle predicted that Alexander would soon defeat Darius III at Gaugamela, "thrice marry" and never return to Macedon.

Lastly, the Oracle told Alexander that he drank too much alcohol and would die young if he didn't temper his excesses.

"If you keep drinking, and do die, your corpse will be brought back to Egypt, and ultimately Siwa, following your death," Alexander was told. "And if your friend and lover Hephaestion pre-deceases you, he may be honored as a hero."

"Alexander was in Siwa to learn his destiny, but I think more had happened than he had come to ask," said Ptolemy when Alexander smiled at him as he left the Oracle and walked into the jarring sunlight. "He began to honor Egyptian temples, gave the go ahead on the construction of Alexandria and, for a short while, didn't seem to drink to excess as much."

The revelation that Alexander was divine wasn't a big surprise to many historians.

"It seems to me that a hero totally unlike any other human being could not have been born without the agency of the deity," wrote Arrian of Nicomedia a few centuries after Alexander's era.

Alexander, who didn't leave the temple until the Oracle was carried out on a litter by four pairs of priests, told his Companions in waiting that he received "the answer which my heart desired" and wrote to his mother that he had obtained "secret information I will communicate to you only when we meet again." Unfortunately, whatever that secret information was has never been revealed and is interred with Alexander's bones, wherever he might be resting. Or with his soul, wherever that is.

During the remaining eight years of his life, Alexander frequently sent gifts to the priests in Siwa and occasionally had more questions for the Oracle in whom he now had an unshakable faith.

Although Alexander would never return alive to see the city he had founded or personally visit the Oracle in Siwa again, his embalmed body (the rites of burning and cremation were growing in popularity, but that wouldn't be Alexander's fate) would eventually be entombed first in Alexandria and then in Siwa after a two-decade stopover in Memphis.

Alexander the Great's visit and consultation with the Oracle in 331

BC was one of the most important and most publicized events of his reign. When I leave the Mediterranean Sea to consult with the Oracle of Ammon on the Spring Equinox, I have no expectations (I never have, or admit that I have, any expectations) but realize that, whatever happens, this is a very important MedTrek milestone.

That's why, after swimming in Cleopatra's Pool and walking in the direction of the temple the day before my audience with the Oracle, I want to quietly explore the temple prior to my meeting.

When I enter the temple just before noon, I climb directly to the Oracle's sanctuary, where a group of touring women is half listening to an English-speaking Egyptian male guide describe Alexander's visit to the Oracle. The women, who are all Russian, regularly interrupt the guide and interject opinions they've picked up from guidebooks. I admire the guide's patience and, as I listen, learn that the group will also be going to view tomorrow's sunrise at the Timasirayn Temple.

The guide explains that during ancient times the sanctum did not have today's windows or any lighting but was completely dark, preventing anyone from actually seeing the Oracle. Then he mentions that at a certain time of year, light shines through the existing "window" and falls directly on the spot where the Oracle sat, a phenomenon that Dustin had mentioned to me.

"The official date of the double window alignment was March 9, or 12 days before the Spring Equinox, but you can still get the idea if you come back this afternoon," the guide tells his group.

When I walk into the outer chamber, I notice a solitary woman meditating in a stone recess in the wall. She's obviously in her own world, not bothered by the loud-speaking Russians, the guide or me. A dark blue scarf hides her face and the vibes from her calm, distant demeanor indicate that she's enjoying her tranquil state and probably isn't even aware of me while I walk slowly and silently around the chamber to soak up the atmosphere of the iconic temple. Ten minutes later she raises her clasped hands and makes a silent dedication before opening her eyes and slowly standing, and almost imperceptibly stretching, on the red-earth floor.

"Excuse me," I say, "but did you happen to be at a truck stop yesterday on the road from Mersa Matruh to Siwa?"

She seems startled by the question, as though she's never heard of Mersa Matruh, or doesn't know what a truck stop is, or has just been rudely approached and interrupted after a meditation session and asked an extremely personal and slightly impertinent question.

"I know it might sound a bit strange," I continue, "but my bus here from Mersa Matruh stopped at a café and I saw a woman who looked a little like you; well, I'm actually not sure what she looked like, but she was wearing a scarf, and I was just wondering if it was you?"

She still looks somewhat baffled and it occurs to me that she might not speak English, that maybe she is with the Russian group. So I ask if she speaks French, German, Italian or Spanish, probably sounding like an Egyptian tout trying to sell her souvenirs. After all, they always greet foreign visitors in a number of languages hoping to elicit a response.

"*Entschuldigung, meine gnädige Frau, wären Sie gestern...*"

She slowly puts up her hand to silence me.

"I did arrive yesterday on a minibus from Alexandria," she says in English with an accent that is neither English, French, German, Italian, nor Spanish. "And we did stop for a break a few hours from here. I just walked in and out as quickly as possible."

"Actually, I was very struck by the regal manner in which you walked in and out of the place, completely aloof from the crowd, looking like a mystic or a goddess," I reply. "It was a very impressive and intriguing performance, and I thought maybe you're a Hollywood actress or a wealthy aristocrat or a model or a coffee heiress...well, I concocted all sorts of theories."

"I thought I was invisible when I walked in that café trying to look anonymous like any other Egyptian woman, so no one would notice me," she says, half smiling. "It's the manner I assume to avoid being hassled or approached by Egyptian men who make a point of flirting with foreigners. I had no idea anyone noticed me. I saw no one, noticed nothing."

"Well, I don't want to bother you, and excuse me if I am, but it was an award-worthy walk-on," I say as noon approaches. "I had all sorts of fantasies about who you might be, but didn't expect to see you again. Do you live in Siwa? Are you the coffee heiress? What are you doing here? And please, if you're not in the mood for a conversation, I completely understand and will leave."

The Egyptian guide sees and hears our conversation and seems to know the woman in the scarf.

"*As-salāmu 'alaykum,*" he says. "Good to see you again, Monika, and welcome back to Siwa."

"*Alaykumu as-salām,*" she replies. "I'll see you tomorrow morning."

Then she turns to me.

"Siwa is very special to me and I always come here during the equinox, special full moons and any other time I feel called," she says in an accent that now sounds Eastern European. "All sorts of special revelations occur here. How about you?"

Because of the scarf and the shadows, I can't see what she looks like or, not that it matters, tell how old she might be, but she conveys a kind of agelessness. I won't be surprised if she's 25 or 65.

"I'm taking a break from a walk across Egypt on the Mediterranean Sea and hope to get an indication of where I should go next and perhaps get a few other questions answered by the Oracle," I reply. "I was out this morning to see the glorious sunrise and met some people who told me all about alignments and other things that I had no clue about."

"That would be Dustin and Robynn, right?" she says. "It's a small community of expats here, and they've made some interesting discoveries."

"I'm going to walk around the temple and get in the mood to meet the Oracle tomorrow," I respond. "And I might come back this afternoon to see the ray of light hit the Oracle's seat. Perhaps I'll see you at the equinox sunrise tomorrow morning."

"I'll be there," she says.

I practice walking meditation while I stroll around the temple and explore most of the nooks and crannies from top to bottom. At high noon, with the temperature in the 30s°C (80s°F) and 24 hours before my scheduled appointment, I find myself on a rampart at one of the highest points meditating about nothing – not even "the goal is the path, the path is the goal" but, truly, nothing – while basking in the sun and dedicating my feelings of calm and contentment to all sentient beings.

Then I return to the Oracle's sanctuary and "The Woman in the Scarf" is still there.

"This is my 139th equinox," I say when I approach her again. "How many have you seen?"

I presume, though I'm not sure, that she divides by two to calculate my age, or maybe she, too, actually keeps track of the number of equinoxes that have occurred since she was born. It's not difficult, of course, because there are two a year indicating the change of seasons in both the northern and southern hemispheres. Most of mine have been in the northern hemisphere, but I also celebrated reverse seasons when I lived in South Africa for three years and during occasional visits to Australia.

"This will be my 73rd equinox," she says, which makes her about half my age. "And my fifth in Siwa, which I've visited twelve times."

We walk four kilometers back to town together and have a mint tea on the way in a hidden garden behind a hole-in-the-garden teahouse. I describe how the MedTrek brought me to Siwa and give her a brief bio about my career as a journalist, including where I've lived and what I've done. I mention that she's about the same age as my daughter and then spin her my hilarious take on *The Woman In The Scarf*, Hitchcock style, and all the amusing tangents provoked by her mystique as she walked into that roadside café.

"The Woman in the Scarf" tells me that she practices quantum hypnosis (whatever that might be), is a channeler (whatever that might entail) and light worker (which presumably is not an electrician) and isn't really of this earth (whatever that might mean). Her name is Monika, she's Polish, mastered English when she lived in London for twelve years, recently left London to live in Alexandria. Most of the people in Siwa seem to know her.

When we reach the center of town, she shows me the best place to have freshly pressed sugar cane juice, and we learn that we're staying at the same hotel. She points to the path that will take me to the top of the Shali, or old town, that abuts the hotel. I thank her for the advice and take the short hike to the top to get another perspective on Siwa.

Naturally, I Google "monika+polish+quantum+hynotist" later that night and learn that she's "an attuned MasterMind developer, transformation and change facilitator, working with advanced and quantum hypnosis, channeling and Ancient Egyptian Light technologies.

"Having spent an extensive time in Egypt on deeply awakening journeys, initiations and research, I'm following my purpose opening the cosmic gateways connections and am honored to facilitate the change for others."

Whoa! A contemporary psychic oracle!

I return to the Temple of the Oracle at 4 p.m. to catch the afternoon light of the setting sun through the window in the Oracle's sanctuary, and, once lit up, I stay, the only one in the temple, until it closes at sunset. The Oracle doesn't appear, of course, but when I leave, I have a sense of calm, completion and coming home and look forward to our meeting the next day.

The Temple of the Oracle has a mythical and mystical reputation, and I've been warned about its impact. It turns out, as I talk to people here and there, that many visitors to Siwa and the temple are deeply affected by it, as indeed, they are affected by similar places in Tibet, the Taj Mahal and sites with a well-known spiritual allure.

Laura Hohlwein, a painter and college professor from California, tells me that she entered into a semi-hallucinatory trance after her visit to the temple, having a long-lasting, repeating vision of a pair of large eyes, very close up, slowly closing and opening while she heard a soft voice whispering over and over "your eyes are closed and your eyes are open.... your eyes are closed and your eyes are open." She has thought for years about the possible meanings of the phrase.

"It was simultaneously reassuring, alarming and inexplicable," she tells me when we meet.

Despite the fact that there is no hot water, I kick off the Spring Equinox dawn, with a shower and shave, at 5 a.m. After enjoying another of my monkish breakfasts of biscuits and Nescafé, I head out for the touted seasonal sunrise in Khaled's minivan with Dustin, Robynn, a few other men and "The Woman in the Scarf," who is dressed in clothes that would fit in nicely with a sophisticated gathering at the Café de Paris in Monte Carlo.

We arrive at the Timasirayn Temple to quietly, almost silently, watch the equinox sunrise over the Temple of the Oracle. There are thirty people this morning compared to only four of us during yesterday's brilliantly clear sunrise. Though there's some grumbling from the Russians, no one is distraught (most people realize they can't control the weather) when intense clouds completely obscure the sunrise. Dustin gives a brief talk about the invisible-today alignment and I consider myself fortunate that I serendipitously came here the day before.

When, an hour later, everyone is ready to disperse and head back to town, I mention that I'll stay behind to climb a nearby flat-topped mountain with tombs that the Romans used for the deceased when they controlled Siwa a few centuries after the era of Alexander the Great.

Monika suggests that I first join her for breakfast at the foot of the mountain at the Taziry (which means "full moon" in the Siwan dialect) Ecolodge and Sustainable Village, where she conducts quantum hypnosis sessions and frequently stays.

We walk an hour to the lodge, and there's no one around at this early hour until a French couple emerges from their room. We introduce ourselves and together rummage and scavenge through the kitchen to find coffee, orange juice and toast. After setting a large outdoor table, we feast on our finds and talk about pretty much everything under the non-existent equinox sun for two hours.

The discussion with Philippe and Virginie, the French couple, ranges from the allure of Siwa, spiritual growth (a hot topic here) and Monika's hypnosis work, which excites Virginie, who's a life coach and just had a QHHT (Quantum Healing Hypnosis Technique) session in Paris.

Virginie asks Monika how she got involved in QHHT.

"I didn't want to be a therapist dealing with people's fears, but a hypnotist enabling them to unlock their potential," she explains.

I feel like someone who's just contracted a previously unheard of disease called QHHT and then typically run into dozens of people who also have it.

The delightful and fascinating breakfast interlude is a pleasant way to kick off spring after the equinox sunrise, about which Philippe and Virginie, friends who are on a quick see-Egypt-in-ten-days tour, are not even aware.

"I can't imagine what she's doing out here with shiny city flat shoes like that," says Virginie, when Monika goes to welcome the owner of the lodge to his own place. "Does she plan to walk up the mountain with you wearing clothes that would be more appropriate for the Ritz Hotel?"

"Hey, I just met her," I say, telling Virginie that I didn't even know what QHHT was twenty-four hours ago and I still don't have a real idea. "The only thing she told me when I implied that this is inappropriate attire for climbing a mountain is that she's visited Siwa twelve times and would never be caught wearing tennis shoes."

# HORSE'S ASS

Following his audience with the Oracle, Alexander and his troops took a straight and direct route via the Qattara Depression to Memphis then left Egypt in mid-April of 331 BC after making arrangements to have the territory governed by a combination of Egyptians, Macedonians and Persians.

Alexander's personality and leadership were revealed just before the fighting began at the Battle of Guagamela in Northern Iraq, near contemporary Mosul, in October 331 BC. His speech in Oliver Stone's film *Alexander* is worth repeating: "You've all honored your country and your ancestors and now we come to this most distant place in Asia where across from us Darius has at last gathered a vast army, but look again at this horde and ask yourselves, who is this great king who pays assassins in gold coins to murder my father, our king, in a most despicable and cowardly manner? Who is this great king Darius who enslaves his own men to fight? Who is this king but a king of air? These men do not fight for their homes. They fight because this king tells them they must. And when they fight, they will melt away like the air, because they know no loyalty to a king of slaves! But we are not here today as slaves. We are here today...as Macedonian *free men*! And all their arms, their numbers, their chariots and their fine horses will mean nothing in the hands of slaves. Some of you, perhaps myself, will not live to see the sun set over these mountains today, for I will be in the very thick of battle with you. But remember this; the greatest honor a man can achieve is to live with great courage, and to die gloriously in battle for his home. I say to you what every warrior has known since the beginning of time: conquer your fear and I promise you will conquer death! Someday, I promise you, your sons and grandsons will look into your eyes. And when they ask you why you fought so bravely at Gaugamela, you will answer, with all the strength of your great, *great* hearts: 'I was here this day at Gaugamela...for the freedom...and *glory*...of Greece!' Zeus be with us!"

Before the battle, Darius offered Alexander half of his empire in return for his promise that he would cease his assault. He refused.

Remarkably, as the Oracle predicted, although the odds were against him – Darius deployed his full force of 100,000 soldiers against Alexander's army of just 47,000 – Alexander did win the battle of

Gaugamela (the name means "the camel's house" because an ancient king once escaped pursuers on a swift camel) and took control of Asia.

Monika and I take a slightly challenging three-hour hike on a circuitous, indirect path up the nearby mountain, towering over Taziry. We traverse across one side of the mountain to inspect the cut-into-the-mountain Roman tombs, which certainly are candidates for Alexander's Siwa grave. I enter and investigate a number of the cave-like tombs, some deep and dark, to "feel" the dead, and think that this would have been a fittingly anonymous common graveyard where the Romans could "hide" Alexander from pilgrims looking to venerate or desecrate his body.

Monika asks me how and why Alexander the Great would have been interred in a place like this, so I give her a bit of background.

"After reigning twelve years and eight months, Alexander died in Babylon on June 10 in 323 BC, a month short of his thirty-third birthday, following a series of victories over the Persians," I begin. "His life ended not on the battlefield, but when he became sick and disabled due to leukemia, malaria, alcohol poisoning or ingestion of a poisonous plant or substance. One historian said it was 'disease, undiagnosable to us.'

I continue: "The historian Plutarch says that 'towards the end Alexander lacked confidence and felt the gods had abandoned him' and 'had become so obsessed by his fears of the supernatural that he interpreted every unusual occurrence as a prodigy or a portent....His court included diviners and priests whose business was to sacrifice and purify and foretell the future.'"

I explain how intriguing it is to imagine that Alexander accomplished as much as he did before he died so young, though in our contemporary times many rock stars (Janis Joplin, Jimi Hendrix, Jim Morrison, Kurt Cobain and Amy Winehouse to name just a few) died at 27 and became, without ever knowing it, members of the 27 Club.

"So for some, I guess, maybe 32 is a ripe old age," I say philosophically.

"It's said," I continue, that Alexander uttered two oft-cited lines when he was near death: "I would rather live a short life of glory than a long one of obscurity" and "In the end, when it's over, all that matters is what you've done."

"He supposedly wanted to return to Siwa after his own audience with the Oracle," I continue. "Following his death, his body was embalmed, placed in a spice-scented gold coffin and slowly brought back in a procession to Memphis while a tomb was being built in Alexandria.

"Priests tended the shrines and tombs in both Memphis and Alexandria, and when the Romans took over, Julius Caesar, Mark Antony and Augustus visited to pay homage. Legends, myths and romance about Alexander flourished.

"The stories make Alexander sound like the first celebrity in the western world. The Roman republican leader Pompey the Great found and wore Alexander's cloak; Augustus traveled to Alexandria to lay a wreath on his coffin; the emperor Caligula took Alexander's armor from his tomb and wore it himself. Accounts of his life were written both while he was living and during a five hundred year period following his death by Callisthenes, Ptolemy, Aristobulus, Nearchus, Onesicritus, Arrian, Quintus Curtius Rufus, Plutarch, Diodorus Siculus, Justin and others.

"Just before he died, Alexander said that he would leave his kingdom 'to the strongest,' though during the next two decades, different territories were ceded to different generals – Cassander took Macedonia, Ptolemy took Egypt, Lysimachus got Thrace and Seleucus reigned in Babylonia.

I conclude: "I think Alexander knew things would be a bit disrupted by his death because at one point he said, 'I foresee a great funeral contest over me,' and indeed Ptolemy, the general who brought the body back to Egypt, recalled, "Within hours, we were fighting like jackals for his corpse. He was a god or as close as anything I've ever seen. In his short life he achieved without doubt, the mythic glory of his ancestor Achilles, and more."

As I finish the story of Alexander, I'm amazed that Monika not only makes the climb to the flat top of the mountain without complaint, but that, wearing urban clothes and shiny shoes, she somehow makes it up and down without getting scathed or dirty. She stops at one point to interview me ("I interview many people I meet about what makes them tick emotionally and spiritually") and asks what I'd say if I had a chance to speak to the world's eight billion people for three minutes.

She records me in the shadow of an overhang of a shallow Roman tomb, and I repeat my daily post-meditation benediction, which most of you have heard before in a slightly different form:

"By the power and truth of this practice
May all sentient beings enjoy calm and contentment and the causes of calm and contentment.
May they be free from suffering and the causes of suffering,
May they find the great calm and contentment that is devoid of suffering,
And may they dwell in the blissful equanimity that is free from anger, aggression, anxiety, arrogance, and assholes."

It seems as meaningful and harmless as anything else I can come up with on the side of a mountain, and I explain to Monika that during the past few years, I've replaced the word "happiness" with "calm and contentment."

From the top of the hill, I look down on Ghâry Lake near the Taziry compound, across to the Darkur Mountain that I climbed yesterday and in another direction to the White Mountain that, unbeknownst to me, I'll climb in a few days. I can also see the Great Sand Sea, the Oracle's Temple, downtown Siwa and mud-brick Shali.

As I frequently say, you never really know someone until you walk together. Among other things I learn about Monika during our mountain climb is that we're both Leos (she was born on July 29 and I was born on July 31) and that she is a hypnotherapist. She has been professionally practicing Quantum Healing Hypnosis Technique for four years and plans to "Fast, Pray, Eat, Love" her way through the upcoming Ramadan in Egypt.

She says she came, like me, to the Oracle at the propitious time of the equinox to hear things, and that her goal is to spread goodwill and love. She ends a long conversation by mentioning some personal issues and says, "you're the first traveler I've ever spoken to about these things... where did you get that skill?"

"It's just the result of being a journalist for decades," I say. "You learn how to encourage people to talk and open up, which almost everyone is eager to do, by just listening. You just proved my point. But I have been wondering, if you don't mind me asking, why you wear a scarf. Is it intended to be a *hijab* or *niqab*?"

I was referring, as Monika knew, to the scarf worn in public by some Muslim women (*hijab*) and the scarf that covers an ultra-religious Muslim woman's entire face (*niqab*).

"I surrendered to the Egyptian way of life not long after I arrived and wanted to blend in and live as an average citizen rather than a tourist," she says. "I said yes to wearing a scarf, though not really for religious purposes. I wanted to know what it was like and to better understand the women wearing it.

"Now covering my head feels very natural," she continues, "It enables me to observe local life and explore corners of Egyptian society not seen by typical visitors. Wearing a scarf is especially natural in conservative Siwa, where women cover themselves from head to toe when they leave their homes, because it shows respect for their local customs and religion.

"The scarf was initially a camouflage that enabled me not to attract excessive attention," she admits. "But it became my silent statement indicating that 'I am here with a purpose, I honor you, I respect your ways.' I love wearing a scarf because I feel a higher level of respect and I notice a palpable shift in my character."

That afternoon, on the first full day of Spring, I return to the Temple of the Oracle of Ammon for the consultation that has been postponed from its original and less auspicious date on the Ides of March.

I imagine myself following Alexander the Great's footsteps up the hill into the inner sanctum atop and cautiously enter the Oracle's now-roofless sanctuary without any of the panache of Alexander the Great, who definitely, as the divine pharaoh and king of Egypt, had a bit more presence than I.

As a precaution, I left the Oracle questions written on papyrus yesterday and would have been content with written responses. Instead I am pleased to enter the room and see the Oracle, at the exact moment that a spot of sunlight appears at precisely the right place on the rock and dried mud wall, sitting in a simple chair.

The Oracle gets up close and personal from the get go.

"You have almost walked enough around, and will have written enough about, the Mediterranean Sea," the Oracle says. "Take kindly the counsel of years and surrender the folly of youth after you complete your walk across Egypt. Reach, but do not walk into, dangerous Libya. Instead proceed to Tunisia, where you will be crowned as The Idiot Emperor of Carthage, Lord of Many Domains."

Alexander never made it to Carthage after he defeated the Carthaginians at Tyre in contemporary Lebanon, but the Oracle tells me that's where my MedTrek should end.

"And while you are in Siwa, do some more self-examination and self-cultivation with another teacher," the Oracle adds. "Walking meditation, Ra and Buddhism are not the only answers and you can look within yourself a bit more if you find someone to guide you."

Then, as an informative denouement, the Oracle confirms that the Romans definitely brought Alexander's remains back to Siwa.

"They brought him back and entombed him high," are the Oracle's exact words to me. "They," the Oracle lets me know, "were the Romans who discreetly placed Alexander the Great on a mountaintop in Siwa. "Find him but let him rest eternally in peace. Keep it to yourself."

"And then?" I wonder silently to myself, as the Oracle seems to read my mind.

"You must seek a Zennier profession to pursue after you complete your 20-year MedTrek and publish *The Idiot and the Odyssey III* in 2018," the Oracle says. "Revisit the people and places you love the most. And when it's all over, because after all you are a mere human, I counsel you to go gently into that good night and enjoy eternal rest."

I wasn't sure of the protocol but I bow, nod in silent thanks and walk backwards out of the sanctuary feeling calm, content and comfortable. It occurs to me that my MedTrek, my life and my world will all end with a whisper or whimper rather than a bang.

I leave the temple and walk slowly back to town, pondering the Oracle's suggestions, and get a glass of rejuvenating sugar cane juice.

Although I agree it's a bit of a stretch, I begin to wonder if "The

Woman in the Scarf" might have been put in my path for a purpose. Is she, a 36-year-old hypnotherapist with shiny flat shoes, sunglasses and a pearl necklace, a human messenger from the Oracle? She definitely seems to open doors wherever she goes but am I supposed to go through one?

It gradually dawns on me that "The Woman in the Scarf" might be the most interesting and intriguing person that I've randomly met on the MedTrek since I encountered the sorceress in Spain (remember her?) well over a decade ago.

While she's only a bit older than my daughter, and has made it clear that she's on a spiritual quest (at one point she says, quite sternly and seriously, "I'm not looking for an adventure or a relationship" and I respond, "I'm in a relationship and you're young enough to be my daughter!"), I start investigating quantum hypnosis online and consider the possibility of having a session to discover or determine if I am as content with my life – the MedTrek, Liz, my kids, my writing, my aging process – as I feel I am. Or am I just fooling myself?

Here's one thing I read about QHHT: "We have all lived multiple Other Lives and we all have a subconscious which contains the answers to any question we may have about ourselves or the life we are living."

Can I determine what other lives I lived? Tap into my own subconscious? Or simply figure out if I'm missing something and kidding myself about my current life, (like I did when I went through a divorce and thought I had it all together, then erupted in tears in front of my daughter after I had a "deep heart acupuncture" session in France)? Am I similarly, if unintentionally, hiding something now? With the MedTrek approaching a conclusion, is it time for a late middle age, or an approaching golden age, identity crisis? Doesn't that crap ever end?

I consider adding Quantum Healing Hypnosis Technique to my Siwa menu to possibly determine if I'm as calm, content and Zen as I think I am. Or find out, maybe, that I'm living a make believe sham. Or, as is often the case, determine where I am in between sham and enlightenment.

I decide to spend a bit more time with this mysterious young woman to consider whether she might be an appropriate vehicle to help me plunge deeper into myself. Without letting her know that I might be a prospective client, I plan to "interview" her to determine if I should hire her for a dose of QHHT. She again tells me her rates, which I think are high by American standards, and makes it clear that this will be a thoroughly professional arrangement. That is, I have to pay.

Each day during my week in Siwa, I watch sunrises and sunsets to honor Ra, the sun god. After watching the sunrise each morning, I frequently walk through awakening downtown Siwa (Siwans tend to be late risers) and shop at the market for local food, like falafel, warm pita bread, sugar cane juice and colorful fruit.

I see Monika the next morning at sunrise at the top of Shali and she asks about the session with the Oracle and wonders what is on my agenda.

Without the equinox to worry about, and with my meeting with the Oracle under my belt, I say I'm ready to find Alexander's tomb after a springy morning stroll around Siwa and a hearty breakfast in the dirt-floored, open-air dining room at the not-yet-buzzing Albabenshal Hotel.

"If I can believe the Oracle, Alexander's body and tomb are within walking distance," I continue. "They are mine to find precisely 2,338 years after the world's most illustrious conqueror was brought back to Egypt."

There are lots of twists, turns and theories about Alexander's last journey across Asia to Siwa, but here are some facts:

Alexander, who requested at the end of his life to be referred as the son of Zeus and Ammon, frequently said that he did not wish to be buried alongside his "human father" at Aegae in Macedon. According to many historians, including Quintus Curtius Rufus, the Roman author of the *Histories of Alexander the Great* in the first century AD, Alexander asked to be interred in the Temple of Zeus/Ammon, as it's known, here in Siwa.

Despite his apparent wishes, a funeral cortege was carrying his remains to Macedon until Ptolemy hijacked the funerary wagon in Syria. Ptolemy, who wound up ruling Egypt, and his soldiers took the body for interment in Memphis, still the center of the Macedon government in Egypt before Alexandria was completed.

According to Plutarch, Python of Catana and Seleucus were sent to a temple of the Greco-Egyptian deity Serapis to ask whether Alexander's body should remain in Memphis or be sent to Alexandria. The answer from the temple oracle prompted Ptolemy to rebury Alexander in the Soma (*soma* means "body" in Greek and gives us words like "psychosomatic"), Alexandria's main mausoleum, in 301 BC.

That Tomb of Alexander became the focal point for the Ptolemaic cult of Alexander the Great and was visited by the likes of Cleopatra, who is believed to have taken gold from the tomb to finance a war, and Julius Caesar when he was in Alexandria in 48 BC. The Roman Emperor Caracalla is said to have "relocated" some of the treasures in the grave when he dropped by in AD 215, but by 400, a local bishop wrote no one could find Alexander's tomb. "Even his own people know not its location," he proclaimed.

When Leo the African visited Alexandria in the 1500s, he wrote: "In the midst of the ruins of Alexandria, there still remains a small edifice, built like a chapel, worthy of notice on account of a remarkable tomb held in high honor by the Mahometans; in which sepulcher, they assert, is preserved the body of Alexander the Great...An immense crowd of strangers come thither, even from distant countries, for the sake of worshipping and doing homage to the tomb, on which they likewise frequently bestow considerable donations."

Naturally there were, and are still, numerous rumors and suppositions about the tomb's location. Although many continue to believe that Alexander's remains remain in the center of Alexandria, a stele says they were moved during the reign of Trebonianus Gallus in the middle of the third century AD to the Pantheon in Rome. That, I presume, is what prompted Seán Hemingway to place the tomb in the nearby Church of Santa Maria *sopra* Minerva.

The fact is that, until now, Alexander still hasn't been found, and the Egyptian Supreme Council for Antiquities has officially recognized over 140 search attempts for Alexander's tomb.

The list includes a search in 1850 by Ambroise Schilizzi, who announced the discovery of Alexander's alleged mummy and tomb inside the Nabi Daniel Mosque in Alexandria. In 1888, Heinrich Schielmann, who uncovered Troy and numerous other ancient Greek cities, attempted to locate Alexander's tomb within the Nabi Daniel Mosque, but he was denied permission to excavate. In 1995, Greek archaeologist Liana Souvaltzi announced that she had found Alexander's tomb in Siwa; in 2011 a program on the National Geographic channel purported that Alexander's body was in the Basilica Cattedrale Patriarcale di San Marco in Venice; and in 2014, Alexander's tomb was "found" at the Amphipolis Tomb in Macedonia.

The Oracle of Siwa told me that Alexander was returned to Siwa in AD 250 and, as you heard, summed it up in just a few words: "They brought him back and entombed him high."

"Look for the heart at the top of the mountain," the Oracle instructed me.

"So I'm going to look for Alexander's tomb today," I tell Monika at the top of Shali. "I don't think it was on the mountain we climbed, but I'll start with the Mountain of the Dead and go from there."

When we return to the hotel Monika introduces me to Luca, an Italian working for the European Union doing research on World War II military battle sites in Egypt, and a young Italian journalist and filmmaker named Ines who wants to interview her about quantum hypnosis. She asks if I want to join them for dinner, and I agree before heading off on my own quest the next morning.

The first place I check for Alexander the Great's tomb is at the tourist-filled Mountain of the Dead (though the local name Gebel al-Musabbarin is better translated as Mountain of the Embalmed) just north of Siwa. Embalmed Alexander could certainly have been entombed here, and I have a delightful time exploring tombs that date from Dynastic, Ptolemaic and Roman times. Most of the tombs have been looted and emptied over the years, and I don't see any rooms or paintings decorated in a style fit for a king or pharaoh.

Then I march to the Tombs of Ballad El-Room, a mound 17 kilometers northwest of Siwa. Many archaeologists posit that Alexander was entombed here by Romans. They quietly brought his remains to this site to keep him off the celebrity tour circuit in Alexandria, where he had become a god in death and attracted too many visitors.

I search for Alexander the Great throughout the Ballad El-Room tombs and find a note in Arabic at the entrance of one tomb that I think might mean something, and, next to it in broad daylight, a five-pound note. Although the Egyptian currency is worth only about 25 US cents it's rare to find money laying around in Egypt.

Are these omens?

I imagine that I've found the answer but it turns out I haven't. The Arabic note, Khaled tells me when I get back to the Albabenshal Hotel, is a sentimental exchange between a mother and her son.

"And the son's name isn't Alexander," Khaled observes.

Besides these discoveries, or non-discoveries really, my most noteworthy encounter of the day is a meeting with a military marching unit on the road to the tombs, not unlike the one I saw in Lebanon.

No, they aren't looking for Alexander.

I meet Monika, Luca and Ines for a three-hour dinner at the Shali Lodge and they tell me they've got a friend, an ace desert guide named Fathi Abdalla, who is a reliable desert safari driver and knowledgeable about everything Siwan. I agree that I'd love to go into the desert and swim in the salt sea and freshwater springs before I resume my search for the tomb of Alexander. We hire Fathi to take us into the desert the next day and I figure he might even have some insight into Alexander's current whereabouts.

Our gallivant in the desert blithely kicks off with a long roll down gigantic sand dunes and ends when I meditatively float in a salt lake before cleaning myself in a freshwater spring. The salt bath has inspired me, since then, to regularly take baths in Epsom salt ($MgSO4·7H2O$) which, if you use the right amount, exactly duplicates the elevated salt level found in Siwa's Brisket al-Marini Lake.

Then Fathi takes us to visit to his Siwa Astor Camp for tea and we chat about all the Roman tombs in Siwa, and my search for Alexander. He informs us of a Berber rumor about a cave at the top of a mountain that is reputed to have a noble buried in it.

He agrees to take me, Ines and Monika to the mountain the next day.

The following morning begins with another sunrise meditation at the top of Shali, and I become transfixed by the only purple house amid buildings that are uniformly of desert-muted, desert-blending natural colors. Who is the radical, I wonder, who brought the royal color purple to the Siwa Oasis?

That afternoon, Fathi takes the three of us to the Adrere Amellal EcoLodge, which is where Prince Charles once stayed with the Friends of Siwa Association. There's no electricity, mobile phones are banned and the buildings in the 40-room resort are constructed from salt rock and illuminated by candles. Fathi tells us to climb the flat Adrere Amellal, which is translated as White Mountain, and catch the sunset, but says nothing more about Alexander.

It's an easy walk to the top that, like the top of the mountain I climbed a few days ago with Monika, is gloriously flat, like a lunar landscape. While Ines interviews Monika for a documentary she's preparing for Italian television, I walk around the mountaintop three times to get wonderful 360° views of all Siwa. There's a top of the world feeling, and, well, I wouldn't mind being entombed here myself.

A large heart has been formed with stones at one side of the mountain, and I recall that Fathi said many people who climb the mountain add stones to expand the heart. I also recall that the Oracle told me to "Look for the heart at the top of the mountain." I promptly find an appropriate rock and make the heart a bit larger.

Fathi had suggested I look for a cave hidden in a crevice and made a crude sketch of the mountaintop in my notebook. I follow his directions, find the crevice in less than fifteen minutes and, when I enter the cave within the crevice, I spend half an hour inside. I photograph evidence that, though I don't see any tangible physical remains, indicates Alexander, or someone of royal stature, had been interred here.

I conduct my initial investigation objectively and scientifically, dispassionately dismissing any notion that this could actually be Alexander's final resting place. But then something inexplicable, an odd feeling of certainty, overwhelms me, and, for the first time since I was a kid, I whisper to myself with absolute conviction "Eureka!" I have found it.

When I meet Ines and Monika coming down the mountain, and later see Fathi, I wonder if I should let them know that I feel certain that I have found the tomb of Alexander? Should I show the photos to the Egyptian Supreme Council for Antiquities when I return to Cairo? Should I propose changing the mountain's name to The Tomb of Alexander the Great? Should I broadcast locally that I found the crevice, explored the cave and discovered the old Berber rumor to be true?

I recall the Oracle's words: "Find him but let him rest eternally in peace. Keep it to yourself."

When we come down the mountain, I book a quantum hypnosis session with "The Woman in the Scarf," despite her extortionist London rates. The next morning she guides me into a meditative state that's comparable to the sensation that I regularly experience during my morning meditations. My mind is empty, there's no noise, I'm capable of doing nothing, I'm totally in the present. But I could have done this by myself.

"You're close, but you didn't go far enough, because you seem stuck in your usual meditative state and content with that," Monika says when the hour-long session is concluded. "Let's try another session tomorrow to see if you can go a bit deeper, or if you're willing to go a bit deeper, and take you to your past and the past."

"Actually, I've got to get back to the MedTrek," I say. "Can't we do it some other time, maybe in Alexandria or London?"

"It's better to do it in Siwa," she says. "There's something special about Siwa. Things happen in Siwa. It's Siwa."

It takes two more Siwa sessions before I experience a time-traveling state to a place that's obviously influenced by my walk around the sea and exposure to Alexander. I see myself walking side-by-side with Alexandros in different places, past and present, reliving some of our earlier conversations, notably the discussions about alcoholism, his father and women. I'm not sure, though, if I am being tele-transported back to his era or if he's being tele-transported to the present day. But we, Alexander and I, are together, and he tells me that he used to see Ammon in his dreams when he was in a similar hypnotic state.

During the session, I see Alexander on his deathbed and he cracks "I am dying with the help of too many physicians," which I think is an appropriately amusing comment not only about the profession of medicine in his own world but also about the health care business today. As soldiers come to pay their last respects, I see him slightly and slowly raise his right hand and make genuine eye contact with each of them.

I'm not quite sure what's going on. Why do I see the scenes with Alexander? What are the messages and guidance coming from my subconscious? What does this have to say about my own life and journey? Why do I have a feeling of comfort, warmth, and security after such a profound experience? Just what is being revealed here?

Whatever happened, wherever we were or whenever it was, the "trip" requires so much energy, or maybe it was concentration, that I am absolutely wiped out and exhausted when Monika brings me back to present reality.

I try to describe my feelings to her, but can't really put them in words. In fact, a photo best captures my tranquilized or traumatized or comatose state. But unlike the sadness and terror I experienced with the heart acupuncture fifteen years earlier, I seem to be actually calm and content with who I am, where I am, what I'm doing, who I'm doing it with and where I'm going.

A couple months later, I get an email from "The Woman in the Scarf" who's observing a full moon at Siwa and has some channeled information from an "esoteric circle session" declaring that Alexander the Great "is well respected and an extraordinary vision of spreading light on Earth. We exist today because of Alexander the Great. If not for him, it is very likely that we wouldn't be here today."

Well, there you go.

"The Woman in the Scarf" will go on to explore the Nile and its temples on a yacht serendipitously called *Alexander the Great* before participating in the fasting, praying and eating rhythm of Ramadan. Here's an excerpt from a story about her in *Egypt Today*:

CAIRO – 10 June 2017: When Polish-born Monika Sleszynska moved to London in her early 20s, the glimpse into Ramadan she gleaned from fasting Muslim colleagues in college didn't make sense to her.

"Why stuff yourself with food late at night and not eat during the day? This was against anything I knew about dieting, which was the only reason I could give fasting any credit," says Sleszynska, who is a solo traveler and return visitor to Egypt since 2012. "Having a taste of the Ramadan in Egypt made me realize how little I knew this religious practice of fasting in my earlier years. I can now see how the month of Ramadan affects the entire year, life and nation."

"The air becomes permeated with sacredness and peace," she explained. "Just a thought of joining others who have been dedicating themselves to a spiritual practice for a month since their childhood by design and participating in a ritual which has been performed for several hundreds of years is thrilling. It makes me realize that I am joining a sacred experience created by billions of souls."

On my last day in Siwa, I walk to Cleopatra's pool for a final swim and a mint tea before again visiting the Temple of the Oracle. When I'm sitting quietly on the tomb I reflect on Alexander's legacy and what happened to him when he left Siwa.

As I said, he bee-lined from Siwa through the desert back to Memphis, and I remember Mary Renault's evocation in *The Persian Boy*: "In spring, Alexander returned to Tyre. He sacrificed, and held some more games and contests. It seemed he was asking the gods' goodwill for a new campaign. When spring turned to summer in 330 BC, the spies reported him on the march for Babylon and the eastern parts of his empire, including Afghanistan, what is now Pakistan and south to the Indian Ocean."

Although it may or may not have had anything to do with his session with the Oracle, chroniclers and historians contend that Alexander went through a life and mood change during this period. They mention increasing loneliness, groundless fears, abundant anger, and growing impatience. They claim he was increasingly suspicious, obsessed by visions of the supernatural, overly reliant on soothsayers and worried about the situation in Greece. Some attribute it to "his inexcusable fondness for drink," others to the impact and adoption of oriental customs.

Indeed, historical descriptions sound like stories you might hear about a drunk after an excessive binge. One of his worst debaucheries led to the destruction of the palace in Persepolis, when he encouraged revelers to set it aflame. Another of his impulsive-while-intoxicated moves was the killing of his once-trusted adviser, Cleitus the Black, in what seems to have been a drunken brawl.

I personally choose to remember Alexandros, after tracing his steps, as one of history's most original and successful military commanders and the creator of an empire that altered the ancient world and would spread Hellenic creativity, ethos and spirit for almost three hundred years.

"The glory and the memory of man will always belong to the ones who follow their great visions," says Ptolmey in a fitting tribute. "And the greatest of these is the one they now call 'Megas Alexandros' – the greatest Alexander of them all."

I leave Siwa and choose to ignore, just as I choose to ignore Alexander's defects and flaws, its sand and dust, garbage and wreckage, noisy street work and the fact that it is hardly a pristine, untouched and undiscovered refuge. I remember it instead as the blessed home of the Oracle; the spot for magic equinoxes; the place Alexander the Great learned he was descended from a god; the spot for rest and rejuvenation from the MedTrek in the middle of the desert; and my first exposure to quantum hypnosis healing technique sessions.

After a week at the Siwa Oasis where my consorting and consulting with the Oracle of Ammon gave me an inside scoop about Alexander the Great's past and a signpost for the future of my MedTrek, I bee-line on a bus to Mersa Matruh on the Mediterranean Sea to resume my hike to Libya.

I smile when my bus stops at the café where I first saw "The Woman in the Scarf," although she's not there on this trip. Then, on arrival at the bus station in Mersa Matruh, I get a cab to the Beau Site Hotel, where I have stored some of my gear.

There are twelve other people staying at the Medside hotel, but it's still a bit too chilly to play in the sand or swim in the water. I walk onto the hotel's beach and avoid the eyes of the Tourism Police manning a desk at the door to sneak out the back door and walk downtown where I seek to get rid of a "virus" on my iPad and iPhone ("I'm convinced both are tapped," I tell anyone who will listen), have a shave and buy a branch of dates. Then I have a leisurely fresh fish dinner and am not surprised to see the armed escort arrive and park outside before I finish the meal. They always act like they've scored a winning World Cup goal when they find me.

Again I'm told that the Egyptian police insist on providing me with an armed escort as I MedTrek west on a coast that will be even more tightly patrolled and controlled by the country's army, navy and air forces.

The next morning, after I meditate on my balcony in rhythm to the rising sun and reflect on my time in a dusty, dirt-floored hotel built out of compressed mud in Siwa, I give the Beau Site a decent load of desert-sanded laundry (most of it worn more than twice) that had accumulated since Al Alamein ten days ago.

I again take off on the seaside behind the hotel to attempt to avoid the early morning watchful eyes of the policemen stationed at the front door. I head west, but within fifteen minutes am stymied by a military base and private homes. I have to walk back past the hotel to the *corniche* and follow the signs west out of town to "BEACHES."

The four-man police escort, in their red pickup, finds me after a couple kilometers and we continue together to sandy Cleopatra Beach, where I pause for a selfie with the queen ("Posing next to Cleopatra at a Mediterranean beach named after her west of Mersa Matruh, Egypt"), and, because of the military presence, they insist that I walk, accompanied by two armed policemen, back toward the main road alongside a lake with some nice looking resorts (one is named Eagles – a big theme in Alexander's time) and housing complexes. I veer, and at this stage it's still early enough in the day that the police don't mind my diversions, towards the Porto Matruh complex owned and managed by the same group as Porto Marina in El Alamein. It's almost the same color scheme but the hotel is closed, and my armed entourage and I continue through the fields toward a mosque.

We walk through a number of uninhabited residential compounds, some of which have been transformed into military barracks for young soldiers during the winter and spring. Despite my police escort, military officials continue to insist that we all, me and my bodyguards, leave the sea and walk on the International Coastal Road a few kilometers inland "for security reasons."

Egyptian soldiers frequently tell us during the day that this Bedouin-inhabited area is unsafe because of "hostile Arabs or uninvited Libyans," though I encounter neither. I keep seeing advertisements for ISIS and wonder why the terrorist group has chosen such a blatant advertising campaign and established retail outlets in Egypt. It turns out that Egypt's ISIS is a large and legitimate company. Great name and no confusing conflict here, because, as I mentioned, Egyptians call the ISIS terrorist group Daesh.

The trend has been set for the whole walking day: bits of main road, a few lovely beaches (there are three main ones west of Mersa Matruh – Cleopatra, Ubayyad and Agiba), dirt roads through little villages with mosques and kids and farmers tending to crops. There is lots of sand, turquoise-colored water, summer-only seasonal housing compounds, and military installations. And I have to keep going inland to get around most of them.

I get to the abandoned Alobodied Beach with the usual deserted apartment complexes and have a long discussion with some soldiers until the military again sends us inland because "there are Arabs living here." I'm a little irritated with the police detail for favoring the road walk to the beach walk and we split up. I go into silent mode for an hour as I MedTrek on the beach until I hit a large complex that has become a "MILITRY" (sic) zone prohibiting MedTrekkers, photos and everything else. The army has taken it over for the season, or maybe forever, and I'm surprised that the ostentatious Carlos Beau Rivage hotel is open next door.

When I finally return to the road, I've lost the police escort after my little escapade. They've either abandoned me or, more likely, can't find me.

I continue solo on the International Coast Road and beach until I get to the long white-sanded Agiba Beach (billboards for Agiba City show an attempt at modernization) with inviting coves that attract fishermen if not (yet) bathers and swimmers. I zip back to Mersa Matruh in a taxi (E £50) and ask to be dropped downtown, which looks mellow and attractive as men laze at cafes and frequent the barbershops.

The Tourism Police, and two vehicles, are waiting in the lobby after I eat breakfast the next day to follow my taxi back to the horseshoe-shaped Agiba Beach with blissfully clear water that changes in color from turquoise to almost white due to the sea sand. Though not quite as dramatic, it reminds me of Zakynthos in Greece.

Considered one of Egypt's most attractive stretches on the Mediterranean Sea, Agiba Beach, to The Idiot anyway, also represents the end of the over-developed Egyptian coast and the beginning of a sparsely populated seaside that extends to the Egypt/Libya border.

That's the direction that I expect to MedTrek today, along a lovely seaside road with very few Bedouins and lots of military bases, though the four-man armed police escort, now led by a new head honcho with a few more stars on his uniform, blithely informs me this won't happen "for security reasons."

Just beyond Agiba Beach the military lookout posts are indicative, by their proximity, of the increase in military control that I've seen building up since Matruh. My armed police escort is against my walking another inch west and an English-speaking Arabic teacher we meet between villages says that it's foolish to walk solo.

"The Bedouins and Arabs will think you're after their women, and

Libyans will think you're easy picking," he said. "I don't feel safe walking here, and you're fooling yourself if you think you're safe."

The concept that I'm chasing Bedouin wives is, from my perspective, the best explanation for practicing caution that I've heard so far.

I send a GPS and take some photographs of the seaside, but I'm well aware this could be the end of the western MedTrek segment in Egypt. I reluctantly return to Matruh with the policemen and en route decide that I must see the Libyan border and the towns of Sidi Barrani and Sallum before I toss in the towel, or *keffiyeh*.

With some frustration, I post:

"Mersa Matruh, Egypt – A constant military presence on the coast and an objection to my walking any further by my armed police contingent have pretty much ended the Egypt segment of the MedTrek.

The Egyptian military and police will not allow The Idiot to continue walking on the Mediterranean coast after he had MedTrekked 45 kilometers west of Mersa Matruh to Agiba Beach "due to security concerns and precautions." They do, however, permit a coastal walkabout in Saluum at the Egypt/Libya border and have given me permission to hike a few parts of the coast with an armed escort tomorrow."

The military and police theoretically restrict my access to the coast between Agiba Beach and Libya, but I casually take some short hikes and ultimately walk past one of the last army outposts in Egypt before arriving in Sallum. When I enter the Bedouin community near the Libya border, I'm met by a police contingent that will accompany me along the sea and up the curvaceous mountain road to the Libyan border.

Although there's no tourist activity, Sallum has a bit of border-crossing buzz and, when I learn that it's the ancient Roman port of Baranis and has a World War II Commonwealth war cemetery, I get the feeling that Egypt's westernmost point on the Mediterranean has seen it all, though Alexander never made it this far.

A Tourism Police officer and I stroll on the seaside promenade and watch a few fisherman and bathers as we approach the high mountain on a windy road that leads to the border crossing seven kilometers away.

Sallum is definitely an end-of-the-road town with just a few people and lots of overloaded trucks going up the zigzag hill road into Libya. I make it as far as the last Egyptian checkpoint, but they won't let me go further to discover if the Libyans will grant me a visa, which, if it occurred, would have made a great news item/tweet in this travel-restricted era.

I am permitted to approach the border, but am told not to risk leaving Egypt and trying to enter the country next door. That, my police handler told me, "might indicate that you're sympathetic to Daesh, and you could be detained if you try to reenter Egypt."

I try to explain that I want to go to the Libya side of the border to see if they'll issue me a visa on the spot and then message President Trump to let him know that Libya is still open to American visitors. But my Egyptian armed police escort isn't too hot on the idea (even most Egyptians don't go to Libya anymore), although they've already been assured that I don't plan to join Daesh/ISIS.

I tell the Tourism Police that after Alexander occupied Egypt, he made an ally of Cyrene, an ancient Greek and Roman city near present-day Shahhat, Libya. It was the oldest and most important of the five Greek cities in the region. It gave eastern Libya the classical name Cyrenaica that it has retained to modern times.

No one seems to care.

Looking down on the seaside town of Sallum and back at the Egyptian coast from the hillside border between Egypt and Libya, I take some photographs before I drop by the police station prior to leaving town. I am again told that the coast, which looks so peaceful from the hilltop, is closed and dangerous. We drive back to Agiba on a road that parallels the coast, which I haven't taken before, and, though there are more military outposts than usual, it's right next to the sea, and there's little traffic. I figure it would be fine to walk on and I'm about to raise that point when, karmically, I receive the following email:

"This replaces the Travel Warning issued on December 23, 2016. A number of terrorist groups, including ISIS, have committed multiple deadly attacks in Egypt, targeting government officials and security forces, public venues, tourist sites, civil aviation and other modes of public transportation, and a diplomatic facility. There are also reports of attacks on security forces in Egypt's Western Desert, the large, mostly uninhabited area west of the Nile Valley, and in Egypt's border areas." – US Department of State

What's next for The Idiot who is on the verge of completing his 20-year project to walk around the Mediterranean Sea? Will he keep trying to walk through Gaza and Sinai or on prohibited parts of Egypt's coast? Will he enter Libya? Should he forget walking and again time travel back to the era of Alexander the Great with more quantum hypnosis? Or perhaps follow the Oracle's suggestion and go directly to Carthage, where he has not been since the 2011 revolution?

After venturing further west on the Mediterranean than Alexander the Great had, I return to Mersa Matruh and, the next morning, enjoy a casual urban ten-kilometer roundtrip walk to Rommel Beach to visit the World War II museum. I walk through downtown with my uniformed minders, return to the hotel and decide to take a bus to Cairo. A Tourism Police agent that I nickname Baksheesh Mahmoud (he's one of the few policemen who keeps asking for *baksheesh*) accompanies me to the station, and I give him a small tip.

On the bus I meet a Russian from Uzbekistan who has 200 camels and says their milk is a health drink and their urine has medicinal value. He offers me a sample. Then I admire a woman's henna handicraft during the ride. In Cairo I spend two nights relaxing near the Pyramids at Le Meridien Hotel, crowded with lots of Chinese tourists who local taxi drivers say they don't appreciate because they always travel in groups.

In Le Meridien lobby I meet travel agent Mohamed Hendy, who is accompanying a faux journalist scheduled to interview me. I immediately cancel the interview when I learn that the journalist wants me to give him $100 to be interviewed. No free press here!

This gives me an opportunity to chat with Mohamed, who has an apartment at Marassi because "it's the most expensive on the Mediterranean and it's the best." He tells me (1) that the derelict and decrepit homes on the coast are in worse shape than usual due to the 2011 revolution and subsequent economic woes and (2) "Egypt was lucky that in 2013 the situation here, punctuated by the tension between the ruling Islamists and the people, didn't result in a civil war, which would have been much worse than what we're seeing in Libya and Syria today."

The palatial Mena House in the shadows of the Pyramids is an ideal spot for my last lunch of Egyptian, Lebanese and other Middle Eastern delicacies before I fly to Paris for a week of French cuisine. A "History of the Pyramids" bronze plaque in the garden indicates that I'm at the exact spot that Alexander the Great stood when he last looked at Egypt's Pyramids before his departure in 331 BC. I grab a taxi to the airport and during the ride the driver demonstrates how to say "I love you" and "I'm in a hurry" with different honks of his horn.

"Welcome to Egypt," he says when he drops me off for my flight.

# MEDTREK MILESTONE #13

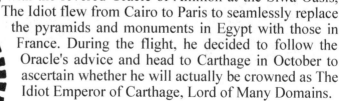

After MedTrekking across Egypt to the Libya border and consulting with the revered Oracle of Ammon at the Siwa Oasis, The Idiot flew from Cairo to Paris to seamlessly replace the pyramids and monuments in Egypt with those in France. During the flight, he decided to follow the Oracle's advice and head to Carthage in October to ascertain whether he will actually be crowned as The Idiot Emperor of Carthage, Lord of Many Domains.

# FOLLOW THE IDIOT

## CHAPTER PHOTOS

## CHAPTER MAP

# Crowned The Idiot Emperor of Carthage

"There are no more worlds to conquer!"
– Alexander the Great

"Men of Macedon, we're going home. May all those who come here after us know when they see this altar, that *titans* were once here." – Alexander the Great

---

After my two glorious MedTrek outings in Egypt, I follow the Oracle's instructions to wrap up my 20-year gallivant around the Mediterranean Sea at Carthage in Tunisia, which I visited frequently from 1997 to 2003 when I was living in the south of France and writing a series of special reports for the *International Herald Tribune*.

During each reportorial trip in those days, I would frequently fetch some fresh Mediterranean air between scores of interviews and rounds of writing in Tunis by visiting the beckoning remains of the ancient city of Carthage and nearby Sidi Bou Said, a hilltop village where every house, every building, almost everything, is blue and white, and each home, according to author Eric Newby, resembles a "*bijou villa*."

Carthage – founded by the Phoenician queen Dido in 800 BC and whose story of her encounter with Aeneas, the founder of the Roman people, is told in Vergil's *Aeneid* – was the powerful capital of an empire that dominated the Mediterranean for almost six hundred years. Alexander, who wanted to be "lord of all," had a serious grudge against the Carthaginians after their lengthy but unsuccessful stand against him in Tyre. And that encouraged him to put Carthage on his intended hit list of future conquests.

"From the Persian Gulf, our expedition will sail 'round Africa into Libya as far as the Pillars of Heracles," Alexander pronounced, producing notebooks that reveal his plans to sail out of the mouth of the Euphrates to North Africa. "From the pillars, all the interior of Libya becomes ours, and so the whole of Asia will belong to us, and the limits of our empire, in that direction, will be those which God has made also the limits of the earth."

Carthage was so important that Alexander even had an alternative Plan B. If necessary, he would construct a fleet of 1,000 ships in Phoenicia for the assault on Carthage and also build a road through Libya, found new cities, erect new temples and monuments and transport a chunk of the Asian population to North Africa.

The image of Alexander going into the sea didn't end there. A miniature painting composed in the late sixteenth century by an Indian artist portrays Alexander as a turbaned king in a bathysphere going for a deep dive in the sea. The portrayal was apparently inspired by a Persian poem that depicts Alexander taking to the water after leading his armies all over the known world.

The Oracle of Siwa requested that I complete my two-decades-long MedTrek in Carthage on Alexander's behalf. Because of the political and social changes that resulted from the revolution known as the Arab Spring when it was launched here in 2011, I'm especially thrilled to be back in Tunisia for the first time in over a decade.

Despite dictatorial leaders like Habib Bourguiba and his successor Zine El Abidine Ben Ali, who was president from 1987 until his ouster in 2011, Tunisia has always been considered North Africa's most progressive country. Polygamy was outlawed in the 1950s, and divorce and abortion are permitted. But it hasn't been a truly global power since 264 BC, when Carthage began to lose its fleets and bases in Sicily and Sardinia.

"There is nothing to fear," the Oracle said to me. "You will be entering Tunisia and Carthage on behalf of Megas Alexandros with my complete protection and support. But concentrate on Carthage rather than walking the entire coast or you'll get into trouble. End your MedTrek in Carthage."

The Oracle's suggested (well, more than suggested) plan fits with the timely conclusion of my 20-year MedTrek but just before coming to Carthage I lunch with a friend in California who insists that, "You won't be capable of stopping the MedTrek even if the Oracle told you to. I bet you'll keep on walking."

We'll see.

Visiting central Tunis for the first time since 2003, I notice troops, police, razor wire and tanks on the central Avenue de France. But the medina, the souk and government offices, or Kasbah, look almost exactly as they did when I was here decades ago, though the hectic sales pressure and badgering by shop owners seems diminished and muted.

My most moving moment in the capital is a visit to the dignified memorial in the Bardo National Museum for twenty-one foreigners and one Tunisian museum employee killed during a terrorist attack on March 18, 2015. The names of the deceased are listed on a mounted marble plaque in the foyer with flags from the victims' ten different countries of origin.

I talk to a Tunisian museum worker who was here the day of the attack and listen to her vivid description and recollection of the surprise and shock she felt – and the subsequent therapy she underwent to help her cope with it.

Then I visit the museum, which has been reconfigured with a new entrance since I was last here, and I'm again enchanted by tiles and mosaics from the Punic period, including one with the head of Ocean and another portraying Odysseus tied to the mast of a ship to rebuff the alluring call of the Sirens.

Seeing Odysseus sparks a reflection on my almost completed twenty-year walk around the Mediterranean Sea. My reverie continues during a coffee at a wonderfully inviting restaurant called Fandouk in the middle of the souk, where I buy a pink-and-blue baseball hat to replace a *Follow the Idiot* cap I give to a young boy.

I meet the owner of Fandouk and discuss the possibility of a party at the restaurant to celebrate the completion of my 20-year walk around the Mediterranean Sea if, indeed, I'm crowned The Idiot Emperor of Carthage, Lord of Many Domains, as the Oracle predicts. We even begin concocting a menu consisting of national dishes representing every country in which I MedTrekked – from Morocco, Spain and France to Lebanon, Israel and Egypt and everywhere in between – during my 1998-2018 walk.

I photograph an *I Heart Tunis* sculpture on Avenue de France before I check into the Royal Victoria Hotel, which used to be the British Embassy. Nearby is the Bab el Bhar archway at the Porte de France that separates the contemporary part of the city from the labyrinthine souk.

My second floor room looks out on the Bab el Bhar gate between the buzzy ancient Arabic souk and the equally buzzy contemporary Avenue de France. A team of workmen is "covering" the archway for restoration, so I got here just in time. I walk the city streets for the first time in more than fifteen years to get the flavor of post-revolution Tunisia. Tunisians, I've always found, are genetically hospitable and friendly, but I personally appreciate them because many, even the police and soldiers, compliment not only my French, but also my French accent, which never happens in France where one former prime minister told me "you speak with the accent and vocabulary of a Spanish cow."

I don't go to Carthage immediately, because I first want to get a sense of the changes on the country's Mediterranean coast before visiting the ancient and historic maritime trading center. Fortunately, I have a free week before I'm scheduled to stand in for Alexander the Great and be crowned The Idiot Emperor of Carthage, Lord of Many Domains. I'll use the time to better get to know my future subjects and meet foreign visitors to my realm.

I get into MedTrek mode by walking, often barefoot, on the beaches north and south of Tunis. I encounter working fishermen, eat fish dinners, observe grand looking camels, see sunbathing flamingoes, pass dilapidated resorts, explore new hotels, stroll on wild and urban beaches, and admire the mostly Russian sunbathers. I am particularly interested in observing the fickle weather, studying the visiting tourists, congratulating hard-working Tunisians and finding a solution to the overwhelming amount of garbage on many of the beaches.

I first follow the rocky coast from Sidi Bou Said in the direction of Algeria to Al Mersa, and the only people I see are fishermen and lots of signs saying in French and Arabic, "Keep the beach clean," which, often, it is not. It's such a delight being back on the Med that I am even transfixed by an octopus as fishermen come in with their catches and sell them on makeshift tables.

After negotiating the rocks and not getting wet (a fisherman at the western end of Sidi Bou Said tells me the coast is walkable but points out one dicey spot), I continue barefoot on the beach through Al Mersa, where there's a no-longer-functioning bathhouse on the sand. There are lots of relatively fancy restaurants and hotels, but most of them are closed after the summer season. I notice that many luxurious apartment complexes have been built and drop by the new Four Seasons in Gammarth Bay. The buzz is that Tunisian tourism is finally making a comeback after a downturn that began with the 2011 revolution.

On reaching Raoued I stop for an hour at a *salon de thé* at precisely high noon after 20 kilometers. I have a long chat with the owner and some customers who compliment my accent and tell me there are no roads accessing the coast for the next fifteen kilometers.

I meet a sweet camel halfway through a sandy MedTrekking day and briefly think I could buy, rent, borrow, steal, beg or hire the darling dromedary as my MedTrekking companion, aide-de-camp and emergency transport in Tunisia. Instead, being true to my feet and quest, I simply chat with my new BFF for a few minutes before walking another mile for a camel (recalling the 1949 "I'd walk a mile for a Camel" cigarette advertisement that was popular in the United States).

I continue on the Avenue Mediterraneé until the road ends and notice that a lot of Raoued Plage projects seem to have been abandoned. But the future takes shape a few kilometers down the beach where an under-construction port, with dykes and a nearby housing project, portends to be "*l'avenir de la banlieu nord,*" or "the future of the northern suburb."

I continue, after fording a river on a sandbar (finding shallow sandbars is now an innate part of my MedTrek abilities) to Kalâat el-Andalous beach and walk inland into a town and commune located 50 kilometers north of Tunis.

After MedTrekking 39 kilometers west toward Algeria on the sandy Tunisian coast yesterday, much of it barefoot, I return to La Goulette in the port in Tunis and begin my walk east towards Hammamet in the direction of the Libya border. My plan is to spend a week hiking to the touristic beaches in Sousse and Monastir.

I allow myself one pleasant distraction during the first days of my MedTrek in Tunisia: I feel compelled to take a break and get $1 daily shaves each afternoon. And I often follow that time out with one of the other delights of walking on the Mediterranean Sea in Tunisia: fresh mint tea and a bottle of sparkling Garci mineral water. Then I buy a branch of fresh dates, an inexpensive market staple in Tunisia, to complete my mid-afternoon respite.

The easy walk on the sand from Nabeul to Hammamet includes a lovely marsh filled with pink flamingos, a naked swim, a 1.5-hour lunch, strolls through chic hotels with infinity pools, walks into resorts closed after the summer season and encounters with Tunisians out for a Sunday afternoon at the beach.

I set up base camp in a spacious, central, vacationy two-story Airbnb in Hammamet with access to everything the town has to offer. Early the next day, I take off on a rainy and blustery morning, heading past the cemetery and the medina along the beachfront promenade. I continue for a few kilometers to the archaeological site of Pupput, a Roman city that today has partly disappeared. A Russian-filled tourist zone with all the usual trimmings, from expansive hotels to beachside bars, has been built over the major part of the ancient site.

Soon after I start on the path, the weather changes from rainy to stormy. I'm not sure if this is an auspicious and favorable omen or a forecast of impending disaster and doom. Or maybe neither.

In any event, I am the only visitor appreciating the intriguing mosaics at the Roman imperial ruins of Pupput during the rainstorm until I meet a Ministry of Culture employee who tells me he trained at the Getty in Venice, Italy. He mentions that Pupput includes a necropolis with 5,000 tombs and walks with me to a number of intricate Roman mosaics, probably from the second and third centuries, featuring fish, serpents and swastikas that have been spared from urbanization. I ask why there are no other visitors and he says, "Russians just want to get tan."

I realize I'm facing an in-and-out-of-the-rain 24-kilometer MedTrekking day through a string of all-inclusive resorts filled with lots of Russians and a very few Germans, all happy to eat and drink to their stomach's content. I find it odd that the "bad" weather doesn't deter the overwhelming number of vacationing Russian visitors from "sunbathing" and taking photographs. They're all on the beach, despite the very windy, blustery day, fighting the waves, standing tall and talking in bikinis, and taking photos of kids modeling for their mothers. I post an amusing "Where Is The Idiot Today?" item featuring a sexy Russian in a bikini under the pretense of conducting a sociological study of Russian vacation habits. In fact, I carefully take notes and photographs to better understand how Russian tourists behave on Mediterranean beaches in Tunisia. The information might come in handy when I'm emperor.

I walk into the Yasmine Port where I have a couscous lunch at Le Cap restaurant and, during one of the more serious thunderstorms, bite into the hottest pepper I've ever tasted. A waiter claims he knew I was American because, he says, "You speak with 'more throat' than Arabs even when you speak French" and tells me that the way to temper the hot pepper is with a spoonful of olive oil rather than a few liters of water. I obediently gulp two big spoonfuls of olive oil to reduce the intense burning caused by the innocent-looking green pepper.

After lunch, I have the wet promenade in Port Yasmine all to myself. I ignore the spa and massages at Alhambra Hotel in Yasmine El Hammamet, the last suburb, and enjoy a wild and windy 10-kilometer stroll on a vacant beach until I get to a place called Essouleum/Bouficha. One good thing about a storm is that it empties many beaches and provides a wide and virginal path for a MedTrekker.

It rarely takes long for the sun to return on the Mediterranean. I amble toward Sousse and Monastir in new weather and the next few sunny days seem to make both Russians and Tunisians much more convivial. A fisherman near Sousse offers me a calamari for dinner and I notice that nuts and fruit, rather than junk food and ice cream, are the best-selling products on Tunisian beaches. I post about Russian female tourists gleefully exercising in the sun.

A few days later, it's another glorious barefoot and shirtless hike in the sun along the now peaceful, tranquil Mediterranean through the hotel-infested beach at Kantaoui Bay. I intentionally stop at the hotel where 38

European tourists were killed in a terrorist attack on the beach in June 2015.

I appreciated and applauded the memorial at the Bardo Museum in Tunis, and I'm scandalized that there is no memorial commemorating the victims here.

"We don't want to remind our guests of a terrible incident that happened here so long ago," an employee of the Steigenberger Kantaoui Bay Hotel tells me in reference to the absence of any memorial commemorating the foreign tourists, including 30 British nationals, killed in a mass shooting by a terrorist here just over two years earlier.

The hotel, which had a different name and management at the time of the attack, certainly hasn't improved security.

The Idiot, with a full backpack, is able to wander in off the beach, get free drinks at an open bar at the pool and use the Wi-Fi for twenty minutes in the lobby without attracting any attention from the security staff. Lax security and a slow police response were partly to blame, says the official report, for the successful terrorist attack in 2015.

My complaints to everyone who will listen about the lack of a memorial and the lack of security result in me being rudely escorted off the premises for making a scene. After this affront, I have a nonchalant, non-eventful day that includes a rare sunburn (gosh, a big toe blister and a sunburn on the same MedTrek outing) and a *shawarma*, which is a shaved meat sandwich on pita bread, while strolling through Port El Kantaoui. I choose that over a sit-down lunch at the Hard Rock Café.

I'm again forced to pose for a selfie with another insistent camel before he'll let me pass a section of Mediterranean seaside north of Sousse. The obstinate camel patrolling the seaside requests, in Arabic, that he and The Idiot "try to make the same facial expression for our selfie."

The next day's MedTrek, which begins just south of the space-age Enfida-Hammamet International Airport, which is used primarily by charters to bring tourists to the hotel-rich coast, illustrates how the Med can go from wild and angry one day to calm and serene the next. Although the sunbathers are limited to mainly Russians at the hotels (The Idiot dropped into one hotel at Palmyra Beach for free coffee and snacks), there are lots of Tunisian fishermen who let their poles do the work – and a young guy who offers me one of his ten octopi.

The advantage of buying fish, or *poissons,* in Tunisia, compared to many other countries in North Africa and the eastern Mediterranean, is that French, rather than Arabic, is used to identify the purchase. That's a big plus for consumers like me who are often very frustrated buying fish without speaking Arabic or Turkish or Greek, and I enjoy talking to the young fisherman about how to cook his octopus.

During the next 33-kilometer-long day, I wind up walking into and through Sousse on beaches, some of them still dreadfully dirty due to the storm, filled with Russians and fish farms, to arrive at the aptly named Monaco Hotel just as I hear the call to prayer at 4:51 p.m.

I'm gloomy, glum and grumpy about the vast amount of garbage I'm finding on the Mediterranean coast in Tunisia. Every time I see a seaside trash heap, I resolutely remind myself that it will all be removed immediately following my coronation as The Idiot Emperor of Carthage next Monday at noon.

The next day's walk into Monastir is a sweet and easy stroll on the seaside sand, and, despite Russian sunbathers and piles of garbage, it's aesthetically pleasing (there are camels, horses and all sorts of other treats) and meditatively satisfying.

I take lots of pictures of daily life on the beach but do have one rude awakening.

The genial general manager of One Resort hotel asks me, after he invites me to have a coffee, why I have a protruding gut with all the walking I do. I blame it on my shirt, but he's skeptical and insists, "No, it's your gut." This makes me feel very self-conscious but doesn't stop me, a couple hours later, from enjoying a leisurely lunch near the palace that Habib Bourguiba, Tunisia's founding father and the country's leader from independence in 1956 to 1987, used to frequent at the edge of Monastir (which gets its name from the Greek word for monastery). I order a dish of spaghetti *aux fruits de mer* and eat it on the Mediterranean seaside while watching fishermen unload their boats before I walk into town and visit a massive mausoleum containing the remains of aforementioned former president Habib Bourguiba, who died in April 2000.

I spend a couple hours walking around the Ribat of Monastir, an Islamic fort built in 796 during the Muslim conquest of North Africa, through the port, and along the beach. Then, I recall the Oracle's advice not to walk too much around Tunisia, and, at some point in central Monastir, realize its time to return to Carthage to prepare for my coronation.

Everything is peachy when I move my base camp to Sidi Bou Said, a little paradise with blue-and-white buildings and cobblestone streets, just a few kilometers north of Carthage. Now, at 7:30 a.m., I'm drinking Nescafé at a table in the courtyard and waiting for someone to bring me a breakfast that, I learn from a British guy who says he works as a translator for the CIA and is taking lessons to perfect his "social media Arabic," is pretty meager.

I spend the day casually walking the course of tomorrow's16-kilometer Run In Carthage so I won't feel compelled to enter the race. The last time I was involved in an organized running race, you might remember, was in Greece, when I participated in the Alexander the Great Marathon from Pella, Alexander's birthplace in ancient Macedon, to Thessaloniki. And, as you'll recall, I walked the entire 42.195-kilometer course and finished second to last in just over seven hours. Today, I stroll solo, and, because there is no one else in the race, feel like I simultaneously come in first and last.

The next day, October 16, I set off down the hill to the Mediterranean, take a right and after a kilometer or two I'm blocked by the presidential palace, which abuts the western side of the Carthage ruins, less than an hour from my hotel in Sidi Bou Said. I knew the palace was there but want to try to negotiate my way through it, which involves a discussion with the numerous guards at the gate.

"You ask too many questions!" exclaims one frustrated presidential palace guard, expressing a sentiment that I've heard before when trying to accomplish something.

"I'm an ex-journalist," I reply. "Incidentally, I'm going to be crowned The Idiot Emperor of Carthage in a few hours so you might want to show me some respect."

He looks at me like I've completely lost it.

I get some photographs of an unfinished hotel development from the beach, a few others of the water and head back up the hill to go around the presidential palace on the Avenue du President Habib Bourguiba. Then, just a couple kilometers later, I'm recognized as the emperor-to-be and given a ten dinar ticket that enables me, during the next few hours, to visit all of the Carthage sights, including the Punic ruins, the museum, the Roman theater, the Byrsa Quarter and the post-Alexander Antonine baths from the second century AD.

Carthage, as you would expect, provides me with some of the best views on the Mediterranean Sea, and before the coronation ceremony begins, I issue a short press release:

"The Idiot, who has been walking around the Mediterranean Sea since January 1998 and MedTrekked a total of 12,667 kilometers, has officially ended his 20-year MedTrek in the ancient city of Carthage on the Mediterranean coast in Tunisia.

As requested earlier this year by the Oracle of Ammon at the Siwa Oasis in Egypt, The Idiot must now serve for the rest of his days as a stand-in for Alexander the Great who died in Babylon in June 323 BC before he was able, as Plutarch wrote, "to sail past the Pillars of Hercules and conquer Carthage."

Following a ceremony later today, The Idiot will henceforth, at home and abroad, in this land and others, be known as The Idiot Emperor of Carthage, Lord of Many Domains.

The Idiot Emperor's first edicts following his coronation are expected to include a total ban on garbage on Tunisia's coast and the introduction of a variety of taxes on the top ten percent of his wealthiest subjects. He also will announce that he will keep and personally maintain many ruins, both Punic and Roman, as reminders of the past.

His first state visit will be to his neighbor in the palace next door, who is the current president of Tunisia. Contrary to current rumors, The Idiot Emperor does NOT plan to change the name of the nearby mosque to The Idiot Emperor's Mosque and he does NOT plan to cover the private parts of any sculptures at Carthage. He will, however, award a subject with a knighthood for picking up garbage and pick up the tab for a Mediterranean dinner at Fandouk in the Tunis souk."

I imagine that you, like an estimated 2.3 billion other people throughout the world, witnessed my coronation live (they say that more people watched the investiture of The Idiot Emperor than the royal wedding or the World Cup final in 2018) or caught the ceremony on YouTube.

Between us, I was a little embarrassed by the overflow of regal splendor and the endless pomp and ceremony throughout the momentous and joyous circumstance, though I was touched that President Trump, the Dalai Lama and so many other foreign dignitaries came to Carthage for the event. I won't again recount all of the details and emotion associated with that once-in-my-lifetime portentous occasion, but simply remind you that, as I said in my inaugural invocation, I hope to be a modest monarch and rule with the deft, skill and noble intention of Alexander the Great, the man who helped get me here.

Following a session to take the first exclusive photos of me as the new emperor, I get some advice from Thich Nhat Hanh, whose book *The Long Road Turns to Joy* is a guide to walking meditation: "Walk upright with calm, dignity, and joy, as though you were an emperor. Place your foot on the Earth the way an emperor places his seal on a royal decree."

I told him I will. Slowly and surely. That's a start.

*TUNISIA TREK*

At the outset it seems that there is more than public opinion on my side.

On the early dark dawn of the decisive day that I was crowned emperor, just after the morning call to prayer, at 4:47 a.m., there is a bellowing, cantankerous, devilish, energetic, ferocious thunderstorm with continual flashes of blindingly bright lightning. The gods and distant observers, from Zeus on majestic Mount Olympus to the Oracle of Siwa in the dry desert oasis, are, I'm told by my soothsayer, applauding me for returning to Carthage on behalf of Alexander the Great. It's the last grand gesture of my 20-year MedTrek.

I look up, to Ra and beyond, and wink.

# MEDTREK MILESTONE #14

The Idiot's 20-year MedTrek is complete after he walked 12,667 kilometers and he is expected to spend the remainder of his days ruling Carthage and Tunisia as The Idiot Emperor, Lord of Many Domains.

On his first foreign trip later this month, The Idiot Emperor will return to Antibes in the south of France where the MedTrek began on January 1, 1998, and symbolically walk around the Cap d'Antibes from Juan-les-Pins to the Picasso Museum.

When he passes the exact spot where the MedTrek began, he'll realize that he walked around almost all of the Mediterranean Sea just to return to where he started.

# FOLLOW THE IDIOT

## CHAPTER PHOTOS

## CHAPTER MAP

# BIBLIOGRAPHY

A partial bibliography of publications cited in "The Idiot and the Odyssey: Walking the Mediterranean," "The Idiot and the Odyssey II: Myth, Madness and Magic on the Mediterranean," and "The Idiot and the Odyssey III: Twenty Years Walking the Mediterranean".

"365 Tao Daily Meditations," Deng Ming-Dao, Harper San Francisco, 1992.

"Alexander the Great At War," Ruth Sheppard, Osprey Publishing, 2008.

"Alexander the Great: The Invisible Enemy," John Maxwell O'Brien, Routledge, 1992.

"The Alexandria Quartet," Lawrence Durrell, Faber, 1968.

"The Anabasis of Alexander, Or The History of the Wars and Conquests of Alexander the Great," Arrian of Nicomedia, Translation by E. J. Chinnock, Hodder and Stoughton, 1884.

"Barcelona," Robert Hughes, Alfred A. Knopf, 1992.

"Be Still and Know: Reflections from Living Buddha, Living Christ," Thich Nhat Hanh, Riverhead Books, 1996.

"The Bull From the Sea," Mary Renault, Pantheon Books, 1962.

"Bullfinch's Mythology: The Greek and Roman Fables Illustrated," Thomas Bullfinch, The Viking Press, 1979.

"Celebrating Homer's Landscapes: Troy and Ithaca Revisited," J.V. Luce, Yale University Press, 1998.

"Coastal Pleasures: Perusing the French Coastline," Elizabeth Billhardt, Editions PC, 1999.

"The Colossus of Maroussi," Henry Miller, New Directions Books, 1941.

"Chronicle of Tao: The Secret Life of a Taoist Master," Deng Ming-Dao, Harper Collins, 1993.

"D'Aulaire's Book of Greek Myths," Ingri and Edgar Parin D'Aulaire, Yearling Books, 1962.

"Deus lo Volt!" Evan S. Connell, Counterpoint, 2000.

"The Dictaean Cave," Georgios I.Panagiotakis, Lassithi, 1988.

"The Eternal Drama: The Inner Meaning of Greek Mythology," Edward F. Edinger, Shambhala, 1994.

"Fidelity: How to Create a Loving Relationship That Lasts," Thich Nhat Hanh, Parallax Press, 2011.

"Fire from Heaven," Mary Renault, Pantheon Books, 1969.

"Funeral Games," Mary Renault, Pantheon Books, 1981.

"The Gold of Troy: The Story of Heinrich Schliemann and the Buried Cities of Ancient Greece," Robert Payne, Funk & Wagnalls, 1958.

"The Great Sea: A Human History of the Mediterranean," David Abulafia, Oxford University Press, 2011.

"Greeks Gods and Heroes," Robert Graves, Doubleday & Company, 1960.

"The Greek Islands," Lawrence Durrell, The Viking Press, 1978.

"A History of Western Philosophy," Bertrand Russell, Simon and Schuster, 1945.

"Homeric Moments: Clues to Delight in Reading The Odyssey and The Iliad," Eva Brann, Paul Dry Books, 2002.

"The Iliad," Homer, Translated by Robert Fitzgerald, Farrar, Straus and Giroux, 1974.

"Journey Into Cyprus," Colin Thubron, Heinemann Educational Books, 1975.

"A Literary Companion to Travel in Greece," Edited by Richard Stoneman, Penguin Books, 1984.

"The Long Road Turns To Joy: A Guide to Walking Meditation," Thich Nhat Hanh, Parallax Press, 1996.

"A Mediterranean Feast," Clifford A. Wright, William Morrow, 1999.

"Mediterranean Europe," Lonely Planet Publications, 2003.

"The Mediterranean in History," David Abulafia, J. Paul Getty Trust Publications, 2003.

"The Mediterranean: Saga of a Sea," Emil Ludwig, Whittlesey House, 1942.

Michelin Country Green Guides (France, Spain, Italy, Greece), Michelin Travel Publications.

"Middlesex," Jeffrey Eugenides, Picador, 2002.

"Myths and Legends of the Ages," Marlon N. French, Hart Publishers, 1951.

"The Nature of Alexander," Mary Renault, Pantheon Books, 1975.

"No-Man's Lands: One Man's Odyssey Through The Odyssey," Scott Huler, Crown Publishers, 2008.

"Odysseus Unbound: The Search for Homer's Ithaca," Robert Bittlestone, Cambridge University Press, 2005.

"The Odyssey," Homer, Translated by Robert Fagles, Penguin Books, 1997.

"The Odyssey," Homer, Translated by Robert Fitzgerald, Doubleday & Co., 1961.

"The Odyssey: A Modern Sequel," Nikos Kazantzakis, Translation by Kimon Friar, Simon and Schuster, 1958.

"The Odyssey For Boys and Girls," Alfred J. Church, The Macmillan Company, 1949.

"On the Shores of the Mediterranean," Eric Newby, Harvill Press, 1984.

"Pan Am's Insider's Rome," Random House, 1972.

"The Persian Boy," Mary Renault, Pantheon Books, 1972.

"The Pillars of Hercules: A Grand Tour of the Mediterranean," Paul Theroux, Hamish Hamilton, 1993.

"Plutarch's Lives," Volume IV, Plutarch, Translation by John Dryden, Revised by A. H. Clough, Little, Brown and Company, 1902.

"Route 66 AD. - On The Trail of Ancient Roman Tourists," Tony Perrottet, Random House, 2002.

"The Rough Guide to Egypt," Rough Guides, 2013.

"Sicily: Three Thousand Years of Human History," Sandra Benjamin, Steerforth Press, 2006.

"Siddhartha," Herman Hesse, Translated by Hilda Rosner, New Directions, 1951.

"A Simple Path," The Dalai Lama, Thorsons, 2000.

"The Song of Achilles: A Novel (P.S.)", Madeline Miller, HarperCollins, 2012.

"The Story of the Iliad," Alfred J. Church, The Macmillan Company, 1904.

"Swim: Why We Love The Water," Lynn Sherr, Public Affairs, 2012.

"Tao Te Ching," Lao Tsu, Translated by Gia-Fu Feng and Jane English, Vintage Books Edition, March 1997.

"A Thousand-Mile Walk to the Gulf," John Muir, Houghton Mifflin, 1916.

"The Tibetan Book of Living and Dying," Sogyal Rinpoche, HarperCollins, 1993.

"Three-Way Mirror: Istanbul, Athens, Rome," Michael Kuser, Citlembik/ Nettleberry Publications, 2010.

"The Tomb of Alexander," Sean Hemingway, Hutchinson, 2012.

"Travels With Herodotus," Ryszard Kapuscinski, Translated by Klara Glowczewska, Alfred A. Knopf, 2007.

"Ulysses Airborne," Mauricio Obregon, Harper & Row, 1971.

"Ulysses," James Joyce, Modern Library, 1934.

"Walking Israel: A Personal Search for the Soul of a Nation," Martin Fletcher, St. Martin's Press, 2010.

"The War That Killed Achilles: The True Story of Homer's Iliad and the Trojan War," Caroline Alexander, Viking, 2009.

"Who's Who in Greek and Roman Mythology," David Kravitz, Clarkson N. Potter Inc., 1976.

"The World of Odysseus," M. I. Finley, New York Review Books, 1954.

"Zen and the Art of Motorcycle Maintenance," Robert M. Pirsig, Bodley Head, 1974.

Various articles by author Joel Stratte-McClure in "Time," "The International Herald Tribune," "European Travel and Life," "People," "The Paris Metro" and other publications.

# ACKNOWLEDGEMENTS

Walking around the Mediterranean Sea from January 1998 to January 2018 was an intriguing and passionate mental, physical and spiritual project. It was a continual joy to share the path with Greek gods, Alexander the Great, contemporary mortals and anonymous readers.

This adventurous exploit would not have been possible without constant inspiration from Homer vis-à-vis Robert Fitzgerald's well-thumbed translations of the *Iliad* and the *Odyssey*. And I would not have been able write the third book in the trilogy without the generous assistance of a variety of people both on and off the path. Key, of course, were the scores of academics, historians and novelists who have, in various ways, been infatuated with Alexander the Great. These range from Plutarch and Arrian of Nicomedia to Mary Renault, John Maxwell O'Brien and Seán Hemingway. Their works, and other books that I consulted, can be found in the bibliography.

I owe a great debt to my pen pal and Stanford classmate Jim Bottomley, who is serving a life sentence in San Quentin State Prison, for frequently reminding me that this book is not a biography of Alexander the Great.

"Keep your third book whimsical, funny and entertaining," Jim, a writer himself, wrote me. "Keep the jokes coming, the interludes, the asides and above all the humor. Readers don't want to read that much about Alexander. They want to read about your current adventures – with all the savory spice you can get in."

I tried, Jim, I tried.

I am truly indebted to the many people who read this manuscript in various incarnations, especially editor Michael Knipe, who was previously a correspondent in the Middle East for *The Times* of London, and Vince Tomasso, a classics professor now teaching at Trinity College in Hartford, Connecticut. Vince has read all three of *The Idiot* books for historical, mythological and grammatical accuracy.

A special thanks is due to author and photojournalist David Douglas Duncan, who died in June 2018 at 102. When I arrived at David's home in the south of France (where we met and were neighbors in the early 1980s) after completing the MedTrek in October 2017, David greeted me with a rough layout of the book cover with the current title. I immediately abandoned my earlier subtitle ("Walking the Mediterranean in the Footsteps of Alexander the Great") when I saw the effort he made.

The third book in my *Idiot* trilogy would not have been completed without critical assessments, astute observations and invaluable input from

Liz Chapin, Lex Hames, John Keeney, Gloria de Luca, Jenni Patterson, Dr. Trudi Pratt ("The Tires Wear Out"), Margaret Sheard (Cyprus), Monika Sleszynska (Egypt), Helen Stratte (my nearly 99-year old mother), Kip Stratte-McClure (my brother) and Luke Stratte-McClure (my son).

I want to thank everyone who walked or talked with me between Greece and Tunisia from April 2013 to October 2017. These patient and tolerant sentient beings included Liz Chapin and Michael Knipe, who MedTrekked with me in numerous countries; Mehmet Kutay, Musa Unal and the Cabbaroglu family in Turkey; Michael and Viola de Glanville in Cyprus; Ibrahim Muhanna in Lebanon; and Michal Shor-Knipe, Sari Amrusi-Yishai and Sara Stratte (my niece) in Israel.

I owe a debt to scores of somewhat anonymous individuals I encountered on the path. These include Maurice, the bodyguard, and "The Colonel" in Lebanon; the policemen and soldiers who escorted and detained me in Egypt; and the dozens of people in Turkey who welcomed me and generously offered me assistance, shelter and food.

I want to thank Anne and Gordon Kling for taking me sailing on three separate voyages off the coasts of Turkey and Croatia and extend my appreciation to a number of authors, curators, professors and scholars who allowed me to interview them or invited me to discuss my works. This august group includes Kathryn Hohlwein, the octogenarian who created *The Readers of Homer,* and many teachers, especially Jim Owens in Florida who annually invited me to give descriptive presentations about the MedTrek to his inquisitive high school classes in Gainesville. Thanks also to Liz Chapin, Michael Knipe, Michael de Glanville, Monika Sleszynska, Sara Stratte, numerous acquaintances and various strangers who politely took photographs of me in some admittedly idiotic poses.

My agent, Felicia Eth, has been particularly patient with my steady progress during the past two decades and my design team, back for a second time, has again been especially creative. Aaron and Jenni Patterson deserve credit for the design and technical features of this book (think QR codes) and its online counterpart, which has again taken my written words to a new level by integrating maps, audios, videos, photographs and various links with the text.

Walk on and ever omward!

*Paris, France, August 15, 2018*

*AMERICA'S BEST TEACHER*

# ABOUT THE AUTHOR

Joel Stratte-McClure, an American journalist/adventurer who lived in France for more than three decades, has been writing about his global trekking and hiking adventures since the 1970s. His work has taken him to more than 115 countries and his articles on a variety of subjects have appeared in *The International Herald Tribune, Time Magazine, The Times* of London, *People Magazine* and numerous other publications.

He is the author of *The Idiot and the Odyssey: Walking the Mediterranean* (2008) and *The Idiot and the Odyssey II: Myth, Madness and Magic on the Mediterranean* (2013). He is currently based in Northern California but regularly travelled to the Mediterranean to gather anecdotes and add kilometers for his third book in this series: *The Idiot and the Odyssey III: Twenty Years Walking the Mediterranean.*

*Follow The Idiot @* www.followtheidiot.com

Made in the USA
Middletown, DE
14 February 2020